The Spirit Sings

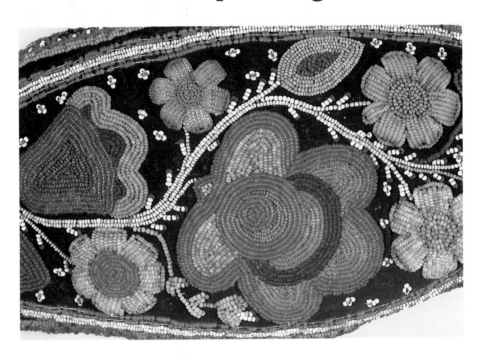

The Spirit Sings

Artistic Traditions of Canada's First Peoples

McClelland and Stewart 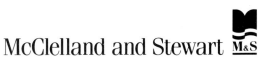    Glenbow Museum

McClelland and Stewart
The Canadian Publishers
481 University Avenue
Toronto M5G 2E9

Every reasonable attempt has been made to attribute
copyright material used in this publication. Information
regarding inadvertent errors or omissions of copyright
information is welcome, and efforts will be made to correct
such errors in future editions.

Lines from *Poems of Rita Joe*, published by Abenaki Press,
are reprinted by permission of the author.

Shell Canada Limited is the exclusive corporate sponsor of
the exhibition *The Spirit Sings*.

Canadian Cataloguing in Publication Data

Main entry under title:

The Spirit sings

Co-published by the Glenbow Museum.
Bibliography
ISBN 0-7710-3355-9 (bound). – ISBN 0-7710-3356-7 (pbk.)

1. Indians of North America - Canada - Material culture. 2. Indians of North America - Canada - Art.
3. Indians of North America - Canada - Religion and
mythology. I. Glenbow Museum.

E78.C2S64 1987   709'.01'1   C87-094638-2

All photographs were taken by Ron Marsh, Glenbow
Museum, *except* the following:

1, 3, 6, 8, 9, 10, 12, 16, 20, 21, 22, 23, 28, 30, 31,
34, 35, 36, 42, 43, 44, 45e, 45h, 48, 49, 51, 53, 54,
55, 56, 58, 60, 64, 65, 66, 69, 70, 72, 73, 77, 88, 92,
97, 100, 101, 102, 103, 104, 109, 112, 115, 116, 117,
119, 121 bottom, 121 left, 124, 128, 132, 135, 138 all,
146, 147, 152, 160, 165, 167, 169, 179, 180, 182,
183, 184, 187, 189, 190, 191, 193, 194, 195, 196,
198, 199, 200, 201, 203, 206, 207, 208, 209, 210,
211, 212, 213, 214, 218.

The publishers make grateful acknowledgement to the Ontario
Arts Council for their financial assistance.

Printed and bound in Hong Kong

1. Half-title page:
Detail of floral beadwork from the top panel
of a Micmac man's cap, late 19th century.
Maine State Museum, Augusta 84.9.1. Pho-
tograph by Greg Hart. L:26.5; W:9.5;
H:10.5.

2. Opposite title page:
Canoe model, Huron-Abenaki, c. 1760.
Musée des Beaux-arts de Chartres, France
11405. Canoe: L:90; Dolls: H:18-24

Models such as this were made for
presentation to Europeans and for the
tourist trade during the early contact
period. Eighteenth century examples are
lovingly made and accurately reflect the
dress and equipment in use at the time.

Contents

3.
Backrest banner, Plains Cree, 19th century.
Courtesy of the Royal Ontario Museum,
Toronto HD 6868. L:112

Banners of this type served in rituals
performed by the Plains Cree while a
buffalo herd was driven into a pound. At
other times these banners decorated the
backrests of their owners.

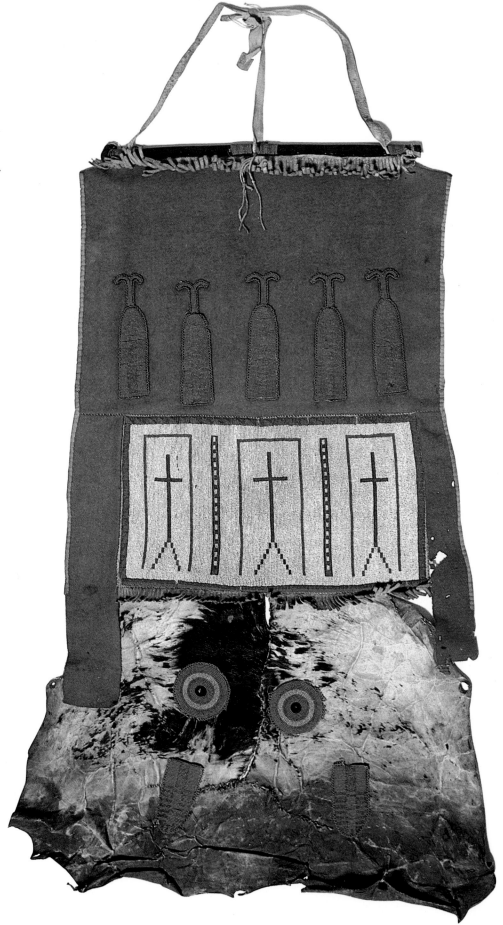

Preface

There are always museum projects just waiting to be done–usually waiting for time and money. For example, Canadian ethnologists have known for a long time that there were important collections of Canadian Indian and Inuit material scattered in museum and private collections around the world. Yet there had never been a world survey of Canadian collections abroad nor an index or inventory of Canadian ethnological holdings outside of Canada. To conduct even a preliminary survey and create an exhibition from international collections would require hundreds of thousands of dollars, a team of scholars with authority in each of Canada's diverse culture areas, and several years of field work.

In April of 1983, when the organizing committee for the 1988 Winter Olympics, to be held in Calgary, asked the Glenbow Museum to mount a major exhibition, the opportunity was seized. Julia Harrison, Glenbow's curator of Ethnology, and the director had returned from a European trip. Ms. Harrison had visited Dr. Christian Feest, the distinguished Americanist, in Vienna in 1981. There was discussion about the wealth of Canadian collections in Europe, largely unknown to Canadian scholars. It was realized that the Olympic environment could mean international co-operation, the possibility of both corporate and government financial support and five years of working time to prepare an exhibition and publications. The decision was made to undertake the project waiting to be done.

A curatorial committee of six scholars was assembled. Each member is a specialist in one of the six major cultural areas in Canada. The Olympic Organizing Committee endorsed the project, calling it the "flagship" of the Olympic Arts Festival while committing $600,000. Plans were begun for international travel and research. What were the goals and objectives?

First, it must be remembered that Glenbow is a museum of art, history and cultural history, and ethnology. It is a major research library and archives. There were many "projects that are just waiting to be done," and therefore many options. It was decided that a project for the Olympic Arts Festival should be an act of social responsibility, addressing an international issue through the medium of the museum and, in this case, the significance and importance of the preservation of aboriginal cultures.

The objectives were then defined – first, to conduct a preliminary survey of Canadian ethnological collections, primarily in the United Kingdom and Europe, and secondly to make a selection of representative artefacts to be borrowed that would illustrate three themes: the diversity of cultures among Canada's native peoples; the commonality of a world-view among those diverse cultures, based on the quintessential necessity of harmony between man and nature; and the continuity and resilience of native culture in spite of overwhelming European influence, oppression, and suppression.

The goal was to increase not only the awareness of but also an understanding of the cultural traditions of Canada's native peoples. This was to be achieved through an exhibition and its interpretation; through publication in print, on television, and in film; and by laying down a foundation for future research in Canadian ethnology that would further this goal of greater understanding. The field notes and the four to five thousand field photographs, together with all the accumulated documentation, would constitute an archive, available to native peoples, museums, universities, and scholars around the world. A significant addition is being made to the Americanist's data base.

The project attracted interest in many quarters. A second venue was established for the national capital, Ottawa, under the aegis of the Canadian Museum of Civilization. Shell Canada Limited came forward as the corporate sponsor, committing $1,100,000 to the undertaking. It is noteworthy that this research and its manifestations have been underwritten by a major corporation, the Olympics, the federal government, the government of Alberta, and the City of Calgary.

As this is written, the exhibition is ten months away. We are aware that we have undertaken one of the most complex museum projects in memory. We have travelled to more than twenty foreign countries, visiting at least 150 museums and private collections. Roughly 665 loans from 90-odd lenders in twenty countries have been negotiated. Twenty thousand square feet of exhibition space has been designed and will soon be constructed. But even at this stage, it has been rewarding to experience exceptional cooperation from our colleagues around the world and in the promise of the exhibition, which we are certain will make a contribution to understanding among peoples.

Duncan F. Cameron
Director

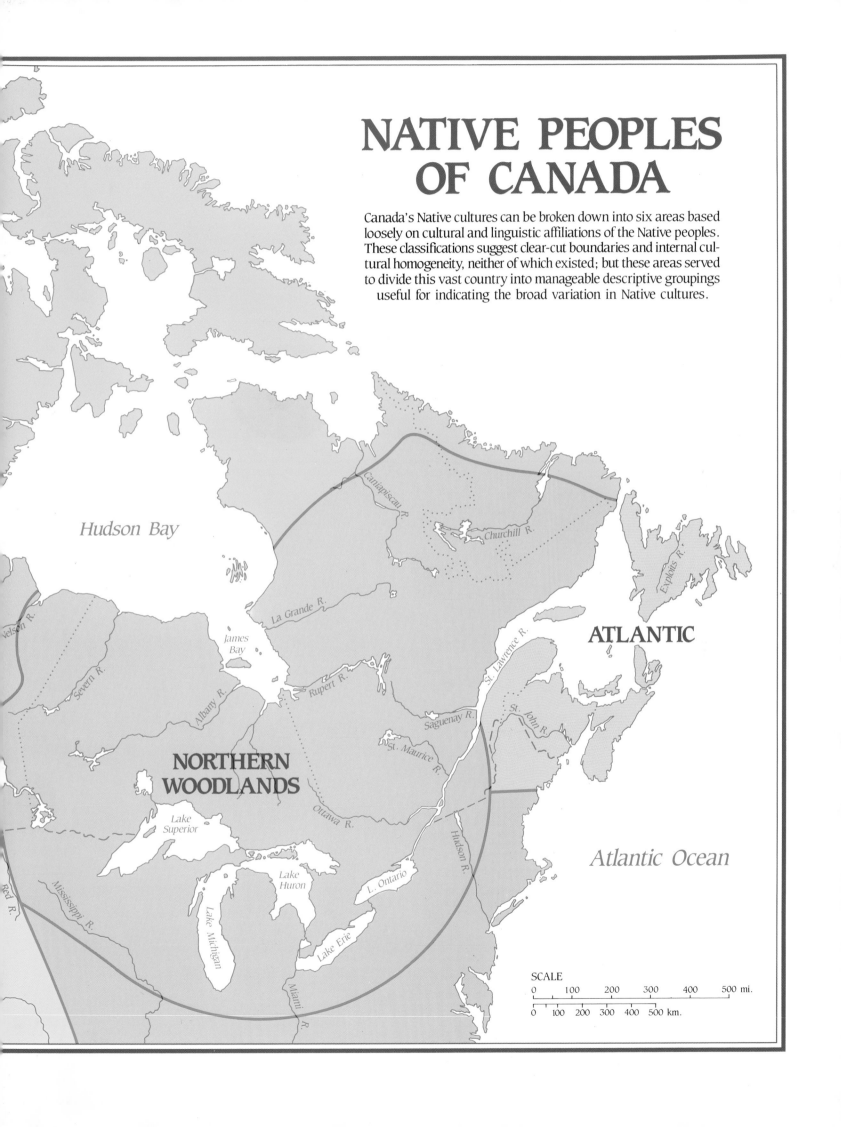

NATIVE PEOPLES OF CANADA

Canada's Native cultures can be broken down into six areas based loosely on cultural and linguistic affiliations of the Native peoples. These classifications suggest clear-cut boundaries and internal cultural homogeneity, neither of which existed; but these areas served to divide this vast country into manageable descriptive groupings useful for indicating the broad variation in Native cultures.

Hudson Bay

Caniapiscau R.

Churchill R.

Exploits R.

La Grande R.

James Bay

ATLANTIC

Nelson R.

St. Lawrence R.

Severn R.

Rupert R.

Albany R.

Saguenay R.

St. John R.

St. Maurice R.

NORTHERN WOODLANDS

Ottawa R.

Hudson R.

Atlantic Ocean

Lake Superior

Mississippi R.

Lake Huron

Lake Michigan

L. Ontario

Red R.

Lake Erie

Miami R.

SCALE

| 0 | 100 | 200 | 300 | 400 | 500 mi. |

| 0 | 100 | 200 | 300 | 400 | 500 km. |

Introduction

This book grew out of an exhibition entitled *The Spirit Sings: Artistic Traditions of Canada's First Peoples*, which opened in Calgary, Alberta, as part of the Arts Festival of the xv Olympic Winter Games.

The exhibition included more than five hundred objects of native Canadian manufacture drawn from national and international ethnographic collections.[1] Some of the finest objects collected in the early contact period of Canadian history were exhibited together in celebration of the native spirit, both communal and individual, from which flows the inspiration to create such objects. The spirit continues in contemporary native experience and expression.

The idea for the exhibition developed out of a visit to ethnographic museums in Europe. Clearly there were significant differences between the North American native collections housed in such Canadian museums as the Glenbow Museum and those held in museums in Europe. It was not that European museums had the best material, but that their collections were older than those of most Canadian institutions; they reflected native cultures as they were before the first wave of Europeans came to the shores of North America. The exhibition's primary purpose was to bring this older material together to emphasize the diversity, continuity, adaptability, and resilience of the native cultures of Canada, which incorporate a world-view distinct from that of mainstream Canadians.

The exhibition, and this book, surveyed some major Canadian museum collections in relation to the native Canadian collections in foreign museums. The overriding strength of Canadian holdings for certain regions became clear in the process.

We also wanted to explore the variety, richness, and depth of aesthetic traditions found among the indigenous populations of Canada at the time of contact. These traditions are somewhat different from those generally associated with the Indian and Inuit peoples of Canada. For example, the introduction of glass beads and European floral patterns caused a dramatic shift in the decorative styles used by certain groups. Similarly, on the Northwest Coast, monumental carving flourished in the post-contact era, as did the production of a wide range of items for trade or sale. However, these new influences were absorbed into rich aesthetic traditions extant at the time of contact.

The meeting of these very different cultural tradi-

4.

Caubvic. Pastel drawing by Nathaniel Dance, 1773. The Knatchbull Portrait Collection, England.

This pastel drawing portrays the young Labrador woman, Caubvic, who was brought to England with four companions by Captain George Cartwright in 1773. Caubvic's parka is richly beaded; she also wears the long tassels of beads worn as hair ornaments, the fashion among Labrador women in the late 18th century.

tions was not without its toll. Not all native groups survived the impact of the European culture, which brought with it new technology, new diseases, and alcohol. Often it was the effects of the latter two, combined with the hostile and at time violent encounters between the strangers, that devastated aboriginal inhabitants of this continent. Such was the fate of the Beothuk peoples of Newfoundland, for example, whose last known member died of tuberculosis in 1829.

Canada's native population has overcome such losses, and the population has been steadily increasing throughout this century. Four hundred years after extensive European contact began on the East Coast, there are nearly five hundred thousand native peoples in Canada possessing cultures distinct from those of mainstream Canadians.[2] The strength of native culture today demonstrates the determined resilience of these peoples in the face of attempts at cultural suppression through government legislation, assimilation through residential school programs, and pauperization induced by the destruction of traditional livelihoods. Changes in legislation and attitude have ameliorated the first two issues, but many native people still occupy the lowest ranks of Canada's poor.

Among mainstream Canadians, there is only a very generalized understanding of the native population. Only when we choose to parade images of Indians in an attempt to portray something unique about being Canadian are native peoples given significant recognition. The popular image of native peoples subsumes a belief that most Indians lived in tipis, wore lots of beads and feathers, chased buffalo (these being traits of the Plains Indians), had totem poles (these are found only on the Northwest Coast), and paddled birchbark canoes (these were used by central and eastern groups). We see the Inuit as a hardy lot living in igloos. It has not generally been part of the Canadian tradition to appreciate the uniqueness, the variety, the complexity, and the contemporary viability of the many native cultures that exist in this country.

During the first years of European settlement of this nation, the Indian was simply blocked from the consciousness of the newcomers: Indians were thought to "have no religion . . . neither art nor literature . . . no clothing . . ."[3] Less than European, their very existence was virtually denied. "The [early] Canadian became incapable of 'seeing' the Indian at all, *except* in so far as he entered into white history."[4] When he did enter our history, he charged to centre stage just returned from the buffalo hunt atop a magnificent steed, feathers and beads flowing majestically behind him. Canada's contemporary native population, who are demanding a greater presence in this nation, appear to some Canadians to be ghosts rising from the dead. A major exhi-

bition of native cultural materials collected during the early phase of European contact would expand our knowledge of the original diversity and complexity of native cultures and would lead to a greater appreciation of the roots of contemporary native populations.

It also seemed appropriate that native Canadians have an opportunity to see this important aspect of their heritage. As a part of the present renaissance of native cultures in Canada, native peoples are demanding the right to interpret their own history. In order to do so, exposure to the wealth and breadth of that history as represented by objects held in some foreign museums seemed crucial. The special events that accompanied the exhibition; the film, video, and slide record of the objects in the exhibition; the interpretive essays, photographs, and collection histories in this book; and the catalogue to the exhibition all contribute to the revitalization and definition of contemporary native cultures.

The authors of *The Spirit Sings* formed the curatorial committee responsible for selecting the objects for the exhibition. They have worked with native peoples across Canada in a variety of cultural programs; they have studied and been employed by Canadian museums, art galleries, and universities, and have a wide variety of academic backgrounds including art history, anthropology, philosophy, and Canadian studies. A meeting of the minds of the group members defined the focus of the exhibition and the text.

Critical to the collective approach was the awareness that the material presented in the exhibition and in the essays is not definitive but only one set of interpretations. It intends to initiate a dialogue with those interested in the subject, most particularly Canada's native peoples themselves. To counterpoint the ideas and interpretations offered by the learned outsider with those of Canada's native peoples is an important aim of the project. As this exhibition developed during five years, the possibility that this will happen soon became more of a reality, as native people and museums begin to forge new and more productive relationships.

Canada's native cultures may be divided into six areas: the East Coast, the Northern Woodlands (here including the Eastern Subarctic), the Northern Plains, the Western Subarctic, the Northwest Coast, and the Arctic. This breakdown is based loosely on cultural and linguistic affiliations of the native peoples (and was influenced by the expertise of the individuals involved in the project). These classifications suggest clear-cut boundaries and internal cultural homogeneity, neither of which existed; but selecting these cultural areas made it possible to divide this vast country into manageable descriptive groupings that were "useful for indicating the nature of broad variations in [native] society, population density, and patterns of land use and ecological adaptation.''[5] It is evident that there was an overlap in these areas, as well as obvious gaps.

Certain areas of Canada could not be given equal treatment for historical reasons. The collections from the early contact period do not contain, for example, much material from the intermontagne region of British Columbia. There was also an imbalance in the physical size of the designated areas. The "Northern Woodlands," as defined here, stretch from the mouth of the St. Lawrence to the northern reaches of Quebec to its western extreme at the lakehead; the "East Coast" includes the much smaller region roughly encompassed by the Atlantic provinces. Moreover, the cultural boundaries of the regions do not coincide with the present-day Canadian border; traditionally, many native peoples have had tribal affiliations straddling the forty-ninth parallel and the Alaska border. However, the emphasis was placed on those groups whose major territories generally fall within the area that became known as Canada. This fact, and the need to keep the curatorial committee to a manageable size, determined the geographic focus of the exhibition.

To add further mayhem, museum resources for the areas varied greatly. For example, there exist in international collections between 250,000 and 300,000 Northwest Coast objects; the tally for the East Coast region is only about 2,500 objects. Such discrepancies are due to many factors that warrant further study. The most obvious include the size of the aboriginal populations at the time of contact, the traditional form of the objects produced by the indigenous inhabitants, their acceptability to the European market and aesthetic, and the ease of access to the regions where quantities of material were made.

The entire project aimed at reassembling early contact period material from Canada's native populations to give some insight into the philosophies and worldviews of these peoples. The reassembly of regional costumes created eloquent statements of how these people saw the world. These costumes included not only the clothing worn to cover the body, but the decoration on that clothing and the accessories worn with it. As Ruth Phillips describes for the Northern Woodlands region, these costumes reflect the aesthetic and symbolic expressions of the people, and suggest perhaps the way they saw the world. The complete costume worn by a member of a Western Subarctic group, for example, expressed the aesthetic sense of its owner or maker, and demonstrated the owner's wealth and social standing. Moreover, as Judy Thompson states, clothing was "closely linked to the soul and personality of its owner,"[6] and allowed insight into the integrated way the corporeal, spiritual, and aesthetic worlds were viewed by these peoples. Bernadette Driscoll demonstrates how the parkas worn by various Inuit groups mirror, in their construction and decoration, the structure of the Inuit world. The fundamental opposition of land and sea, male and female, light and dark, man and animal are shown to be integral to the form of the parkas and the aesthetic of their decoration. Often, ideas were layered just as adornment and decorations were layered to produce many levels of meaning and aesthetic expression.

All the essays deal in some way, either directly or implicitly, with transformation. The process of turning a sheet of birchbark into a canoe, a piece of alder into a grease bowl, or porcupine quills into a beautiful armband, not only requires great manual skill and creative expression but also articulates, in the final object, the symbolic and metaphorical qualities of the raw materials and the designs used. For example, among the Copper Inuit, the ermine is considered to be ''smart and sneaky'' and its attachment to dance hats may have been to imbue the wearer with these qualities to protect him against unexpected attack by human or spiritual forces.[7] When the Micmac of Nova Scotia began to produce a great volume of material for trade with Europeans in the mid-nineteenth century, "many traditional designs were retained,"[8] and the meaning of the designs was transferred to the non-traditional objects. Eventually, the meaning of the designs was lost, but "the beauty of traditional designs was still potent."

Just as many ideas went into any object, so many forms of expression were as integral to objects as were the paint and shells applied as decoration. An object produced for use in a traditional context was one part of a complex whole, including the songs that were sung over it, the dances in which it was worn, and the myths and legends that governed its form and use. These were as essential as the object itself. Usually, however, the object alone was collected and preserved; now these objects hold the key to the thinking and motivation of their makers and users. Thus, one aim of the exhibition and this book was to reintegrate the object with its original context by examining the mythology, oral tradition, and commentary as recorded in the accounts of the early Europeans who met these people. Although many of the early accounts do acknowledge the strength and unique nature of the cultures of these aboriginal populations, it must be noted that the Europeans who recorded this commentary could not help but reflect their ethnocentric views in their assessment of these peoples. This bias must be kept in mind when working with the records, but it does not invalidate them. They remain a valuable and, at times, the only source of information about these objects and the people who made them.

Most of the native peoples who owned and used

these objects lacked a written language and thus little was recorded in their own language or even in their own words about these possessions. Yet through the spirit and aesthetic that emanate from the objects, we can gain some understanding of the objects and of the people who made them. This insight, integrated with the European voices who commented upon them, provide a basis for greater understanding of the cultures of Canada's native people at the time of contact with Europeans.

This integrative process needs to include commentary by the descendants of these peoples who continue to manifest much of that same cultural expression. This imperative exists because of the adaptive nature of the culture of Canada's native peoples. The essays demonstrate that none of the native peoples of Canada lived in isolation prior to contact; they were all part of elaborate intergroup trading networks. This integration did not, however, dilute the individuality of the groups; each retained its own language, while freely borrowing and trading costumes, rituals, hunting practices, and technologies. Canada's native peoples, at least those not devastated by disease and alcohol, survived the European onslaught because they were used to borrowing, adapting, and integrating. "White contact stimulated new ideas, introduced new goods and even greatly accelerated the pace of cultural change . . . [but] for the vast majority of tribes, there was time to develop attitudes and adaptations about the presence of whites which involved *negotiation and selection borrowing* rather than absorption into white culture and society."[9]

Fine examples of this strategy are the items created for a rapidly growing eighteenth- and nineteenth-century tourist market. The exquisite birchbark boxes decorated with elaborate porcupine quillwork in nested sets suited to a Victorian lady's dressing table served no purpose in the Micmac world but to be sold to the newcomers who cherished and paid fine prices for them. The market was identified and the product created; Micmac integrity remained because those things with which the people parted incorporated only implicitly the essence of what it is to be Micmac. Only much later, when populations were severely reduced, were items of great cultural value sold or given away. In general, the native populations' determination to retain their unique cultural identities through an often strategic adaptation to the presence of the white man made possible their survival into the twentieth century and predicted the recent renaissance of those identities.

Another theme underlying the essays is the history of European contact. This history varied from region to region not only in intensity but also in motivation and the period in which it was begun. Though archaeological evidence demonstrates that sporadic European

5.
Figurine, Tanaina type, late-19th century type. Indianer Museum der Stadt Zurich, Switzerland 7(204). H:39.5

By the 1880s and 1890s the Tanaina, although still manufacturing traditional skin clothing, had substituted glass beads for the earlier quillworked motifs. This was also the case for Kutchin and other western Athapaskan groups, but Tanaina work was often characterized by diagonal beaded lines radiating from a central vertical line on shirt fronts and backs, sheaths, pouches, etc. – a motif possibly developed from earlier, much smaller, markings in ochre.

contact with North America had been going on for centuries, repeated and extensive contact did not begin until the first half of the sixteenth century on the East Coast of Canada, and not until the twentieth century with some Inuit groups.

As the centuries passed, the reasons for coming to the cold, harsh lands of North America changed. Contact and subsequent early settlement on the East Coast were perpetrated by the cod trade, a bountiful resource discovered by voyages attempting to find a passage to the riches of the Orient. The search for the Northwest Passage took the Spanish to the West Coast of North America in the mid-sixteenth century. Later expeditions came to both coasts in the name of science — collecting information on the flora and fauna, the latter category including the human inhabitants of the continent, in concordance with the thinking of the day. The fur trade spurred exploration of the north and central interior regions of the continent from the early-seventeenth century onward. Traders and merchants were followed quickly by missionaries, military and government officials, and general adventurers. Long after most aboriginal groups had had extensive contact, settlers spread across Canada in large numbers. Finally, the imposition of territorial sovereignty in Canada's northern regions prompted concerted government attempts to secure contact with all the native inhabitants within the boundaries of Canada.

Underlying this exploration was an economic motive, either national or personal. Many came seeking to better themselves by means of wealth to be taken home or by establishing a new life in this strange land. Europe had been in a protracted upheaval since the fifteenth and sixteenth centuries, when "the growth in power of the business classes sufficiently undercut the last remnants of the feudal economic and social order and promoted the development of centralized nation-states."[10] During the same period, the Protestant revolution took hold, legitimizing the new-found business ethic. The native North Americans had "to cope with the instability of strangers who [emerged from this environment] and exploded . . . in an engulfing wave of settlements."[11]

Life in the ''New World'' was profitable and less bound by class structures than life in Europe, but it incorporated European cultural traditions and values. This perspective persisted and even in the twentieth century offered little room to acknowledge the aboriginal cultural traditions that greeted but did not stop this ''engulfing wave.''

The newcomers had varying effects. At least one eastern group was annihilated partly through genocidal campaigns against the aboriginal inhabitants of this land; other groups suffered significant population reduc-

tion through the more random but nearly as devastating effects of disease. The Europeans quickly realized, however, that the aboriginal inhabitants of the new land could serve useful purposes. Some were employed as guides; others as suppliers of furs and other marketable products; and others as teachers of the skills necessary to survive the harsh climates of North America. But by the nineteenth century it became advantageous to remove the aboriginal populations of certain areas from the land, to open the land to agricultural settlement. This was achieved through treaties that concentrated native populations on reserves, rather than through genocide.

In the central regions of Canada the effect of the Europeans was often felt long before they appeared. Manufactured goods traded through aboriginal networks quickly became part of the cultural inventory. Many native peoples also became suppliers for the fur trade; and, after trading posts were established in an area, settlements often concentrated around trading posts, which supplied basic items of food and clothing. This shift greatly changed the lives of these peoples as they became dependent on an economic system controlled in distant lands.

Many of the newcomers to the continent were presented with gifts of welcome by the indigenous inhabitants; other visitors acquired a variety of objects through purchase, gifts, and, at times, plunder. Some items were collected as specimens for scientific study, as curiosities, or for their aesthetic appeal. Why and what objects were acquired changed over the years according to the motivation and the ideology of the collector. For example, J.A. Jacobsen, a Norwegian entrepreneur, was sent out in 1881 by the Museum für Völkerkunde in Berlin to obtain Northwest Coast material before the culture was completely annihilated by European contact.[12] Jacobsen visited various points on the coast, amassing a collection of nearly 2,400 objects, from a large Haida pole to stone clubs to masks and ceremonial items.[13] The director of the Berlin museum contracted Jacobsen for two reasons: to ensure that proper documentation was made of these important cultures, and so that he would not be outdone by other agencies sending out expeditions to the region. Jacobsen returned to the coast with his brother in 1885, this time to collect objects that he could sell to museums.

Another collector was an Italian, Giacomo Beltrami. An explorer and an adventurer, Beltrami saw himself as venturing into unknown and dangerous territory when he travelled in 1823 to the Great Lakes area of North America. There he collected a variety of souvenirs including drums, birchbark containers, and costumes, which eventually found their way into the city museum in his home town of Bergamo.

The Danish Fifth Thule Expedition set out in 1921 to make a thorough scientific exploration of the peoples and regions of the Central Canadian Arctic. During the expedition, an extensive ethnographic collection was amassed along with various botanical and zoological specimens; these became part of the National Museum of Denmark. Another collection put together in the name of science was part of the Royal Scottish Museum holdings of Athapaskan and Inuit materials. These were acquired largely by employees of the Hudson's Bay Company throughout the Arctic and Subarctic in the mid-nineteenth century. Of particular note is the large collection of Bernard Rogan Ross, whose intention it was to photograph the people from whom he collected and to record their languages. Unfortunately, very little of his documentary material survived.

Scientific explorations of an earlier era included the study of aesthetics and religion. Such was the orientation of artist George Catlin, who travelled among various Plains groups in the 1830s. During these trips he painted many of his famous images of these people and collected various artefacts, some of which found their way into the Smithsonian collection in Washington, D.C. Catlin's aim in his drawings and paintings was "to rescue from oblivion so much of their primitive looks and customs as the industry and ardent enthusiasm of one lifetime could accomplish . . ."[14] Catlin's aesthetic sense undoubtedly played a role in his selection of objects.

Many of the artefacts found in museums today passed through several hands upon their arrival in Europe. An excellent example of this is an Athapaskan suit now in the Reiss Museum in Mannheim, West Germany. It was apparently collected by Baron von Wrangell between 1829 and 1834 in Alaska, and sent as a gift to the Russian czar. From Petersburg it went to the Duke of Leuchtenberg, who gave the suit to the King of Bayern. Eventually, after the king's collection became state property, the suit came to the Museum für Völkerkunde in Munich. Later, it was given to Arthur Speyer, Sr., a German collector, in exchange for other objects. Finally, in 1968, Arthur Speyer, Jr. gave the suit to the Reiss Museum in exchange for a figure from New Guinea. The history of this itinerant piece, and its frequent role as a gift, indicates the high regard in which such objects were held, if one assumes that, among the aristocracy, any object given as a gift implies it is significant and unique.

Native people quickly realized the commercial value of their cultural materials and demanded high prices for the objects for sale or barter. (There was obviously a large selection of items available for Jacobsen, as he came home with a collection of more than two thousand items.) However, items of high value were sometimes given away as gifts. These were likely made for a special occasion, as the nature of the gift would seem to serve no purpose in the cultural inventory of the group from which it came. An example of great intricacy and detail is a model canoe with a full array of miniaturized accoutrements sent by a group of St. Lawrence Indians to the Cathedral at Chartres in France as an *ex voto* offering. Another such gift was made by Jane Nevin of the Whycocomaugh reserve, Cape Breton, Nova Scotia; it was a pair of moccasins with the crown of St. Stephen beaded on them for Queen Victoria's Jubilee.

Some objects are well documented as to why, when, where, and by whom they were made; for others no such information was recorded. A Blackfoot shield was collected in 1846 by Captain Thomas A. Clairborne; he recorded from what the shield was made and the inspiration for the designs that appear on it and on its cover. "The warrior dreamed of holes in the ground, with snakes in them, of a curious bird, and of a storm, all of which is painted on the shield."[15]

The canoe at Chartres was sent by a group of Abenaki, but whether they made it is uncertain. An item in the Ashmolean Museum, Oxford, England, collected before 1660 — its early date making it of great interest — presents many problems because of the lack of information about it. Generally, it would thought to be Cree; but upon re-examination it has been suggested that it may come from the St. Lawrence Gulf area. Further speculation was suggested that it is a woman's rather than a man's garment, and authorities are uncertain as to whether it was influenced by European ideas or manifests purely aboriginal style.

The Spirit Sings demonstrates, however, that sufficient pieces of the puzzle exist to make coherent statements about much of this material. These statements add a great deal to the full picture of native tradition in Canada in the past and today.

Each essay makes a unique contribution to its field of study. Ruth Whitehead presents a framework for looking at the most meagre remnants of the Beothuk peoples that gives us an undying sense of their humanity. It is in our awareness of the final tragedy of the Beothuk that we come to know one of the most critical and eloquent themes of this project — the humanity, despite our cultural diversity, that we share with the artisans who created these objects — reason enough to have mounted this exhibition.

Judy Thompson, in her essay on the Western Subarctic, skilfully pulls together for the first time information and data on the rich aesthetic expression of the aboriginal inhabitants of the regions of Northern British Columbia, the Yukon, and the Northwest Territories, an area considered barren and harsh and which has not been given much academic attention in the study of art and aesthetics. Ruth Phillips' discussion of the costume of the Woodlands describes aesthetic principles of these groups. This, in conjunction with her integrative discussion of the resplendent costumes worn by these people, emphasizes the need to see these objects as parts of a much larger cultural whole.

Much has been written about the contemporary art works of the north, and Arctic archaeological work has been one of Canada's most exciting and fertile areas of research. But what of the ethnographic record, the living people at the time of contact, and the objects that they made and used in everyday life? Bernadette Driscoll's essay explores the milieu that produced among the Canadian Inuit a wealth of clothing and items of personal adornment from this period.

The dynamic nature of life on the plains and the parallel character of its cultural traditions, particularly in the post-contact period, is a major element of Ted Brasser's essay. He traces the roots of various cultural patterns to the Missouri River valley and explores their dissemination and adaptation across the Northern Plains, incorporating elements of the mythological, ceremonial, and artistic traditions of the two areas.

Martine Reid examines the motivation of the artists who produced the rich array of complex works of art found on the Northwest Coast. She suggests that these works are an integration of three elements: form, context, and content. The artist moulds his creation into a form coherent with the content or meaning of the images he wishes to imply or convey. He must also marry his creative genius with the context within which he produces his work. A major element of that context in Reid's discussion is the nature of the social structure of the society in which he lives.

All the essays explore themes particular to their region, but they share a few key themes. Implicit in all the texts is the concept of the peoples' unity with the spiritual and animal worlds, and with the environment, all of which were integral to their survival. Any aesthetic sense incorporated this sense of wholeness; this is integral to any objects produced. A defined ordering of the world and a sense of one's place within it is evident in the eloquent beauty and strength emanating from all the objects discussed here and in the exhibition. It was these objects that captured not only the eye of the European collectors but the seminal spirit of their creators. It is these objects, housed in museums around the world, that, when brought together, reveal the strength, richness, and complexity of Canadian native cultural traditions.

Julia D. Harrison
Curator, Ethnology

6.
Westcoast man from Nootka Sound.
Watercolour by John Webber, 1778. Peabody Museum, Harvard University 41-72-10/497. Photograph by Hillel Burger.

This man is wearing a nose-ring ornament and a circular cloak made of shredded red cedar bark. His face is decorated with facial paintings or tattooing.

I Have Lived Here Since the World Began

the World Began

Atlantic Coast Artistic Traditions

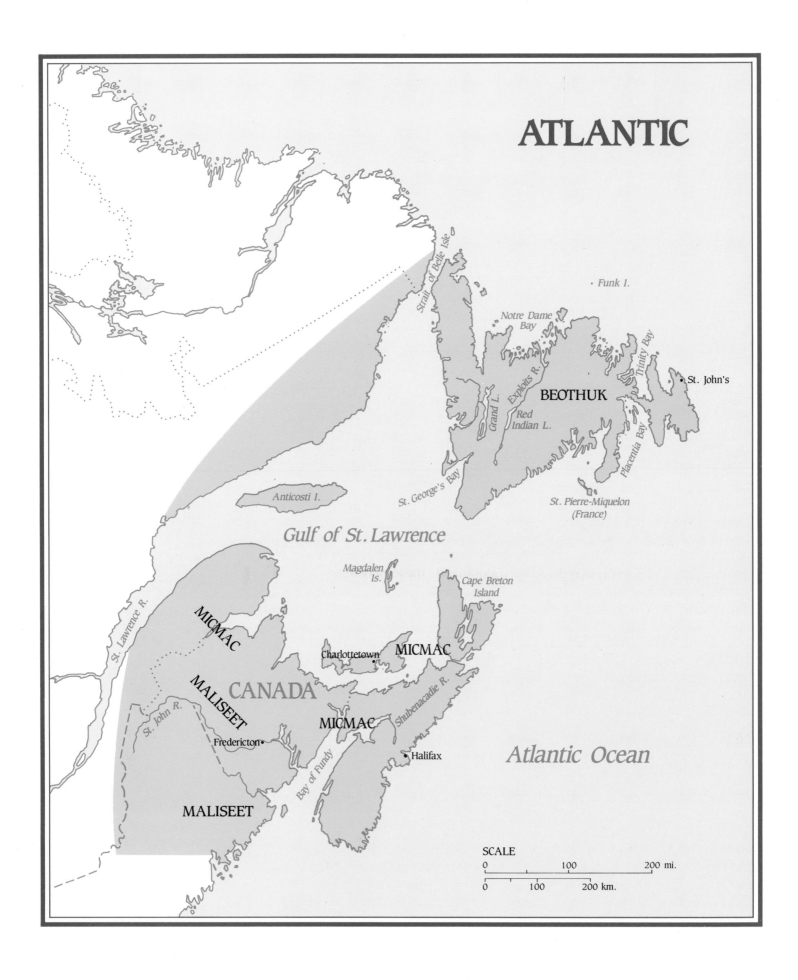

ATLANTIC

Funk I.

Notre Dame
Bay

Strait of Belle Isle

Grand L.

Exploits R.

BEOTHUK

Red
Indian L.

Trinity Bay

St. John's

Placentia Bay

Anticosti I.

St. George's Bay

St. Pierre-Miquelon
(France)

Gulf of St. Lawrence

Magdalen
Is.

Cape Breton
Island

St. Lawrence R.

MICMAC

Charlottetown

MICMAC

MALISEET

CANADA

MICMAC

Shubenacadie R.

Atlantic Ocean

St. John R.

Fredericton

Bay of Fundy

Halifax

MALISEET

SCALE

| 0 | 100 | 200 mi. |
| 0 | 100 | 200 km. |

They came to a wigwam. It was a long wigwam with a door at each end. The man inside the wigwam said, "I have lived here since the world began."[1]

O nce, Atlantic Canada was ice, its massive blue glitter rising forever into the cold sky.[2] In some places the ice gripped even the edge of the sea; but farther out, on what one day would be the drowned lands, the Grand Banks offshore, there were still pockets of plants and animals, a refugium of life. Then, as the earth warmed again under the sun, and the ice groaned and heaved its mountains into the water or melted quietly down to the raw rock, the living things followed its retreat. The world began again.

Some eleven thousand years ago, people appeared in these lands, trailing the herds of animals that fed off tundra moss and grasses near the ice edge. One of the earliest living sites of these Paleoindian hunters was high on a ridge of red sandstone overlooking the grazing plains near what is now Debert, Nova Scotia.[3]

Between these first people and those next known, a gap of several thousand years exists. The ice continued to melt northwards, and people may have been living in southern Labrador even earlier than eight thousand years ago.[4] All along the coasts of Atlantic Canada, these Maritime Archaic peoples had developed techniques that enabled them to hunt on the sea and the sea ice as well as on land. In an extensive Maritime Archaic cemetery at Port-au-Choix, Newfoundland, these people sleep surrounded by the bones of seals and caribou, strings of Great Auk beaks, and whistles made of the wing bones of swans.[5]

The ice moved north and the climate and ecology of eastern Canada changed. Many culturally distinct peoples moved in and out of the area during the following millennia, but our understanding of these ebbs and flows is not complete, and we may never know which of these groups were the ancestors of the native peoples living in Atlantic Canada in historical times.

"Our Home Is This Country"

By 1500 A.D., when a permanent European expansion into the New World began, Newfoundland appears to have been occupied by the Beothuk, with the Maliseet in southwestern New Brunswick and the Micmac spread throughout northeastern New Brunswick, Nova Scotia, and Prince Edward Island. The Micmac and Maliseet were closely related and spoke Eastern Algonkian languages, while the Beothuk probably spoke a form of Central Algonkian, and were perhaps distant cousins of the Montagnais Indians of present-day Labrador and Quebec.[6]

The Beothuk, the Micmac, and the Maliseet called themselves simply "People." *Beathu* is the word for "person" or "human being"; the plural, *Beothuk*, we use as the name for both the tribe and the language. The

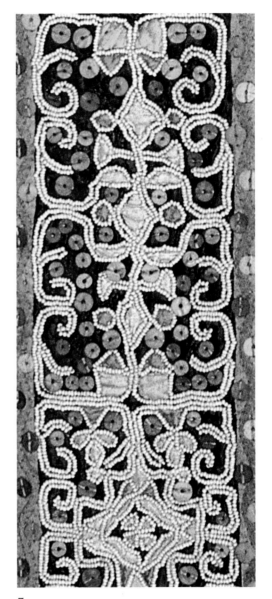

7.
Detail of Micmac beaded sash. Collected before 1856 by Vojta Naprstek. Náprstkovo Museum, Prague 22273.

term "Beothuk" was not in use before the 1820s, however, for until that time no one thought to enquire of a Beothuk about nomenclature. The Europeans, the Maliseet, and the Micmac simply called the Beothuk "Red Indians" — a term that gradually encompassed all native peoples of North America — because of their custom of painting their bodies and possessions with red ochre.

The Micmac and Maliseet word *lnu'k*, meaning "people," is used today to designate a native person only. The word "Micmac" derives from *nikmaq*,[7] a salutation that means "my kin friends" in the Micmac language. According to Marc Lescarbot, a Frenchman who lived in the New World for a year in 1607, this was the greeting used in conversation with Micmac Indians,[8] whom he referred to as "Souriquois," from the Souricoua River[9] in their territory. Later Frenchmen called these people *notres niqmachs*, and eventually, through misunderstandings, errors in transcription,[10] and English pronunciation, this became Micmac, and the tribal designation.

The Maliseet acquired their present tribal name from the Micmac, who called them *mali'sit*, meaning a person who "doesn't speak like us." The Maliseet called themselves *Wulustukw keuwiuk*,[11] roughly "the people of the beautiful river," the St. John River and its tributaries, along which their camps were strung like beads on a necklace. (Lescarbot and his contemporaries referred to them as *Etchemin*; the derivation of this term is uncertain.)

The Beothuk, the Maliseet, and the Micmac, living in similar northern maritime environments, created material cultures — tools, clothing, shelter, transportation — with many parallels, as would be expected. After all, they were using the same raw materials to hunt the same animals (except for the moose, which is not found in Newfoundland). Yet each of the three peoples exhibited a unique tribal stamp and flavour, diverse responses to common problems and experiences. Their histories were also to be different.

Documented history of the original inhabitants of North America begins with the Beothuk; yet of all the peoples represented in this exhibit, the Beothuk alone are not here to tell their story.

> You are doubtless aware that three of the Aborigines of this Island were brought to St. John's about two years ago, and two of them died very shortly after. . . . The third, a woman about 18 or 19 years of age is still alive. . . . She states that the whole number of her tribe did not exceed 15 persons in the winter of 1823, and that they were obliged by want of food to separate into three or four parties. Of these fifteen, two were shot down by some of our settlers, one was drowned, and three fell into our hands, so that only nine at the utmost remain to be accounted for.[12]

8.
Beothuk *Dancing Woman*, pencil sketch by Shanawdithit, a Beothuk captive, c. 1827-1829. Collection of the Newfoundland Museum, St. John's. From James Howley, *The Beoethucks*.

The silence of the Beothuk still speaks with a terrible eloquence of the disastrous way in which differing cultures can react and overreact to each other. Only a handful of artefacts remains of the Beothuk culture, distinguished by its unusual canoes with high crescent-moon ends, delicately beautiful pendants of carved ivory and bone, and a lavish use of red ochre. That handful comes largely from Beothuk burials and items made or drawn by one Beothuk woman captured by the English in the last decade of Beothuk existence.

The work of the Micmac and Maliseet, on the other hand, reflects, above all, these peoples' intense interaction with the Europeans through trade, which brought about pervasive changes to native life. Almost all the existing material culture of these two groups was made to be traded or sold. To compare a tiny ochred birchbark dish from a Beothuk grave and a lushly beaded red-wool tea cosy that a Micmac woman made and lined with magenta silk is to appreciate the wrenching cultural and economic upheaval necessary to adapt a neolithic culture to a nineteenth-century European world.

"We are the Mi'kmaw, as Old as the Sea"

What was life like for "the people" — Beothuk, Micmac, and Maliseet — before the arrival of the Europeans changed it forever? In 1740, the Abbé Maillard interviewed a Micmac shaman and chief named Arguimaut[13] as he sat with his councillors and elders in a summer wigwam on Isle St-Jean, now Prince Edward Island.[14] The Abbé provides the only record of the aboriginal people of this region and period as they describe the life-ways of their ancestors. "Father, before your arrival in these parts where God decreed we should be born, and where we have grown like the grasses and the trees you see around you, our most constant occupation was to hunt all sorts of animals so as to eat of their flesh and to cover ourselves with their skins."[15]

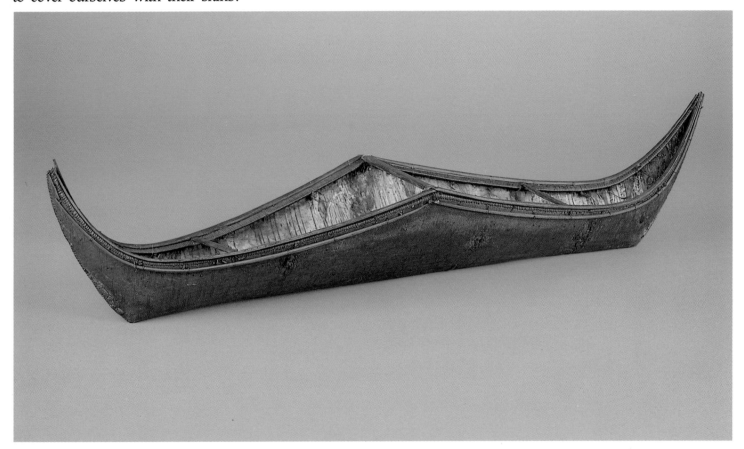

An all-encompassing interest in and understanding of animals was necessary for survival. Within the gestalt of the landscape, the lives of people and animals were everywhere entwined, both dreaming and awake. Animals were considered not as people, but as "persons," with whom one might have a relationship. An animal could become one's spirit-helper, and at need a human could take on that animal's form and power. Songs, stories, and mime dances consolidated these relationships. There were strictures and taboos about animals, those one ate and did not eat, and how one disposed of their remains.

It was a religious act among our people to gather up all bones very carefully and either to throw them in the fire (when we had one) or into a river where beaver lived. . . . All the bones of game we got from the sea had to be thrown in the sea so that the species would always exist.[16]

9.
Beothuk canoe model, taken in 1827 from a tomb erected 1819-1820. Made by the family of Nonosbawsut and Demasduwit. The Trustees, National Museums of Scotland, Edinburgh UC288. L:80.6; W:23.5; H:18

Heat and light were of paramount importance; the sun and its symbol, fire, dominated their rituals. Seventeenth-century creation myths of the Micmac[17] tell that the sun divided the earth into several parts, separated by great lakes; in each part "he caused to be born one man and one woman." Both Micmac and Maliseet addressed the sun as "Grandfather," considering it to be the oldest male ancestor and provider. "The Voice" that told the Beothuk they were created from an arrow or arrows stuck into the ground[18] is likely the sun. (A Montagnais version of the arrow story, in which the sun appears as a deity, was noted in 1605.[19])

10.
Beothuk *Mamateek and Food*, pencil sketch by Shanawdithit c. 1827-1829. Collection of the Newfoundland Museum, St. John's. From James Howley, *The Beoethucks*.

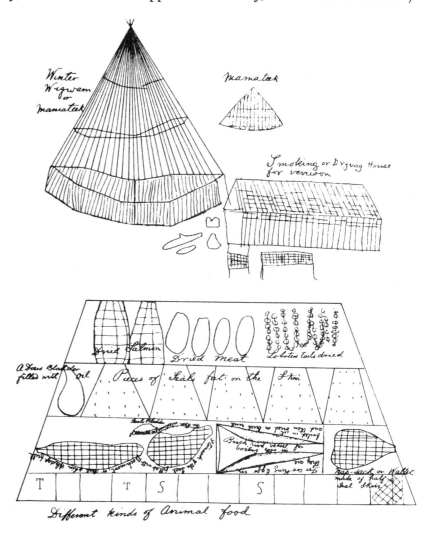

Chief Arguimaut described for the Abbé Maillard an important winter's-end ritual celebrating fire and the sun as life giver. This narrative gives us our most vivid image of the lives and world-view of these people.

> To preserve the fire, especially in winter, we would entrust it to the care of our war-chief's women, who took turns to preserve the spark. . . . When it lasted the span of three moons the fire became sacred. . . . We would suck in the smoke [from pipes lit with it] and one by one puff it into the face of the woman . . . telling her that she was worthy above all to share in the benefits of the Father of Light, the Sun, because she had so skillfully preserved his emanations.
> Then we would dance around the fire, and this is what we would sing: "O Fire, light our pipes and grant that by sucking in your goodness under the cover of the smoke that hides you from our eyes, we may become strong and vigorous and always able to know our servant-women and the wives of our bed. . . . Grant that hunger and thirst and illness may never overwhelm us to the point where

we are no longer indifferent to those ills as we should be. You, woman, by the great care . . . you have paid . . . to this spark of fire, have become the principal wife of our chief, if you are not so already. And now we summon this chief, who has broken so many heads, both human and animal, to come forward, and here in our presence he will stretch out his great fur, and you, woman, will lie under it first and he shall follow you.[20]

A bonfire was then lighted, and every kind of beast, bird, and fish cooked and eaten. Thus were food and warmth and fertility celebrated.

The Algonkian languages of "the people" differentiated between things animate and inanimate. Their languages mirrored their belief that not only were most living organisms animate, but that such things as stars were, as well, and special features of the landscape. Land, sea, and sky were imbued with animate power, and all who moved therein, whether corporeal or incorporeal, inhabited "a landscape of numinous events."[21] The Micmac and Maliseet called this power *mntu*; we translate the word imperfectly as "spirit" or "mana." Power could be acquired or lost: a tree was considered animate until it died, yet its dead wood, shaped into a bow or a bowl, became animate again by suffusion in the power of its maker, and by the importance of its function. Similarly, an arrow was animate, as was a snowshoe, a mask, or a woven sleeping mat. The land also held conscious manifestations of power, the *mntu'k*, who could be benevolent, malevolent, or indifferent.

In this animist cosmology, the three peoples used ritual — formal and informal manipulations of what they saw as the natural law of their world — in order to survive. Everyone could interpret and act out dreams, and recognize and accumulate "found" power-objects: strangely shaped or coloured stones, anomalies such as a bone with a curious lump on it. These objects were kept in medicine pouches, made into amulets, or sewn on clothing.

The decoration of clothing or the body was an intrinsic part of the way in which power was accrued, assimilated, and stored: "Both magic and decoration overlap so often and so deeply that they are almost inseparable; decoration is used to express and enhance magic, and magical thoughts are often contained — consciously or subconsciously — in decorative motifs and devices."[22] Personal manipulation of power might also include minor hunting magic and weather control through certain ritual actions or abstentions. Beyond the manipulations of magic that are small-scale and personal — for oneself and one's immediate family — are those that require enormous power and the ability to control it.

Persons adept in controlling power were the shamans, who were the "interface" between the people, animals, and *mntu'k*, and the power that was the ground of being for all. They strove to keep these relationships harmonious, performing curing ceremonies for the sick and initiating necessary actions to renew the land after famine: perhaps, suddenly, the caribou had changed their migration route; perhaps the wind kept the pack-ice and the seal herds away from land; perhaps the moose did not bunch up ("yard") because there was no snow during a mild winter. Had the people offended? Was some enemy at work? The shaman entered deep trance and sought his answers.

The ritual differed among the people; but combinations of fasting, enduring pain, drumming, and chanting were used by the shaman so that his spirit might escape the body and take flight. His blood pulsing to the drum, he passed through the cries of ravens, the rising thunder of hooves, the enormous silences of empty valleys, of ages and seasons like a river flowing over the land. Swimming beneath the earth or climbing to the sky-world, he embarked on a journey fraught with dangers.

11.
Beothuk male image, found in the grave of a four-year-old boy. Collection of the Newfoundland Museum, St. John's VIII-A-412. L:19.3; W:5.6; H:3.7

What he found at journey's end, we can only guess at.

An English expedition up the Exploits River, Newfoundland, in 1820 came across "a tree upon a projecting point just above a cataract, about forty feet in height, the bark of which was stripped off leaving only a small tuft on the top and from that downwards were painted alternate circles of red and white."[23]

12.
Micmac petroglyph, Kejimkujik National Park, N.S. Photograph by Olive Kelsall. The Nova Scotia Museum, Halifax.

This Beothuk creation immediately recalls Adrian Tanner's description[24] of the "made trees" of the Mistassini Cree rituals, "a tree from which all the branches have been removed, and which is then decorated, sometimes by cutting away bands of bark and sometimes by painted designs." This image of a sacred tree or pole is "essential to the beliefs and ritual practises of shamanism because it connects the three fundamental zones of the shamanistic cosmos; its roots penetrate the Underworld, its branches rise to the Sky."[25]

The site of the stripped and painted Beothuk tree, with its crowning tuft of branches, was thought by the Englishmen who saw it in 1820 to have "the appearance of a place of observation." If one extends this definition to include the spirit world, then perhaps they were right. This point of land above a waterfall, with its "made tree," may have been the site of one of the last spirit flights made by a Beothuk shaman, in a land where all balances were now fatally disrupted.

"We Are at Home Everywhere"

To move from the metaphysical to the physical world required, for the people, only a short step. Secure within the reciprocal relationships that ritual established with their world, they took from it what they needed for survival. The material cultures of all three groups show this very clearly, in their ingenious uses of animal, plant, and mineral materials.

Animals gifted them with more than meat. Fur and hides were used for clothing, animal sinew for sewing, and animal bones for awls and painting tools. The people incorporated into their costume animal hair, feathers, shells and bone, teeth, claws and dewclaws, quills, beaks, tails, horns — even the entire skins or stuffed bodies of small animals. These elements lent the animal's power or particular characteristics to the wearer.

Clothing was largely made by women; the materials, cut, and construction seem to have been much the same for all three peoples. Men and women wore a loincloth of supple leather, attached to a belt; leggings of some thicker hide; and moccasins. The favourite arm coverings were detached "sleeves" of beaver fur. Each covered an arm and a portion of the front and back torso. Both sexes had untailored outer robes, usually of beaver fur, moose, or caribou, which were thrown blanketwise over the shoulders; women added to this a body wrap of hide, girdled around the waist. Children wore smaller versions of adult costume, and infants still in baby carriers were swaddled in swansdown or fox fur.

Animal skins used in clothing included bear, walrus, seal, lynx, rabbit, mink, skunk, muskrat, squirrel, wildcat, wolverine, weasel, beaver, moose, caribou, bird skins with the down left on, as well as the skins of certain fish. To move — particularly in ceremonial clothing — was to experience the click and clash of teeth and dewclaws, the swaying of feather tufts. The power of the animal was conjured into clothing through the incorporation of its physical matter. In Micmac and Maliseet stories — including some about the Beothuk — many characters have animal names, and seem to shimmer between their human and spirit-helper shapes. Enwrapped as they were in the multiple, magical animal essences of costume, this is understandable.

This magical binding or association could also be accomplished by working the animal's image, in paint or embroidery, on an object. Both Micmac and Maliseet represented "upon their garments certain figures of wild beasts, birds or other animals such as are supplied by their imaginations."[26] There is a single eighteenth-century reference[27] to Beothuks painting on skins the figures of men and women, fish, and "fanciful scrawls."

13.
Detail of Micmac designs of parallel lines, in ribbon appliqué, on a 19th-century woman's peaked cap. From the collection of the Earl of Elgin and Kincardine, KT, CD, Scotland.

Maliseet and Micmac had their "fanciful scrawls" as well: borders or bands of parallel lines, "lace-like designs," and groups of "broken chevrons."[28] Geometric designs sometimes encoded magical protection, skills, or strengths received in dreams. "Indians believe in dreams," noted LeClercq in 1675,[29] and these dreams had to be acted out, made real, and sometimes incorporated as design work into personal possessions or clothing.

Both realistic and geometric motifs were painted and embroidered on clothing. Micmac and Maliseet worked in the four ritual colours: red, white, black, and yellow. If the Beothuk sometimes worked designs on their clothing, in all likelihood it would have been done over the ground of red ochre with which they painted everything. This red-ochre coating was both abstract decoration and perhaps also the potent life force of blood.

Micmac and Maliseet women used porcupine quills for embroidery, appliqué, wrapping, and weaving, or by oversewing, as they did with bird quills.[30] Oversewn lines of moose or caribou hair seem to have been used to create designs. The porcupine is not found in Newfoundland, but there is evidence that Beothuk women made similar use of bird quills and dyed lengths of split spruce root.

There are no surviving examples to show us Micmac, Maliseet, or Beothuk clothing from this early period. What little we know has been interpolated from chance sentences in sixteenth- and seventeenth-century records, and from the few fragments of "traditional" yet post-contact clothing that survived the introduction of cloth.

Apart from moccasins and the occasional tobacco pouch, the Micmac and Maliseet left no post-contact leather items. While most of our knowledge of Beothuk costume rests on two drawings by a Beothuk captive and on the occasional written description, we can examine three surviving pairs of moccasins, a legging, and a fragment of robe fringe — all probably from the early 1800s. These give a good idea of what pre-contact clothing looked like. Long hostility between Europeans and Beothuk prevented them from making wholesale use of cloth.

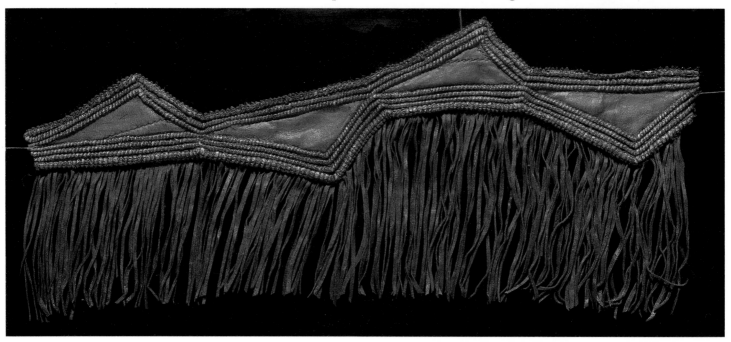

14.
Beothuk robe fringe, c. 1819-1820. Courtesy of the Trustees of the British Museum, London 2583. L:48.6; W:20.5

Note the parallel borders of rolled intestines and the pieced triangles.

The robe fragment is a fringed edging from a wrap taken in 1827 from a Beothuk tomb erected between 1819 and 1820.[31] It is a narrow rectangle of caribou leather, cut along the long axis at top and bottom to form triangles. A border of three raised parallel lines follows the edge of each upper triangle; a border of four lines follows the lower edges. The lines appear to be lengths of small rolled-up intestines, laid on the surface and oversewn so tightly that a corrugated effect is produced. A band of fringed leather falls from the lower edge, and the whole piece was rubbed with ochre, probably mixed with seal fat.

The three pairs of moccasins come from an undated child's burial of the post-contact period.[32] They are of considerable interest, as their construction differs from that produced by groups that surrounded the Beothuk. All are of caribou leather: a sole, a vamp, and a cuff with a leather tie. The sole folds up and is stitched to the vamp in a straight ungathered line across the toe, then along the sides of the vamp to the point at which the cuff overlaps the vamp. The sole is then stitched to the cuff, and the remaining length of vamp is tucked behind the cuff as a tongue. A single vertical edge of one cuff has been decorated with bird-quill overlay, sewn on with sinew, and then resewn with split spruce root, which was passed through the original awl holes.

The piece of leather included in the child's burial has been described as a shroud, robe, or burial bag. It is, however, a woman's left legging,[33] the only complete piece of adult Beothuk clothing known. It is made up of five pieces of beaver hide, with the fur removed.

The outside of the legging is painted with ochre. Bird claws[34] and bone pendants – probably two of each, originally – were attached to the outer edge. Each seam has had lengths of peeled and split spruce root passed through awl holes over the sinew thread that was used to stitch it together. Spruce root is beautifully white when first peeled, and would have produced a decorative contrast to the red ochre paint.

These few remnants of Beothuk costume tell us so much: the use of caribou, beaver, bird, and seal implies a wide range of hunting technologies, tanning, and tailoring, and the tools necessary for all. Bone pendants and bird claws on the legging and the blood-red ochre coating on all the objects speak of the animist world-view of these people. It is the decorative use of prosaic materials such as intestines and spruce root, however, that intrigues us: lacking moose and porcupine, Beothuk women found these rather unexpected substitutes for the usual quill and hair used in embroidery. Roots and guts? one asks – yet they are beautiful.

15.
Beothuk child's moccasins of caribou hide painted with red ochre. Collection of the Newfoundland Museum, St. John's VIII-A-392 a,b. L:12.5; W:4.8; H:5.3

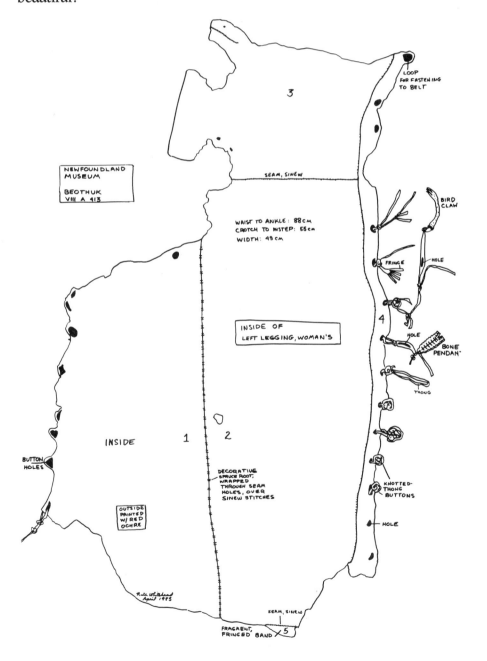

16.
Beothuk legging of pieced beaver skin, with bone and bird-claw pendants. Drawing by Ruth H. Whitehead. Collection of the Newfoundland Museum, St. John's VIII-A-413. L:88; W:49

"As This is All We Own"

The plant world also had much to give the three peoples; they harvested many trees for their wood and plants for medicines, dyes, and food. The root of the black spruce (*Picea mariana*), for example, was used for much more than decoration. Spruce root makes excellent cordage: the wigwam frame of spruce poles was lashed together with it; debarked and split, it became thread for sewing the bark wigwam cover.

With bark of the white birch (*Betula papyrifera*), the people constructed everything from wigwam (or Beothuk *mamateek*) to torches, moose-callers to shrouds. Birchbark was water-repellent. Cut, folded, and sewn, it could be made watertight. Water could even be boiled in a birchbark pot: it was the perfect lightweight container.

The peoples' most ingenious use of birchbark was to make it a container for themselves. The birchbark canoe was the most complex creation of their respective material cultures. Samuel Champlain recorded that in the early seventeenth century, the canoes of the Indians were all made alike, "from Saco [Maine] along the whole coast as far as Tadoussac [Quebec]."[35] This was generally true of size, materials, and construction techniques; yet Beothuk, Micmac, and Maliseet canoes were tailored to the demands of their marine or riverine environments, and thus there were very specific differences.

"The old form of Malecite [*sic*] canoe used on the large rivers and along the coasts appears to have had rather high peaked ends, with a marked overhang fore and aft."[36] In 1602, the English appropriated what was probably a Maliseet canoe and took it back to Britain; it was "open like a Wherrie, and sharpe at both ends, saving that the beake was a little bending roundly upward. . . . It carried nine men standing upright, yet it weighed not at the most above sixtie pounds."[37]

17.
Maliseet canoe model of incised birchbark. York-Sunbury Historical Society Inc. Museum, Fredericton. 1973.18.3 L:38.5; W:11; H:3.2

These narrow, high-beaked canoes were excellent river craft, capable of squeezing through the tightest rapids. After European settlement, when the Maliseet withdrew more and more from the coast to the interior waterways, this shape became more exaggerated, moving farther away from the ocean-going Micmac form it once may have resembled.

The Micmac canoe was built for the sea. Its high, rockered ends, hogged sheer — the convex line of the gunwales amidship — and its broad beam kept out breaking waves and gave it stability. Such canoes were up to twelve metres long.[38] Other types included war canoes, built for speed, and a small river canoe, in which the sheer eventually flattened out.

"The unique appearance of Beothuk canoes was largely due to their very high and curved end sections and their hogged and sometimes pointed sheer."[39] There were probably two distinct types. The first and oldest had a straight bottom and incorporated a keelson, "a long shaped pole, placed in the centre of the bark hull; the bark sides were folded upwards on either side of the keelson at an angle of approximately 45 degrees forming a deadrise."[40] It was V-shaped in cross-section. A second type had a profile like a crescent moon: "The Beothuk bent the keelson into the desired curve and cut two half-moon-shape bark sections for the sides."[41] The bark sections were sewn along the keelson underneath which made the canoe more seaworthy.[42]

Both birchbark and spruce root were involved in decoration. Spruce root was often dyed, then sewn into the bark to form ornamental patterns, even on something as large as a canoe. Spruce root was used as a substitute for porcupine quills in both line embroidery and wrapping techniques. Birchbark was painted and embroidered. Seventeenth-century wigwams were embellished with "a thousand different pictures of birds, moose, otters and beavers, which the women sketch there themselves with their paints."[43] Bark containers were ornamented with quills, which were probably wrapped around the bowl's wooden rim or oversewn in lengths by the root that lashed rim to bowl.

Birchbark was also decorated by an incising technique. Bark gathered when the sap is rising[44] has a darker inner layer, which can be scraped away to show the lighter colour beneath. All these decorative techniques were to be of great importance in later times, after the arrival of Europeans created a market for ornamental work.

From plant material, women also created textiles, containers, and cordage. Basswood bark, cedar bark, rushes, reeds, cattails, nettles, Indian hemp, sweetgrass, beach-grass and wood fibres were worked in a variety of ways. Most of the three peoples' knowledge of these techniques did not survive the seventeenth century, however, and only a few fragments of mats and bags remain.

Men worked wood into snowshoes, toboggans, sleds, baby carriers, bowls and spoons, war clubs and shields, and the haftings for tools and weapons. They also excelled at working stone and bone. The Beothuk do not appear to have smoked, but both Micmac and Maliseet made tobacco pipes from wood, bone, stone, antler and even lobster claws, birchbark, and reeds. Micmac men, said Lescarbot, "do make pictures of beasts, birds and men as well in stone as in wood,"[45] to decorate their pipes and other creations.

18.
Detail of 19th-century Maliseet canoe paddle, with incised geometric motifs. York-Sunbury Historical Society Inc. Museum, Fredericton. 1969.2062.1 L:190.5; W:15.2; H:2.4

The Maliseet and Micmac played the bowl game *waltes* at least as early as 1600. A *waltes* set is the only traditional item made and used today as it was centuries ago: six "dice" of ivory or moose leg-bone are placed in a shallow wooden dish, usually made of a maple burl. The bowl is slammed against the ground to toss the circular dice — convex and unmarked on one side, with a decorated flat surface on the other. Scores are kept with carved wooden sticks or reeds representing different values.

The world of the people, through its animals, plants, and minerals, provided them with everything necessary for a comfortable life, but all

19.
Micmac ocean-going canoe, incised birchbark. Collected 1879 from the island of St. Pierre, off the coast of Newfoundland. Museum für Völkerkunde. Vienna 8437 L:525; W:90; H:33.5

three peoples seem to have hungered for beauty as well, once basic needs had been satisfied, and for novelty. This may have been an impetus for establishing native trade routes, such as the ones that brought exotic stones and copper, musk-ox hair[46] or buffalo fur to Atlantic Canada as early as two thousand years ago. The habit of trade and the desire for things new and different were to burgeon with the coming of Europeans.

"And I Will Relate Wonders to My People"

The arrival of the European traders and fishermen, with their metal knives and copper pots, woollen fabrics, glass beads, guns, and strange intoxicating drinks generated an enormous excitement. The people were consumed with curiosity. "We are people," they said. "What are you?"

> When there were no people in this country but Indians, and before any others became known, a young woman had a singular dream. . . . A small island came floating in towards the land, with

20.
Micmac or Maliseet tobacco pipes and crooked-knife handle. Watercolour, 1862, from L.L. Hawkins's *Illustrated Gleanings of Aboriginal Ornaments from the International Exhibition of 1862*, Plate 57. Courtesy of the Trustees of the British Museum, London R6869.

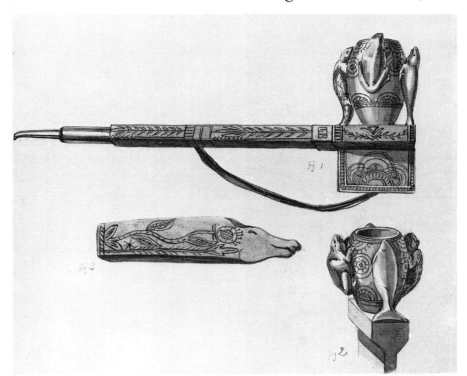

21.
Micmac or Maliseet powder horn. Cow's horn acquired in trade and incised with floral and geometric motifs. Watercolour, 1862, from L.L. Hawkins' *Illustrated Gleanings of Aboriginal Ornaments from the International Exhibition of 1862*, Plate 55. Courtesy of the Trustees of the British Museum, London R6869.

tall trees on it, and living beings. [The shamans] pondered the girl's dream but could make nothing of it. The next day an event occurred that explained all. What should they see but a singular little island, as they supposed, which had drifted near to the land and become stationary there! There were trees on it, and branches to the trees, on which a number of bears . . . were crawling about. . . . What was their surprise to find that these supposed bears were men.[47]

Thus the Micmac told their descendants of the coming of the white men.

When did these first encounters take place? We know that after 985 A.D., the Norse were journeying along the coasts of Labrador and Newfoundland, and perhaps down the Strait of Belle Isle into the Gulf of St. Lawrence. Some of them reported meeting a people with whom they traded red cloth and milk for furs, and with whom they later fought.[48] Were these the ancestors of the Beothuk or Montagnais, or even the Micmac? All one can say is that they were Indian; unlike the Inuit, they wore untailored clothing, which they let fall when running away from the Norse.[49]

Intensive exploration of the "New Found" world of Atlantic Canada did not begin until the 1500s, after John Cabot's 1497 voyage reported the enormous shoals of codfish off Newfoundland. A Portuguese colony under Fagundes is said to have been established on Cape Breton Island in 1521. "Because they lost their ships there was no further notice of them except from some Basques who continued to seek and barter on that coast the many things to be had there."[50]

What were these Basque traders after? First and most obviously, furs. After canoeing out to European ships, Micmac wearing lustrous beaver-fur robes were immediately offered anything and everything for what they considered to be their old clothes. It didn't take them long to learn the rules of this new trade: in 1534, when Jacques Cartier sailed into Chaleur Bay on the New Brunswick coast, he was besieged by Micmac in canoes, waving furs on the ends of poles and screaming "*Nape'u, tú dameu a cierto!*" ("Man [cock], give me something!")[51] The fur trade was in full swing.

By 1583, for example, Étienne Bellenger had made several voyages to the New World; in that year, he brought home from the Atlantic coast of Nova Scotia, "Buff hides reddie dressed upon both sides bigger than an Oxe; Deere skynes dressed well on the inner side, with the hayre on the outside; marterns enclyning unto sables; beavers skynnes verie fayer as many as made 600 beaver hattes; otters skynnes verie faire and large."[52]

Records are less clear for Newfoundland. Anchored off the Funk Islands in 1534, in order to load his ship with auks, Cartier recorded the Beothuk term for these birds: "called by the natives *Apponath.*"[53] This is the first hard evidence that not only had contact been made with the Beothuk before 1534 — Cartier had made at least one voyage to Newfoundland before 1532 — but that this contact was an amiable one.

The tone of these early encounters with native peoples varied — according, one supposes, to the individuals involved on either side. In 1536, a scant two years after Cartier's expedition, an English ship sighted Beothuk, who fled when the ship's boat was sent after them.[54] In 1583, several of Bellenger's men were murdered by a Micmac band, who also stole his pinnace, the smaller boat with which he had hoped to explore the coast.[55] Richard Whitbourne recounted that, for payment, the native people of Newfoundland assisted the French and Basque codfishers and whalers in gutting fish, butchering whales, and rendering their oil; this is thought by many scholars to be mere propaganda for the colonists Whitbourne hoped to entice.[56] Whatever the case, it is at this point that

22.
Micmacs in traditional 19th-century dress. Thought to be Christian Morris and her adopted son Joe. Courtesy of the Public Archives of Nova Scotia, Halifax.

Beothuk relations with Europeans began to take a different form from the type experienced by the Maliseet and Micmac.

"Stories Told of Indians and White Men"

To begin with, this whale- and cod-fishery off Newfoundland was so structured that there was an enormous European presence in the area during the fishing season, but almost none of the hundreds of ships over-wintered. As colonization was discouraged, every winter for years the Beothuk were free to roam through deserted European camps, examining their constructions and fingering their discarded garbage. In 1594, about forty Beothuk were camped in St. George's Bay, hard by the wrecks of two Basque vessels, which they probably were in the process of stripping.[57] Ultimately, the annual autumn departure of the European fishery meant there was no need for the Beothuk to develop trade with Europeans; they simply appropriated what they needed as soon as the last ship sailed over the horizon.[58] Eventually they grew bolder and began helping themselves *before* the season ended. Whitborne told that before 1622 a ship anchored near his in Trinity Bay had been robbed by Beothuk; the crew in turn raided a Beothuk camp consisting of three tents, three canoes, and three birchbark pots "standing each of them on three stones, boyling, with twelue Fowles in each, euery Fowle as big as a Widgeon, and some so big as a Ducke."[59]

> They had also many such Pots so sewed, and fashioned like leather Buckets . . . great store of skins of Deere, Beauers, Beares, Seales, Otters, and diuers other fine skins which were excellent well dressed; as also great store of several sorts of flesh dried. . . . They all ran away naked, without any apparell, but onely some had their hats on their heads, which were made of Seale skinnes, in fashions like our hats, sewed handsomely with narrow bands about them, set round with fine white shels. . . . All their three Cannowes, their flesh, skins, yolks of Egges, Targets, Bowes and Arrows and much fine Okar and diuers other things [the Europeans] tooke and brought away.

Here we have one of the first detailed descriptions of Beothuk material culture. It is ironic that even before the words were written, this band had lost most of its possessions to the pilferage and retaliation that, over the years, would spell doom for the Beothuk.

John Guy, who established one of the first overwintering English colonies in about 1610, met a party of Beothuk in Trinity Bay in 1612; the Beothuk were cautious but friendly. "One of them, blowing in the aqua-vitae bottle, yt made a sound, which they fell all into a laughture."[60] After the initial encounter, Guy's party came across a probable "dumb-barter" site: "An old boat sayle, three or fowre shell chains, about twelve furres of beavers most, a foxe skinne, a saple skin, a bird skinne, & ane mitten set everye one upon a severall poule: whereby we remayned satisfied fullie that they weare brought theather of purpose to barter with vs. . . . Because we were not furnished with fit things for to trucke, we took only a beaver skin, a sable skin and a bird skin."[61] Guy's men were not set up for trading; they were themselves trapping.

For the Beothuk, the simple barter of the very early contact period never developed into full-blown trade, as it did for the Maliseet and Micmac.

> The nature of the 17th and 18th century Newfoundland economy discouraged the sort of European-native contact which might have resulted in mutual adaptation to each others' presence . . . [via]

Indian agents, missionaries and fur traders. These Europeans did not exist in insular 17th and 18th century Newfoundland.[62]

Such was not the case on the mainland, where Basque and French traders had been plying their wares successfully for at least a hundred years. In return for furs, both Maliseet and Micmac received woollen clothing, blankets, hats, shoes, ribbons, beads, and all manner of metal goods, of which the large copper cooking pots were a great favourite. A Micmac burial (between 1570 and 1590) included twenty-two pots, as well as axes, a saw, fish hooks, adzes, caulkers, daggers, spear heads, swords, awls, a wine cork, a ceramic apothecary jar, trade beads, and wool blankets.[63]

Long before 1689, when the young English boy John Gyles was captured by the Maliseet, European goods had become a way of life. Many native technologies had fallen by the wayside. Moccasins, for example, were the only traditional clothing still being made in any great numbers. Even Gyles, a slave, had a wool blanket.

> If [Maliseet] parents have a daughter marriageable, they seek a husband for her who is a good hunter. . . . If the man [has] . . . a gun and ammunition, a canoe, a spear, a hatchet, a monoodah [pouch], a crooked knife, looking glass and paint, and pipe, tobacco and knotbowl to toss a kind of dice in, he is accounted a gentleman of plentiful fortune.[64]

The Maliseet husband's gun and ammunition, spear head, knife blade, axe, mirror, and paint, even his tobacco, were all made by Europeans. His "plentiful fortune" depended on the new fur-trade economy.

In the early years of contact, both Micmac and Maliseet used their knowledge of coastal and inland waterways — and of the ancient trade connections — to become middlemen in the fur trade, bargaining for moose

23.
Maliseet wigwams. *Indian Camp, New Brunswick*, watercolour on paper by William Robert Herries (1818-1845). Purchased with a grant from the Government of Canada through the Cultural Properties Import and Export Act 1983 and funds from the Marguerite and Murray Vaughn Foundation and the Samuel Endowment. Beaverbrook Art Gallery, Fredericton. L:36.5; W:24.4

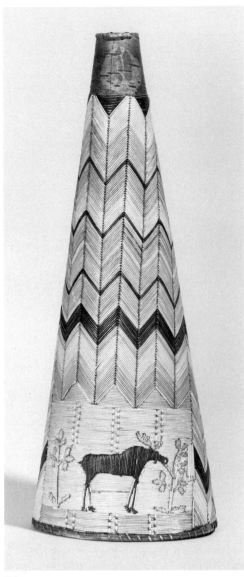

24.
Micmac quillwork moose-caller, with a
moose worked in black quills on a
background of chevrons, early 19th century.
Pitt Rivers Museum, Oxford 1954.9.71.
L:33.5; D:12.3

and beaver from unacculturated groups in the Gulf of St. Lawrence and the Gulf of Maine. In 1606, Messamouet, chief at La Hève, in what is now Nova Scotia, sailed his shallop to Saco to trade "kettles, large, medium and small, hatchets, knives, dresses, capes, red jackets, peas, beans, biscuits, and other such things" for furs, which he would then transport back to the French sphere of influence.[65] Chief Messamouet informed his would-be clients that he had been to France [before 1580], as the house guest of the Mayor of Bayonne.[66] Both Micmac and Maliseet were by this time fluent in pidgin Basque, the trade language of the Gulf of St. Lawrence, and were accomplished shallop sailors.[67]

"I Was Free Before, in Spaces to the Stars"

This native entrepreneurship, which may have been in place quite early in the 1500s, did not survive long into the 1600s, as French and English explorers moved farther south and north along the coasts. The shock of cultural contact was severe. It is estimated that, between 1600 and 1700, from 70 per cent to 90 per cent of the native population died from epidemic diseases unwittingly introduced from Europe, and from the toxic and sociological effects of alcohol.[68] The year 1607 marked the first time European guns were used by native against native, as an alliance of Micmac, Maliseet, and Montagnais raided into Maine. Nor was it to be the last time. Under the pressure of the gun and the fur trade, animal populations also dropped, in some cases almost to extinction, reducing both the people's bartering power and their traditional supplies of food and clothing.

Micmac and Maliseet men were accounted worthy, in pre-contact times, if they could feed their families well. By 1740, the Abbé Maillard noted, standards of worthiness had expanded to include one who paid his seasonal debt to the European trader. As their priest, Maillard tried to encourage them to work hard during the trapping season, and "finally gain some credit."[69] Then, said his parishioners, "we would have furs enough to pay for all the supplies and materials, etc., we borrow every autumn." This was a completely different economic structure, and it was difficult for people to adapt.

Furs were becoming scarce, however, and the influx of Loyalist settlers during the 1780s forced the Maliseet and Micmac from the food-rich coastal areas into the barren interior. The constant warring of the French and English across native territory during the first half of the century had exhausted the peoples, and the survivors were falling prey to epidemics of smallpox and to starvation.

From this it can be seen that even the most amicable trade relations were fraught with danger. In Newfoundland, the Beothuk chose isolation, or had it imposed upon them. They took what they needed from the seasonal fishermen and learned quite a lot about European technology without the risks of face-to-face meetings. Inspired by European constructions, their architecture underwent a brief florescence: there are reports of rectangular Beothuk buildings, "framed neatly in the fashion of English fishing houses. The lodgement of the rafters on the beams and the necessary joints were as neatly executed as in the houses commonly inhabited by our fishers."[70] The Beothuk discovered how to forge iron, stealing traps and pots for raw material; they often burnt European boats to get at the nails used in their construction. From stolen iron they made their own arrow- and spear heads. A recently excavated Beothuk site at Boyd's Cove, Newfoundland, shows that from about 1650 to 1720 — when the English set up a salmon fishery and fur-trapping operation six kilometres away — life was largely undisturbed and the European pickings fairly rich: to date, more than 1,324 metal objects have been recovered from that site alone.[71] But this scavenger economy, as the abandonment of Boyd's Cove shows, was no longer viable once intensive settlement by Europeans began. "Their repeated thefts resulted in Europeans taking punitive measures against them. . . . In the short term, it may well have been a more adaptive decision to steal rather than to trade, but in the long run it might have proved fatal."[72]

By the 1700s the coasts were no longer safe places for the Beothuk. Micmac and Maliseet were driven away from the sea by European population pressures; the Beothuk withdrew into the interior of the island of Newfoundland to escape European guns. Their ocean-going canoes now sailed only brooks and lakes. There, cut off from the bird islands, the sealing grounds, and the food resources of the sea, with European nets catching the spawning salmon on the lower reaches of every stream, illness and malnutrition took its toll. The Beothuk had to rely on the autumn migration of caribou for food and furs. But as their numbers

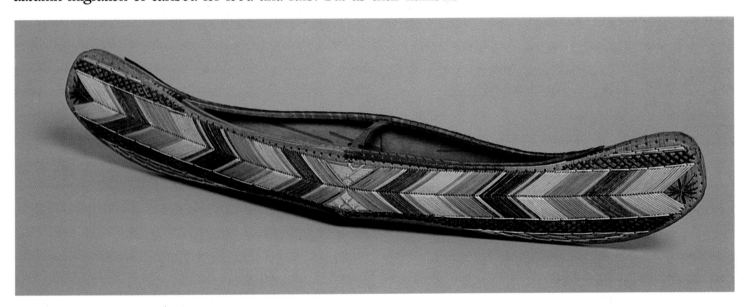

25.
Micmac quillwork canoe model, purchased from *Tuscarora Indians, N.Y., 1840*. The Peabody Museum of Salem, Massachusetts E4212. L:48; W:9.9; H:10

A good example of the type of Micmac souvenir art for sale at places such as Niagara Falls.

26.
Micmac quillwork chair seat, c. 1850-1860. Canadian Museum of Civilization, National Museums of Canada, Ottawa III-F-267. L:40.5; W:32.5

diminished, they could no longer maintain or use the thirty to forty miles of caribou fences along the Exploits River. The more people they lost, the less there was to eat.

Although this was happening to the Maliseet and Micmac as well, they had recourse to governmental assistance. The Beothuk's only contact with Europeans was with settlers, and this was almost always hostile.

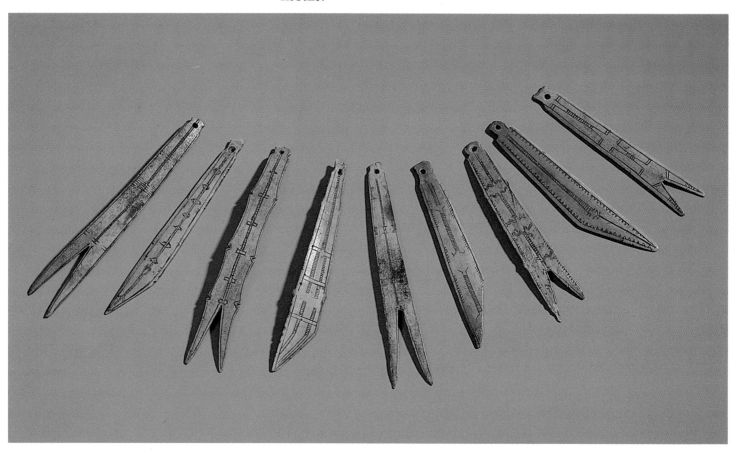

27.
Beothuk pendants, of caribou bone and walrus ivory. Collection of the Newfoundland Museum, St. John's. L:3-15 (range)

When we went up the brook in February 1790 in search of the Indians, we set out fully resolved to kill all we should meet. . . . Thomas Taylor said, we will give them fair play; if they run we won't fire. They all ran off. . . . Three of us remained at the wigwams. . . . In the dusk of the evening I asked Thomas Taylor to go down to the landwash and burn their canoes to retaliate for their burning a punt of ours. We went to the spot where they left their canoes, and putting two of them into the third, set fire to them. . . . Before we left the spot we set fire to three of their wigwams out of four, to be revenged on them for burning a winter-house in the Mouth of the Exploits River. The wigwams we burnt were covered with sails the Indians stole. We got about 100 deer skins. . . . In the wigwams we found a Tin Tea-kettle, an Iron Pot, several Traps, some of our Salmon Nets. The Beds of the traps they worked into spears and arrows; some of the nets were picked to pieces to make rope.[73]

Burnt inside each wigwam was the winter's supply of caribou meat, "40 or 50 of these [twenty-five-foot] square packages," full of pressed and frozen meat. The pot, the tea-kettle, and five hundred arrows were thrown into the brook, and then the settlers returned home. This was not the only raid, and such losses of homes, canoes, food supplies, tools, and clothing contributed heavily to the deaths of entire bands.

To give them their due, the colonial authorities in St. John's were anxious to establish good relations with the Beothuk, and made several attempts to search them out in the interior. In August 1768, Lieutenant John Cartwright's expedition up the River Exploits had as one of its aims, "to surprise, if possible, one or more of these savages, for the purpose of effecting in time, a friendly intercourse with them, in order to promote their civilization, and render them in the end, useful subjects of His Majesty."[74] No "savages" were encountered. Lieutenant David Buchan's journey up the Exploits in the winter of 1810–1811 ended in tragedy, with the death of two of his marines who had been left hostage with the Beothuk, and the subsequent forced abandonment by the people of the winter camps in which he found them.[75]

In September, 1818, this same band, now considerably diminished, cut loose from John Peyton's wharf in Lower Sandy Point his "large open boat, loaded with the season's produce . . . ready to proceed to market."[76] This was a heavy loss, and in March 1819, Peyton took a band of men up the Exploits, with the permission of Governor Hamilton, to "search for his stolen property, and if possible try and capture one of the Indians alive."[77] Thus began the last chapter, the last decade of Beothuk history.

Peyton and his men came upon three *mamateeks*, and the inhabitants fled before them. One was a woman, Demasduwit, said to have given birth to her first child two days previously; unable to keep up with the others, she was captured. Her husband, Nonosbawsut, tried "by oratory" to persuade the men to free her. They refused. Nonosbawsut threw himself against the odds of ten to one — those ten armed with guns — and Peyton's men killed him. Demasduwit was taken back to Twillingate, and then on to St. John's. Her baby, left behind, died on the second day.[78]

The government eventually ordered Demasduwit — referred to as Mary March for the month of her capture — to be returned to her people. "Whatever it may be that operates so fatally on savages separated from their native habits, spared not poor Mary. She left St. John's with a bad cough and died of consumption on nearing the Exploits."[79] Buchan, now a captain, took her coffined body up the river and left it at the deserted camp.

Demasduwit had a niece, Shanawdithit, who was captured with her mother and sister in 1823. The other two women soon succumbed to tuberculosis; Shanawdithit, also consumptive, lived until 1829. From this Beothuk woman we have the *other* side of this story, an eyewitness account of her people's last twenty years, "nearly all the information we possess regarding her tribe."[80] For Shanawdithit became the "interesting protegé" of William Cormack, president of the Boeothick Institute, and the first white man to walk across Newfoundland (in 1822). Each learned enough of the other's language to communicate. On her death, Shanawdithit left Cormack a granite pebble, a quartz crystal, a length of her hair. Her legacy also included his reams of notes on their conversations, maps and pictures she had drawn herself, a complete Beothuk costume, some mythology, history, and vocabulary. (Not all of this has survived.)

When Shanawdithit was taken away from them in 1823, there were thirteen members of her family still alive in the interior. "Here ends," wrote Cormack, "all positive knowledge of her tribe, which she never narrated without tears."[81]

In 1827, Cormack made a second trip across the Newfoundland interior, this time searching for Beothuk in the company of a Micmac, an Abenaki, and a Montagnais. They came to Red Indian Lake, "looked down on the lake from the hills at the northern extremity, with feelings of anxiety and admiration: no canoe could be discovered moving on its placid surface in the distance."[82]

> My party had been so excited, so sanguine, so determined to obtain an interview of some kind with these people, that on discovering from appearances everywhere that the Red Indians . . . no longer existed, the spirits of one and all of us were very deeply affected. The old Mountaineer was particularly overcome. . . . The wreck of a [canoe] lay thrown up among the bushes at the beach. . . . Had there been any survivors, nails being much prised by those people . . . such an article would no doubt have been taken out for use again. All the birch trees in the vicinity of the lake had been rinded, and many of them and of the spruce fir . . . had the bark taken off, to use the inner part of it for food.

Cormack went on to tell that one night he and his men had camped on the foundation of an old *mamateek*, on an exposed point of land thrusting out into the lake.[83] The Micmac and the Abenaki became very uneasy. "From time immemorial none of the Indians of the other tribes had ever encamped near this lake fearlessly." Their fire was a single minute point of light in miles of darkness; the water held a terrible emptiness. The Red People were gone, but everywhere the land was filled with their ghosts.

"I Lay My Body Upon the Ground"

We tend to concentrate on the history of the Beothuk simply because so little else remains. What did they leave behind them? "A few fabulous fragments," to quote Cormack, "traces enough left to cause our sorrow that so peculiar and so superior a people should have disappeared from the earth like a shadow."[84] European collections hold less than twenty Beothuk artefacts, most of them acquired by William Cormack.

On his 1827 journey, Cormack stumbled on the tomb in which the Beothuk had laid Demasduwit in her coffin, Nonosbawsut, and their child. He opened the grave, taking two skulls and some grave goods:

> There were two small wooden images of a man and a woman, no doubt meant to represent husband and wife; a small doll, which was supposed to represent a child (for Mary March had to leave her only child here, which died two days after she was taken); several small models of their canoes; two small models of boats; an iron axe; a bow and quiver of arrows were placed by the side of Mary March's husband; and two fire-stones . . . lay at his head; there were also various kinds of culinary utensils, neatly made of birch rind and ornamented, and many other things.[85]

Cormack gave the Royal Scottish Museum one canoe model; it is the best surviving example of the older type of canoe and is exquisitely made. Three birchbark containers from this burial are in the same collection; a wooden bird image and "the pelisse of the Chief's infant daughter" have been lost.[86]

A larger version of one of the Edinburgh bark containers is held by the Ethnography Department of the British Museum (Figure 28).[87] Both it and the robe fringe described earlier came from the Demasduwit grave. A second bark container, two bone pendants,[88] and some shell beads in this collection are demonstrably Beothuk, but lack provenance.

The Oslo University Museum owns a Beothuk harpoon head, and the National Maritime Museum in Greenwich, England, has a canoe model made by Shanawdithit.[89] The Nova Scotia Museum in Halifax holds a bone pendant, taken "from a woman's grave, interior of Newfoundland," in about 1850 – possibly the Demasduwit burial or one of the nearby graves seen by Cormack in 1827.[90] In Montreal, the McCord Museum's collection includes three bone pendants[91] and some shell beads from a man's grave discovered near Rencontre in 1847; the National Museum of Civilization in Ottawa has more than fifty bone and ivory pendants, all from poorly recorded Newfoundland sites.

The largest collection of Beothuk work – comprising objects in birchbark, bone, ivory, shell, spruce root, wood, metal, and other scavenged European materials – is housed at the Newfoundland Museum in St. John's. This museum also holds Shanawdithit's surviving maps and drawings, with annotations by Cormack.

Of all the things they made, most fascinating are the Beothuk's curious bone and ivory pendants. Until excavations at Boyd's Cove in the 1980s, these were known only from burials; most date to the period after the arrival of Europeans. Several in the Ottawa collections are worked with metal files.[92] Pendants are connected in some way with magic, either as personal amulets – two were found attached to the woman's legging described earlier – or possibly as ritual objects used by shamans.

Caves on Long Island in Newfoundland's Green Bay have yielded three groups of thirty to thirty-six elaborate pendants, not associated with human burials.[93] It is possible that these packaged and buried pendants were shamans' medicine bundles. Some of the pendant forms may represent bears, parts of bears, or "mammalian figures,"[94] perhaps either bear or human. This would certainly fit the shamanic world-view in which bears are powerful spirit-helpers. There is also a marked similarity between human hand and foot bones and the equivalent bones of bears, which may have been of great magical significance. Four of the Ottawa pendants clearly represent skeletal human finger-bones in a very realistic style. The large elaborate forms in the three bundles mentioned earlier may also represent an increased concentration on magic as a bulwark against the European incursion.

While *The Spirit Sings* was being researched, an oddity was noted in the construction of the large bark container in the British Museum. A second band of bark had been added to project above the original rim, in order to increase the dish's depth. More bizarre was the fact that this band had not reached all the way around, so it had had to be pieced, by the insertion of a small bark strip, sewn to either end with

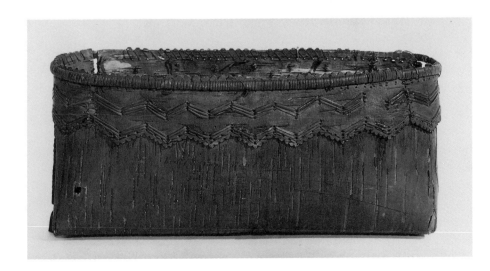

28.
Beothuk container, *Red Indian Meat Dish for Deer's flesh found in the Chief's tomb at Red Indian Lake 1827 by W.E. Cormack.* Pieced from three birchbark sections. Courtesy of the Trustees of the British Museum, London 6976. L:15.5; W:13; H:17.3

spruce root. This is neither functional (it weakens the dish), nor practical (it is faster to cut a strip the right length), nor decorative. This raises the question: why not simply make another dish? Does this reflect a scarcity of bark? Cormack did note that birches around Red Indian Lake and other areas had all been rinded.

The robe fringe from the same tomb was pieced together in part from scraps of leather; the joins can be seen running beneath the decorative border. Was this tell-tale evidence of Beothuk poverty, or simply coincidence worked upon with modern hindsight?

That the desperate circumstances of their last years are apparent in surviving Beothuk material seems to be confirmed with a terrible finality in the grave-gifts of a four-year-old boy,[95] the Newfoundland Museum's most important Beothuk collection. The body was surrounded by three model bark canoes,[96] much smaller than that from Demasduwit's burial, miniature bark dishes, a packet of food, and a wooden male image,[97] which recalls the wooden figures from the Demasduwit site. Also included were three pairs of moccasins.

The tiny vamp of one moccasin had been cobbled from three scraps of leather; one fragment of hide was not even from the same species of animal. Piecing, patching, and repairs are evident in three of the five moccasins still intact; and the moccasins had been repaired, not with caribou sinew, but with stiff, thick spruce root. A clumsy spruce-root knot and repair was placed right beneath one heel, to hold the worn leather together.

The child had been covered with a folded piece of leather, now dried hard and brittle. Careful examination showed it to be the woman's legging discussed earlier. It was put together from five pieces, some repaired or patched. This is such an odd thing with which to shroud a body; in the light of this it seemed probable that the mother, in burying her child, and having nothing else to cover him with, had simply removed one of her leggings and folded it twice to drape like a blanket from his neck down over his feet.

Some Naskapi women in the interior of Labrador told Mina Hubbard in 1905, "We are poor, and we live among the trees, but we have our children."[98] In the end, the Beothuk did not even have that comfort.

"There Would Be Food Today, When My Father Sold Our Work"

The Micmac and Maliseet narrowly escaped the same fate. "I learned on enquiry from many elderly people, who stated themselves to be childless, that they had had from 8 to 12 children each, who had died in infancy. . . . During my visit to the Miramichi the children were suffering dreadfully from dysentery, and while at Burnt Church a death occurred almost daily."[99]

Ethnographers of the early nineteenth century felt that within a few more decades these people, too, would become a "vanished race." Yet somehow they survived: as military allies, first of the French and later of the English, as Roman Catholic converts under the protection of their resident priests, and as necessary partners in a fur-trade economy — forms of protection not available to the Beothuk.

As the fur trade declined, the Micmac and Maliseet were able to live by creating new commodities to trade and to sell, and by exploiting the new market provided by growing white settlements. Their manufactures were practical items, which were used until they fell apart and were thrown away, or items of a primarily decorative type. The former included canoes, snowshoes, storage boxes, feathers for beds and pillows, axe handles, ship fittings, barrels, wagons, and functional baskets.

It is the decorative objects made for the souvenir trade that survived to grace present-day collections. Traditional technologies, raw materials, and designs were combined with the new European media and patterns to produce a beautiful body of artwork, with the Maliseet and Micmac stamp firmly upon it.

As early as 1600, women had found buyers, in the seasonal fishermen, for their quillwork. "The Indians fix the price to the fishermen according to the kind of skin and its fantastic ornamentation. . . . It is made from Porcupine quills, white, red and violet, and sometimes with their wampum."[100] A single costume of quilled caribou leather,[101] collected before 1650 and thought to be from the Gulf of St. Lawrence area, is all that remains of this type of quillwork; such techniques disappeared during the seventeenth century.

Micmac women expanded the simple quillwork on the rims of bark containers, and created a mosaic art that covered entire obverse surfaces of bark items. The ends of quills were inserted into holes in the bark and pulled down tight to lie in parallel rows, thus creating a design. Geometric motifs were most common, but only two design names have survived: an eight-pointed star called "Eight-Legged Starfish" and a fan shape called "Northern Lights."[102] Early works were coloured with organic dyes. After the invention of inorganic aniline dyes around 1863, quillwork items showed off the new vibrant colours by using fewer geometric shapes, placed on a white background. Most of these items were designed for such European needs as hat cases, jewellery boxes, and flowerpots.

Lidded boxes form the bulk of surviving collections, followed by birchbark canoe models with quilled sides and rims. The very smallest of these little canoes seem to have been sold as containers for maple sugar, at tourist attractions such as Niagara Falls. Canoe models may have been a trade item as early as 1675, for LeClercq noted that quills were used to decorate "their canoes, their snowshoes, and their other works which are sent into France as curiosities."[103] Maliseet women do not appear to have made this type of souvenir art, which has become the hallmark craft of the Micmac.

The second most prevalent item in museum collections is the moccasin. Thousands were made and sold, not only for their comfort as footwear, but as an essential part of snowshoeing gear. They were collected for their beauty as early as 1638: "Their moccasins are rounded in front, and the sewing redoubles at the end of the foot, and is puckered

29.
Maliseet moccasins, part of a costume made for Mrs. Frank Hazen, c. 1884. The New Brunswick Museum, Saint John 5989. 7a,b. L:23.5; W:11.2; H:6

as finely as a chemise [with] the seams being ornamented with quills of porcupines, which they dye red and violet."[104] By 1699, ornamented moccasins seem to have been made primarily for trade: moosehide moccasins painted and edged with quills "are only for sale to those who wish to procure them for display in their own land."[105] Moccasins continue to sell to the present, but by the 1700s, leather vamps and cuffs had been replaced with coloured wools, and paint and quillwork decoration had given way to glass beads and ribbon appliqué.

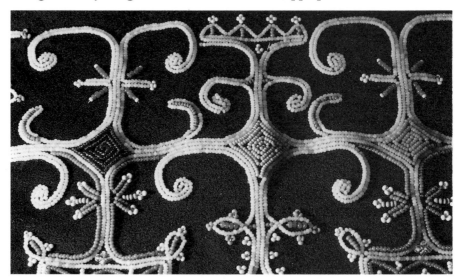

31.
Micmac double-curve motif, in beadwork on a 19th-century woman's peaked cap. (Detail of Figure 30.) Photograph by Ruth H. Whitehead. Courtesy of the Trustees of the British Museum, London 1929.12.16.7

30.
Micmac women's peaked caps have straight edges at the base, as in this 19th-century example. Courtesy of the Trustees of the British Museum, London 1929.12.16.7. L:41.5; W:20.5

During this time of cultural transition, materials changed but many traditional designs were retained, probably for their protective power. The borders of parallel lines once painted on leather were replicated in ribbon appliqué; the "lace-like" painted and quilled patterns became the familiar double-curve motif still used by Maliseet and Micmac women in their beadwork. Only the realistic animal art failed to survive the change-over, until it resurfaced in nineteenth-century tobacco pipe bowls: hunting and its spiritual bonding of animal and man had given way to mere trapping. Gradually, both the power and the meaning behind surviving designs also were forgotten, as more and more of the people became Roman Catholics.

The beauty of traditional designs was still potent, however, and materials familiar to the European eye — ribbon appliqué and beadwork — made moccasins very marketable. In addition, purses, belts, glove cases — indeed, any fabric or fabric-covered item that could be ornamented — sold well, particularly during the Victorian era, with its passion for decoration.

For themselves, Micmac and Maliseet women beaded curious peaked caps; their lower edges were straight for the Micmac and curved for the Maliseet. Skirts and jackets had rich parallel-line appliqué; suspenders, belts, and leggings were elaborated with silk ribbons, glass and metal beads, and shiny sequins of copper and tin.

Their men's blanket robes were similarly adorned, sometimes with matched leggings, moccasins, belts, and ornamental sashes. By the nineteenth century, men no longer wore robes, but affected a military-greatcoat style. These originated with the yearly "presents" of military coats given by Europeans to their Indian allies. Women lavished beads and appliqué on them, adding as much as fifteen kilograms to their weight. The earliest examples are covered in a double-curve motif of white glass beads; the simple curves of earlier times were heavily elaborated with coloured beads as the nineteenth century progressed, these motifs finally merging with European floral renderings of fat blossoms and leaves. Both Micmac and Maliseet men wore magnificent eared headdresses, thought to be based on dogs' heads. Dogs were admired for their courage, and their brains were eaten raw by men to absorb their ferocity.[106]

A technique of embroidering dyed moosehair directly onto birchbark or cloth-covered bark was taught to native women by the Ursuline nuns of Quebec.[107] Micmac and Maliseet used it on family clothing and on made-for-trade souvenir art, from cigar cases to table-cloths and chair upholstery; however, as European floral motifs predominated, there is no way to identify tribal origin.

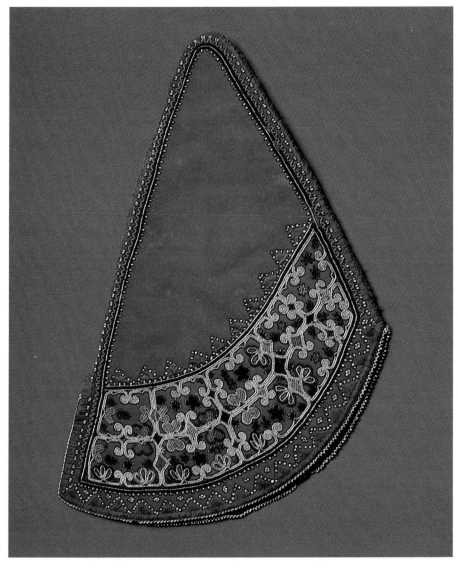

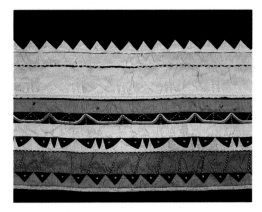

32.
Maliseet women's peaked caps have curved edges along the base. This cap's base is reinforced with birchbark and has a lining of blue silk. Saffron Walden Museum, England 1969.30. L:40.6; W:32

33.
Detail of ribbon appliqué from a Micmac woman's skirt, made c. 1845 by Mary Morris Thomas. The Nova Scotia Museum, Halifax 10.7

A final commodity was the wood-splint basket. Baskets were created for practical uses, such as gathering eggs, as well as ornamental wall pockets and whimsies. The sale of such items provided an income for both Micmac and Maliseet during the nineteenth century.

Micmac and Maliseet souvenir art has turned up in collections all over the world, taken home by tourists, settlers, missionaries, and the military. Captain James Cook spent the winter of 1758–1759 in Nova Scotia, and acquired a small quillwork box, which he gave to friends in Bath, England.[108] (They mistakenly thought it was a souvenir from Tahiti.) Vojta Naprstek, for whom the Naprstekovo Museum in Prague is named, took back to Czechoslovakia before 1856 a magnificent Micmac beaded sash.[109] Between 1851 and 1860, Micmac women gave parting gifts of their work to Scottish neighbours emigrating from Nova Scotia to New Zealand. These moccasins, quilled boxes, and letter cases are now in the Waipu Hall of Memories Museum, on New Zealand's North Island. In 1840, Samuel Huyghue obtained a Micmac chief's costume,

which he took with him to Australia in 1851.[110] In Lübeck, the Museum für Völkerkunde has a quillwork box labeled "Santo Domingo," suggesting it was acquired there; records show that sea captains often carried cargoes of Indian work to sell in foreign ports.[111] A Maliseet man's costume, made in about 1780, recently surfaced in Lancashire, whence it was probably taken by an English officer who was returning home.[112]

Famous collectors include the Netherlands' King William III, whose cabinet of curiosities held a Micmac quilled box. The French in the New World sent a model of a Micmac canoe to Versailles as one of the eighteenth-century contents of a "birthday box" for the Dauphin. Queen Victoria received numerous presents of moccasins, quillwork, and basketry.[113] Moses Perley, a New Brunswick Indian Agent, was presented to the Queen wearing full Maliseet dress. For her 1897 Jubilee, Micmac Jane Nevin sent Victoria two pairs of moccasins, with purple-velvet vamps and cuffs edged with écru silk, purple quilted satin linings, and beadwork crowns on each toe.[114]

Two of the nicest royal collections are at Osborne House, Victoria's summer residence on the Isle of Wight. Here are deposited many of the Micmac and Maliseet gifts to the Prince of Wales and to Prince Arthur, on their respective Canadian tours of 1860 and 1869. These include meticulously dressed dolls in canoes, tobacco pipes, carved spoons, moosehair embroidery, and a large quillwork box, with fourteen quilled panels inside. One panel sports the Prince of Wales Feathers as a central design, worked in black and white quills.

The oldest surviving example of souvenir art is a Micmac birchbark canoe model more than five feet long; formerly part of the Tradescant Collection in the Ashmolean Museum, Oxford, it is now held by the Pitt Rivers Museum in the same city. This model[115] is thought to be the "very ingenious little boat of bark" Georg Stirn saw on a 1638 visit to John Tradescant's house in Lambeth outside London.[116] By the nineteenth century, international exhibitions featured Indian work, and dealers sold consignments of it in Europe as well as locally in North America, with Niagara Falls a prominent retail outlet.

The attraction this work had for Europeans can clearly be seen in the quantities that were bought up, even by persons of modest income. One such was Juliana Ewing, who spent two years in Fredericton, New Brunswick, between 1867 and 1869. Mrs. Ewing bought a full-sized canoe, two pairs of snowshoes, and innumerable moccasins for herself and her husband, but she also shipped home to relatives in England a variety of Micmac and Maliseet items, such as the argillite tobacco pipes by Maliseet artist Peter Polchies:

> Tell Regie to make up his mind whether he will have a *beaver*, or an *indian* — or a *tortoise* on the front of the bowl of the pipe — so that I may give Peter orders when the funds admit. I am sending Maggie one with a beaver. . . . I think the pipes are really curious. It is all hand work of course.[117]

Also dispatched were "bits of beadwork," a "pair of *tiny* snowshoes," "a small and simple basket," a " 'sweet' thing in moccassons [sic] for nephew or niece," a "rosary of Indian workmanship [and] a wooden *cross* for Charlie of indian work," the promised "pipe of peace for Regie — & moccassin [sic] slippers for Brownie — & a miniature canoe for Stephen . . . an indian spectacle case of large dimensions for the dear pater!!"[118]

> We send Maggie a little card case of indian work — & Regie a cigar case of ditto — & a piece of canoe birchbark for the museum. I saw some *pipes*, but all the indians things are very dear — & the pipes

34. (opposite)
Micmac man's military greatcoat, back view. Note the yoke shaped like an animal hide, with neck and forefeet. This chief's costume was collected in Nova Scotia in 1840, and taken to Australia in 1851. By courtesy of the Museum of Victoria, Melbourne, Australia X8938.

35.
Maliseet chief's coat, made by a Micmac woman c. 1870-1880. Collected in 1893 from Chief Frank Francis, Tobique Reserve, New Brunswick. Peabody Museum, Harvard University 94.15.10/50793. L:106; W:58

36.
Maliseet wall hanging, made by Agathe Athanase, Rivière-du-Loup. Quebec, in 1893. This large piece has a number of small whimsies attached: 45 baskets, snowshoes, a moccasin, a small bottle wrapped with splints, 22 flowers, a bow and arrow, a bark bowl. Quills spell out *With Fond Love To Thee, Remenber* [sic] *Riv du Loup* [sic] *Canada, Indian Work*. Peabody Museum, Harvard University 94.33.10/52510. Photograph by Hillel Burger.

37.
Micmac wood-splint basketry whimsies. National Museum of Natural History, Smithsonian Institution, Washington, D.C. 21 5628-21 5634. L:0.5-6 (range)

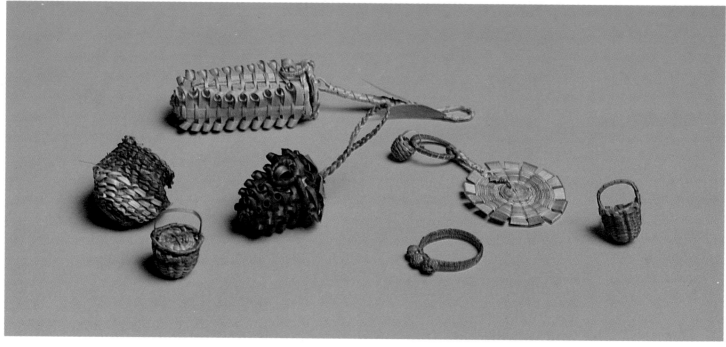

38.
Micmac man's cap, made by Mary Ann Geneace, Richibucto, N.B. The New Brunswick Museum, Saint John 15351. L:27; W:14; H:12

A magnificent example of floral-motif beadwork of the latter half of the 19th-century.

particularly so. . . . The Melicetes [sic] who are *here*, work in basket work & in *coloured* beads. I got 2 strips of *their* coloured bead work & Sarah & I "ran up" 2 red velvet bags & trimmed them with these strips for tobacco bags for Brownie and Steenie.[119]

(Mrs. Ewing's tobacco bags represent a combination of European and Indian work, which sometimes makes tribal identification difficult.)

In a letter to her mother in April 1868, she reports both the purchase of more Indian work, and the poverty of the makers:

The sqaw [sic] has been making the blotting case — & Peter brought it today — & I am very much pleased with it. . . . I would like to have got an envelope case & canoe, but they are so difficult to pack . . . so we got a few *flat* things. The blotting case is a good specimen, as it is made of the lovely birchbark; & they were all got direct from Indians we know. A sqaw [sic] with a sad face of rather a high type called to beg the other day — she could hardly speak English. She said, "Sister, me no ate today." So I gave her some bread and butter, which she gave at once to the boy with her, and went away."[120]

All this rich decorative work, this riot of colours and textures, was conceived and executed under such sad, impoverished conditions. "Almost the whole Micmac population are now vagrants [and] the sufferings of the sick . . . surpass description. . . . whole families were subsisting upon wild roots and eels, and the withered features of others told too plainly to be misunderstood, that they had nearly approached starvation."[121] Yet these same people were producing tea cosies in multi-hued quillwork, lavish beadwork and delicate moosehair embroidery for their European patrons' use. A sense of design, an eye for beauty and symmetry was bone-deep in the Maliseet and Micmac; not even the most wretched period of their history could eradicate it.

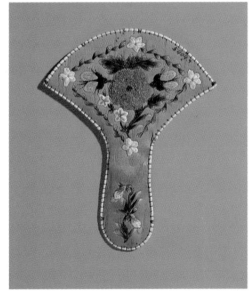

39.
Maliseet fan handles. The New Brunswick Museum, Saint John 5404.8 and 5404.9 L:14.5; W:11.5

Maliseet women made birchbark fan handles, embroidered with moosehair in floral motifs. European retailers added the feathers.

40.
Two Micmac tea cosies, one in double-curve beadwork, the other in porcupine quillwork, c. 1850-1870. The Nova Scotia Museum, Halifax 85.47 and 69.3.2

41.
Maliseet tea cosy, made to be sold. The New Brunswick Museum, Saint John 11444. L:39; W:11; H:28

The birchbark base is covered with red wool and embroidered with dyed moose hair. The finishing touch is the commercially made tassels at the top.

"A Heritage of Honour Sustains Our Hopes"

> The man in the wigwam began to beat on bark and to sing. . . . He said, "Do you want to see the fish come?" He took out a shell whistle. The [sea] bottom was very clear. They could see all kinds of fish. "These are my fish," he said. "They come from all those parts people throw away on the shore. I sing for them and they come back."[122]

For the groups along the Atlantic coast, over whom the wave of European arrivals first washed, the remaining fragments of documentation and objects are a mere handful when compared with those from other parts of Canada. Still, these objects bring back a living awareness of the original peoples in the early historic times.

The Beothuk, the Micmac, and the Maliseet were related by a kinship that lay deeper than the shared constraints of a northern maritime environment and common elements of material cultures. They were related in ways that, ultimately, extend to all of us, through those things that all human beings share: not only the usual uproars of life and death, but the attributes of curiosity, inventiveness, an appreciation of beauty, and a sense of humour. Stories such as that of the Micmac girl lying in her wigwam at night, looking up through the smoke-hole at the stars, and asking her sister, "What kind of husband would you like to have, one with big eyes or one with little eyes?"[123] or the Beothuk men blowing noises into the aqua-vitae bottle and laughing under a sun now more than three hundred years set, show us this kinship more truthfully than any common genealogy.

There is a further bond: all of us hunger to create and to be remembered. The Abbé Maillard recorded an old woman's speech at a feast: "Let the riversides, I say, for I call them to witness for me, as well as the woods of such a country, attest their having seen me."[124] The worldview of Micmac, Maliseet, and Beothuk included much more than woods and rivers. Ultimately, their vision and the way they translated it into what we consider their works of art still speak for them, still show their curiosity and inventiveness, their sense of beauty. This will most vividly attest their having lived; this will be their memorial.

Ruth Holmes Whitehead
In memory of G.W.W. Richardson

Like a Star, I Shine

Northern Woodlands
Artistic Traditions

42.
Chippewa Mode of Travelling In the Spring and Summer. Watercolour by Peter Rindisbacher. West Point Museum Collection, United States Military Academy, West Point, New York.

The dress and equipment of an Ojibwa family in the 1820s is carefully described in this painting. The woman wears a strap dress and carries her baby in a cradleboard by means of a burden strap across her chest. The father and son wear neck and hair ornaments of feathers and bear claws.

Art in Woodlands Life: the Early Pioneer Period

Like a star
I shine.
The animal, gazing, is fascinated by my sight.
Ojibwa hunters' song[1]

Art of the early historic period from the Canadian Woodlands is a fragmentary but rich legacy. For the people of this region the power of beautiful objects was a central feature of life. The meaning of such objects lay as much in the songs sung over them and the actions accompanying their presentation as in their intrinsic beauties of form and design. Decorated objects were but one facet of a complex set of aesthetic expressions, including song, oratory, dance, and dramatic mime. A wampum belt was displayed during an eloquent oration that explained its meaning. A quilled ornament was worn at a feast made brilliant by rich dress, dancing, and music; a carved war club was used with gesture, song, and costume to dramatize the brave exploits of a warrior. Indeed, it was the rich imagery and elegance of Indian oratory, not visual art, that most impressed contemporary Europeans.[2]

The objects in modern museum collections have long been separated from the words and songs that once belonged to them. Some of this context is preserved, however, in the eyewitness accounts written by early European visitors. Equally precious are the oral traditions that have remained a vital part of Indian life to this day and have been recorded by ethnographers and their native consultants. The objects and texts illuminate one another and allow us to recapture a sense of the total aesthetic expression. Today we gather them together — the war club, the wampum belt, the pipe, and the quilled ornament — as things of beauty in themselves and also as fragments of a distinctive vision of the universe and the meaning of human presence in it.

The history of Woodlands Indian art during the post-contact period has been one of creative adaptation to the intrusion of European cultures. The early part of the contact period — from Cartier's first voyage up the St. Lawrence in 1535 to the middle of the nineteenth century — provides us with our best opportunity to gain understanding of symbolic meanings and of the way in which artistic style expressed these meanings before the full impact of European influence was felt. Such insight is vital both to the interpretation of the art of the late prehistoric period, which we know only from mute archaeological finds, and to an appreciation of the period from 1800 on, when white settlement greatly accelerated the pace of change in art and life-style. The focus of this essay, then, will be on the art of the Canadian Woodlands during the first three centuries of white contact.

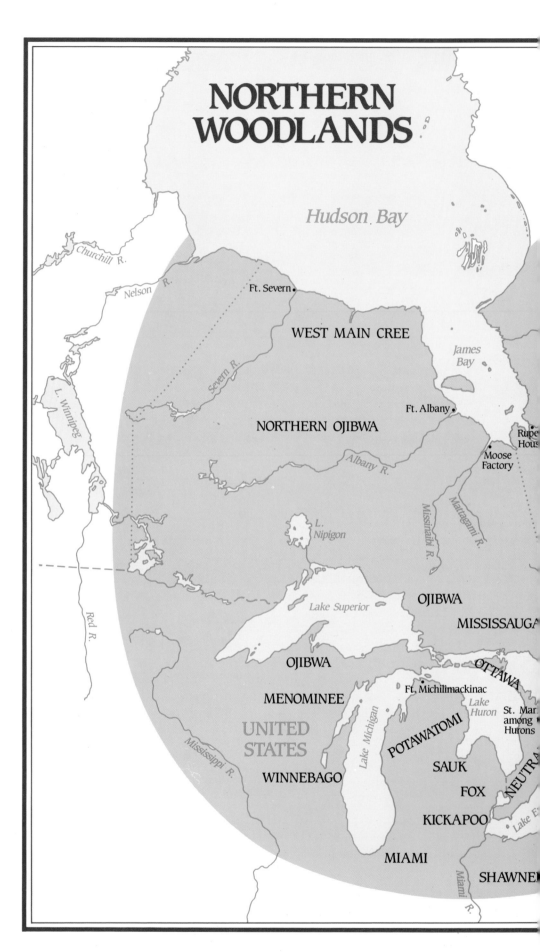

NORTHERN WOODLANDS

Hudson Bay

Churchill R.

Nelson R.

Ft. Severn

WEST MAIN CREE

James Bay

Severn R.

Ft. Albany

NORTHERN OJIBWA

Rupe
Hous

L. Winnipeg

Albany R.

Moose
Factory

Missinaibi R.

Mattagami R.

L.
Nipigon

Red R.

Lake Superior

OJIBWA

MISSISSAUGA

OJIBWA

OTTAWA

MENOMINEE

Ft. Michilimackinac

Lake Huron

St. Mar
among
Hurons

UNITED
STATES

Lake Michigan

POTAWATOMI

NEUTRA

Mississippi R.

SAUK

WINNEBAGO

FOX

KICKAPOO

Lake E

MIAMI

Miami R.

SHAWNE

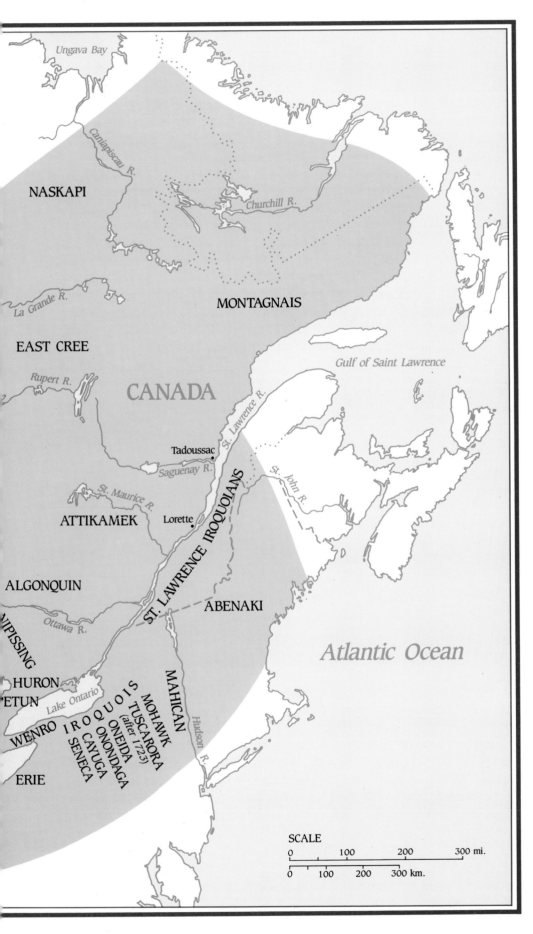

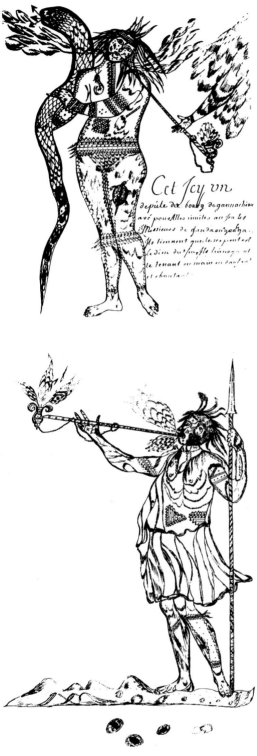

43.
Four early images of Northern Woodlands Indians from the "*Codex Canadensis*" attributed to Louis Nicolas, drawn about 1680. The figures illustrate the importance of body decoration throughout the region. Representations of personal guardian spirits were often incorporated, as seen in the turtle and snake tattooed or painted on the Iroquois man, upper right.

When Europeans first sailed up the St. Lawrence early in the sixteenth century they encountered peoples who had occupied the land for nine thousand years or more and who were ethnically, linguistically, and culturally diverse. The art traditions of the Canadian Woodlands can be grouped into three main regions; the Iroquoian, the Great Lakes, and the Eastern Subarctic.[3] The Iroquoian-speaking peoples, who include the Huron of Ontario and the Iroquois of New York, were farmers and hunters who lived in large semi-permanent villages. They excelled at the arts of political alliance and war, and waged successful campaigns against many neighbouring peoples. From the early seventeenth century they were in direct contact with Europeans and were early recipients of the wealth and imported goods introduced through the fur trade.

In the Great Lakes, where the climate was less favourable to agriculture, people relied more on hunting and gathering than on farming. The peoples living north of the Great Lakes – all speakers of Algonkian languages – led a semi-nomadic life, travelling in small family groups by canoe and snowshoe to harvest the foods of the forest and lakes (Figures 42 and 44). The peoples of the colder Subarctic region, who also spoke Algonkian languages, lived entirely by hunting and gathering. European contacts were first established with the Eastern Great Lakes and Subarctic peoples in the seventeenth century; the French reached the Central Great Lakes in the mid-seventeenth century, and by about 1670 the British fur traders of the Hudson's Bay Company had established forts on James Bay.

44.
A Southeast View of Cataraqui (Kingston, Ontario) taken in 1783 (detail). Watercolour by James Peachey. Public Archives of Canada C-13120.

Forts throughout the Great Lakes were regularly frequented by Indians to trade and receive treaty gifts. As shown here, people wore body paint, ornaments, and carefully dressed hair as well as their best clothes when they went visiting. Ostrich feathers, muslin shirts, and trade-cloth caps were popular in the late eighteenth century.

In a brief essay, it is not possible to investigate exhaustively the many distinctive artistic traditions of Woodlands Indians, but striking similarities in world-view, ritual practices, and visual symbolism underlie regional diversity. These elements of continuity may be due in part to the relatively small aboriginal population of the Eastern Woodlands at the time of contact. Even more significant was the mobility of Woodlands bands. In a single year people travelled hundreds and even thousands of miles by foot and canoe through the territories of neighbouring bands to hunt and fish. Even before the arrival of European settlers, groups of people moved in response to extraordinary events, such as soil exhaustion, game depletion, and the failure of annual animal migrations.

The typical scene of a family travelling by canoe is brought vividly before our eyes by a model made as an *ex voto* offering for the cathedral of Notre Dame de Chartres (Figure 2). Such canoes were "of a very elegant form . . . so light and slender that one wonders how they can carry five or six people, their dogs, their tents, and all their moveables."[4] Canoes were often decorated with painted designs, like those on the model, during the early contact period. The double-curve motifs typical of the Eastern Subarctic are used on the model;[5] among the West Main Cree one frequently saw "figures of serpents, fish, guns, and other things sketched out upon [canoes]."[6]

A second glimpse of Woodlands aboriginal life is displayed on a large birchbark box probably made by a Huron woman about 1800.[7] It is embroidered in coloured moosehair with such skill that the artist has virtually "painted" a complete Woodlands landscape in which we see lake and forest, the canoe with its dog and its human passengers, the bark wigwam, and the campfire with its trade kettle hanging from a tripod. During the nineteenth century such scenes rapidly became stereotyped on the great quantities of wares produced for tourists. On the finest early examples, however, there is a quality of fresh and lively self-portraiture in which native people attempt to depict what was typical of their own way of life for outsiders. These were new art forms that arose in direct response to the challenge of culture contact.

During the early contact period artistic cross-fertilization and innovation resulted not only from European influence but also from traditional intertribal trading and gift-giving relationships. From prehistoric times native people attended annual trading gatherings, during which they exchanged surpluses of local products as well as luxury goods from remote parts of the continent. Certain groups specialized in skilled manufactures. The Huron, for example, prized the painted skin clothing and amulets made by neighbouring Algonkians and the woven mats of the Ottawa (Figure 86). In 1623, the missionary Sagard saw Mississauga women "making reed mats extremely well plaited, and ornamented in different colours. These they traded afterwards for other goods with the savages of different regions who come to their village."[8] French visitors compared the outstanding quality of these mats to "Turkey carpets," and wrote that they were "wrought as tapestries are wrought in France."[9]

Artistic ideas were also spread by the increasing number of multi-ethnic Woodlands communities. Intensified warfare expanded the traditional practice of adopting war captives. It also created many dispossessed people who took refuge among alien groups, bringing with them their distinctive artistic traditions and techniques. By the late eighteenth and early nineteenth centuries, when many of the works of Woodlands Indian art in our museums were collected, wars, epidemics, the fur trade, and white settlement had created multi-ethnic Indian communities throughout the Canadian Woodlands.[10] The styles and forms of many of the art objects produced during that period must necessarily represent a blending of a number of different artistic traditions. The use of wampum belts, for example, though originally an Iroquoian custom, had spread throughout the Great Lakes and into the Subarctic by the late eighteenth century.[11] Thus, rigid classifications of ethnic styles in Woodlands art may well be a phantom of our own academic habits rather than an accurate reflection of native art traditions.

Art and Cosmology

Throughout the Woodlands a common set of cosmological beliefs guided the conduct of life. Myth cycles explained that the universe originated in the will of a remote creator god, associated by many Woodlands peoples with the sun. Both the Iroquoians and Algonkians made ritual acknowledgement of the sun in numerous ways that included regular sacrificial offerings and prayers. The Great Lakes peoples also associated the sun with war, and the ritual torture and killing of war captives by the Iroquoian peoples was very probably a sacrifice to the sun.[12] The sun is one of the most widespread motifs of Woodlands Indian art (Figure 45). It is the central image painted on Naskapi and Eastern Cree ceremonial hides, which were exposed to the rays of the rising sun in order to absorb power.[13] In such Eastern Subarctic compositions the sun is frequently represented iconographically by a circle or a series of concentric circles with projecting rays.[14] Organically curving lines spiral out from this central image, suggesting the connection between vegetable and animal growth and the power of the sun.[15] A very similar motif appears on a number of Algonquin, Iroquoian, and Central Cree embroidered pouches and moccasins. A remarkable deer-antler headdress of a type said in myth to have been worn by Iroquois chiefs also displays a red sun disc. It is placed above a pair of opposed hooked lines, symbolic, in Iroquois art, of the great world tree, the central axis of the universe above which the sun is located.[16] In the Eastern and Central Great Lakes sun symbolism is implied by the widespread custom of wearing round, shining discs of shell and metal, often engraved with sun motifs (Figure 45(i)).

The Woodlands peoples also revered the spirits of the seasons. The seasons are identified with the winds that blow from the four corners of the earth, and they ensure the regular changes of weather on which all life depends. Ritual offerings of tobacco were regularly made to the four cardinal directions when the pipe or calumet was smoked. The presence of these spirits was very real. The seventeenth-century Montagnais told Father Le Jeune, for example, that although they were not sure what form the spirits of summer and winter took, "they were quite sure they were living, for they heard them, they said, talking or rustling, especially at their coming, but they could not tell what they were saying."[17]

The four directions are symbolized by an equal-armed cross, which, when superimposed on a circle, becomes a symbol of the earth itself. This motif was probably placed on objects to propitiate the spirits of the seasons; it is often seen painted on Indian canoes in early European depictions.[18] The cross superimposed on an explicit sun circle is also a cosmic map, locating the sun at the top of a vertical axis at the centre of the cosmos. Other geometric motifs found in Woodlands art may have symbolized the individual wind directions. The north wind was represented by the Ojibwa, for example, by horizontal parallel lines containing groups of three short oblique lines.[19] Interpretations of this kind, though rarely recorded by Europeans, indicate that symbolic meanings may lie behind geometric motifs now often regarded as merely decorative.

Belief in an animist universe was fundamental to all Woodlands religious systems. Phenomena as diverse as climatic manifestations, features of landscape, flora, and fauna were believed to be possessed of a soul and spiritual power that could respond to human wishes. People made frequent offerings to these spirits, called *orenda* by the Iroquois and *manitos* by the Ojibwa. As one eighteenth-century Great Lakes fur trader explained:

> The Indians have many superstitions with respect to this mountain which, with every other remarkable or dangerous place on the borders of the lake or interior country, has its genii, to whom they never fail to make a speech, accompanied with a present of tobacco and sometimes their silver ornaments whenever they pass.[20]

45.
Composite montage of sun motifs.
a) *Naskapi painted hide,* mid-18th century, Canadian Museum of Civilization, National Museums of Canada, Ottawa III-B-588. L:105; W:118
b) *Pouch,* Iroquois type, Staatliche Museen Preußischer Kulturbesitz, Museum für Völkerkunde, Berlin, FRG IV-B-3.
c) *Pouch,* Algonquin, collected 1820-1867. Museum für Völkerkunde, Vienna 11981. L:12
d) *Mittens,* Huron type. Hunterian Museum, Glasgow E105.
e) *Moccasins,* The Trustees, National Museums of Scotland, Edinburgh UC 290, 290 a.
f) *Drum,* collected 1823. Museo Civico di Scienze Naturali, "E. Caffi", Bergamo, Italy. Collezione G.C. Beltrami 31. D:40.1
g) *Wampum gorget,* 18th-century type. The Museum of Anthropology and Ethnography, named after Peter the Great, Leningrad 1901.23. D:17
h) *Pipe (detail gorget),* early 19th-century type. Courtesy of the Trustees of the British Museum, London Dc80.
i) *Silver gorget,* 1798-1800. McCord Museum, McGill University, Montreal ME984.301. D:15

The prominence of sun motifs in many artistic media throughout the Northern Woodlands reflects the central religious importance of the sun spirit.

Animist beliefs also lie behind the elaborate burial offerings practised across the Woodlands. Woodlands people buried their dead in their finest clothes side by side with kettles, weapons, and food so that the souls of these objects could accompany the human soul and satisfy its needs during the difficult journey to the afterworld.[21]

Because animals, too, had spirits, they could be killed by humans only if they gave themselves voluntarily. Respect for the bones of the animals was an essential way of acknowledging this gift. Father Sagard, who lived among the Huron in the 1620s, vividly illustrates the Woodlands way of thinking about animals:

When I threw [fish bones into the fire] they scolded me well and took them out quickly, saying that I did wrong and that I should be responsible for their failure to catch any more because . . . the spirits

a

b

c

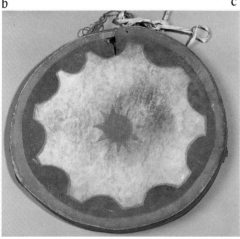

d

e

f

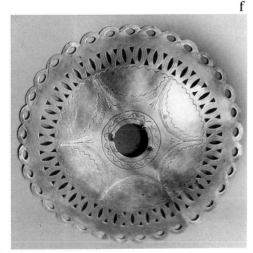

g

h

i

of the fish themselves whose bones were burnt . . . would warn the other fish not to allow themselves to be caught, since their bones also would be burnt.[22]

The animal spirits were thought to belong to two great classes, those of the air and those living on or below the earth. Throughout the Great Lakes and adjacent areas, the most powerful spirits of the sky world were the thunderbirds, mythic beings that caused lightning and thunder by flapping their wings and flashing their eyes.[23] They brought the spring rains and were especially powerful protectors of warriors. Thunderbirds were locked in perpetual warfare with equally powerful underwater deities, imagined as large, horned, and long-tailed cats, the *Misshipeshu* or underwater panthers. The servants of the underwater panthers were horned serpents, whom the thunderbirds hunted as food for their young.[24] Horned serpents, too, were powerful *manitos*, and one early observer remarked that "there is no animal you see oftener painted on their faces and bodies[25] (Figure 43).

The opposition of all-powerful beings of the upper- and underworlds characterizes Woodlands cosmologies. Throughout the region, and especially in the Subarctic, people venerated the bear as an underworld being parallel in importance to the underwater panther of the Great Lakes. The underwater panther, too, is probably closely related to the long-tailed amphibious beings depicted on proto-historic and historic-period Iroquoian pipes and to maned horse-like beings on some later pipes from the Great Lakes.[26] Like the thunderbirds, all these underworld *manitos* were powerful guardian spirits who could bestow great gifts on human beings. They had dominion over plant life, the locus of medicine, and over metal and shells, the wealth of the earth. These great power animals, the thunderbirds, underwater panthers, and other long-tailed beings, bears, and snakes are among the most frequent subjects of art in the Great Lakes and adjacent regions.

Plants, too, could contain spirit and power. As one missionary to the Montagnais noted, language itself expressed this belief: "they have different verbs to signify an action toward an animate or toward an inanimate object; and yet they join with animate things a number of things that have no souls, as tobacco, apples, etc."[27] Toward the end of the historic period floral motifs showing European stylistic influence came to dominate Woodlands textiles; indeed, floral imagery has been regarded as entirely of European origin. Yet the belief in the animate nature of plants (and their importance as power substances) is a pre-contact feature of native religion; stylized depictions of plants and flowers that do not reflect European influence are found in early contact-period art, particularly from the Eastern Subarctic.[28] Thus it is reasonable to assume that when a native woman represented a plant or flower, whether in a traditional or a Europeanized style, she understood it not only as a decorative motif but also as a power image.

Survival and success depended on gaining access to powers inherent in the natural world located in plants, animals, and minerals. Such powers are usually translated into English by the term "medicine," although the concept bridges Western notions of both the natural and the supernatural. Possession of medicine and the knowledge of its use was a gift bestowed by the spirits. People actively sought the indispensable blessing of direct contact with the *orenda* or *manitos* and the gift of medicine power. This contact was made possible above all through dreams and visions.

The Reality of Dreams

For the native people of the Woodlands, dreaming was the touchstone of reality, the ultimate proof of truth, and the supreme guide to action.

46. (opposite)
Painted bag, Northern Great Lakes type, c. 1720. On loan from the State Castles and Gardens Wörlitz-Oranienbaum-Luisium, GDR. L:38 (without fringe); W:16.5

Bags such as these held tobacco and other important articles and were tied to or folded over a belt. This bag is unique both because of its double panel of netted quillwork and its representation of a land animal on one of them, rather than the more usual thunderbird.

47.
Gunstock Club, Eastern Great Lakes type,
late 18th-century type. Société du Musée et
Vieil Yverdon, Switzerland OO.01.2. L:66.5;
W:8.5

Clubs were often engraved with images and
designs that form a record of an individual's
visionary experience. The original owner of
this club, probably collected by General
Haldimand, had powerful underwater spirits
as protectors.

During sleep the soul was believed to be free to travel out of the body
and to communicate with the souls of other people, spirits, and objects.
Soul travel revealed future events and the efficacy of courses of action.
Belief in knowledge gained through dreams was as much an article of
faith to Indians as was the Divine Revelation or the validity of logical
proofs to the Jesuits. A debate between these two very different systems
of knowledge is reported by the missionary Le Jeune, who was urged
by a Montagnais man to take native beliefs seriously. Le Jeune asks if
a dream has to be followed even if, for example, it requires one person
to kill another. The Montagnais replied that "just as he believed us when
we told him something, or when we showed him a picture, so likewise
we ought to believe him when he told us something that was accepted
by his people."[29]

The mention of a picture is revealing. The Jesuits found pictures to
be a persuasive medium of propaganda because native people were
accustomed to using visual representation to record dreams. Visual images
validated the dream experience and preserved the power it conferred.
Dream representations could be abstract or representational, as is clear
from information about such widely separated peoples as the Naskapi
and the Ojibwa.[30] Individuals also sought special visions at crucial
moments. At puberty, in many parts of the Woodlands, young men and
some young women separated themselves from the community and fasted
in order to receive a vision of a guardian spirit who would protect and
guide them throughout life. A rare early account of such a vision was
recorded among the Huron in 1642. A sixteen-year-old youth, after fasting
for sixteen days, "suddenly heard this utterance, that came from the Sky!
'Take care of this man, and let him end his fast.' At the same time,
he saw an aged man of rare beauty who came down from the sky,
approached him, and, looking kindly at him, said: 'Have courage, I will
take care of thy life.' "[31] Similar experiences have been recounted by Great
Lakes people down to this century.

The medicine bag, containing power substances revealed in the vision,
was a tangible outcome of dream experiences. Among the West Main
Cree, "when a young man has done dreaming and fasting, he sets to
work collecting ingredients for what he calls his Conjuring or Medicine
Bag, which consist in different roots, barks, weeds, grasses, dyed quills
and small bits of wood made into knick-knacks of different shapes, according to what he dreamt. For each of these he composes a song, without
which they would have no efficacy as medicine."[32] One Cree medicine
bag was "ornamented with paint, beads, [and] brass tags" and contained
"medicines for his family, beaver teeth, bears claws, eagles talons, the
beautiful red foreheads of woodpeckers, and many other kinds of
feathers."[33] Each medicine was associated with specific qualities, such
as invisibility to the game or sureness of aim.[34] Medicine bags were
thought to possess autonomous power capable of giving warning of
approaching enemies or of harming unauthorized persons (especially
women) who examined their contents. On war parties or voyages an
adult man always carried his medicines, which were carefully enclosed
in painted and woven bags[35] or wrapped in layers of cloth and birchbark.[36]

Smaller bags contained tobacco or individual charms; often they were
adorned with depictions of a guardian spirit or with symbolic designs
revealed in a dream (Figure 46). Scattered clues to the symbolic meaning of certain abstract designs can be found. An equal-armed cross composed of red dots or groups of dots symbolized sunbeam illumination
for the Naskapi.[37] The seventeenth-century Montagnais said that the "eyes
of the Genii of Light" (helper spirits of shamans) took the form of two
parallel oblique lines.[38] Patterns and ornaments revealed in dreams were

painted on the dreamer's skin and worn on the body (Figures 43, 70, and 73).

The sculptural effigies of anthropomorphic and animal beings carved on weapons, bowls, spoon handles, and pipes were also probably inspired by visions of guardian spirits[39] (Figures 48, 49, 79, and 80). They, too, are rendered in styles ranging from naturalism to near-abstraction.[40] Effigy bowls and spoons were used at feasts honouring personal guardian spirits; the carved images on pipe bowls were oriented to face the user and may have aided contemplative acts of prayer and meditation[41] (Figures 48 and 80). The preciousness of objects adorned with dream-inspired images echoes in the words of a Montagnais shaman converted to Christianity in 1642: "I have thrown away my drum; and yesterday I sold to the French a superstitious robe that I had had painted, as I had seen it in a dream, for my health."[42]

Shamanism

Some individuals in every community were able to achieve especially frequent and powerful visions. Their main techniques for contacting the spirits — drumming and singing — were not essentially different from those used by ordinary individuals, but were more effective because shamans had especially powerful helper spirits and medicine bundles. Shamans could divine the cause of illness or gain knowledge of distant events through trances, often achieved by the ritual of the shaking tent. A wonderfully succinct statement of the role of the shaman was made by the Montagnais shaman Pigarouich in 1637. It occurs in the course of one of the many debates between native people and missionaries during the early historic period in which traditional Indian ways of contacting the unseen were pitted against the new Christian gospel:

> I am going to tell thee what I do; I give feasts at which all must be eaten, I sing loudly during these feasts; I believe in my dreams, — I

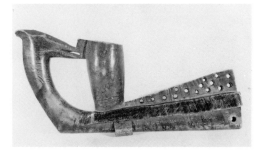

48.
Pipe bowl, Mississauga, before 1796. Courtesy of the Western Reserve Historical Society, Cleveland 43.2871. L:23; H:11

Pipe bowls were often made of wood in the Eastern Great Lakes during the early historic period, and often carved as effigies of underworld power animals.

49.
Bowl, probably Oneida, early 19th century. The Cleveland Museum of Art 84.12. Purchase from the J.H. Wade Fund. L:19.8; W:14.4; H:8.7

A simplified, fully rounded style employing naturalistic proportions characterizes most Northern Woodlands wood carving. Anthropomorphic and animal effigies on feast bowls and spoons honoured the guardian spirits of the owners.

50.
Drum, Ojibwa, before 1823, Museo Civico di Scienze Naturali ''E. Caffi,'' Bergamo, Italy. Collezione G.C. Beltrami 31. D:40; H:4

One of the most beautifully painted Ojibwa shaman's drums, this may also be the earliest collected. The lines radiating from the spirit image probably represent the light radiating from the spirits seen in visions.

51.
Shaman's drum, painted by Paul Kane in his sketch-book about 1845, probably on Manitoulin Island. Pencil and watercolour. Courtesy of the Royal Ontario Museum, Toronto 946.15.31

An Ojibwa shaman adapted a military drum to his own use, painting on it a chart of the cosmos, with the underworld and its animals divided from the upper-world containing the sun, moon, and sky beings by a round *axis mundi*. A nearly identical drum, probably the original of the painting, is now in the Museum of Mankind, London.

interpret them, and also the dreams of others; I sing and beat my Drum, in order to be lucky in the chase and to cure sickness; I consult those who have made the Light; I kill men by my sorceries and with my contrivances; I take robes and other gifts for curing the sick; I order that these should also be given to the sick themselves. Tell me, what dost thou find bad in all that?[43]

Shamans, like ordinary people, had depictions of their helper spirits on their ritual equipment and personal possessions, often made with special care by expert carvers and craftswomen. Drums and rattles used to call the spirits were sometimes painted with especially elaborate spirit representations (Figures 50 and 51); another theme is a balanced composition of spirits of the upper- and underworlds. Such diagrammatic visual schemae seem to express the ease with which the soul of a powerful shaman could travel through both realms and call upon their powers (Figure 51).

Sometime during the eighteenth century a highly organized society of shamans known as the *Midewiwin*, or Grand Medicine Society, developed in the Central Great Lakes.[44] The *Midewiwin* was dedicated to curing, but it also promised its members a safe journey to the afterworld. The society held annual initiation ceremonies, during which the new members were "shot" dead by the sacred cowrie shell contained within an otter medicine bag, and were then mystically reborn into a new life. The *Midewiwin* was a popular institution that spread throughout the Great Lakes and into adjacent regions.[45]

Midewiwin members recorded their songs and ritual procedures on incised wooden boards and birchbark scrolls by means of schematic diagrams and images. The graphic style of these scrolls and song boards is the culmination of an ancient pictographic tradition that has its roots in rock painting and a long-established system of totemic markings. The latter, symbolizing clan affiliation, were usually simple animal outlines. They were used on personal possessions, grave markers, and in travellers' messages inscribed on the bark of trees. The simplified, fluid, economical outlines of animals, plants, and humans are often rendered with great elegance on *Midewiwin* song boards and other objects, transforming a functional and mnemonic system of notation into graphic art[46] (Figure 52).

The Great Lakes *Midewiwin* practitioners employed a number of curing techniques and rituals, including the handling of hot objects, "shooting," and bragging in song, also used by Iroquoian curing societies. In the early contact period, Huron and Iroquois medicine societies also made use of elaborate masquerades in their rituals, some of which closely resemble those of the nineteenth- and twentieth-century Iroquois False Face Society. Members of this society wear wooden masks carved in the likenesses of forest spirits, whose help in preventing and curing disease had been procured for mankind during the mythic period by the creator.[47] This type of curing ceremony was present among the early Iroquoians. The Jesuit missionary Le Mercier, for example, witnessed a "dance for the recovery of a patient" in 1637, at which "all the dancers were disguised as hunchbacks, with wooden masks."[48]

52.
Midewiwin Songboard, Ojibwa type, late 19th century. The Vatican Museums, Vatican City State Am 3231. L:55.5; W:22.2

The eye of the Woodlands artist easily transformed line into contour. Here the trick is played by the two otters that curve around the ends of the songboard, slipping easily from two into three dimensions.

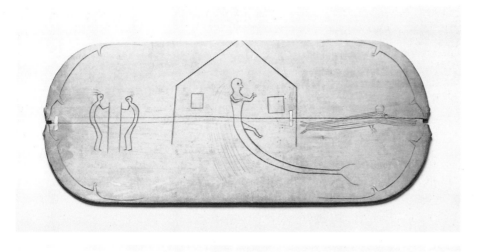

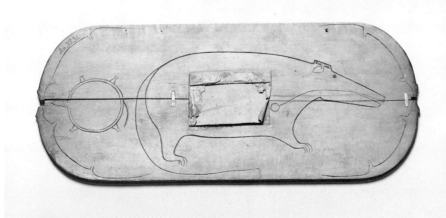

Other types of masks and religious sculptures used during the early contact period have disappeared because of the disruptions to traditional village life and religion brought about by missionary activity and European colonization. The seventeenth-century Huron made great use of carved and plaited corn-husk images. During one of the many devastating epidemics introduced by the Europeans, Huron shamans "ordered that those who would be delivered entirely from this disease should hang at their doorways large masks, and above their cabins figures of men similar to those scarecrows that in France are placed in the orchards."

And, indeed, "all the cabins of Onnentisati were almost covered with images."[49]

Feasts and Festivals

Visual representation, aesthetically enhanced, made the private, transitory experiences of dreams concrete and public. The special powers controlled by individuals were shared with the wider community through feasts and festivals, which provided the broad ritual and celebratory framework within which public validation of important events took place. These events included major rites of passage such as the acquisition of a name, a boy's first animal kill, his successful vision quest, marriage, and death. Feasts were also given in response to specific needs or crises: a successful hunt, a dream, an illness, the initiation of war or of peace, the torture of war captives, or the honouring of a man's personal medicine bundle (Figures 53, 54, and 55).

Preparation for feasts involved activities that incorporated both ritual and aesthetic elements, including the ritual purification of the sweat bath and the purification and renewal of the wigwam through the artistic laying of a new spruce-bough floor.[50] Invitations were issued in the form of colourfully dyed quills. Guests wore fine garments and ornaments, and carried to the feast a personal, decorated wood or bark bowl and spoon.

53.
Iroquois Dance, illustrations to *Aventures du Sr. C. Le Beau . . . ou Voyage Curieux et Nouveau Parmi les Sauvages de l'Amérique Septentrionale*, c. 1738. Public Archives of Canada C-14780.

The scene of Iroquois men and women inside a long house dancing in a circle around a musician accords with written descriptions of the early contact period. Dances were held for many reasons such as curing illness, or fulfilling a dream. Outside the house two women are shown weaving a mat.

54.
Chippewa Scalp Dance. Watercolour by Peter Rindisbacher. West Point Museum Collections, United States Military College, West Point, New York.

War dances called forth special costume and ornaments. Clubs were displayed as part of the costume assemblage and feathered ornaments, associated with the thunderbird, patron of warriors, were prominent. The display of scalps, held aloft on poles, may represent an offering to the sun and other spirits of the sky world.

The sacrificial pole, the white dog often used in sacrifice, and the bones remaining after the meal were all ritually decorated (Figure 55). Feasts were celebrations and included not only the consumption of an immense meal, but also speeches, songs, dancing, dramatic performance, and a magnificent display of body decoration, ornament, and clothing.

The central importance of feasts in Woodlands life was recognized by Le Jeune in 1639:

> I do not know how to characterize feasts, as regards our Savages. They are the oil of their ointments, the honey of their medicines, the preparations for their hardships, a star for their guidance, the Alcyon of their repose, the spring of their activities and of their Ascwandics, — in short, the general instrument or condition without which nothing is done.[51]

A twentieth-century student of ritual reminds us that a celebration, etymologically, implies the presence of many people, vivacity, and the "effervescence" generated by a crowd:

> When artists, craftsmen, songsmiths, and musicians are invited or commissioned to "make" something for a celebration, their work is inevitably informed by lively memories of that effervescence. . . . In a way such "makers" become the articulators of the otherwise inchoate celebratory "spirit", and the ephemeral events they choreograph, or the permanent artworks . . . they shape or construct, become a kind of shining language in which a society formulates its conception of the universe and its cultural philosophy.[52]

The festive dress of the Woodlands peoples is indeed like a "shining language" through which many of their beliefs about the universe are vividly expressed.

55.
Cree Indians celebrating a Dog Feast, Rupert's Land, 13 Sept. 1857. Watercolour by Major George Seton. Public Archives of Canada C-1063.

On the back of his sketch Seton wrote that the participants were "tricked out in red and green blankets, bright handkerchiefs and ribbons and in all the finery of the sort that they can muster." Such feasts, he notes, took place in oblong enclosures marked by willow branches. A short pole, seen in the drawing, was placed in the centre with an ochre-painted stone at its foot upon which the participants placed offerings.

Costume

> Their feasts are also very extraordinary. . . . They are all dressed in their best. The men have their hair braided up in a worked fillet, bunches of curious feathers being stuck up in it, their faces painted with black and red across the eyes, mouth, nose etc. . . . The women are no less industrious in equipping themselves to the greatest advantage: the embroidered cap, sleeves, smock, hair dressed, and breast plate put on; the hands and face washed, the latter finely painted, and bits of swan's down stuck in the hair.[53]

Festive costume was the most important single category of visual artistic expression. It was a complex assemblage including not only clothing, but also ornaments and various kinds of body decoration. The pouches, knife sheaths, burden straps, and weapons worn on the body were also elements of costume, for they contributed to the individual's self-presentation.

Early historic period costume from the Canadian Woodlands presents many puzzles to the researcher. Most forms of body decoration survive only in generalized early European depictions and descriptions. No examples remain of several garment types described in early accounts, and we often lack documentation that would permit us to attribute examples we do have to specific ethnic groups. Here, as elsewhere, we must combine information from early European sources with collected examples to form an idea of the clothing types and ornaments worn in the three subdivisions of the Woodlands region.

The Iroquoian Peoples

The sixteenth- and seventeenth-century clothing of the Iroquoian peoples is known only from descriptions by early European travellers. In 1542, according to the Sieur de Roberval, the St. Lawrence Iroquoians wore "skinnes upon them like mantles and they have a small payre of breeches, wherewith they cover their privities, as well men as women. They have hosen and shoes of lether excelently made. And they have no shirts: neither cover they their heads."[54] More detail is given by Le Beau in the early eighteenth century: during the pre-contact period Iroquois men wore a breechclout consisting of a rectangle of tanned deerskin drawn between the legs and folded over a belt so that panels hung down in front and behind, leggings cut with a wide outer flap, moccasins, and a hide robe. In colder weather or on journeys, a sleeveless tunic "peculiar to the Iroquois and Hurons" and separate sleeves tied behind the shoulders were added. By Le Beau's time, the tunic had been discarded in favour of European cloth shirts. Women wore knee-length skirts tied around the waist, European shirts, leggings, and moccasins. This clothing was ornamented with dyed porcupine quills, and "prettily worked" headbands, garters, and belts decorated with moosehair and quills[55] (Figure 56).

Huron clothing appears to have been similar and was painted, Sagard tells us, "in patterns and a mixture of colours with very good effect."[56] Champlain describes broad stripes of red, brown, and yellow and also mentions that there were specialists expert at painting skins. It was the opinion of the Europeans and of the Hurons themselves, however, that the neighbouring Algonkians were "the best clothed and painted and the most prettily bedecked of any."[57] This clothing was sought after in trade by the Hurons and other Iroquoians and must have spread Algonkian decorative motifs to the neighbouring peoples.

As trade materials became more available, Woodlands people made leggings, breechclouts, skirts, and robes out of woollen cloth instead of hide. But — with the exception of the shirt — the cut and arrangement

56.
Iroquois Women from the Historiae Canadensis . . . by F. Du Creux, 1664.
Public Archives of Canada C-99228.

An idea of Iroquoian women's dress at the time of contact can be gained from this early engraving. Painted hide leggings and skirts were worn with wampum necklaces and armbands and quilled ornaments.

of garments did not significantly alter until the nineteenth century (Figure 57). The full glory of mid-eighteenth-century Iroquoian and Eastern Great Lakes clothing is seen in portraits painted of Indian leaders and of allied white officers wearing Indian dress (Figure 58). Later, the traditional way of life based on hunting and warfare was lost; the Iroquois and Huron, like other native people, gradually adopted the tailored coats, trousers, long skirts, and smocked blouses worn by white people in the first half of the nineteenth century.

57.
A Huron and Abenaki of Canada,
anonymous watercolour, before 1776.
Braunschweigisches Landesmuseum, FRG.

Ribbon-appliquéd clothing, trade-silver ornaments, and a European hat combine with brilliant face painting and traditional Woodlands garment types to produce the typical dress of the late 18th century.

58.
Portrait of Sir John Caldwell, oil on canvas, late 18th century. King's Regiment Collection, National Museums & Galleries of Merseyside, Liverpool.

Military officers involved in the North American wars of the 18th century fought side by side with Indian allies. On his return to Europe, Sir John Caldwell had himself painted in the costume that was typical of the Eastern Great Lakes Indian men during this period. He displays the pipe tomahawk and wampum belt that were essential tools for the making of war and peace.

Two sets of clothing created just before the middle of the nineteenth century display both radical alterations in the cut of Indian clothing and the continuation of ancient decorative traditions. A man's suit made by the Lorette Huron comprises a blanket-cloth hooded capote, which Indian men on the lower St. Lawrence had begun to adopt from the French settlers during the eighteenth century, and a splendid matched set of accessories (Figure 59). The black-dyed deerskin leggings, moccasins, pouch, and mitts are finely embroidered in coloured moosehair. The Huron of Lorette were one of the oldest Christianized Indian communities in Canada. The floral designs for which they are famous combine European needlework traditions originally learned from the Ursuline nuns at Quebec and Trois Rivières and an ancient, more stylized, curvilinear design tradi-

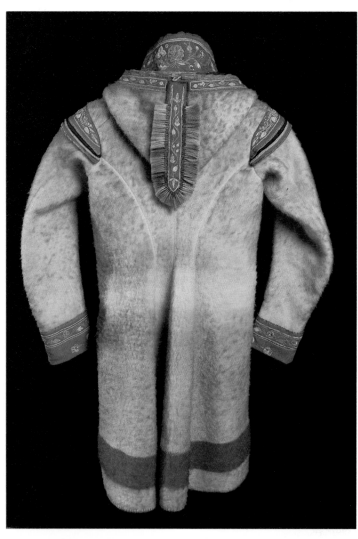

tion. The remnants of this ancient tradition can be seen in the typical Huron arc-and-dot border design and, more clearly still, in the highly stylized floral motifs of earlier examples of Huron moosehair embroidery.[58]

A similar absorption of European clothing traditions is seen in a woman's outfit made at the Christian Mohawk village of Caughnawaga, near Montreal, probably during the second quarter of the nineteenth century.[59] The rich clothing of the Caughnawaga Mohawk was remarked by a late-eighteenth-century visitor who commented that, "they are extravagantly fond of dress, and that of the most expensive kind."[60] The silk dress in brilliant colours has a modified European cut, but it was worn over a wrapped underskirt, a longer version of the older hide skirt. This underskirt is trimmed along the edge with ribbon appliqué cut in a sawtooth pattern. Women used bright strips of ribbon to decorate the borders of cloth garments, just as their ancestors had used paint to decorate those of hide. In the intricate cut-and-sewn contours of the ribbon appliqué they probably preserved ancient aboriginal painted designs. This costume would have been made even more bright and splendid when worn with the massed trade-silver ornaments that had replaced the shell and wampum of the early contact period.

The Great Lakes

The Great Lakes region is the cultural crossroads of the Iroquoian, Mississippi Valley, and Central Subarctic regions. The variety of pre-contact garment types worn by Central Great Lakes peoples reflects the coming together of different traditions. Precise information is lacking for many ethnic groups, but we do know that most Great Lakes men wore only breechclouts, leggings, and moccasins through much of the year. Early French travellers reported that the Ottawa and some other groups wore even less. It is probable that, in this region, a loose deerskin shirt with set-in sleeves was worn in colder weather, decorated with ochre for everyday wear and with fine shell, metal, quilled, and feather ornaments for festive occasions[61] (Figure 61). In the Western and Northern Great Lakes, the traditional female garment was the "strap dress," consisting of a side-folded, knee-length deerskin fixed over the shoulders with straps, and worn over leggings and moccasins. In cold weather, separate sleeves were tied across the chest over this dress (Figure 42).

In the Great Lakes, as throughout the Woodlands, women kept their babies well protected in cradle boards, which could be carried on the mother's back while travelling or hung on a tree while she worked. These were made of wood with protective curved hoops around the upper portion (Figure 60). A "moss bag" of hide or cloth was attached to the board to contain the baby and the powdered dried wood or moss used to absorb moisture. Parents lovingly ornamented cradle boards for the

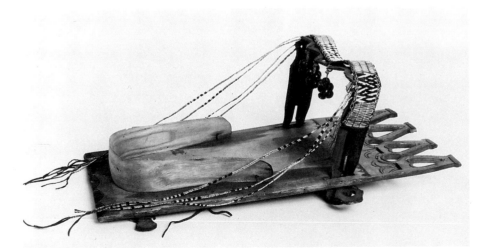

59. (opposite)
Man's suit, Lorette Huron. National Museum of Denmark, Department of Ethnography, Copenhagen Hc 146a, b, e, g. Coat (a): L:106; Leggings (b): L:65; W:28.5; Sash (e): L:150; W:16.5; Pouch (g): L:59; W:24

Clothing decorated with moosehair embroidery by the Lorette Huron was popular with European tourists to Canada in the middle of the 19th century. This particularly fine costume includes black-dyed deerskin leggings and was collected by Mr. Dollner before 1847.

60.
Cradleboard, Ojibwa type, before 1825. Stoneyhurst College on loan to the Museum of Mankind, London. L:54; W:24

The original ornaments remain attached to this cradleboard and it is further decorated with quillwork, engraved lines, perforations, and paint.

61.
Man's shirt, eastern Great Lakes type, early 19th-century type. National Museums & Galleries on Merseyside, Liverpool 12865. L:80.5; W:56 (bottom)

It is very unusual for so fine a set of gorgets and quilled and feather ornaments to have remained attached to a garment in a museum collection. Often personal ornaments were buried with their owners.

protection and entertainment of the child as well as for beauty and for show. They hung beads and ornaments from the hoop and suspended panels of netted quillwork in front to trap evil in the web-like patterns of the netting. The board itself was painted and carved with engraved and pierced designs. Such ornaments reflected the prowess of the baby's father, the skills of its mother, and their wishes for the child's future success. "If the father is a good hunter, he has all his adornments placed on the cradle; when the child is a boy, a bow is attached to it; but if it is a girl, only the mere ornaments are on it."[62]

An extensive description of Central Great Lakes dress written by Isaac Weld at the end of the eighteenth century shows the extent to which trade materials were in use by that date, and the close similarity between Central Great Lakes and Iroquoian clothing. Women's dresses, skirts and leggings were often made of trade cloth; blue and scarlet were the preferred colours.[63] Women ornamented legging seams "with beads, ribands, &c. when the leggings are intended for dress"; the front and back flaps of the breechcloth were also adorned with beads and ribbons with the "utmost ingenuity of the squaws" (Figure 62).

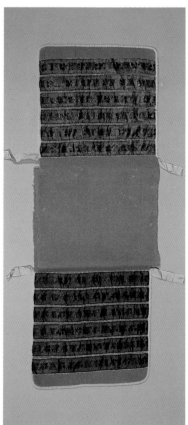

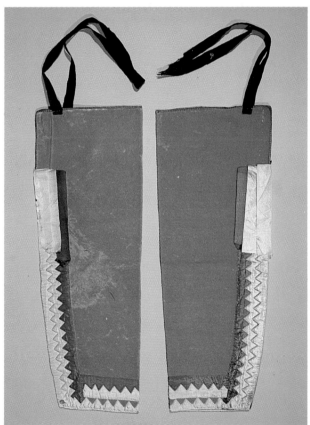

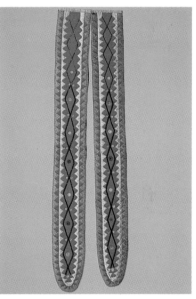

62.
Man's costume, Ottawa, early 19th century. Berne Historical Museum, Switzerland, Can. 1a, 1b (a, b), 1c, 1d, 1h (a, b). Blanket (1a): L:151; Leggings (1b): L:69; Breechcloth (1c): L:153; Belt (1d): L:97; Garters (1h): L:62.5

Broad bands of ribbon and bold zigzag contours probably reproduce in trade materials the designs of earlier periods. This costume also includes a cumberbund and bandolier straps borrowed from European military uniform.

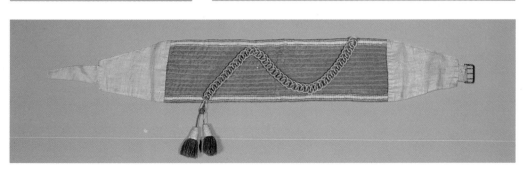

63.
Coat, Mississauga, c. 1844. National Museum of Natural History, Smithsonian Institution, Washington, D.C. 178398. L:118; W:62 (Shoulders)

This coat belonged to the Mississauga missionary, Reverend Peter Jones, author of a history of the Ojibwa that records many traditional beliefs and practices. The punched decoration is found on early Great Lakes hide shirts; the quilled thunderbirds and serpents belong to pre-Christian religious imagery.

The moccasins, leggings, and breech cloth constitute the whole of the dress which [men] wear when they enter upon a campaign, except indeed it be a girdle, from which hangs their tobacco pouch and scalping knife, &c.; nor do they wear any thing more when the weather is very warm; but when it is cool, or when they dress themselves to visit their friends, they put on a short shirt, loose at the neck and wrists, generally made of coarse figured cotton or callico of some gaudy pattern, not unlike what would be used for window or bed curtains at a common inn in England. Over the shirt they wear either a blanket, large piece of broad cloth, or else a loose coat made somewhat similarly to a common riding frock; a blanket is more commonly worn than any thing else.[64]

These observations are borne out by men's coats collected during the early nineteenth century. Many display a European cut, shoulder capes, and collars combined with traditional decorative and symbolic motifs in quill and beadwork (Figure 63).

Moccasins worn by both sexes in the Central Great Lakes were of smoked deer or moose skin "rendered a deep brown colour." They were cut of one piece with a central vamp seam. The ankle flaps and seam were "tastefully ornamented with porcupine quills and beads," and the flaps were edged "with tin or copper tags filled with scarlet hair, if the moccasin be intended for a man, and with ribands if for a women." Such ornamented moccasins were "worn only in dress, as the ornaments are expensive, and the leather soon wears out; one of plain leather answers for ordinary use."[65] (Figure 83) Among the "dress" occasions dances were prominent, and the metal "tinklers" attached to the moccasin cuffs made a pleasant noise. It is possible that these tinklers, which early writers specify were placed on dance moccasins, served like rattles and drums, to call the attention of the spirits.

The Subarctic
The cut of the clothing worn by the Subarctic peoples reflects the harsher climate of this region. Well-tailored fitted clothing provided protection and was worn in layers in cold weather. In winter Naskapi men wore "a jacket of [caribou] deer skin, worn with the hair next to the body, and a coat of the same material reaching to the knees, with the hair outside. Leather breeches, leggings, and moccasins protect the lower extremities; and the hands and arms are defended from the intense cold of those regions by gloves and gauntlets reaching as far as the elbows."[66] Over these garments Subarctic people wore cloaks of fur before the introduction of trade blankets. Seventeenth-century descriptions tell us that the neighbouring Iroquoians greatly prized Attikamek and Algonquin cloaks woven of the furs of small animals such as rabbits and squirrels.

Early contact period Montagnais and East Main Cree clothing was probably very similar to Naskapi examples. In 1800, James McKenzie, travelling through the Eastern Subarctic, reported that Eastern Cree peoples and the neighbouring Attikamek and Algonquins "differ but little in their dress, manners, and language."[67] The summer coats of Naskapi men had flared skirts constructed by the insertion of triangular gussets and were beautifully painted[68] (Figure 64). The neighbouring Eastern Cree peoples probably wore similar garments, but no documented examples survive.

Striped patterns such as those described for the early-seventeenth-century Montagnais are probably the oldest Subarctic motifs. "The women paint colored stripes . . . from top to bottom, which are about as wide as two thumbs, and are equally distant from each other." They painted stripes horizontally around sleeves as well.[69] Examples of Naskapi painted clothing collected during the eighteenth century display denser and more

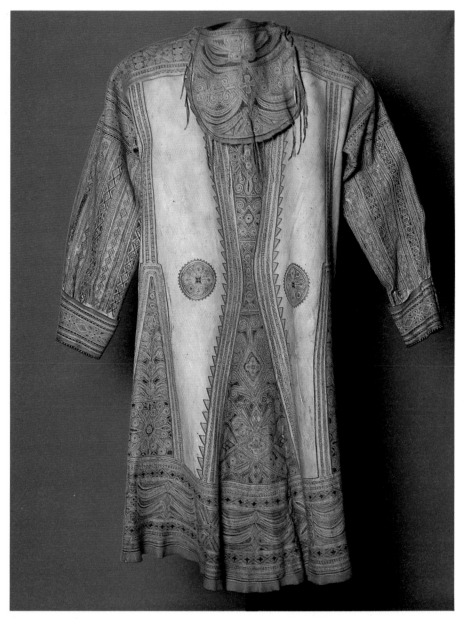

64.
Coat (back view), Naskapi, Pitt Rivers
Museum, Oxford 52.5.01.

The dense and complex painted designs on
this coat contrast with the simpler and
clearer pattern of the 18th century. The
change may be due in part to exposure to
European printed textiles.

65.
Painted hide, Napaski type. By courtesy of
the Trustees of the British Museum, London 1984.AM.17.1. L:198; W:131

The central motif of this unusual and un-
documented painted hide is a sun image
similar to those painted on Naskapi
shaman's robes. The overall composition is
reminiscent of oriental carpets and textiles,
and it is possible that this hide may have
been made for a fur trader or European
visitor.

complex painted patterns combining stripes, triangles, and double curves.
The double-curve motifs have been interpreted as representing caribou
horns and vegetation, but the later painting style was probably also
influenced by imported textiles traded or merely seen in fur-trade forts.
The design of a splendid large rectangular painted hide, for example,
appears to combine the overall composition of an Indian chintz with traditional Naskapi motifs (Figure 65). During the late nineteenth century,
the Naskapi were copying design ideas from trade fabrics and kerchiefs —
suggesting that other borrowings had probably been made during the
preceding century.[70]

The winter clothing of men in the Central Subarctic was also layered,
consisting of a "Cloase Coate nes't their skin and a Loose coate over
flying open before."[71] A group of long, loose painted coats from the Central
Subarctic conforms to these descriptions of cut and construction. The
skin-painting traditions of this region are not well understood;
documented examples are extremely rare, and northern Ojibwa and Cree
art styles blend in the area south of James Bay. Compared to the flowing, integrated curvilinear designs of the Naskapi, Central Subarctic skin
painting was rigidly geometric, composed of stripes, circles, crosses,
squares, and triangles. A combination of solid elements and linear border
designs was used.[72] Elaborate ornaments of woven and netted quillwork
were also applied to the shoulder seams, neck, and wrist edges of coats
(Figure 66).

66.
Painted coat (back view), Central Cree
type, early 19th century. National Museum
of Ireland, Dublin 1892.20. L:123

Central Cree coats were less tailored than
those of the Naskapi and were decorated
with rectilinear patterns and rows of
repeated geometric motifs. Elaborate quilled
ornaments were attached to the cuffs,
shoulders, and neck.

Women throughout the Subarctic wore the strap dress with separate sleeves,[73] "open under the armpits and fastened together at the angles behind and before by a string or breast-plate prettily adorned with beads, brass, quillwork, or the like."[74] Belts and garters, important elements of Central Cree costume, were made of hide decorated with woven or embroidered quillwork.[75] Women's belts were wider than men's and they incorporated glass beads and had "several ornaments depending from the lower edge in form of a fringe."[76] Attached quilled ornamentation on clothing was a long-standing tradition throughout the Subarctic. In the seventeenth century, for example, Montagnais women made their leggings with a fringed border, "occasionally fastening to this a few matachias," or quilled ornaments.[77]

Moccasin-making was a considerable part of a woman's work, for the average adult wore out fifteen to twenty-five pairs a year. Subarctic moccasins were nearly always cut with set-in vamps; women were so skilled that they handled the hide as if it were linen, gathering the moccasins "around the toes like the hand-band of a shirt and in as neat a manner."[78] On festive occasions, the Cree wore special moccasins whose vamps were embroidered with quills and beads.

Throughout the fur-trade period, Cree men and women wore peaked hoods of cloth richly adorned with silk-ribbon appliqué and bead embroidery.[79] These hoods had probably been introduced by the seventeenth-century French.[80] The exception were the Naskapi, who wore round caps of red and blue trade cloth. By the middle of the nineteenth century, East Main Cree and Montagnais clothing of painted hide had been largely superceded by clothing of European trade cloth. On leggings, hoods, moccasins, and pouches, European-influenced floral motifs sewn in silk embroidery thread and glass beads appear to have replaced porcupine-quill decoration by the end of the nineteenth century.[81]

A pair of dolls made for the early tourist trade about 1800 exactly reproduces the dress of West Main Cree women as described by the early fur traders (Figure 67). The dolls illustrate the construction of individual garments and show the way these garments were combined with ornaments. They testify to the pleasure taken in a rich array of contrasting textures, patterns, and colours. Painting on hide, woven and embroidered quillwork, beadwork, and European cloth are brought together in one brilliant assemblage. Another pair of dolls collected in the 1880s among the Naskapi shows the mixture of traditional painted hide and trade-cloth clothing worn during the period of transition between traditional hide clothing and European-influenced dress in the Eastern Subarctic.[82]

For Woodlands people, the wearing of hide clothing was in itself an act imbued with meaning. Animals were believed to give their skins to human beings voluntarily, and the decoration of the skins honoured the animals. In the Eastern Subarctic — and probably throughout the Woodlands — people believed that power could be transferred from the animal to a human wearer through the proper treatment of the animal's skin. The East Main Cree used the intact head skin of an animal for the hood of a child's or a man's winter coat in order to invoke the animal's protective power for the wearer.[83]

Although European trade goods were incorporated into aboriginal clothing and ornament very soon after contact — and in some areas even before direct contact — for many years these materials enriched rather than altered existing clothing traditions. European cloth, metal, and beads appeared at first as almost magical substances, imbued with the same beauty and power as the gifts of the spirits. The Naskapi word for fine

67.
Pair of Dolls, Cree type, c. 1800. The Horniman Museum and Library, London 1976.459 and 1976.460. H:35.5; H:33

Although the dolls themselves were made in England between 1770 and 1790, their dress accurately reflects the costume of late-18th-century Cree women. One wears a side-fold dress and the other a tunic with side-sewn seams. Separate sleeves and leggings are worn, together with a splendid array of quilled and beaded neck ornaments, hair binders, belts, and garters.

European cloth translates literally as "skin of a *manito*," and the word for glass beads means "*manito* berry."[84] These new materials were readily adapted to the existing concept of clothing and ornament as a means of enhancing personal efficacy. The availability of the new materials brought about a flowering of Woodlands art that lasted for two hundred years and more. Native people were highly selective in the choices they made from among the range of available trade goods; their preference for certain colours and surface textures was based on ancient aesthetic and symbolic traditions. Blue, black, and red cloth were preferred colours, in accordance with the long-standing popularity of red vegetable dyes and ochres and the dark colour produced in hides by smoking and dyeing.

> Trinkets or ornaments for dress, though ever so gaudy, or ever so neatly manufactured, they despise, unless somewhat similar in their kind to what they themselves are accustomed to wear, and fashioned exactly to their own taste, which has remained nearly the same since Europeans first came among them.[85]

In the making of costume, raw materials were given shape and pattern. A great many different craft skills were employed: artisans made shells into polished wampum beads, minerals into paint, plants into dyes; and they cut and sewed whole animal hides into garments. In the animist world-view of the Woodlands Indians such transformations paralleled the magical transformational acts of *manitos* recounted in myth and seen in dreams. Ritual acknowledgement of the sacred sources of power therefore accompanied the activity of the artist or craftsperson, as it did that of the hunter or farmer.

The transformations that Woodlands people worked on their own bodies were equally dramatic and expressed connections with the super-natural in many ways. The application of red ochre to human skin and animal hide — the most widespread form of decoration — invoked protective medicine power. Red ochre was symbolically and perhaps magically identified with blood and the life force. Shaping and marking the body by tattooing, painting, hairdressing, piercing the skin, and attaching ornaments also made references to the sacred. Self-decoration was part of a quest for beauty with which to please both spirits and the human community.

Body Decoration

Early European travellers in the Woodlands were often amazed by the lack of clothing worn by native people. Nakedness was taken as evidence that Indians were living in an uncivilized state of nature. Champlain, for example, found it strange that when he was received by a group of Algonquin women at Tadoussac in 1603 they cast off their garments before performing their songs and dances although "retaining their ornaments of matachias which are beads and braided cords made of porcupine quills dyed of various colours."[86] To native people, however, ornament — including body paint, hairdressing, and tattooing — was as significant an outward sign of culture as clothing; a person who was thus adorned would not have been considered undressed. Face painting in particular was "such an essential ornament that they consider themselves undressed without it even if everything else is complete."[87] Although relatively little attention has been paid to the ephemeral arts of body decoration, they were important ritual and aesthetic expressions and the intended complements to clothing.

Body decoration was a statement of social identity. Special emphasis was given to self-adornment when people attended large social gatherings and when they travelled through foreign territories. Young men intent on establishing themselves in the community and with the opposite sex were said to be most concerned with self-decoration. Charlevoix complained of a Great Lakes Indian man to whom he gave a passage in his canoe:

> This young man fell a dressing himself before he embarked, and at every three strokes of his oar, took up his looking glass to see whether

68.
Burden strap, Iroquois, late 18th century. The Museum of Anthropology and Ethnography named after Peter the Great, Leningrad 1901-1920. L:555 (overall); L:66 (embroidered section)

This unusually wide burden strap is embroidered in a classic design composed of alternating blocks of colour and pattern unified by a bold meander line.

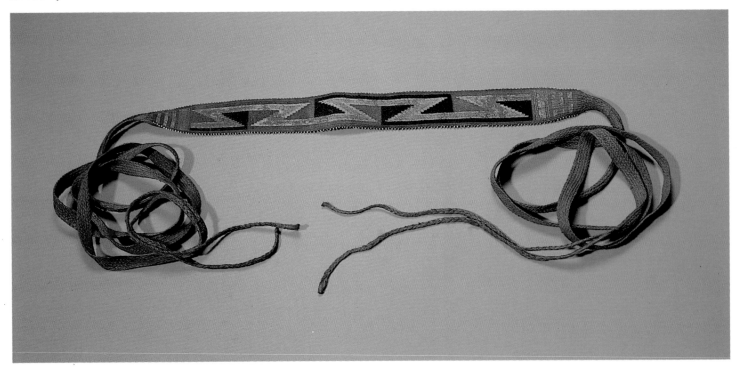

the motion of his arms had discomposed the oeconomy of his dress, or whether the sweat had not changed the disposition of the red and other colours with which he had daubed his face.[88]

It was noted that the Montagnais "have their faces painted when they make visits,"[89] and that the Ojibwa carried their "pigments and oil with them on a journey" and used them "to paint and stain themselves, especially when they are approaching or passing through another tribe. . . ."[90]

Inter-village games such as lacrosse provided other occasions for self-adornment, especially for the young. The white captive John Rutherford was loaded with all the ornaments his Indian family possessed so he might cut a fine figure on one such occasion.[91] Young Huron men wore all their finest ornaments when courting young women. Early accounts stress the great variety of styles of hairdressing, body painting, and ornaments. This variety implies that body decoration afforded considerable opportunities for inventiveness and individual self-expression.[92]

Body decoration was also intended to please and honour the spirits. New clothes and quantities of ornaments were worn by young men of the West Main Cree when beginning the vision quest. At dances asking the blessings of the spirits before the departure of a war party and at the feasts held on its return, both the warriors and their captives were painted, ornamented, and finely dressed. Prisoners taken by the Iroquois, Huron, and Ojibwa were led to these victory celebrations painted and bound with embroidered and ornamented ties.[93]

When hunting, too, an individual confronted the supernatural and sought the co-operation of the animal spirits. Some of the most fascinating information about the power attributed to dress and ornament has come from the Eastern Subarctic. Among the Naskapi and East Main Cree, the decorations applied to clothing and hunting equipment were dream-inspired and believed to be necessary to please the spirits of the animals and to show them respect. Decoration of snowshoes, toboggans, and other equipment also ensured that the spirits of these objects co-operated with the hunter by functioning properly.[94] In more recent times, Naskapi women continued the apparently pre-contact custom of presenting their husbands with decorated headbands bearing dream-inspired motifs, which were worn to please and attract the animal spirits. It seems highly probable that the early contact period Iroquoian practice of adorning that part of the burden strap worn across the forehead or chest with complex embroidered designs may be derived from a similar set of beliefs[95] (Figure 68). Decoration on bows, knife sheaths, snowshoes, and other equipment made during the early contact period by Great Lakes and Subarctic tribes may also have its origin in a desire to propitiate animal spirits.

Finally, at the end of his life, an individual prepared to meet death fully adorned.

> He is decked with all the ornaments owned by the family. . . . They dress his hair with red paint mixed with grease, and paint his body and his face red with vermilion; they put on him one of his handsomest shirts . . . and he is clad with a jacket and a blanket, as richly as possible; he is, in a word, as properly garbed as if he had to conduct the most solemn ceremony. They take care to adorn the place where he is [lying] with necklaces of porcelain and glass beads . . . or other trinkets. His weapons lie beside him, and at his feet generally all articles that he has used in war during his life.[96]

According to ancient Woodlands traditions, people were buried in fine clothing and accompanied by their personal possessions — early contact period Iroquoian graves contain great quantities of valuable glass beads. Burial was perhaps the best example of the belief that costume art height-

69.
Chief Oshawana, Ojibwa. Daguerrotype, c. 1838. Courtesy of the Royal Ontario Museum, Toronto HD 6360/2

An early photographic image captures the highly personal assemblage of silver and wampum ornaments of an eminent Ojibwa chief who had been one of Tecumseh's principal warriors.

70.
Bust of a Mohawk Indian on the Grand River, pen and ink sketch by Sempronius Stretton, 1804. Public Archives of Canada C-14827.

Popular types of nose and ear ornaments are shown here together with examples of Iroquois face painting, trade silver and hair dressing c. 1800.

ened a person's powers — in death as in life — for the voyage to the after-world was regarded as the most difficult of all journeys.

Ornaments

The set of ornaments worn by a man or a woman accumulated over many years (Figure 69). Many of the elements were associated with important life transitions or events. In many parts of the Woodlands, the first permanent act of body decoration was the piercing of the nose septum, the ears, or both at the naming celebration held when a child was a few months old (Figure 70). In the Central Great Lakes, this act was performed by a shaman at a feast offered to the sun or some other spirit.[97] The almost universal custom of wearing shell, stone, and metal ear and nose ornaments in this region thus seems to be associated with *manito* protection as well as increased personal attractiveness. A grown man might have a row of perforations around the ear into which bones, brass screws, or silver ornaments were inserted. The ear rim was also cut and wrapped with brass wire; on special occasions downy feathers, symbolizing sky power, were fixed to these ornaments (Figures 70 and 73).

A long-standing symbolic association between white shell and the supernatural world appears to underlie the ritual role played by wampum and its later analogue, silver.[98] From prehistoric times, one of the most important ornaments worn by prominent men was a large disc or "gorget" of sea shell, sometimes plain and sometimes engraved. A general identi-fication between gleaming, round discs and the sun seems implied; on both shell and trade-silver gorgets, sun images are often found[99] (Figure 45(g), (h), and (i)). In the Great Lakes, the sun was also associated with war, and shining gorgets were therefore particularly appropriate orna-ments for warriors. At the same time, Woodlands myths recount that shell, like metal, was the gift of the underworld spirits.[100] The popular-ity of round gorgets may have been due in part to their polyvalent nature as symbols that contain references to both supernatural realms.

The Iroquoians also made medallions of shell wampum beads that incorporated images of the sun. A wampum gorget, probably collected in the eighteenth century, displays a sun emblem formed of white beads against a purple background, and is the only known surviving example of the great circular "plates" of wampum described by seventeenth-century writers[101] (Figure 71). De Quen describes the presentation of such an ornament by a Mohawk chief to welcome a group of Jesuit mission-aries, and makes clear its power as an emblem of peace. The chief's finest present "was a large image of the Sun, made of six thousand por-celain beads, — its purpose being, as he said, to dispel all darkness from our councils, and to let the Sun illumine them even in the deepest gloom of night."[102] The light of the sun, a metaphor for openness, right con-duct, and power, is conveyed visually through the medium of shell. Belts of wampum beads woven with symbolic motifs were more common than plaques and discs, and served the same diplomatic purposes. They probably carried similar symbolic associations with supernatural power (Figure 77).

Hairdressing

Early observers were impressed by the variety of individual styles of hairdressing. Among seventeenth-century Huron men:

> Each follows his own fancy. Some wear it long and hanging over to one side like women, and short and tied up on the other, so skill-fully that one ear is concealed and the other uncovered. Some of them are shaved just when the others wear a long moustache [lock]. I have seen some who had a large strip, closely shaved, extending across

71.
Wampum gorget, Mohawk type, 18th-century type. The Museum of Anthro-pology and Ethnography named after Peter the Great, Leningrad 1901-1923. D:17

Discs of wampum representing the sun were described by 17th-century European visitors to the Iroquois, but this is the only known surviving example. Such gorgets were highly valued as gifts; the act of giv-ing such an object called upon the sun as witness to the openness and purity of in-tention of the parties to an agreement.

72.
He who travels Everywhere, a warrior, Ojibwa, 1835. Oil on canvas by George Catlin, 1835. National Museum of American Art, Smithsonian Institution, Washington, D.C.; Gift of Mrs. Joseph Harrison, Jr.

The symbolism of personal ornaments is made clear by the anecdote Catlin related about this painting: "While he was standing for his portrait . . . there were some ten or fifteen of his enemies the Sioux, seated on the floor around the room; he told me to take particular pains in representing eight quills which were arranged in his headdress, which he said stood for so many Sioux scalps that he had taken with his left hand, in which he was grasping his war-club. . . ."

the head, passing from the crown to the middle of the forehead. Others wear in the same place a sort of queue of hair, which stands out because they have shaved all around it.[103]

The French were much struck by the seventeenth-century Mississauga who, like the Ottawa, "wear their hair fastened up above their forehead, more erect than the wigs of our ladies, and they keep it erect like that by the use of a hot piece of iron or hatchet."[104] Warriors also wore feathers in the hair at the crown of the head as signs of war powers received from the thunderbirds (Figures 42 and 72).

In the Great Lakes during the late eighteenth century a popular style of men's hairdressing was the one given to the captive John Rutherford when he was adopted into an Ojibwa family. His Indian father, he wrote, "shaved my head, leaving only a small tuft of hair upon the crown and two small locks which he plaited with silver brooches interwoven, making them hang over my face.[105] Woodlands people may have believed that power was concentrated in the hair and in particular in the long lock that was left at the crown of the head. The scalp lock was the trophy sought by warriors and may have symbolized the taking of trophy heads in related prehistoric Woodlands cultures.

Woodlands Indian women wore their hair long and dressed it in a variety of styles, braiding it, shaving the hair to enlarge the forehead, or "clubbing" it into rolls over the ears. Rich ornaments of wampum and eel skin were worn by the Iroquoians of the early contact period, and Cree women made lavish use of beaded cloth streamers. Both sexes rubbed the hair with animal grease and red pigment to make it shiny and stiff. Down, which also symbolized protective upper-world power, was worn at feasts by both women and men.[106] Hairdressing emphasized the vital significance of the head symbolically, through the incorporation of silver, shell, down, feathers, and ochre, and also aesthetically, by creating striking alterations of mass and volume and of the contours of the face. During mourning and menstrual seclusion, women abandoned the grooming and annointing of the hair – a further illustration of the connection between hairdressing and personal well-being.

Body Painting and Tattooing

Body painting was a universal practice throughout the Woodlands. It was a favourite subject of the European writers, and there are many detailed descriptions of individual and regional styles. The seventeenth-century Montagnais applied polychrome pigments to their faces in a manner that reminded Father Le Jeune of European carnival maskers:

> There were some whose noses were painted blue, the eyes, eyebrows, and cheeks painted black, and the rest of the face red; and these colors are bright and shining like those of our masks; others had black, red, and blue stripes drawn from the ears to the mouth. Still others were entirely black, except the upper part of the brow and around the ears, and the end of the chin. . . . There were some who had only one black stripe, like a wide ribbon, drawn from one ear to the other, across the eyes, and three little stripes on the cheeks.[107]

A contemporary group of Ojibwa from Lake Superior painted their faces "in different colours with oil, very prettily; some had one side all green, the other all red, others appeared to have the whole face covered with natural lacework and others again were quite different"[108] (Figures 70 and 72). A century later, it was noted that the Ojibwa favoured black

73.

Sa Ga Yeath Qua Pieth Tow
(Sagayenkwaraton) (detail). Oil on canvas by John Verelst, 1710. Public Archives of Canada C-92418.

This portrait of a Mohawk chief who was one of "four kings" who journeyed to London to meet with Queen Anne in 1710 is one of the best existing records of early contact-period tattooing. It also depicts the moosehair-embroidered belt and the belt pouch worn by Iroquois men in the early 18th century.

and red paint for their faces.[109] Farther north, too, among the West Main Cree, men attending a feast had "their faces painted with black and red across the eyes, mouth, nose etc. . . . Sometimes it is longitudinal, or down the face; at other times it is in squares or circular spots; or one side of the face red, the other black, and many other varieties."[110]

The patterns of body painting appear to have been inspired by visionary and dream experience and thus honoured guardian spirits. Colour and pattern were also dictated by the occasion and were applied differently for everyday wear, feasts, war, and mourning. An opposition between red, the colour associated with life enhancement and celebration, and black, the colour of danger and death, is suggested by the customs of peoples across the Woodlands.

As with hairdressing, women's body painting was less elaborate than men's. Early contact period Iroquois, Cree, and Great Lakes women adorned the parting of the hair with red ochre.[111] Cree women favoured red paint but also made use of black and used simple motifs: "a round spot on each cheek is very common, but they frequently paint the eyebrows, and sometimes a stroke is seen under each eye, and another down the nose."[112]

During the early contact period, tattooing the body was a widespread practice (Figure 73). In the Central Great Lakes region tattooing was initiated at puberty. After a successful vision quest, a representation of a boy's guardian spirit was tattooed on his skin.[113] Some peoples, like the Neutral, practised especially elaborate tattooing. They "cause to be made a thousand different figures with charcoal pricked into the flesh, upon which previously they had traced their lines, — so that sometimes one sees the face and breast ornamented with figures, as are in France the helmets, breastplates and gorgets of military men; and the remainder of the body is appropriately decorated."[114] Similarly, among the late-eighteenth-century West Main Cree, "breasts, backs, hands, arms, and faces are marked with a variety of figures, some resembling birds, others beasts, and fishes; while others have borders, flourishes or plain lines according to their fancies."[115] In the Eastern Subarctic, tattooing was less elaborate; the Naskapi made use of simple short lines on cheek and chin similar to those of the neighbouring Inuit.

Pouches

By the end of the eighteenth century, elaborate tattooing had all but ceased in the central Woodlands, probably because more clothing was worn and covered much of the body. However, the same repertoire of motifs used in tattooing is found in another important element of Woodlands Indian costume, the decorated pouch. The intriguing possibility exists that, in the course of the eighteenth century, some of the symbolic motifs previously used in tattooing were transferred to the outsides of pouches — containers of medicines worn close to the body. Images of guardian spirits such as thunderbirds, underwater panthers, and horned serpents are the motifs most frequently depicted on pouches collected during the eighteenth century, as they apparently had been in tattooing (Figure 76). Representational motifs such as suns, turtles, fish, and beavers also occur on pouches, as do the "borders, flourishes, and plain lines" found in tattooing. It is likely that at least some of the geometric motifs found in both tattooed and pouch decorations are symbolic; zigzag and wavy lines, for example, probably represent the power emanating from the *manitos* of the upper- and underworlds in the form of lightning and turbulent water.[116]

The typology of Woodlands bags and pouches is a complicated subject, as is the variety of ways in which they were ornamented. An early account describes and contrasts styles of pouches worn by the

74.
Twined basket, Northern Great Lakes, early 18th century. On loan from the State Castles and Gardens Wörlitz-Oraneinbaum-Luisium, GDR. H:22; C:42-54

This basket–one of only few surviving examples–is unique in its use of motifs resembling those on painted bags and quillwork from the Northern Great Lakes and in its use of porcupine quills for false embroidery.

75.
Moosehair-embroidered pouch, Huron or Iroquois. Staatliche Museen Preußischer Kulturbesitz, Museum für Völkerkunde, Berlin, FRG IV-B-1. L:18.3; W:15.5

The intricacy of many geometric designs on early moosehair false-embroidered pouches and burden straps is achieved by reversing the colours of the mirror image of the initial design unit.

seventeenth-century Huron and the neighbouring Algonquins:

> The Savages wear their pocket, wallet, and purse behind the back, in the form of a pouch, which they hang about the neck by means of a leather thong, and in which they put their tobacco and the other little necessaries that they use most frequently. This pocket, or pouch, is generally seamless, and is made by the Huron women as artistically as a piece of needlework; the Algonquins often make it of a whole skin.[117]

The comparison to needlework appears to be a clear reference to the moosehair and porcupine-quill false embroidery at which Huron and Iroquoian women excelled in the early contact period. Several small rectangular pouches embroidered in this way illustrate the type that is probably being described (Figure 75). An old, unique example of a twined basket decorated with porcupine-quill false embroidery displays motifs

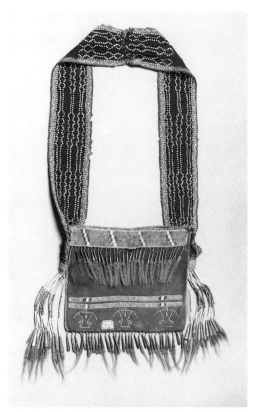

76.
Pouch, Ojibwa type, c. 1800. Natural History Collection of the Town of Winterthur, Switzerland IX.2.134. L:67 (total)

The nearly perfect condition of this and other objects in the Rieter Collection at Winterthur makes it possible to appreciate the bright colour and clarity of design admired by Woodlands Indians and Europeans in early contact-period textiles. Thunderbirds are among the most popular motifs of warriors' pouches.

77.
Eight wampum belts drawn by S.D.S. Huyghes at the Huron Council House at Lorette in 1848. By courtesy of the Museum of Victoria, Melbourne, Australia.

The keeper of the belts explained that #1 was used to rally eight allied tribes for war, #2 symbolized an "open path'' and was used to inaugurate a grand chief, #3 was a "pledge of peace with eight nations or villages," and #4 was a war belt, #6 was worn by the grand chief on state occasions, and #7 was used to make peace. (#5 and #8 were not explained.)

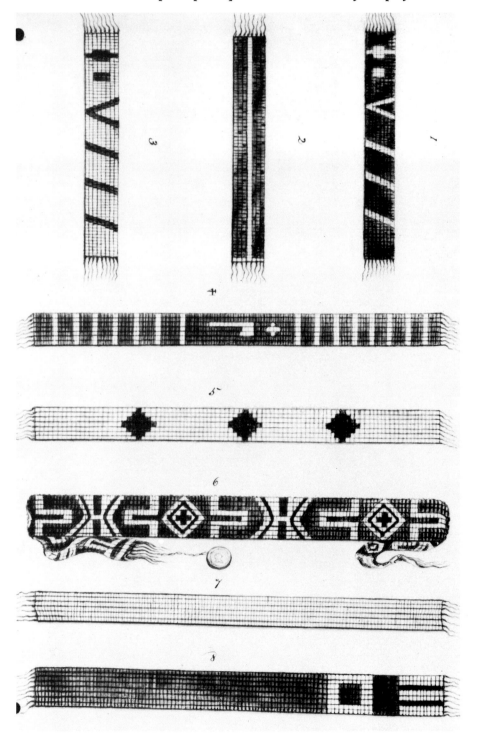

resembling those on eighteenth-century painted bags probably collected in the Northern Great Lakes[118] (Figure 74). This basket suggests that an even wider range of weaving and decorative techniques existed during the early contact period. Another type of pouch used by Eastern Great Lakes peoples is the belt pouch, a rectangular hide container with an opening in one side, which was folded over the belt. In concept, this is similar to the pouches made of whole animal skins used in many parts of the Woodlands, which were also hung from or folded over a belt (Figure 73).

Another type of bag or pouch collected during the early eighteenth century or perhaps earlier is a rectangular hide container with a panel of netted quillwork suspended from the bottom. Images of thunderbirds are frequently worked in this panel, and the painted decoration of the two sides may include images of the sun, thunderbirds, and geometric motifs (Figure 46). These painted bags probably originate in the Northern Great Lakes, for the painting style resembles that found on coats of the region. Among the West Main Cree, a small, rectangular pouch was worn suspended around the neck and ornamented on one side with bands of woven porcupine quills or, later, beads.[119]

During the wars of the eighteenth century, Indians of the Central and Eastern Great Lakes fought alongside European soldiers. This led to the emergence of a new style of shoulder bag made of dyed-black or smoked dark-brown skin modelled on military bandolier bags[120] (Figure 76). Although the bags are innovative in construction, the embroidered designs continued long-established iconographic traditions. The compositions often resemble those found in the pendant panels of netted quillwork on earlier painted hide pouches. The new square and rectangular formats of the bag fronts challenged eighteenth-century craftswomen and stimulated a number of splendid new decorative solutions. Some Iroquois bags were made with woven panels of glass imitation-wampum beads, like those formerly worn as hair ornaments by Huron women (Figure 78), and others were covered with dense rows of quill embroidery or pieced moosehair false embroidery.[121]

A striking parallelism in the ornamentation of the human body and the skins of animals is revealed by our survey of clothing and body decoration. Just as red pigment was rubbed onto areas of the body, it was applied in amorphous patches to pouches and clothing. Contemporary descriptions of body painting speak of animal motifs, figures, stripes, "lacework" and "flourishes" in red, green, black, and other colours; the same repertoire of designs is also present in the painted and embroidered decoration of hide clothing and pouches. The analogies can be extended. We read of the decoration of scalp locks with silver, beads, and shell. So, too, the red-dyed animal-hair tassels are attached to moccasins and pouches, strung on beaded thongs and wrapped with cones of brass or tin. Wampum strings were attached to the human hair and body as well as to the fringes of garments. Fine ornaments of woven and embroidered quills and beads were worn around the neck, wrist, and waist, and also sewn across the seams of leggings and coats (Figures 56 and 66).

The most archaic forms of decoration on articles made of hide appear to be relatively simple patterns of stripes and dots, which were still in use among the Eastern Cree peoples in this century. The connection between ritual and decoration among these peoples may offer clues to the possible symbolism underlying the act of decoration in general; after successful hunts and at periodic feasts, the skins of slain animals were ritually adorned with ochre stripes and dots, beads, and ribbons as a sign of respect to the spirits of the animals.[122] The many parallels that exist between the ritual treatment of animals by these people and other Wood-

78.
Pouch, Iroquois type, before 1778. Braunschweigisches Landesmuseum, FRG VM7250. L:69.5 (overall)

A vogue for shoulder bags with fronts made of imitation glass wampum beads existed at the end of the 18th century. The geometric designs they display resemble those on belts and ornaments made of shell wampum beads.

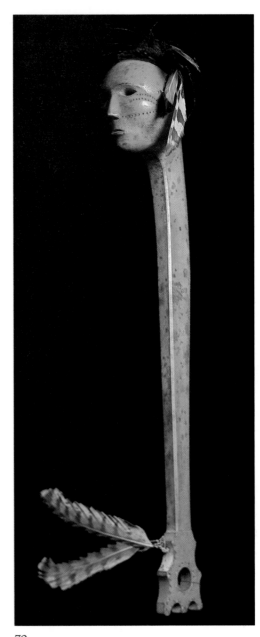

79.
War club, Iroquois type, 1847-1854. From the collection of the Earl of Elgin and Kincardine, KT, CD, Scotland. L:65

Skill in the carving of naturalistic effigies developed during many centuries of artistic activity in the Woodlands. This club also displays an assemblage of symbolic materials and paint that has often disappeared from similar pieces collected during the early contact period. It probably once had inlays of shiny material in the eye sockets.

lands groups makes a shared attitude towards decoration probable. The further parallels between body decoration and hide-clothing ornamentation suggest that the two have a common inspiration. They point to an identity between the human and animal realms.

It is clear that the individual elements of clothing and body decoration were not originally independent artistic creations. The artist of the early contact period created an ornament or garment to be a part of an ensemble, both aesthetic and symbolic. Time has fragmented the original unity of early contact period Woodlands art. When we see a headdress or quilled ornament displayed in isolation, we must remember that, according to the original intent of artist and wearer, these would have formed part of a dazzling and colourful array of clothing, paint, and ornament. By reassembling the complete costume – at least in the imagination – we can appreciate dress and body decoration as complete symbolic and aesthetic expressions.

The Aesthetics of Woodlands Indian Art

> They are fond of painting, and practise it with considerable skill, considering that they have no rules of art nor fitting means; yet they make pictures of men, animals, birds, and other things in caricature, both in perspective on stones, wood, and other similar substances, and painted flat upon their bodies. They make these not for idolatry, but to enjoy looking at them, as an ornament for their calumets and pipes and to decorate the front of their lodges.[123]

The European observers who recorded so wide a range of information about the Indians of the Woodlands during the early contact period tell us little about native ideas of beauty. To these men of the seventeenth century the stylizations of Indian painting and sculpture were rude, and native taste in dress barbaric. They concluded, with Sagard, that the native peoples had no "rules of art."

Woodlands languages have no words for "art" or "artist," and the use of these terms in discussions of Woodlands Indian objects and their makers represents the imposition of essentially Western concepts on native culture. Art-making was neither the specialization of a small group of people within society, nor was it separable from function and ritual activity. Native ideas of beauty were tightly linked to criteria of technical excellence and usefulness.[124] However, substitutes for the term "artist," such as "craftsperson," "maker," or "creator," lack the important dimension of aesthetic expression that is present in the objects and genres under discussion. The term "artist" is used here to refer to that aspect of a person's creative activity that was governed by aesthetic considerations in addition to the dictates of ritual and practical use.

Although we lack explicit statements of ideals of beauty by Woodlands Indian artists and patrons, their taste and stylistic choices are embodied in the objects they made. By studying these objects, we can identify consistent approaches to the handling of space, colour, line, texture, and form. Five aesthetic preferences can be observed: naturalistic three-dimensional representation; the use of rich and dense ornament; luminous surface; asymmetrical design; and figure-ground reversal.[125]

The Naturalistic Effigy
The expert skill with which Woodlands artists created sculptural effigies of animal and human forms is rooted in ancient, prehistoric Woodlands artistic traditions. The earliest collected clubs and pipes display carved, rounded, and lifelike birds, animals, anthropomorphic heads, and figures; stylistically similar effigies are found in prehistoric clay and stone pipes.

All are thought to portray protective guardian spirits.[126] Three-dimensional guardian spirit images occur, too, on war clubs, spoon handles, and bowls in both pre- and post-contact art (Figures 79 and 80).

These effigies are rendered with accurate proportions and a refined, simplified naturalism of form. The fine detail of hair, eyebrows, and flesh folds is smoothed out to eliminate the highly specific or individual. The simplified forms of body and face form a base on which symbolic ornaments, such as inlaid shell or glass eyes, feather ornaments, tattoo markings, and paint, were applied, although these are not always present today. These effigies were intended to evoke the real presence of the *manito* in the human realm, for in Woodlands belief a representation embodied some part of the thing represented.[127]

This belief in the presence of a being in its visual image is evident in the reactions of seventeenth-century Indians to the baroque Christian religious art to which they were exposed by the Jesuits. Le Jeune describes the astonishment of the Huron on seeing the Jesuit chapel at Quebec. They asked him if the statues of saints were *ondaqui* (spirits), and if the tabernacle was their house and the altar clothes and ornaments their dress. They also laughed when three separate statues were identified as the mother of God, asking how one man could have three mothers.[128] On a darker note, Le Mercier found it hard to combat the belief that the Christian sacred images were causing outbreaks of disease among the Huron, and the missionaries had "some difficulty in making [the Indians] believe that these were only flat paintings."[129] For Woodlands Indians,

80.
Pipe, Iroquois or Delaware type, before 1710. National Museum of Denmark, Department of Ethnography, Copenhagen E Gc4. L:47; H:10

This pipe, which was in the Royal Danish Collection, is one of the earliest collected from the Eastern Woodlands. The insertion of the stem in the mouth of the effigy on the bowl is typical of the visual punning found in northern Woodlands art.

naturalistic style was an aesthetic means of giving permanent and convincing form to transient visionary experiences of the immanent supernatural beings.

The Aesthetic of Ornament

Early observers often spoke of Woodlands Indian dress as gaudy. To their eyes, the contrasting patterns, colours, and textures characteristic of native costume and other art forms lacked the qualities of clarity and unity of medium that were ideals of the European classical tradition. They were also struck, as Champlain's description of young Huron women shows, by the sheer quantity of ornaments that were worn:

> They are laden with quantities of wampum, both necklaces and chains . . . and also with bracelets and ear-rings. They have their hair well combed, dyed and oiled . . . sometimes they fasten to it plates a foot square covered with the same wampum, which hang behind. In this manner gaily dressed and adorned, they like to show themselves at dances, where their fathers and mothers send them, forgetting no device that they can apply to bedeck and bedizen their

daughters; and I can assure you that at dances I have attended, I have seen girls that had more than twelve pounds of wampum on them, without counting the other trifles with which they are loaded and decked out.[130]

The Woodlands concept of ornament was additive — more was better — and the massing of individual elements proportionately increased the attractiveness of the presentation. Aesthetic pleasure — derived from the heaping up of brilliance, colour, and pattern — was enhanced by the identification of precious materials, such as shell, with supernatural power. Ornaments also represented prestige and wealth as the products of women's industry and skill, and, during the fur-trade era, a luxuriance of glass beads and trade cloth was also evidence of men's hunting prowess and economic success.

An anecdote recounted by a Hudson's Bay Company trader poignantly illustrates the great value placed on ornaments by Woodlands people. The story tells of a canoe accident during which a mother sacrificed herself to save her husband and children. As a last act, "holding the canoe with one hand she untied her belt and gave it with her other ornaments to her husband, then letting go her hold, sank down and was drowned."[131]

The dazzling display seen in the total costume assemblage also governs the design of individual ornaments, garments, and pouches. The most splendid surviving set of seventeenth-century quilled ornaments — stitches and weave intact and dyes still brilliant — was collected at Hudson Bay about 1660 (Figure 81). These ornaments set before us a virtuoso exhibition of skill; an array of different techniques, including wrapping, twining, and netting, produces a series of shifting internal contrasts in pattern, which provide visual interest and pleasure. A similar effect was achieved by the late-eighteenth-century creator of a splendid pendant from the Great Lakes region. Its central image of a human figure is woven of glass wampum beads and edged with braided, woven, and embroidered multicoloured quills, and hung with metal cones and scarlet-dyed deer-hair tassels (Figure 82).

The new materials available to Woodlands craftswomen after contact allowed them to create an even wider range of textures and patterns. Artists regularly chose to combine as many different techniques, patterns, and materials as possible within one piece in order to create an

81.
Set of quilled ornaments, Central Cree, 1662-1676. Dean and Chapter of Canterbury Cathedral, England B58. Neck ornaments L:88; Belt: L:82; Garters: L:27

These ornaments were collected during one of the first voyages to Hudson Bay. They testify to the technical excellence and love of rich ornament that was present among the Central Subarctic peoples at the time of contact.

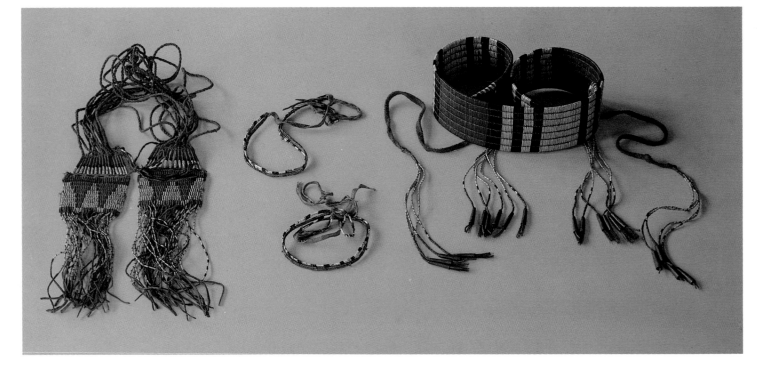

effect of maximum richness and visual interest. During the historic period, as before the coming of the Europeans, a lavish display of ornament was a means of bringing together power and beauty in a potent and inseparable mixture.

Luminosity

The metaphor of light is central to Woodlands Indian thought. In Indian speeches recorded during the early contact period, light is related to knowledge, wisdom, and far-sightedness. The ultimate source of light, and of all these virtues, was the sun. Both the seasonal cycle, on which successful hunting and farming depended, and the powers of warriors depended on the sun and sky worlds.

The symbolic association of shining and reflective materials, such as polished shell, metals, crystal, and glass, with supernatural beings has already been noted. Further evidence of the way in which the new trade materials were incorporated into traditional symbolism is indicated by the Naskapi word for mirror, which translates as "see soul metal." Similarly, the Iroquois word for glass bead is also the word for eye.[132] Two of the earliest sculptures brought to Europe from the Eastern Woodlands, a club and pipe carved with human effigies, incorporate this symbolic reference in the embedded glass beads that serve as eyes (Figure 80). The use of these beads endows the effigies with the visionary qualities attributed to shamans and leaders.

Shining objects are often found as parts of medicine bundles, for they were regarded as precious gifts bestowed directly by the *manitos*. This association is illustrated in an anecdote of two young Ojibwa women, who were struck with awe by the sight of a piece of shining yellow metal at the base of a cliff that "exactly fronted the rising sun. After examining it for some time, it occurred to the eldest girl that it belonged to Gitchi Manitou, the Great Spirit, upon which they abandoned the place with precipitation."[133] The association of light with supernatural power is more general, however. Light-reflective metals were also associated with underworld spirits; native people who found pieces of pure copper beneath the water kept them "as so many divinities, or as presents which the gods dwelling beneath the water have given them, and on which their welfare is to depend. For this reason they preserve these pieces of copper, wrapped up, among their most precious possessions."[134] Narratives of visions commonly describe *manitos* in general as radiating light,[135] and spirits are often represented in sacred art with rays emanating from their heads (Figure 50).

A preference for luminous surface can be found throughout Woodlands art. Carved wooden and stone objects such as pipe bowls and clubs were polished and rubbed with oil to produce a shiny surface. Descriptions of painting on animal hides and the human body also stress the shininess of the paint, which was mixed with oil to make it glossy. It is probable that, as in many cultures, a glowing skin was evidence of health, vitality, and well-being, and the generalized taste for shining surface may have reflected these associations. The great popularity of shiny trade-silk ribbon in the early historic period is consistent with the taste for luminous surface that informs all of Woodlands art.

Asymmetrical Design Distribution

There is a widespread tendency across the Woodlands to subdivide and treat the surfaces of objects in an asymmetrical manner. Characteristically, the front and back or upper and under surfaces of containers and utensils and the left and right sides of garments display different motifs or colours. Western textiles and decorated objects, by contrast, are usually covered by a continuous composition or by repeats of the same motif.

82.
Ornament, Ottawa or Wyandot type, before 1838. Saffron Waldon Museum, England E392. L:65.0;. Gorget: D:7.0

The array of different materials, textures, and techniques combined in this ornament satisfied the Woodlands Indian's taste for maximum contrast, density of pattern, and liveliness.

On pairs of Naskapi and Great Lakes moccasins, for example, right and left cuffs display different geometric motifs (Figure 83). Iroquoian moose-hair embroidered pouches often have different designs on their two sides; a Great Lakes finger-woven bag displays horizontally oriented zigzag motifs on one side and vertically oriented chain motifs on the other.[136] Similarly, the two sides of bark containers, legging borders, and breech-clouts are often decorated differently (Figure 84). Even headbands and the straps of shoulder pouches are often divided in the centre into contrasting right and left design fields. Although Europeans usually dismissed such compositional schemes as "barbaric," one early-nineteenth-century observer of Great Lakes face painting noted that, "in the care with which everything like symmetry or harmony in form or colours was avoided, there was something evidently studied and artistical."[137]

The tendency towards asymmetry in visual art may be related to the spatial structuring that was a fundamental aspect of Woodlands cosmologies. The division of the universe into upper and lower realms, the central vertical axis — the great World Tree of Iroquoian mythology — that joined the layers of the cosmos, and the quartering of the earth's surface by the cardinal directions, established clear spatial zones vital to an individual's sense of orientation.

83.
Moccasins, Eastern Great Lakes, late 18th century. From the King's Regiment Collection. National Museums and Galleries on Merseyside, Liverpool 1958.83.12. L:26

The asymmetrical design typical of Woodlands art is seen here in the contrasting patterns used on the moccasin cuffs. The moccasins were collected by an American Loyalist army officer who served at Michilimackinac during the American Revolution.

84.
Rogan, Ojibwa, c. 1823. Museo Civico di Scienze Naturali, "E. Caffi," Bergamo. Collezione G.C. Beltrami 53. L:16; W:8; D:10

Bark containers, like many other objects made by Woodlands Indians, are often decorated with contrasting designs on the front and back. The meander lines on one side of the container as well as the zigzag and chain motifs on the other are typical of Great Lakes textiles but are not usually seen on rogans.

In all ritual acts it was necessary to acknowledge the loci of power in the earth, heavens, and the four corners of the cosmos by directed gesture and the blowing of tobacco smoke. Native people were conscious of the particular directional *manito* they confronted when they set out to hunt or travel and in the Subarctic particular designs were displayed on clothing and tools to please and placate these spirits. Native people's keen awareness of spatial structure and geographical directions is witnessed by the many references to the unerring precision with which they mapped their journeys by observing the positions of the sun and celestial bodies. Communal life also required a strong awareness of the directional orientation of one's own body; people slept in the wigwam or longhouse in a strict order guided by place in the family grouping, with specific categories of kin to the right and left.

The careful division of the surface of decorated objects and the application of contrasted colour, pattern, and motif to the separate surfaces appears to reflect the strong sense of spatial structure that was part of the Woodlands world-view. There is a further possibility that, on some objects, asymmetrical design is a modelling of the arrangement of cosmic forces. Woodlands mythology often explains the creation of the world as a result of the interaction of the "positive" and "negative" forces of sky and earth. A related sense of complementary dualities underlies much ritual and artistic expression. Man's well-being is dependent on the blessings of both realms. Some decorative schemes, then, may express more than a simple awareness of directionality. They may also express a mimetic balancing of the powers that were believed to reside in the different directions. Such an interpretation appears to be particularly relevant to the Central Great Lakes, where many objects display on their front and back surfaces motifs related to the two great powers of the upper- and underworlds, the thunderbird and the underwater panther.[138]

The Aesthetic of Positive and Negative Space

The design of some Woodlands Indian objects, particularly textiles and carvings, sets up a careful interplay between the figure and the space that surrounds it. The artist draws the eye of the viewer both to the shape of the central image and to that of the "empty" space around it. Four examples in very different media illustrate this approach. A series of pre-contact Iroquoian antler combs with elaborately carved handles

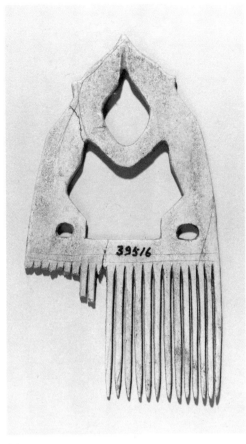

85.
Antler comb, Cayuga, post 1600. From Prince Edward County, Ontario. Courtesy of the Royal Ontario Museum, Toronto 39516. L:13.6; W:7.3

A visual emphasis on the negative spaces between the forms of the animals is notable here and in many other early historic Iroquoian combs.

86.
Rush mat, Ottawa, 1851-1853. Museum für Völkerkunde, Vienna 131694. L:94; W:39.5

A pattern of thunderbirds emerges and recedes in this optically active woven pattern. The visual effect is perhaps intended to express a belief in the ability of supernatural beings to transform their appearance and to manifest themselves to people at will.

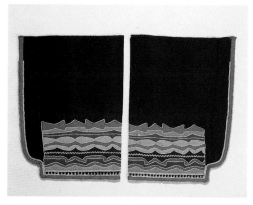

87.
Leggings, Northern Ojibwa or Cree type, mid-19th century type. Canadian Museum of Civilization, National Museums of Canada, Ottawa III-M-60 a, b. L:32.5; W:23.5

Linear patterns used in early contact-period painted decoration often reappear as the contour lines of fur-trade era ribbonwork appliqué. The new materials made possible greater density of pattern and a wider range of colours.

display representations of animals, human figures, and architectural elements that may represent clan animals and longhouse officials[139] (Figure 85). We perceive the spaces between and around the figures as independent formal elements existing in the same spatial plane as the figures, rather than receding into the "background." Much the same phenomenon occurs on a rush mat from the Central Great Lakes, woven in a repeated pattern of thunderbirds (Figure 86). Here, too, the figures come forward and recede as we look at them, so that figure and ground become interchangeable, alternating perceptions.

The *sgrafitto* technique used to decorate birchbark containers across the Woodlands requires the scraping away of the dark outer layer of the bark to reveal patterns in the lighter underlayer. Early examples of such containers set up similar tensions between the emerging lighter "background" forms and the receding darker motifs of the surface (Figure 84). The aesthetic of figure-ground reversal is perhaps most pronounced in ribbon-work appliqué. In the beautiful ribbon-work borders on a pair of woman's leggings from Northern Ontario, the overlapping cut edges of the ribbon define readable contours not only for the top strip of ribbon, but also for the ribbon onto which it is sewn (Figure 87). The negative space, or background, becomes as prominent an element of the composition as the figure or foreground.

The interplay the artist sets up between foreground and background in these three examples can be regarded as a purely aesthetic play of form and colour. The way an artist solves such problems, however, may reflect characteristic ways in which her culture "sees" the relationship between human beings and their environment. In Woodlands art, the human or animal figure does not stand out against a receding background as it would in post-Renaissance Western art; rather, it is held in a tension or equilibrium with the other elements of the composition, including the "vacant" space. The aesthetic of "figure-ground reversal" is consistent with Woodlands beliefs that human beings exist in a reciprocal, balanced relationship with many other beings. It is also in harmony with the animist world-view, according to which not only people and animals but also other phenomena have animate presence. If the very wind was a real person to the peoples of the Woodlands, no space could be considered truly "empty." In some art works, too, the aesthetic of figure-ground reversal allows us to see identifiable figures emerging from undefined abstract shapes and forms. A concept of the transformability of matter and of the immanence of *manitos* in the world around us seems implied in these visual plays.

The early historic period art of the Woodlands Indians contains many examples of a need to give outward visible form to beliefs about the correct relationship of human beings to one another and to the supernatural forces that surround them. These "rules of living" are embodied in symbolic systems, of which visual artistic images are one manifestation. The arts of the Woodlands peoples also provide abundant evidence of the joyous creativity and skill with which artists enhanced symbolic expression, lending it the commanding, seductive power of beautiful form and surface. The "rules of art" these artists followed were the product of many generations of artistic activity. At the core of this achievement was the creation of styles harmonious with the values and world-view of the makers. It was no less an achievement that, during the early historic period, visual artists responded to the tremendous impact of contact with European culture with outstanding inventiveness and creativity.

Ruth B. Phillips

By The Power of Their Dreams

Artistic Traditions of the Northern Plains

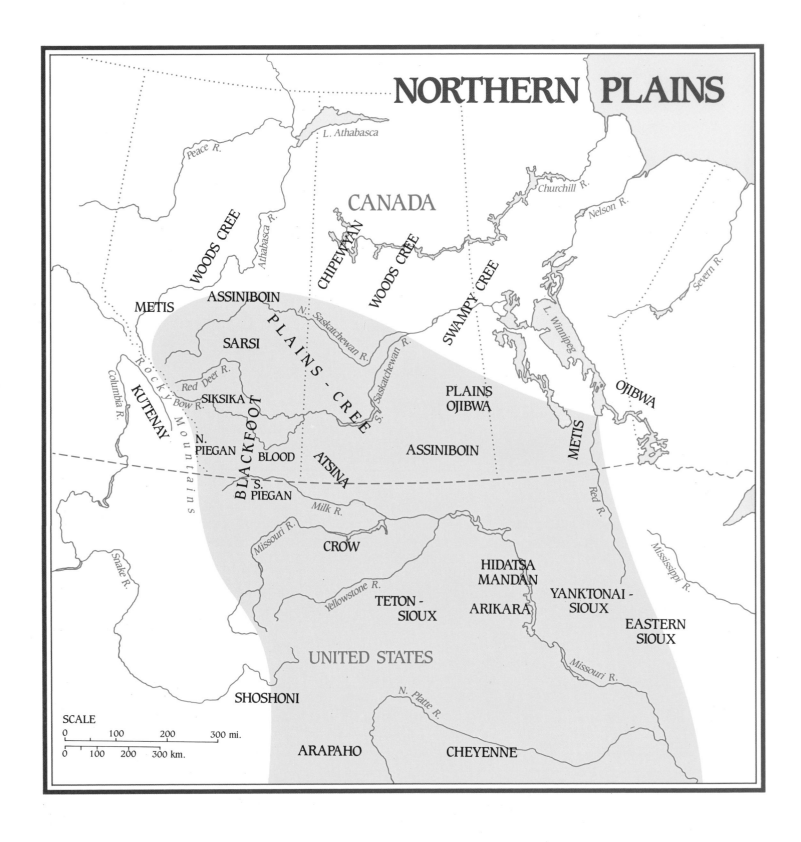

NORTHERN PLAINS

We think of the Canadian Plains as an ocean of grass, rolling towards a far-away horizon, a near-abstract landscape under the "big sky." In fact, however, a fair portion of the northern Plains is a hilly parkland of lakes and aspen groves, a transition zone between the open plains in the south and the boreal forests north of the North Saskatchewan River. A few more rivers twist their way out of the forested foothills of the Rockies, meandering through wide and wooded valleys east to Lake Winnipeg.

This is the new earth made by Old Man after the Great Deluge.[1] Sitting on his raft, Old Man sent four of his animal friends down to recover some of the original earth. He spread the mud on the water and directed the wolf to run along the margins of this tiny island. As a result, it expanded until the present surface of the earth was formed.

Thus the universe acquired its final form, divided into three major realms: Sky, Earth, and Underwater. Native traditions deal primarily with the subsequent events on the island called Earth; but for their sacred powers its inhabitants remained dependent upon the life-giving forces of the sky and the dark deep, ruled by the Sun and by Our Mother, the Earth. Inhabiting remote regions of their realms, these two rulers expressed their powers through a multitude of spiritual beings such as the thunderbirds and Morningstar above, and the horned snake and other monsters below.

Apparently in response to the creation of the earth, these spirits acquired visible representatives closer to the earth's surface, such as the birds in the sky and the animals that live in the water. Divided by the surface of the new earth, the two power realms thus evolved into two strata.

Old Man changed the wasteland of Earth into a home for the animals emerging from underwater and for the birds from above. But when he added mankind, his own creation, he changed the animals as well, for he intended man to be a hunter, not the animals' prey.

Numbering in the millions, buffalo were the dominant inhabitants of the Grasslands, but the Parklands offered a larger variety of game. In wintertime, when The-One-Who-Comes-With-Blizzards reigned on the open plains, the buffalo, elk, and many other animals sheltered in the parklands and the river valleys.

The life and well-being of most animals were looked after by their spiritual ancestors. The buffalo spirit was chief of the grass eaters, the wolf spirit of the meat eaters, the beaver spirit of the long-tailed water mammals, the thunderbird of the summer birds and flying insects. From these and other guardian spirits all parts of nature derived their sacred powers.

88.

Indian Hunters Return. Oil by Charles M. Russell, 1900. Montana Historical Society, Mackay Collection, Helena.

Many years of personal acquaintance with the Native people enabled the artist to create this realistic picture of a traditional winter camp of Northern Plains Indians.

Wishing the people to share in these powers, Old Man advised them to learn from the animals.[2] Perhaps that is why the people formed nomadic bands, following the animals on the open plains in summer, retreating into the forests and the valleys during the winter. Having joined the people long ago, wolfish dogs carried their modest possessions.[3]

Native creation myths convey the message that, unlike the animals, man was a latecomer without inherent spiritual power. He depended upon gifts of power gradually transferred to him by animal spirits and other associates of Sky and Underworld. Some Blackfoot Indians still remember that "the old people survived by the power of their dreams," and according to Cree Indians, "it was impossible for men to survive without the assistance from spirits." Through dreams and mystic experiences people were given sacred power, game, and success in all enterprises in return for the consecration of daily activities through ritual practices; the lords of nature were generous to those for whom hunting was a sacred occupation. Dreams also provided the native artisan with images painted, carved, or embroidered on garments and utensils.

This world-view was most pervasive among the Indians who had migrated from the harsh northeastern forests into the Parklands after the mid-nineteenth century. It found a less intense but more colourful expression in an annual cycle of communal ceremonies among the Indians who had been enjoying nature's abundance on the Northern Plains for many centuries.

Evidence of these people's diverse origins survived primarily in their different languages. The Blackfoot tribes, Atsina, Cree, and Plains Ojibwa, speak Algonkian langauges originating from the northeastern boreal forest. The Sarsi came down from the north, speaking a language of Athapaskan derivation. The Assiniboin or Stoney speak a language belonging to the Siouan family, formerly centred in the upper Mississippi region.

After the introduction of the horse in the 1740s and the subsequent arrival of European traders, Northern Plains Indian culture acquired its distinct character. Metal tools, glass beads, and other coveted imports replaced time-consuming native craft work; the horse as a beast of burden and a mode of hunting made life more comfortable and freed time for the elaboration of annual ceremonies, horse raiding, and warfare. Ceremonials and warfare provided important stimuli for art expressions suited to the nomadic way of life.

The Plains Indians, in colourful costume on horseback, feather head-dresses streaming in the wind, have captured the imagination of the entire world. Attracted by the sense of freedom and dashing bravado of these latter-day knights, the industrial city dweller saw them as the apotheosis of the American Indian, if not of the noble savage himself. Yet it is a curious fact that this Plains Indian emerged only after the coming of the white man. Fine artefacts were created during that most fascinating but poorly understood period in which the native people were adjusting their way of life to changing conditions. This essay will concentrate not so much upon the golden age of historic Plains Indian culture as upon its antecedents.

"The ground on which we stand is sacred ground; it is the dust and blood of our ancestors."
     Plenty Coups, Crow[4]

Once there was a Blackfoot woman who had given birth to many children, but life was hard and all her children had died. In her grief she had mutilated several of her fingers. What could the future bring a woman without children to look after her?

Standing under the burial tree of her last child, she saw a small whirlwind twisting through the grass towards her. When it was close by she saw a small boy running in the centre of the dust whirl. The boy said to her, "Mother, don't cry any more, for I will be your next child. When I am born you must cut off a piece of my navel string, wrap it up with sweetgrass, and hang it around my neck. Then I shall not die."[5]

The navel string was cut with a sharp stone arrowhead, never with a metal knife, for that belonged to the world of the white man. Praying for his long life, the midwife then painted the child's body all over with red ochre.[6] The navel string was put in a small decorated bag. For Blackfoot boys these bags were shaped like an aggressive snake; those for girls represented the patient lizard (Figure 89). These animals were believed never to be sick and to enjoy a long life; they shed their skins much as children changed their names at four stages in their lives.

Similar navel-string charms were used by all tribes of the Northern Plains. In 1832 the artist George Catlin purchased some from Sioux women, "but in every instance they cut them open and removed from within a bunch of cotton or moss the little sacred medicine which, to part with, would endanger the health of the child."[7]

The bag was attached to the baby's cradle for good luck; with its brilliant colours, the bag served as a focus of interest for the child. Cradles on the Eastern Plains were like those used in the Great Lakes region: flat wooden boards with a footrest on which the swaddled baby was held by means of straps. Protecting the baby's face was a wooden bow, attached to the sides of the board and held in place by straps of elaborate quillwork reaching down to the lower rim of the board (Figure 90).

89.
Navelstring amulet, Blood, c. 1900.
Courtesy of the Glenbow Museum, Calgary
AF 4684. L:12.5; W:8

Its lizard shape indicates that this amulet was for a girl. The fossil snail shell attached to the lizard's nose is a good-luck charm.

90.
Cradleboard, Eastern Sioux, 1830s. National Museum of Natural History, Smithsonian Institution, Washington, D.C. 73311. L:117; W:47

Wooden cradleboard with incised decorations and quillworked cover. Attached at the bottom are fragments of two decorative straps, formerly running up to the protective hoop.

Quillwork covers and carved decorations along the top of the boards beautifully expressed the love with which families received their children; new life was considered sacred in those days. The covers on Eastern Sioux cradles frequently show symbols of the great spiritual guardians of life, thunderbirds and long-tailed underwater panthers, worked in dyed porcupine quills wrapped around strips of birchbark. Similar cradle ornaments of the Plains Ojibwa show geometric patterns in loom-woven quillwork.[8]

Farther to the west, the Plains Cree, Assiniboin, Blackfoot, and Sarsi used a moss bag similar to those used throughout the northern boreal forests.[9] Soft moss lining in these bags absorbed all fluids and was changed daily. Elaborate cradle boards, such as those made by the Kutenai and Flathead across the Rocky Mountains, were desirable trade items on the Northwestern Plains. Moss bags and cradle boards enabled the people to transport their babies on their wanderings in search of game.

For many thousands of years small bands of hunters followed the buffalo herds, seasonally moving their camps from Parklands to Plains. Still visible are the many rings of field stones used to hold down the skin covers of their conical lodges. These tipis were small, their size limited by the weight a dog could haul on the A-shaped, wooden travois. A tipi cover made of about six buffalo skins was a heavy load for a strong dog.

Conical dwellings were characteristic of boreal-forest people, and suggest that these ancient buffalo hunters were of northern origin.[10] More evidence is provided by the designation as the "seat of honour" the position opposite the tipi's entrance, which is another northern circumpolar custom.[11] Colourful paintings on some tipi covers represented the animal spirits from which the tipi owners had acquired their sacred powers. In 1809 Alexander Henry saw Cree tipis "painted with red and black figures. These devices are generally derived from their dreams." On Blackfoot tipi covers he saw that "the buffalo and the bear are frequently delineated, but in a rude and uncouth manner."[12] Apparently, Henry did not appreciate the stylized, monochromatic images, in which the animals' joints were marked and certain internal organs pictured in a tradition widely spread in the northern parts of North America and Siberia.[13] Several other cultural aspects indicate that the people exploiting the Northern Plains were essentially Parklanders, who had modified northern, Subarctic traditions in their adjustment to the regional ecology.

Evidence several thousands of years old has been found of organized, communal hunting techniques associated with rituals; later these involved corrals or pounds and buffalo jumps in the foothills. Such activities required the co-operation of several of the widely dispersed bands, and suggest that there may have been other social contacts as well.

Contacts with people living beyond the Northern Plains gradually increased over the centuries, starting with the import of flint and obsidian, used in the manufacture of lance– and arrowheads. The picture becomes more detailed after about 200 A.D.,[14] when migrants from west of the Rocky Mountains appear to have settled in the foothills country. Other groups arrived from the east, reinforcing the general Woodland heritage in the regional Plains culture. Derived from Eastern Woodland prototypes, distinctive pottery styles developed, and communal hunting techniques improved. Every part of the buffalo not used for food was put to some other purpose. Hide was used for clothing, tipi covers, straps, shields, trunks, and bags; bone was a strong material for skin scrapers, awls, paintbrushes, and other tools; horns were made into spoons; sinew made excellent sewing thread because it swelled when wet, thus helping to make seams waterproof. Even the buffalo's dung was useful as fuel on the open Plains where firewood was in short supply.

The world-view of these people was undoubtedly derived from that prevailing in the circumboreal forest. Success in hunting depended upon a private and sacred interaction with the animal spirits. Band leaders were hunters who had acquired strong spiritual powers in this manner.

These bands were small, consisting primarily of male relatives and their families. Trained in the manufacture of ceramics, clothing, and decoration techniques, women played an important role in the spread of art traditions through their marriages into the neighbouring bands. Prehistoric objects made of skin, bark, and similar perishable materials have not survived, but a Woodland heritage is evident in artefacts of early historic origin.

However, an expanding network of intertribal trade introduced cultural influences from the middle Missouri River region. Reflecting these contacts, the first burial mounds appeared about 700 A.D., suggesting the emergence of an élite in the formerly egalitarian society of the hunters.[15] This élite may have acquired their prestige in a pattern of ritualized warfare that was coming in from the southeast.

More than 2,000 years ago, agriculture developed in the lower Mississippi Valley, allowing the people there to settle in semi-permanent villages. Complex societies flourished and waned in the southeast and, by 900 A.D., large groups of migrants from that region had spread a Mississippian culture pattern far and wide.[16] Its reverberations were felt as far as the Northern Plains. Thus any discussion of the Plains people must include a description of the essential aspects of Mississippian culture as it appeared in its south eastern homeland.[17]

Mississippian communities in the south east were ruled by chiefs descended from aristocratic lineages, probably claiming descent from the Sun and other cosmic deities. The chiefs, representing of these deities, officiated at an annual cycle of communal rituals focused upon fertility and warfare. Related to these rituals was the ostentatious distribution of wealth, which stimulated the production and dissemination of artwork. The members of this élite were buried in mortuary shrines and burial mounds, and the burial rituals also involved the display of large quantities of sculpture, shell masks, ceramic human-head effigies, spiral-painted pottery, and ceremonial effigy pipes.

The artwork and its decorations reveal a complex cosmology in which winged beings competed with horned water reptiles. This cosmic war between Sky and Underworld was re-enacted by human warriors in a ritualized form of warfare in which enemies were beheaded and captives carried off into slavery. Intertribal contacts of a more pleasant character were based on a ritual kinship between strangers; adoption practices of this type were experienced by several early European explorers.[18]

The Northern Plains people were at the periphery of Mississippian expansion, yet the cultural impact upon the Plains hunting society was considerable. Important intermediaries in the diffusion of south eastern cultural elements were the Mandan and Hidatsa, who had established their earth lodge villages on the middle Missouri River by 900 A.D.[19] These villages became major centres in an extensive network of intertribal trade. The villages were visited annually since prehistoric times by large groups of nomads from the Central and Northern Plains, middlemen in trade contacts with remote tribes along and beyond the periphery of the Plains.[20] Intertribal trade at the Mandan and Hidatsa villages persisted well into the nineteenth century.[21]

Early records by Europeans describe the native trade as primarily an exchange of the villagers' crops for products of the hunt.[22] In return for deer skins, buffalo robes, and dried meat, the nomads received corn, beans, squash, and tobacco. In addition there was a lively exchange of decorated apparel. These articles were not necessarily manufactured by the native traders, nor did they all reach their final destination among the Mandan and Hidatsa. Thus, intertribal trade resulted in distributing craft work and other culture elements over great distances, levelling cultural differences and spreading new fashions. The Upper Missouri River style of clothing and decorative art, characteristic of much of the Northern Plains during the historic period, may well have made its first appearance during this early period.[23]

Yet intertribal trade must have been the vehicle for a more complex cultural interchange between the villagers and the nomads. The diffusion of Mississippian culture into the Northern Plains must have been part of the intangibles exchanged, in addition to corn and skins. Evidence of this process survived in the many Plains Indian myths and ceremonial organizations that originated in the Missouri River village tribes.[24] The distinct character of Northern Plains cosmology, ritualism, and art had its roots in the melding of northern attitudes towards the game spirits with the cosmic structure and ceremonialism that came from the southeast. In the public liturgy born from this cultural contact, the Northern Plains Indians still honoured the game spirits as of old, but the focus had shifted to man's role in the annual renewal of nature's creative forces.

The Assiniboin Indians of southern Manitoba annually travelled a well-established trade route to the Missouri River villages.[25] Their linguistic relationship with the Mandan and Hidatsa may have sped the assimilation of Mississippian culture elements. Between 1000 and 1500 A.D., several hundred burial mounds were constructed on the northeastern Plains; some were used by the Assiniboin as late as the 1770s.[26] The élite were buried with the products of widespread trade contacts: pipes from southwestern Minnesota, stone tablets from the lower Missouri, shell masks from the lower Mississippi Valley, copper items from Lake Superior, dentalium shells from the West Coast, as well as local pottery, birchbark containers, eagle-bone whistles, and the painted skulls of buffalo and other mammals.

Many of these items — ceremonial pipes and other sacred objects — may have been associated with "medicine bundles" given by spirits in the legendary past. Highly developed in the Mississippian heartland, these ritual units also attained prominence in the ceremonials on the Northern Plains. Among the riverine villagers, these sacred objects were owned by clans or by the tribe as a whole, but in their assimilation into the religious customs of the nomadic hunters, medicine bundles and their sacred powers became individual property.

91.
Buffalo effigy of green quartzite, found near Ardmore, Alberta. Courtesy of the Glenbow Museum, Calgary AX 70. L:25; H:14

Buffalo sculptures were probably used in hunting rituals during the Late Mississippian period.

Incised patterns decorate some of these Mississippian imports: spirals on pottery, thunderbirds, turtles, lizards, and buffalo figures on ceramics, stone tablets, and elk-antler bracelets.[27] Presumably, such figures were also scratched and painted on more perishable materials. By means of these symbols, Mississippian cosmology was grafted on the world-view and rituals of the northern buffalo hunters. The role of Sun and his son, Morningstar, the cosmic struggle between thunderbirds and water monsters, virility derived from the elk spirit, and many other concepts can be traced to the southeast.

Mississippian influence was not restricted to the Northeastern Plains people. Incised catlinite tablets, stone pipes, and some very fine stone buffalo effigies found their way through North Dakota into Saskatchewan and Alberta.[28] The stubby legs of the stone buffalo allowed them to stand securely on the uneven surface of an earthen altar (Figure 91). Other stone sculptures, including human heads, have been found in eastern Montana and southern Saskatchewan.[29] On boulders in the same region, human faces were incised with tear lines coming down from the eyes.[30] This "weeping-eye" motif is frequently found on Mississippian shell masks from burial mounds in the Northeastern Plains (Figure 92). Its symbolism is related to lightning flashing from the eyes of the thunderbird.

"Weeping eyes" survived in skin paintings made by Crow Indians, on the masks used in the Fool's Dance of the Assiniboin, and on horse masks of the Plains Cree. Though not always made of stone, buffalo effigies survived in rituals of the Plains Cree, Crow, and Cheyenne, and in those of the Kiowa, who once resided in the upper Missouri River region. Buffalo-shaped stones were used as hunting charms by the Blackfoot, who also made elk-antler bracelets until the early nineteenth century.[31]

Human-head effigies representing a spirit called Double Face figured in the Sun Dance of the Assiniboin and in sculpture on Sioux pipes. Human-head effigies in Mississippian art have been associated with head-hunting. The practice of this custom earned both Sioux and Assiniboin the name of "cut-throats" in early historic times.[32]

The ceremonial function of all these objects indicates that the major element of Mississippian export was of a spiritual nature. The wholesale transfer of rituals and their regalia from one tribe to another was an important aspect of intertribal contacts. The Mississippian practice of adopting trade partners spread throughout the plains and created a vast network of ritual kinship relationships. This practice survived in the "give-away" ceremonials of recent times.[33]

Efforts were made by Middle Missouri River people to migrate north-westward into the Canadian Plains during the early 1700s.[34] When the unfavourable climate defeated their farming initiatives, they abandoned their earth lodge settlements. Crow Indians, who lived in southern Alberta until the 1770s, and perhaps the Atsina in Saskatchewan may have been their descendants. These people may have introduced the cultivation of tobacco and associated beaver-bundle rituals among the Blackfoot tribes.[35] They may also have played a role in bringing ceremonials from the Missouri River that survived in the historic warrior societies on the Northern Plains.

The so-called "medicine wheels" on the Northern and Central Plains appear to have been related to an elaboration of burial rites on the North-eastern Plains; they were the western extension of a mortuary cult that prevailed throughout the Eastern Woodlands. Medicine wheels usually consist of a burial cairn of boulders, surrounded by a circle and radiating spokes of fieldstones.[36] These monuments range from ten to thirty metres in diameter, and regular tipi rings are usually found nearby (Figure 94) Blackfoot and Plains Cree interpret some of them as modified tipi

92.
Shell mask. Courtesy of the Royal Ontario Museum, Toronto 915-11-1. L:12

Masks of this type were made of shell from the Gulf Coast, evidence of the widespread trade during the Late Mississippian times. This example from southern Manitoba marks the northern boundary of its distribution. The "weeping eye" motif around the eyeholes represents falcon-eye markings with lightning symbols zig-zagging downwards.

rings, serving as memorials to important and well-remembered chiefs. While some of these medicine wheels may have functioned in tribal ceremonies, less convincing are suggestions that they were used for astronomical observations.[37]

Similar stone arrangements formed the outline of large human and animal figures.[38] Several of these mosaics were made in the historical period to commemorate local events (Figure 93). These petroforms may be derived from early eastern prototypes, some of which have been found in the forests of eastern Manitoba.[39]

Possibly created in this late prehistoric period are the so-called "rib stones." Located on high hills, these glacial boulders of up to 1.5 m long suggest resting buffalo. Ancient artists made vertical grooves running down both sides, like ribs, from a central groove along the upper ridge. Occasionally a face with horns is incised at one end of the central groove, and many small pits are pecked all over the surface.[40]

Most rib stones are on the Alberta Plains, but some are found in Saskatchewan, Montana, and the Dakotas. Undoubtedly they were part of the spiritual relationship between the people and the buffalo, for representing skeletal details is a well-known feature of shamanic art. The skeleton was intermediate between the killed game and its rebirth for

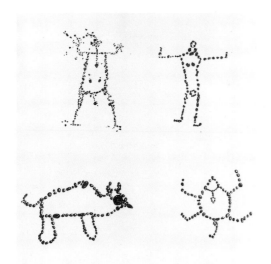

93.
Boulder monuments of the Northern Plains.

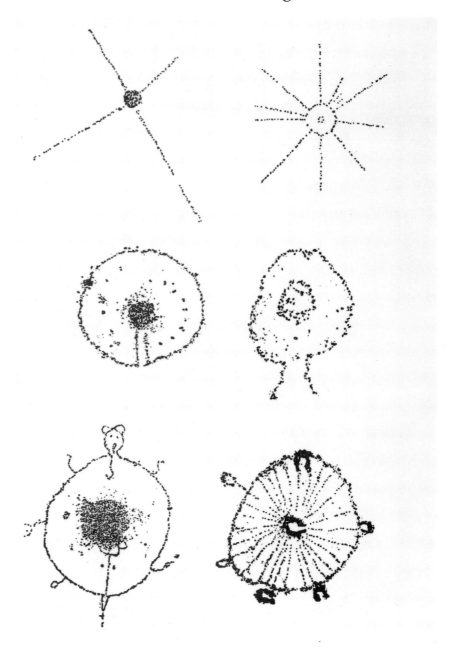

94.
Medicine wheels of the Northern Plains.

the respectful hunter.[41] Powerful spirits resided in prominent boulders throughout the ancestral north eastern homeland of the Cree Indians.[42] It would be natural for these Indians to approach the rib stones on the plains with similar attitudes, even though these monuments were probably made before the Cree arrived in the region.

Rock art included pictures incised and painted on the surface of cliffs. Most of the pictographs found on the Northern Plains are believed to have been created after 1500 A.D., and form the roots of representational art in the historic era (Figure 96). Though widespread, rock-art sites usually are of modest size and content; however, they include the murals at Writing-On-Stone in southern Alberta, which is the largest and most impressive rock-art site east of the Rocky Mountains.[43] The artistic value of these pictures was recognized only in recent times; the Indian aimed at recording important events on the rock's surface.

Incised petroglyphs predominate on the Northern Plains, and the pointed hammer stones used in their creation have occasionally been found nearby. Different in style and technique are the painted pictures found along the slopes of the Rocky Mountains, presumably made by Kutenai Indians who lived there in early historic times.[44]

Early rock-art expressions consist of carefully executed animal pictures, occasionally in association with a human figure. They suggest a spiritual relationship between the animal spirits and the artists, who may have created these pictures while praying for a vision.[45] Petroglyphs depicting animals with boat-shaped bodies and human figures hiding behind large circular shields extend northward into southern Alberta.

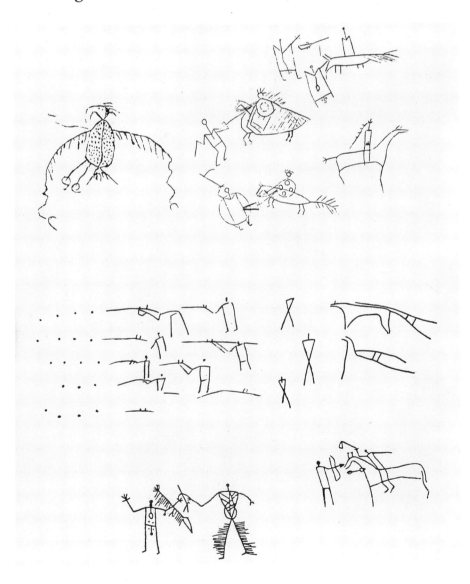

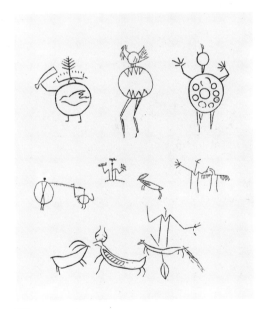

95.
Rock art of the Northwestern Plains, early style.

96.
Rock art of the Northwestern Plains, late style.

These are probably the work of Shoshoni Indians who temporarily penetrated the area during the late seventeenth and early eighteenth centuries.[46] The emphatic depiction of the symbols decorating these large shields appears to indicate a spiritual focus, as does the portrayal of human figures with horned heads and raised arms. The "lifelines" and rib markings occasionally indicated in the animal and human figures reveal the persistence of ancient circumpolar art traditions.

Rock-art human figures developed into several types. Stick figures and humans with pointed shoulders gave way to figures drawn with rectangular or hourglass-shaped bodies; the latter are similar to paintings on buffalo robes and skin tipi covers in the historic period.

Animals were pictured in profile, but human figures were normally shown in frontal position. The most striking feature of these renderings is the almost total lack of composition. Each figure is treated in isolation, sometimes superimposed on older pictures. Remarkable also is the extremely rare appearance of buffalo figures,[47] except on the Roche Percée in southeastern Saskatchewan.[48] The presence of horses and guns in this rock art indicates that it persisted after about 1730. Pictures of all other animals rapidly decreased after that date; the animated scenes of warfare that succeeded them suggest a shift in cultural orientation. Warfare increased as a result of dramatic developments initiated far beyond the eastern and southern horizons.

Descriptions of Plains Indian culture usually focus upon its colour and vibrance after the arrival of horses and the fur trade. However, the elaborate developments in the historic era resulted from the interaction of these European imports and ancient cultural traditions.

The Inhabitants of the Plains are so advantageously situated that they could live very happily independent of our assistance.
Duncan M'Gillivray, trader, 1790s.[49]

Competing with British traders on Hudson Bay, the French established trading posts as far west as Lake Winnipeg and the lower reaches of the Saskatchewan River by the 1730s. Along aboriginal trade routes, the Cree and Assiniboin Indians of these areas carried the desirable imports far beyond the European outposts.[50] As early as the 1690s, they travelled as far as Fort Churchill with furs from the Western Parklands. This was sufficiently lucrative that they resisted efforts by more western Indians to establish direct contacts with the trading posts. Through these native middlemen, the first firearms reached the Blackfoot Indians long before trading posts were established in their territory.

While French and British guns slowly made their way westward, horses were arriving from the Spanish settlements in the far south. About 1730 horses reached the Shoshoni in Wyoming, enabling these Indians to expand their range on the Northwestern Plains. The aggression of these invaders most likely was stimulated by a desire for firearms. After Spanish authorities refused to provide such weapons to the native people, the Shoshoni may have tried to force their way through to French trading posts. Certainly all the tribes in the region realized that the acquisition of horses and firearms would place them in a powerful position in relation to neighbours who possessed only one or the other.[51]

Guns and horses initially spread through intertribal trade and, inevitably, met at the old native market in the Mandan and Hidatsa villages on the Missouri River; in exchange for guns the riverine villagers received horses from the nomads of the Central Plains.[52] However, the guns did not grow in the Mandan gardens. They were supplied by native middlemen from the Northern Plains. While the Assiniboin controlled this link in the traditional trade connections, their Cree allies carried guns west, up the Saskatchewan River.

Faced by Shoshoni raiders on horseback, the Blackfoot called upon the Cree for help in about 1733.[53] Ten guns brought victory to the Blackfoot in a decisive battle; not long afterwards they acquired their first horses.[54] Thus, in the gradual transition from vague rumours to eye-witness reports, the 1730s may well serve as the regional start of the historic era. For the native people, this period brought accelerating access and exposure to a wide range of products and ideas imported by the Europeans. The second half of the eighteenth century saw the rapid development of the new way of life commonly associated with the Plains Indians.

During their annual expeditions to and from the eastern trading posts, the native middlemen frequently turned to trapping as well, using their firearms to expel the old inhabitants of the Parklands and adjoining forests. Apparently forced by these newcomers, the Sarsi moved to the Plains about 1700. Thirty years later Cree bands occupied the North Saskatchewan River system as far west as the foothills and were aware of the ocean beyond the Rocky Mountains.[55] By the 1750s Assiniboin bands were scattered from southwestern Manitoba to eastern Alberta. Intriguingly, the northwestern migration route of these Assiniboin Indians coincides with the distribution of stone-buffalo effigies and incised stone tablets on the Canadian Plains.[56]

The Assiniboin of southern Manitoba and Saskatchewan, who had traded with the Missouri River villagers since prehistoric times, became increasingly oriented towards life on the open Plains.[57] A cultural divergence developed between them and their relatives who had moved into the Northwestern Parklands.[58] A similar division among the Cree bands took place during the 1790s, when the native middleman was cut out by the establishment of trading posts on the North Saskatchewan River. Thus the Cree and Assiniboin are not "tribes" in the usual sense of communities with a common culture and territory.

Pressed by the Cree and Assiniboin and requiring year-round pasturage for their horses, the Blackfoot tribes abandoned their winter camps in the Parklands to make the Grasslands their more permanent home. In expanding their territory on the Plains, they forced the Shoshoni and Crow to move south into present-day Montana.[59]

Like the Assiniboin and Cree, the Blackfoot were divided into many independent bands but, traditionally and historically, they formed three tribes: the Blackfoot proper, or Northern Blackfoot; the Blood; and the Piegan. The bands within each tribe were united by "warrior societies," which drew members from all bands. Most Blackfoot men and many women belonged to these organizations, which fostered loyalties beyond one's own band.[60] The Sarsi and Atsina united their bands into tribal systems through similar sodalities. It is true that the regional Cree and later Plains Ojibwa adopted warrior societies as well, but each of their autonomous bands had its own fraternity, without members from other bands.

Trading posts were about the only European settlements on the Northern Plains until well into the nineteenth century. The native population had a long time during which to adjust to European influences, without the interference of colonial administrators and white settlers. Moreover, the fur traders preferred to establish most of their posts along the northern margins of the Plains, within reach of the northern trappers and the North Saskatchewan River, which they used for transportation.

From the traders' point of view, business with the Plains Indians was of limited importance, providing mainly wolf skins, dried meat, and horses. The Indians were not inclined to change from hunting buffalo to trapping beaver, and the long transportation route of the Canadian fur trade made heavy buffalo skins unprofitable. Indeed, several early traders complained that the Plains Indians had few needs that could not be met by their traditional exploitation of the buffalo herds and other natural resources.

The Indians saw the fur trade merely as a new twist in the ancient intertribal trade; before doing business, the trader had to participate in lengthy ceremonies to establish ritual kinship with his customers, who thereafter expected him to be generous. These expectations were later transferred to the Canadian government, when Queen Victoria was adopted as the Great White Mother.

Metal knives, needles, axes, and kettles allowed the natives to give up the manufacture of stone and ceramic tools and utensils; commercial dyes replaced native paints; textile fabrics and glass beads made inroads into the native use of skins and porcupine quillwork. As these imports were considered prestige items to the Indians, there developed a gradually increasing dependency on the white man's goods.

How gradual this process was is evident from the observations of early traders. In the 1720s metal knives, axes, and metal arrowheads were highly valued possessions owned exclusively by native middlemen in the fur trade;[61] in the 1770s native pottery was still in general use on the Northwestern Plains,[62] and as late as 1810 metal kettles were still scarce there.[63] By the early nineteenth century, garments of cloth were replacing aboriginal skin dresses on the Northeastern Plains, and glass beads were replacing porcupine quills in their decoration.[64] Maintained in their decoration of ceremonial objects, quillwork and painting acquired a sacred quality.

However, along with these trade goods, the Europeans unwittingly introduced smallpox and other diseases to which the native population lacked immunity. The Plains tribes lost more than half their population in a smallpox epidemic that swept across most of western North America in 1781. Thereafter, similar epidemics ravaged the native societies about once a decade. These epidemics were a significant factor in the process of cultural change.

The native interpretation of the first epidemic and a coincidental decrease in game offers us a rare glimpse of the traditional world-view, recorded by David Thompson, who arrived shortly after the disaster. According to the Indians, "the Great Spirit having brought this calamity on them, had also taken away the Animals in the same proportion *as they were not wanted, and intimating the Bisons and Deer were made and preserved solely for their use; and if there were no Men there would be no Animals*."[65] However, as the population passed through this deadly bottle-neck, many of the old ideas and customs disappeared forever.

A new way of life emerged, made up of fragments of the old world-view changed to function in new contexts, increasingly motivated by the achieving of war honours and acquiring material wealth, to be ostentatiously displayed in warfare and tribal ceremonies. Much of this colourful paraphernalia and ceremonialism undoubtedly originated in ancient times, but owed its survival to a reinterpretation of symbolism in terms of warfare.

Horses enabled the Indians to transport larger tipis and comfortable furnishings (Figure 97); with greater mobility, game became more easily available. The resulting leisure time was devoted to expanding and elaborating ceremonialism, decorative arts, and warfare. Medicine bundles still transmitted blessings and the sacred powers promised by the spirits;

but the topic of conversation was the prestige of their owners, derived from the generous compensation given by them to the bundles' former owners. Wealth from horses and the fur trade made it possible to become the respected owner of medicine bundles without the rigorous efforts needed to acquire such spiritual gifts in a vision.

Wealth and its prestige motivated Blackfoot parents to have a "child of plenty," a child always dressed in finery, provided with ponies and play tipis, initiated in ceremonial roles at an early age and guaranteed high social status in years to come. And while the parents socialized on a grand scale, there were slaves, mainly women, to do the work.[66] Captured in warfare, such women were used as payment in the transfer of a medicine bundle; the thunder spirit had compensated for the stealing of a woman with the gift of the first medicine pipe. That was long ago, and so was the egalitarian character of Plains Indian society. Wealth derived from horses and the fur trade shifted the centre of regional culture from the horticultural villagers to the equestrian nomads.

97.
Moving Camp. Oil by John Clymer, 1972.

In addition to being a very fine picture, this painting is also a tribute to the ethnologists who record the information and collect the artefacts utilized by the artist in his creation of this scene.

Yet these people were still hunters, and it was the abundance of game that had enabled them to adopt the cultural values, complex ceremonialism, and art forms of late-prehistoric sedentary horticultural societies. This situation reminds us of the native cultures on the West Coast, where an abundance of fish allowed the people the leisure to create great art associated with complex ceremonials. Historic Plains Indian culture presents a similar example of cultural elaboration attainable by hunting societies, provided that the natural resources were more than adequate. However, the adoption of the horse gave changing Plains Indian culture an unusual and fascinating twist.

Whereas the introduction of metal tools increased the efficiency of native technology, the introduction of horses fundamentally altered the Plains Indian way of life. The care of large numbers of horses, the need to herd, pasture, and protect this new wealth, forced the Plains Indians to change practically all aspects of their daily life.[67] The result was something that was no longer a pure hunter society but not yet a pastoral one, such as that of the Kazaks and Mongols of central Asia.

Like those Asian herders, the Plains Indians were nomads and derived prestige from warfare and wealth from horses. Hunting was the favourite sport of the Asiatic herdsmen, but here is the essential difference: hunting remained a necessity for the Plains Indians. Laplanders changed from being reindeer hunters to reindeer herders in medieval times, but historical events prevented similar developments among the buffalo hunters of the plains. Instead, the new riches were utilized in the elaboration of the existing culture, particularly on the Northwestern Plains; the more eastern Assiniboin and Cree bands remained relatively poor in horses.

The relative importance of horses is but one facet of the cultural divergence between the Indians of the Northwestern Plains and those of the Northeastern Parklands. The continuous influence of the ancient culture of the Woodlands people had been strongest in the northeast, where the Assiniboin had been intermediaries in the spread of late Mississippian culture as well. By comparison, the western Blackfoot Indians had occupied a relatively isolated cultural backwater.

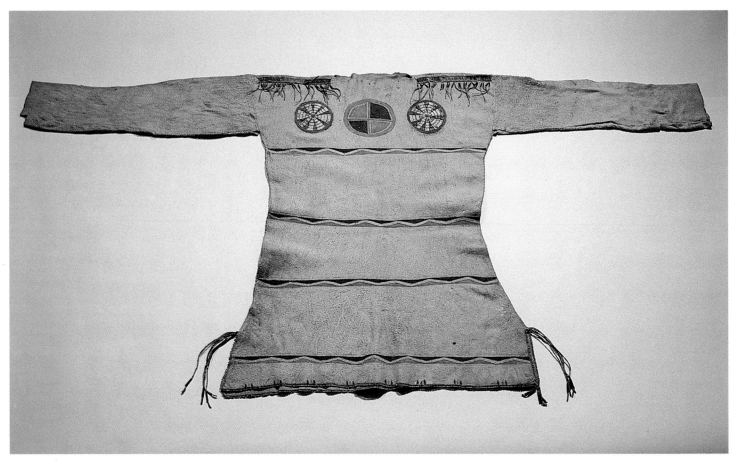

98.
Mooseskin shirt, Parklands Cree type, early 18th century. Kungl Livrustkammaren, Stockholm LRK 45/560. L:40; W:193

This shirt, decorated with paintings and quillwork, dates back to the early 18th century, and most probably originates from the northeastern margins of the Plains.

Regional differentiation was accelerated by the involvement of Cree and Assiniboin people in the fur trade. Their western expansion through the Parklands was facilitated by the acquisition of horses by Western Parklanders, which had forced the latter to make the Grasslands their year-round home. Thus, whereas most of the Cree and Assiniboin reinforced their cultural orientation to the Parklands and its fur bearers, the Blackfoot and Sarsi, as well as some Cree and Assiniboin bands, became true Plains Indians with only marginal involvement in the fur trade. Whatever remained of their old Parkland culture was adapted to the new way of life.

The distinction between Northwestern Plains and Northeastern Parklands peoples is evidenced by two regional art traditions, found in artefacts, pictures, and observations made in the early nineteenth century. Frustrated by poor documentation of these early artefacts, some ethnologists tend to reject the notion of tribal differences within these regional art traditions.[68] This may be acceptable for small tribes such as the Sarsi, who, intimately associated with the Blackfoot, were indistinguishable from the latter in much of their culture.

However, many of the early explorers did mention differences observed by them in the arts and crafts of the various tribes. Perhaps the best description is that of the artist George Catlin in the 1830s. He observed that "there is, certainly, a reigning and striking similarity of costume amongst most of the Northwestern tribes; and I cannot say that the dress of the Mandans is decidedly distinct from that of the Crows or the Blackfeet, the Assiniboins or the Sioux; yet there are modes of stitching or embroidery, in every tribe, which may at once enable the traveller, who is familiar with their modes, to detect or distinguish the dress of any tribe. These differences consist generally in the fashions of constructing the head-dress or of garnishing their dresses with the porcupine quills, which they use in great profusion."[69]

Catlin's summary might fit any tribal society, but he went on to qualify the regional similarities, pointing out that apparel was frequently captured in warfare or exchanged among the different tribes, leading to the spread of new fashions.[70] This was an important observation, because the intertribal exchange of finished products may have given an unduly strong impression of regional similarity in arts and crafts. Neither would the spread of new fashions have affected tribal differentiation; rather than imitating such novelties, each tribe undoubtedly adapted them to fit its own art style.

The regional variety of art expressions of the Northeastern Parklands people suggests that traditions from all directions had met and intertwined there since prehistoric times. Moreover, in the historic period, cultural differences were increasing among the independent and now widely dispersed Cree and Assiniboin bands. Depending upon the location of any given band, their arts and crafts might reflect contacts with people of the Boreal forest, Great Lakes, Central or Northwestern Plains.

However, when Alexander Henry reached southern Manitoba in the 1760s, he noticed that the dress and other apparel of the local Cree was "very distinguishable" from those of the northern forest and Great Lakes Indians, and very similar to the fashion popular among the Assiniboin Indians.[71] From this observation we may deduce that Northeastern Parklands arts and crafts had a distinct character, although this is hardly evident from the few surviving early artefacts. This northeastern style area extended southward to include some Sioux groups.

Early historic artefacts from this region indicate that the men wore skin caps (Figure 99), tailored, short skin shirts (Figure 98), and long skin coats.[72] Early pictures show the use of buffalo robes and leggings, worn gartered below the knee. The "side-fold dress" of the women was a skin tube sewn down one side; the top was folded down over the bodice and supported by leather shoulder straps.[73] The folded-over portion was decorated with painted designs or cut into long quill-wrapped fringes (Figure 100). Separate sleeves could be attached in cold weather. The side-fold dress appears to have been a regional variation of the strap dress originally worn by people of the Great Lakes in the east to the Shuswap west of the Rocky Mountains.[74] Moccasins were of the softsole type, with a toe seam and vamp.

The painted and quillwork decorations of these garments were similar to patterns used by the northeastern forest Indians: parallel straight lines, rectangles, triangles, and circles combined into geometric compositions, frequently with bilateral symmetry. Circular patterns on the front of men's shirts were to become popular throughout the Northern Plains during the nineteenth century. Loom-woven quillwork, netted quill wrap-

99.
Cap, Parklands Cree, c. 1800. Staatliche Museen Preußischer Kulturbesitz, Museum für Völkerkunde, Berlin, FRG IV-B-8607. H:23

A cap of painted skin with loom-woven quillwork along lower rim. Attached are three feathers with quillworked strips along the shafts. Originated before 1800, presumably from Cree Indians in the Manitoba Parklands.

100.
Side-fold dress, Plains Cree type. Peabody
Museum, Harvard University
99-12-10/53046. Photograph by Hillel
Burger. L:118

This dress was acquired by Lewis and
Clark on the Upper Missouri River,
1804-1805. By that time this type of garment was already old-fashioned and disap-
pearing.

ping, and decorative perforations of skin garments betrayed influences
respectively from the north and the Great Lakes; robe paintings included
the large feathered circle design of Sioux origin. Paintings on tipi covers
included large anthropomorphic thunderbirds.[75] Tattooing was common
on men's upper bodies and on women's faces.

Birchbark containers were decorated with scraped and incised designs.
Similar techniques were used on rawhide objects along the eastern and
western margins of the Northern Plains.[76] The apparent relation to bark
decorating and the location of this art form may indicate that it originated with the Parklands people (Figure 101).

Wood carving was a minor art form on the Plains, found primarily
along its eastern margins. It was essentially an extension of Great Lakes
art traditions. During the 1820s a beautiful war club of the gun-stock
type was acquired by Paul, Duke of Württemberg, apparently from
Eastern Sioux or Western Ojibwa Indians (Figure 102). The careful sketch
in the duke's diary shows some feather pendants, which have since disappeared.[77] Carved on the upper part of the handle are the figures of
thunderbirds above their enemy, the long-tailed horned panther. Another

war club of this type was found among the Plains Ojibwa in Saskatche-wan.[78] Its considerable age suggests that it was an heirloom from the eastern homeland of these people.

Painted robes, feather work, and other apparel obtained from the Man-dan and Hidatsa were very popular on the Northeastern Plains;[79] in return, the Missouri River villagers received birchbark containers decorated with incised, curvilinear designs.[80] These designs may represent the first regional experiments with a floral art style of French-Canadian origin. Adopted and transformed by native artisans, this new art style gradu-ally made its way west, changing the direction of native art developments.

In the northwest, the change from a Parklands to a Plains orienta-tion took place before the arrival of Europeans, and little evidence of the old Parklands tradition in arts and crafts survived the subsequent rapid cultural change. Transmitted by the Assiniboin, Crow, and Atsina, fashions popular among the Missouri River villagers became prevalent throughout the Northwestern Plains, and the art tradition developing in the region was therefore designated the Upper Missouri River tradition.[81] It should be remembered, however, that an unknown but certainly large part of the decorated apparel disseminated by the Mandan-Hidatsa was not of their own creation; the Upper Missouri art tradition includes a variety of tribal styles. Moreover, the centre of cultural florescence gravitated from the Missouri River villagers to the nomadic tribes of the Central Plains when horses and other European imports improved the living conditions of the buffalo hunters.

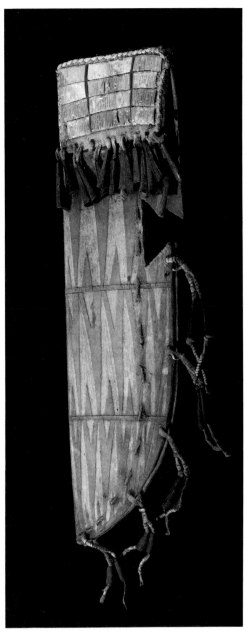

101.
Knife sheath, Eastern Sioux type, before 1828. Peabody Museum, Harvard University 99-12-10/53027. Photograph by Hillel Burger. L:27; W:8

Knife sheath of rawhide, the upper part decorated with bird quills, the lower part first painted orange and then partially scraped, leaving orange patterns on white background.

102.
Warclub, Eastern Sioux type, 1820s. Private Collection. L:62.6

A wooden warclub with metal point inserted. Acquired by Paul, Duke of Württemberg, during his travels in the 1820s, presumably from Eastern Sioux or Western Ojibwa Indians.

The diminishing influence of the Mandan-Hidatsa during the nineteenth century was reflected in the tribal art styles of the Plains Indians. Collections from the Northwestern Plains indicate that stylistic developments among the Blackfoot, Sarsi, and Atsina were diverging from those of the Mandan, Hidatsa, Crow, and western Sioux. Stylistically intermediate between these two subgroups were some of the Western Cree and Assiniboin bands.

Skin shirts worn by the men during the early nineteenth century tended to be long and semi-tailored; however, in later years, a shorter poncho-type shirt became popular.[82] These poncho shirts had a flap or bib hanging from the neck, front and back. Among the northern tribes this flap was rectangular; the Sioux and their neighbours preferred a triangular shape. Leggings were made of complete deer skins, folded lengthwise. Knee-length leggings were worn by women.

The strap dress of the women was observed by early traders and remembered in native traditions. By the 1830s, however, the long deer-tail dress was in general use. This dress consisted of two large elk skins sewn together so that the tails fell over the wearer's chest and back.[83] A reinforcing yoke was frequently sewn over the upper part of this dress. Moccasins were of the soft-sole, side-seam type; but a two-piece type with rawhide sole became popular by the 1850s.[84] The origin of all these fashion changes supports other evidence suggesting that, though distinct, the Northern Plains people remained dependent upon cultural innovations of a more southern origin.

Painting was perhaps the most distinctive decorative art of the Northwestern Plains people. Mixed with hot water and sizing, earth paints were applied with pointed sticks or wedge-shaped tools of bone, porous enough to hold the paint. Blackfoot Indians coloured many of their skin garments with red ochre or black paint, a custom that has survived only on ceremonial objects in more recent times.[85] Their buffalo robes were painted with a number of narrow parallel bands of smaller geometric design units in different colours. A related design consisting of columns of horizontally placed arrow figures was painted on Plains Cree robes. The feathered-circle design was popular on robes among the Assiniboin and their Sioux relatives (Figure 103).[86] Geometric paintings also decorated tipi linings and parfleches, rawhide, envelope-shaped containers on which the designs appear to have been created by continuously subdividing the space, with a strong tendency to symmetry.[87]

These conventional geometric patterns were painted by women; male artists produced pictographic paintings related either to religious symbolism or to warfare. Symbolic designs painted on tipi covers, shields, drums, and ritual paraphernalia usually originated from visions and dreams. In such paintings the spiritual identity of animal figures was indicated by details representing joint marks, kidneys, and the lifeline running from the mouth to the area of the heart. Thunderbirds were identified by white spots, representing hail, on their upper bodies.[88]

Picture writing of war records decorated buffalo robes, shirts, and tipi linings and covers. The figures were drawn in forceful outlines with little detail, in a style clearly related to that of similar pictures scratched on the surface of rocks. As these were historical records, aesthetic considerations were of secondary concern to the painter.

Unlike the archaic style of picture writing that survived on the Northwestern Plains, a more elaborate and realistic style developed on the Central Plains in the 1830s, perhaps as a result of meetings with visiting white artists.[89] Increasing attention was given to proportion, body movement, detail, and colour. Many of the robes now in museum collections were painted with commercial pigments, which had been imported by traders since the 1770s.

103.
Quillworked robe, Assiniboin. Peabody Museum, Harvard University 74-25-10/7895. Photograph by Hillel Burger. L:253; W:184

Occasionally a design, usually painted, was executed in quillwork, as illustrated by this buffalo robe, acquired among the Assiniboin in the mid-19th century. The feathered circle design represented a shield in Assiniboin symbolism, while the column of red-painted horse quirts may refer to horses given away.

The large buffalo-skin robes frequently had a seam along the longitudinal centre, resulting from the manner of skinning the heavy buffalo carcass. This seam was covered with a strip of quillwork; rosettes placed in this strip were interpreted by the Sioux to be symbols of the four major wind directions.[90] Large rosettes, centrally placed on the front and back of men's shirts, appear to have been introduced by the Assiniboin in the early 1800s.[91] Among the Blackfoot, rosettes replaced rectangular panels of quillwork decoration that were used to decorate the shirts.[92] Strips of quillwork were sewn over the shoulders and along the sleeves of shirts, as well as along the sides of leggings. Designs in these strips tended to mark the shoulder and elbow joints, though this correlation with joints was less obvious on the leggings.[93]

Quillwork designs were geometric, consisting of straight lines, bars, squares, crosses, triangles, diamonds, and hourglass forms. Diagonal lines were frequently stepped and made up of many small squares. A block pattern spread over three lines of quillwork strips was very popular. Design units of this type appeared throughout the Northwestern Plains; tribal distinction resulted from the ways in which these units were combined and, to some extent, from the range of colours preferred by each tribe.

Wrapping, sewing, and plaiting were the principal techniques used in quillwork. Plaiting of diagonal and diamond patterns is usually attributed to the Missouri River villagers and the Crow, but narrow strips of plaited quillwork are found on early Blackfoot shirts as well.

Glass beads were introduced by the white traders, who found that white and blue beads were most popular with the native women.[94] The early "pony beads" were fairly large and did not lend themselves to small or complex patterns in bead embroidery. Strips of alternating blocks of blue and white beads were popular on men's costumes by the 1830s; patches or red colour were produced by incorporating red trade cloth into the beadwork patterns. Most of this early beadwork was done in a loose overlay or spot-stitch technique among the northern tribes, though a lazy stitch was used for the wide, curved breast band decorating the Blackfoot woman's dress.[95]

By 1850 steel needles became generally available, enabling the women to utilize the smaller "seed beads" in more complex and more colourful patterns, usually on a white or light-blue beaded background. After an early experimental period, distinct tribal beadwork styles developed during the second half of the nineteenth century.[96] The flat surface of overlay beadwork remained characteristic of the northern tribes; the ribbed effect of the lazy-stitch technique prevailed among the Sioux and their neighbours (Figure 104).

104.
Gun case, Assiniboin type, c. 1900.
Saskatchewan Museum of Natural History, Regina 87 6477. L:120; W:60 (incl. fringe)

Although this gun case of beadworked deerskin was acquired from Blackfoot Indians, the beadworked designs suggest an Assiniboin origin.

Many beaded designs were derived from traditional painted and quillwork patterns. Floral designs of Red River Métis origin also became popular. As beadwork expanded, time-consuming quillwork gradually disappeared, particularly after trade cloth replaced skin in the manufacture of garments.[97]

Beadwork appears to have stimulated the creativity of Plains Indian women as nothing before. No longer taking their inspiration from the Missouri River villagers, the Plains Indians started to influence native art beyond the Plains. Blackfoot influence can be traced in the beadwork of the Kutenai, Flathead, and other tribes west of the Rocky Mountains; Crow beadwork inspired the Nez Percé and Umatilla of the Columbia River region. Borrowings of this type were an aspect of ongoing intertribal contacts; decorated apparel was traded far and wide (to frustrate future museum curators trying to identify tribal art styles).

Symbolism in native art has been a subject of controversy among ethnologists, some of whom maintain that most native art expressions were "as devoid of meaning as the pattern on the average white man's necktie."[98] Indeed, native art lost much of its ancient meaning after the buffalo were gone. By the time ethnologists started their studies, native art, though still vigorous, expressed memories of a way of life that had disappeared.

Loss of and change in symbolism undoubtedly started long ago, and reflected the dramatic changes in native culture. After the holocaust of the early epidemics, the spiritual world-view eroded and was replaced by a drive for material wealth and prestige. Symbolism of decorated apparel, once indicative of man's relationship with the spirits of nature, was reinterpreted in terms of warfare and military heraldry.

Symbolic art was created of skin, porcupine quills, earth paints, and similar gifts from Our Mother, the Earth. The white man's glass beads did not share in her sacred powers: they had no life of their own, and with them came disease, liquor abuse, and other social evils. Feelings of this sort inhibited a transfer of symbolism to the new form of artwork. However, some of the old meanings were recorded by early travellers and preserved in native traditions.

Native symbolism was expressed by means of colours, intricate featherwork, and headdresses, painted and quillwork designs, and fringes on apparel. Only prominent warriors were entitled to have their costumes fringed with scalp-hair tassels. The manufacture of such a dress was a ritual event, participated in by invited comrades, each of whom contributed scalp locks for this purpose. Paul, Duke of Württemburg, recorded that a dress of this type was worth about thirty horses.[99]

Returning from an enemy encounter, warriors painted themselves black if they had killed their opponents. Blackened scalp shirts of the Blackfoot referred to such exploits.[100] Black or dark-brown parallel stripes painted on shirts and leggings also related to war honours, though their precise meaning differed from tribe to tribe.[101] The Blackfoot chief Crowfoot invited the Reverend Edward Wilson to count the stripes on the chief's dress: he had hit, or "counted coup," on one hundred and forty-three enemies.[102]

More ancient may be the interpretation of such stripes as the trail of the weasel, honoured as a ferocious fighter and patron of warriors.[103] A similar change in symbolism is suggested by the interpretation of painted stripes around the upper part of Blackfoot painted tipis. Traditionally they represented the trails of the animal spirits who had given the tipi paintings in dreams, but on war tipis they referred to battle honours.

Even more prestigious than the scalp-lock costume was the weasel-tail suit of the Blackfoot (Figure 105). This was treated as a sacred medicine bundle, ritually transferred to new owners, and daily honoured with incense.[104] The legendary Scarface received this costume from Sun as a reward for killing enemies.[105] In addition to the fringes of weasel fur and the battle stripes, the costume was decorated with painted figures of tadpoles. Able to transform itself, the tadpole was a complex symbol. In this instance, the tadpole is associated with Old Man, the primeval culture hero: disguised as a frog, he killed an underworld enemy of mankind. This victory was repeated in the defeat of evil by Scarface; all men who inherited the weasel-tail suit were expected to follow his example. In more recent times, however, the tadpole design merely represented battle wounds. As part of the widespread respect for the aggressive weasel, shirts fringed with weasel pelts were also used by the Assiniboin and Crow Indians. The use of eagle and hawk feathers on Sioux shirts carried a similar war symbolism.

Many other decorative elements not only symbolized an association with spirits but also conveyed the magical protection and spiritual power believed to reside in the decorated objects, be they moccasins, snowshoes, headdresses, or shields. Alexander Henry observed that, among the Cree, men's moccasins were decorated; women's were not.[106] Moccasins and snowshoes used in hunting were decorated to please their spirits as well as the spirits of the game.[107] In a legend of the Plains Cree we are told of snowshoes that sang as the hunter walked home;[108] Blackfoot Sioux, and presumably other Plains Indians, believed that lost moccasins would return home by themselves. Painted decorations or quillwork on the soles of moccasins were originally intended to please the spirits, a notion that survived in the northeastern boreal forests. However, the wealthy horse owners on the Plains reinterpreted this symbolism to indicate that they no longer needed to walk.

Similar ideas pertained to the decorated moccasins of Plains Indian warriors. During the 1830s Prince Maximilian noted that Blackfoot and Atsina decorated the two moccasins of a pair in different colours,[109] and also the designs on each moccasin were often different (Figure 106). A similar change in decorating has been found on early Arapaho moccasins. The military heraldry of such decorations was recorded among the Atsina.[110]

Moccasin decorations were frequently associated with their owners' visions. The patterns were intended to be seen from the wearer's angle of view and they served to concentrate his thoughts during meditation. This is most obvious in a pair of Assiniboin moccasins, showing a thunderbird surrounded by symbols of hailstones and lightning (Figure 107).

The heavy rawhide shield of the Plains warrior was one of his most treasured possessions; it was also one of the most individual expressions of Plains Indian art, because visionary experiences and power

105.
Shirt, Blackfoot, c. 1840s. Courtesy of the Trustees of the British Museum, London Q72 AM 14. L:150; W:185

Deerskin shirt, decorated with paintings, quillwork, and fringes of weasel fur. Quillworked panels were distinctive on Blackfoot shirts of the early contact period, but their symbolism was lost when other fashions were adopted.

dreams inspired its creation. The dream symbols painted on or attached to the shield were kept hidden by a cover, and were revealed only in battle. These decorations were thought to protect the warrior, which is the reason the shields remained in use long after the introduction of firearms.

On a more general level of symbolism, the circular shield represented Sun, the great sky warrior; eagle feathers surrounding the shield symbolized the sun's rays. These feathers were frequently attached to a strip of red cloth, which expressed the intention to shed the blood of enemies. The shield would be hung outside its owner's lodge in order to strengthen its sacred powers through exposure to the sun.

The origins of some of these shields were preserved in legends. A Blackfoot myth tells of a man who killed his wife, wrongly believing her to have been unfaithful. The buffalo brought her back to life and gave her three sacred shields before returning her to her remorseful husband. One of the three shields was sold to a museum by its last native owner, because he had failed to learn its ritual when it was transferred

106.
Moccasins, Blackfoot, 1840s. Courtesy of the Trustees of the British Museum, London Q85 Am 33. L:23; W:12

The different quillworked patterns on each moccasin of the pair convey a symbolic statement, perhaps relating to war honours.

107.
Moccasins, Assiniboin, c. 1900. American Museum of Natural History, New York 50-1969. L:26; W:10

The beadworked design on these moccasins relates to the owner's dreams of the thunderbird.

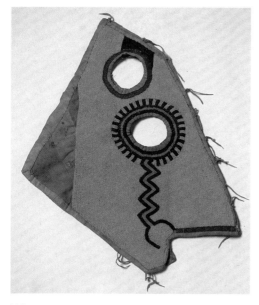

108.
Horse mask, Plains Cree, late 19th century. Courtesy of the Royal Ontario Museum, Toronto HK 239. L:54.6; W:46

The lightning design on a sky-blue background related to its symbolic association with the thunderbird.

109.
Chief Shot on Both Sides. Oil by Winold Reiss. Courtesy of Mr. W. Tjark Reiss, Hudson, New York.

The head chief of the Blood Indians is wearing the One-Horn-in-Front headdress, decorated with quillwrapped strips along the eagle feathers.

to him.[111] He was unable to profit from its sacred power.

Shields and many other objects related to the old way of life were kept as prestigious ornaments. Backrests of outstanding warriors among the Plains Cree and Plains Ojibwa were decorated with sacred banners formerly used in rituals associated with the buffalo hunt.[112] The designs embroidered on these banners symbolized the enclosure or pound used to corral the buffalo (Figure 3). The famous Cree chief Poundmaker earned his name through his initiation in these hunting rites.

Horse masks were believed to convey success in warfare. Those of the Plains Cree frequently showed lightning symbols zigzagging down from the eyeholes, suggesting the survival of the Mississippian weeping-eye motif and its association with the thunder spirit (Figure 108).

Indeed, the horse was described as a gift from Thunder in some myths; according to other traditions within the same tribe, the horse originated in the underworld.

These conflicting origin myths resulted from only partially successful efforts to classify the horse in the native world order. The first encounter with a horse was recalled by an elderly Indian in the 1780s. "We all admired him, he put us in mind of a Stag that had lost his horns; and we did not know what name to give him. But as he was a slave to Man, like the dog, which carried our things he was named the Big Dog."[113] Dogs and horses were slaves to human beings, in contrast to the "pure" animals, who were associates of the spirits in nature. However, the Indians' admiration for and love of horses were strong enough to overcome philosophical objections, to some extent. The prevailing association of the horse with Thunder and Sky allowed songs of "horse medicine" to become part of Blackfoot rituals in honour of the sacred medicine pipe, and horses replaced slave women as payment for a medicine pipe bundle. The capture of horses, rather than slaves, become a major aim in warfare. Parties of predominantly young warriors would risk their lives for the wealth and prestige that came with successful horse raids. "Gambling" was their euphemism for these enterprises; gambling and the glory won by the survivors dominated the new way of life.

> They have many mysteries and ceremonious dances, in which they make great use of drums, rattles, and shrill whistles.[114]

Plains Indians always liked to go on extended visits, attending the ceremonials of neighbouring and distant tribes.[115] Presents and ideas exchanged during such visits stimulated change and innovations in ritualism, arts, and crafts. Horses enabled the people to increase these intertribal contacts, stimulating the surprisingly rapid emergence of a new and distinct regional culture pattern.

Seasonal activities of hunting and gathering remained essentially unchanged, and many fragments of the past survived in the cycle of annual ceremonies. Yet changes were noticeable in the combination and reinterpretation of these fragments, and in the motivations of the participants.

In spring, when the ice broke up in the swollen rivers, the beavers left their inundated lodges for the first green grass on higher ground. The beaver was recognized as chief of water animals and the veneration in which it was held may have been a cause of the Plains Indians' refusal to trap beavers for the fur traders. In honour of these "underwater persons," the owners of the beaver medicine bundles among the Blackfoot, Sarsi, and Atsina performed their rituals before leaving the winter camps.

Musical instruments used in these rituals were restricted to the rattles beaten on buffalo hide, symbolizing the beaver's tail striking the water's surface. The spherical rattles were made of rawhide, preferably from the scrotum of a buffalo. In ancient times, figures of mythical beings were incised on the rawhide. Following a night-long ceremony, the beaver men planted the sacred tobacco seed.[116]

These rites were considered to be the most ancient in the native liturgy, although the Atsina claimed that the Blackfoot had borrowed the ceremony from them.[117] The beaver rites and associated tobacco cultivation may have been inspired by spring ceremonials among the Hidatsa on the Missouri River. The Blackfoot likely became acquainted with this cult when some of the Hidatsa migrated onto the Northwestern Plains in the early 1700s; ultimately they became known as Crow Indians.

When the birds returned in spring the buffalo left the protection of the river valleys, drifting into the open Plains. Following in their trail were wolves, grizzly bears, and human hunters.

As the bringer of rain and new fertility, the first thunder of spring was joyfully anticipated. It was the sign for the owners of medicine pipes to open their medicine bundles, sing the many songs in honour of Thunder and the other Sky Persons, and bless the people.[118] There was an obvious symbolic relationship between all these rituals and the locale of their performance. Those for the Underwater Persons were held when the people were still down in the valley, in a sense below the surface of the earth. In contrast, Thunder's gift of the medicine pipe was celebrated when the people had emerged and wandered on the high open Plains.

The actual object of veneration in the medicine pipe bundle was a long wooden wand, decorated with feathers, weasel fur, and bells. In 1846, artist Paul Kane acquired an example from the Plains Cree chief Kiakikasacuwe.[119] Covered with the head and skin of an eagle, this impressive piece pronounces its association with the thunderbird (Figure 110). Based upon his field sketches, Kane later painted the Cree chief holding this sacred object.[120]

110.
Medicine pipe, Plains Cree, 1846. Manitoba Museum of Man and Nature, Winnipeg H4.42-2

This sacred medicine pipe stem is covered with the skin of an eagle. Acquired in 1846 by Paul Kane from "The Man Who Gives the War Whoop," a Cree chief at Fort Pitt.

The chief's responsibility for the medicine pipe bundle was not accidental, even though in Kane's days the office of pipe keeper was increasingly taken by other prestigious band members. Once the mediator between the spirits and his people, the chief was becoming a mediator between white officials and his tribe. In the old days the medicine pipe was the chief's standard and, according to native tradition, "the people followed the Medicine Pipe." As pipe keeper, the chief, his clothing, horse, and tipi were all painted red, and his hair was tied into a large knot over his forehead. This peculiar hair-do, representing a single horn, can be traced back to Mississippian figurines; it was a shaman's symbol in native North America as well as in northern Asia.[121] Each of the three Blackfoot tribes had an elaborate headdress with one horn projecting from the front (Figure 109); a similar horn decorates a horse mask of the Blood Indians.[122] These items probably originate from this long-forgotten shamanistic context; they owed their survival to their reinterpretation as war medicines.

In the diary of his travels during the 1840s, Paul Kane left us the first eyewitness account of a medicine pipe ritual among the Blackfoot Indians.[123] From this and later reports we learn that the ritual required the use of seven drums; their painted decoration and sound were associated with the thunder spirit.[124] During the ritual the participants danced with the sacred pipe-stem, carrying it like a war trophy. The stem was hollow and a pipe bowl could be attached for smoking, but the sacred wand was seldom used in this way. The medicine bundle contained a regular pipe for this purpose.[125]

Such details suggest that the so-called medicine pipe was not a pipe at all. One of the medicine bundles in the Blood tribe contained a lance that was also referred to as a pipe.[126] The sacred pipe-stem in the Blackfoot beaver bundle appears to have a similar origin; according to tradition, this object was the arrow used by the legendary Scabby Round Robe to kill an enemy chief.[127] In 1690 Henry Kelsey saw a medicine pipe-stem of the Assiniboin Indians; it had "eagle feathers split and layed on like the feathers of an arrow."[128] Could it be that the medicine pipe originated as a sacred weapon, carried by the chief when leading his people?

A similar origin has been suggested for the ceremonial pipe or calumet of the Central Plains and Great Lakes regions. That pipe was referred to as an arrow by some tribes, and it was used as a substitute for the ceremonial exchange of arrows in establishing friendship between individuals and nations.[129] Originating among the Pawnee in the late seventeenth century, the calumet ritual spread far and wide as part of a revitalistic movement. Through time and distance the medicine pipe of the Northern Plains people acquired a different role, but its common roots are evident.[130]

The association of friendship arrows and pipe-stems was linked with the symbolic connotations of tobacco smoke as an incense for the spirits. Pipe smoking was a device to concentrate one's thoughts, frequently upon subjects of a spiritual nature, but also in preparation for important discussions.[131] Pipes were offered in prayer to the spirits, the mouthpiece pointed first towards the four directions, then upwards for Sky Persons, and downwards for Earth.

War leaders offered such pipes to smoke when they invited men to join their war parties. On such occasions the red crests of pileated woodpeckers decorating the pipe-stem were allowed to stand up, because the crest of this bird always comes up when it is angry.

Pipe bowls attached to these decorated stems were usually carved of red catlinite acquired from southern Minnesota, or of a local shale or soapstone. Sculptural traditions surviving among the Sioux were given a new impetus by religious cults spreading from the Great Lakes region during the seventeenth century; these were reflected in effigy carvings of animal and human forms on pipe bowls. According to a Sioux Indian, "these different effigy pipes are not the representation of different animals or represent man, but they are the animal soul or man soul. They are . . . the conception of the inner life rather than the effigy of any particular animal or man."[132] The effigies faced the smoker and represented his guardian spirit; they were to be contemplated by the smoker while he meditated on his dreams.

An exceptionally fine example of such a pipe was presented to James Bruce, Earl of Elgin, while he was governor-general of Canada between 1846 and 1854 (Figure 111). The flat wooden stem and its chip-carved ornaments suggest a Western Ojibwa or Eastern Sioux origin in the Western Great Lakes region. Effigy pipe-bowl carving was still very popular there in the 1840s, but the flying eagle represented by the grey stone bowl is unique.

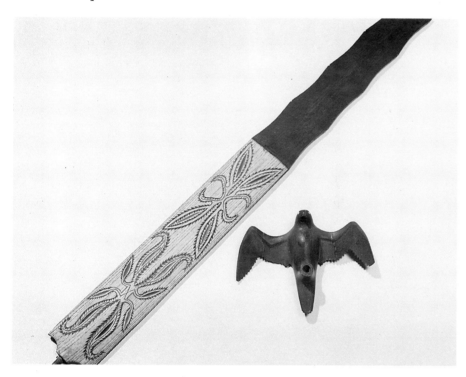

111.
Ceremonial pipe, Western Great Lakes, c. 1850. From the collection of the Earl of Elgin and Kincardine, KT, CD, Scotland. Bowl: L:14; W:19; Stem: L:94

The greyish stone bowl carved in the form of a flying eagle is unique. This ceremonial pipe was made for and presented to Lord Elgin while he was Governor General of Canada, 1847-1854.

Pipe bowls were often decorated with pewter inlay. Channels were carved into the stone surface, which was then tightly wrapped with leather before the molten metal was poured into the channels. This casting technique has a long history in native art, starting among the East Coast tribes in early colonial times.[133]

Pipes decorated with bear effigies were used by members of the Sioux bear cult; these people had acquired power from the bear spirit — power in warfare and in the curing of wounds. In their ritual performances, these shamans personified bears; in daily life, they could be recognized by certain decorative elements of their make-up. Bear-paw patterns on their moccasins identified them with the powerful spirit of the underworld. Bear power made these men fearsome in warfare, although their only weapon was a dagger with a handle made from a bear jaw.[134] Such weapons were known to most Northern Plains tribes; the earliest known example dates from the 1820s.[135]

After the breakdown of the old way of life during the epidemics of the late eighteenth century, new ceremonials became popular and played a role in the reintegration of native society. A well-known example of such a ceremony is the Sun Dance. Significant details of this ceremony had their roots in rituals of the Missouri River village tribes; but it was probably among the Cheyenne and Arapaho that it developed a form attractive to the nomadic Plains Indians.[136] The ceremony appears to have been adopted by the Blackfoot during the early decades of the nineteenth century.[137]

Each tribe modified and adjusted the ceremony to its own ritual pattern, but all recognized as its essential purpose the recreation of the sacred world order. Like most other rituals, the Sun Dance re-enacted mythical events in which mankind had acquired certain blessings and powers. By repeating these events in a ritualized manner, the powers were invigorated and nature itself was renewed. Unlike the future orientation of the "Great Religions," tribal ideology emphasized that everything was good in its natural form — and should stay that way. For untold centuries the present was experienced as a continuation of the past, a perpetuation of the sacredness of life in all its manifestations.

112.
Sun Dance headdress, Blood-Blackfoot, 19th century. Denver Art Museum, Colorado 1938.223.2b.

Sacred headdress of the holy woman in the Blackfoot Sun Dance. The parts making up this headdress refer to blessings received from Sky and Earth.

The obvious time for the Sun Dance was midsummer, when the life-giving powers were at their strongest. At this time, too, the buffalo assembled in large numbers, allowing the bands to camp together for a short period. The tribal summer camp was the occasion of festivities for various cults and fraternities, and the Sun Dance was added to them.

Preparations for the Blackfoot version of the Sun Dance started after a respected woman had made a vow to the sun to act as the "holy woman" during the celebration; the woman made the vow in the hope of receiving spiritual help in a crisis.[138] While a messenger notified the other bands, the woman and her husband made their first sacrifice: many horses and trade goods purchased a *natoas* bundle, which contained the paraphernalia used by the holy woman during the ceremony. During the transfer ritual, the mythical origin of each garment and object was recited in song. The traditions associated with some of these objects illustrate the rich symbolism and complex metaphysics inherent in art expressions of native origin.

The Blackfoot Sun Dance or "Medicine Lodge" ritual re-enacted the mythical experiences of two women and provided the people with access to the power sources of Sky and Underwater, the spiritual realms.[139] Tailfeather Woman, the human wife of Morningstar, dug up the forbidden turnip. She looked into the hole and saw the camp of her people down on Earth. Feeling lonely, she turned to Spider, who provided a long rope for her and her baby son to get down to Earth. The rope broke when they were almost down; in his fall, the baby received a scar on its face.

When he was a young man, Scarface made his way back to his grandfather, Sun, who removed the scar upon his request. Without the scar, the young man closely resembled his father, which led Sun to rename him Mistaken Morningstar and to instruct him in the details of the Sun Dance rites. With these gifts, Mistaken Morningstar returned to Earth. His symbol, which resembled a Maltese cross, guaranteed the truthfulness of rituals; marked on sacred objects, it confirmed their genuine sacred nature.

In discussing this mark in sacred paintings on tipi covers, Blackfoot informants called the mark *apunni*, a term referring to the outstretched wings of a moth or butterfly. It also means "to go about telling news." An *apunni* on a tipi was an indication that the tipi painting and its associated ritual had been given by spirits in a dream. The soft buzzing of butterflies was believed to announce such a power dream; the butterfly was a messenger of spirits who would come to the dreamer with gifts. As such, there is an association of the butterfly with Mistaken Morningstar: he, too, was a messenger, bringing the gift of a communal ritual from the source of all Sky powers. The butterfly was his representative in the transfer of blessings from the spirits.

This intimate association of Mistaken Morningstar and the butterfly was emphasized on a elk-skin robe of a holy woman, acquired from the Blackfoot in the 1840s (Figure 113). The close resemblance of the alternating crosses and butterflies, and their repeated juxtaposition, emphasize their relationship in native cosmology. Mistaken Morningstar's cross is red because he had *natojiwa*, sun power. The butterfly is green, which, like blue, indicates an association with the thunderbird, lord of most winged beings. The two figures are placed in four rows, four being the sacred number, and they are beautifully integrated with horizontal stripes, the traditional Blackfoot robe decoration.[140] These stripes represented the trails of the weasel, who long ago instructed a woman in this type of decoration.[141]

Although only implied in the story of Morningstar's family, the transfer of sacred powers from spirits to people through sexual intercourse is a frequent theme in Blackfoot mythology, and in the re-enactment of the event in transfer rituals. In the mythical past of this warrior society, women played an important role as intermediaries with the spirits and in the founding of cultural institutions. The story of Elk Woman also asserts that sacred life has love as its origin.

Hearing an elk whistling in the woods, a woman could not resist its temptation. Transformed into a man, the elk seduced her, but the powers of her husband forced the elk to give her up. The elk compensated the couple by giving her a sacred elk-skin robe and a headdress. In making the headdress, the elk used eagle feathers to represent his antlers, but he also requested several other animals to contribute their power symbols.[142] These gifts were added to the beaver medicine bundle of the woman's husband, who attached a phallus-shaped container of tobacco seeds to the headdress. The seeds were referred to as "children," suggesting a fertility symbolism (Figure 112). Attracted by the beauty of the headdress and robe, the holy women used to borrow them for use in the annual Sun Dance; eventually they were allowed to keep them as a separate medicine bundle. It was probably at this stage that the headdress was identified as a symbol of the *natoas*, the turnip dug up by Morningstar's wife, which led to the origin of the Sun Dance. Several plumes in the headdress represent the leaves of the turnip. The decorations added to the elk's robe have been mentioned already. However, an animal skin was never considered to be merely raw material; its decoration was always a gesture of respect for the animal's spirit, whatever its other symbolic functions.

113.
Painted robe, Blackfoot, 1844. Etnografiska Museet, Stockholm 1854.2.27. L:196

Elkskin robe of the holy woman in the Blackfoot Sun Dance. The painted designs refer to spiritual intermediaries in the transfer of blessings from the spirit world to mankind.

These Blackfoot traditions convey the message that the sun and the elk provided mankind with access to the creative powers of the sky and the earth, celebrated in the annual dance. However, these traditions also raise many unexplained questions. The elk's headdress and robe indeed may have been used in the dance in part because of their beauty, but that does not explain the interrelation of the two myths.

Blackfoot traditions do include a few fragments that may help to connect the two stories. There was an elk spirit called Windmaker,[143] and the generic term "trotter," used for the elk and all members of the deer family, is related to "earth trotter," the literal meaning of the Blackfoot name for "spider." These and other fragments may suggest a relationship between the elk (the earth) and the winds in the sky. Intermediate between the two realms was the spider; he was an earth trotter, but he also floated on his web in the sky; in the myth, the spider helped Morningstar's wife to return to earth.

Blackfoot traditions no longer elaborate on these details; in order to retrieve the full meaning of the myths we have to cast our net more widely. Myths and rituals spread through intertribal contacts, but it is at their source that we may discover parts of their original meaning lost in the process of adaptation.

The elk's tempting whistle, his virility and power to seduce, and his association with the woods leave no doubt about his origin. Down the Missouri River, in the former heartland of late Mississippian cultures, several tribes identified the elk with the spirit who gave "the breath of life" in the creation of the earth. That spirit called up the four winds (symbolized by a design resembling a Maltese cross), and caused the woods to grow from the hair he shed on the ground. The myths of the Pawnee Indians explicitly identified the elk and the spider as two aspects of the same spirit, providing a connection between the realms of the sky and the earth. The Spider was the Central Plains equivalent of Old Man in Blackfoot mythology, the trickster and bringer of culture to mankind.

The Sioux explain the elk's power to arouse the sexual passion of women by referring to the polygamous behaviour of the bull elk in nature.[144] In imitation of his whistling cry, young men blew on wooden flutes decorated with elk effigies when courting (Figure 114); when in love they painted their robes with the figure of an elk or a spider.

The minor role of the elk as wind maker and seducer of women in Blackfoot mythology was but a vague remembrance of this complex Mis-

114.
Elk effigy flute. National Museum of Natural History, Smithsonian Institution, Washington, D.C. 200,588.

This effigy whistle portrays the head of a bull elk calling his mates.

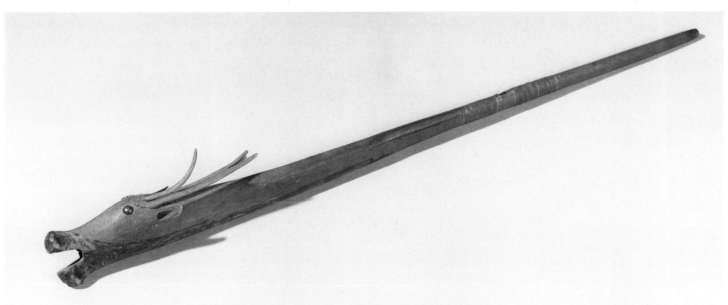

115. (opposite)
Wooden wand, Eastern Sioux, early 19th century. Private Collection. L:42; W:28

This wand was used as a magic mirror by members of the Elk Dreamers cult.

sissippian theme, eroded by time and distance. However, it does reveal the original connection between the two founding myths of the Blackfoot Sun Dance.

The focus of both legends is less upon the spiritual gifts than on the great intermediaries, Scarface (Mistaken Morningstar) and Elk (Spider). Behind these two were Morningstar and Old Man, and an analysis of Blackfoot mythology suggests that they were both sons of Sun and Our Mother, the Earth. This link clarifies why a headdress and robe given by Earth could symbolize Sky. The holy woman in the Sun Dance did not only represent the wife of Morningstar; she was also Our Mother, the Earth. Like women in a victory dance she wore the garments of her husband, Sun, the Great Warrior. In essence, the Sun Dance was a celebration of all creation, resulting from the love between these two primeval sources of sacred power.

Far from being an exclusively solemn affair, the Sun Dance was also an occasion for socializing, games, horse races, honouring upcoming warriors, feasting the visitors, and courting the girls. Every night the courting flutes could be heard around the summer camps of the Assiniboin and Sioux Indians.

A mirror decorated with elk and thunderbird symbols was also powerful in charming the Sioux girls. Flashing the mirror was supposed to send a beam of the hypnotic power of the spirits to the girl. The thunderbirds were lords of the four winds called up by the elk in the creation myth; they were also renowned womanizers in the myths, making restitution for their pranks by giving medicine pipes to several tribes.

In Sioux ceremonial practice, young men who dreamed of the bull elk and his amorous successes joined the Elk Dreamers, a cult group that acted out dreams in dance performances.[145] Wearing elk masks, they carried hoops and magical mirrors to "shoot" elk power at the women in the audience. Once glass mirrors became generally available, their flashing undoubtedly added to the excitement; yet the shooting of elk power did not require this pretty flash of mirror light. This is apparent from an example dating back to earlier days (Figure 115).

This magic mirror was made of white pine, its shallow carved decorations painted red and blue. The style and symbolism of these decorations unmistakably indicate an Eastern Sioux origin of the 1820s, if not earlier.

On one side of the mirror the bull elk is shown, shooting his power over a harem of twenty-three does, which form a circle around a decorative interpretation of the thunderbirds as lords of the four winds. Man's utilization of these powers seems to be the subject of decorations on the other side of the mirror. Here we see a circle of thirty-one women and three headless men, surrounding a large rosette. This central rosette may be interpreted to be the magic mirror itself, shooting its beams of elk power at the audience. Further study of Sioux legends may explain the three men, who seem to have lost their heads in the excitement.

> Indians, whose chief ornament consisted in the paint on their faces, voyageurs with bright sashes and neatly ornamented moccasins, half-breeds glittering in every ornament they could lay their hands on . . .
> Paul Kane, Fort Edmonton, 1847.[146]

Influencing and to some extent counteracting the spread of Plains Indian culture were the reinforcements of the Northeastern Woodlands heritage, which continued throughout the historical period. From the 1790s on, various Ojibwa bands migrated westward, forced to move by the waning importance of the fur trade in the Great Lakes region; most of these bands included a mixture of Ottawa, Cree, and Métis. They moved into southern

Manitoba and the adjoining parts of Saskatchewan, where they were called Saulteaux or Bungi. Interaction between these Plains Ojibwa and the regional Plains Cree extinguished many cultural differences, though not those relating to religion and ritual. It is true that the Plains Ojibwa adopted a version of the Sun Dance, but the focus of their religious life remained upon the *Midewiwin* cult, or Medicine Dance.

The ethnographic record of this cult begins with nineteenth-century reports from the Great Lakes, and *Midewiwin* practices recorded since that time were concerned with the curing of disease and the ensuring of good health. It is well known, however, that the cult emerged in the Western Great Lakes region during the early decades of the eighteenth century, when there was great demand for the furs of such animals as otter and beaver.

Descriptions of *Mide*-like rituals dating back to the eighteenth century are vague, but there is some evidence that the cult elaborated on ancient hunting rituals.[147] Probably the *Midewiwin* initially endeavoured to respond to the greater demands made upon the game spirits as a result of the fur trade.

In those early days the cult was referred to as the Black Dance.[148] Hunters used to paint themselves black, and the medicine bags and ceremonial skins surviving from that region and period are also black. Their uniform shape, size, and decoration identify these objects as the paraphernalia of a popular cult, most likely an early version of the *Midewiwin*.[149]

Responding to the spiritual needs of the native people, the *Midewiwin* rapidly spread west among the Eastern Sioux and several Missouri River tribes. Negative aspects of European contact among these tribes were still largely restricted to the drastic decline of fur-bearing game, which may explain why they practised an early version of the cult, which focused upon man's relationship with the spiritual lords of the animals.

By the end of the eighteenth century, however, the fur traders left the Great Lakes region for more profitable regions out west, and the Great Lakes Indians were left to face the destructive aspects of American and Canadian expansion. The native communities were ravaged by diseases, malnutrition, and a host of related social evils. Not surprisingly, there grew a preoccupation with health in Ojibwa Indian rituals.[150] The shift from honouring the game spirits to curing disease was facilitated by the intimate association of animal spirits with disease. Throughout native North America, disease was believed to result when animal spirits were offended by the improper conduct of hunters.[151]

Among the Ojibwa, cured patients joined the *Midewiwin* after initiation into the lowest of four degrees; they moved on to the higher degrees after instruction in secret knowledge and the payment of prescribed fees. Each member received a "bag of life," made of a whole animal skin and ornamented with beads or quillwork.[152] This bag contained the medicine conducive to the promotion of *pimadaziwin*, the good life, the health of body and mind. With these medicine bags new life was "shot" into patients, comparable to the shooting act of the Sioux Elk Dreamers.

The *Mide* lodge represented the universe; its spiritual inhabitants were represented by wooden figurines standing in the lodge during ceremonies. Herbal medicines were stored in the cavities of some of these sculptures.[153] Other wooden dolls were made to move or dance in demonstrations of magic. Similar wooden effigies were used throughout the Great Lakes region in shamanistic acts, as love charms, and as family guardians of health.[154] Mnemonic figures incised on bark scrolls and wooden boards recorded the many incantations. The *Midewiwin* cult was perhaps the most elaborate expression of shamanistic ideology in North America.

The Eastern Sioux preserved in their version of the Medicine Dance many features reflecting its original focus upon the game spirits. For example, their ceremonials included the eat-all feast, in which the participants consumed large quantities of game broth. It was believed that the extravagant consumption of game pleased the game spirits, who would increase the game population as a result. The rims of the wooden bowls used by the participants were decorated with carved effigies of voracious animals.[155] Eat-all feasts and the effigy bowls used on these occasions were common throughout the Eastern Woodlands, of which the Eastern Sioux culture represented the westernmost extension.[156]

The Ojibwa *Midewiwin* shifted the focus of their rituals from propitiation of the game spirits to the curing of disease. These Indians had moved west in search of better trapping ground; but by the time they reached southern Manitoba the game was decreasing there, as well. A new cult was formed. The Wabano revived an ancient shamanistic relationship with the animal spirits. Members of the cult used mnemonic prayer boards decorated with a profusion of animal figures, which represented spiritual guardians[157] (Figure 116). Such a prayer board is carried by one of the dancers in Peter Rindisbacher's picture of an Indian scalp dance, painted while he was in southern Manitoba in about 1823 (Figure 117).

In the wake of Lewis and Clark's famous explorations, American traders expanded their activities; the Missouri River formed a relatively easy route into the Northern Plains. In their large keelboats, these men shipped tons of trade goods upriver and returned to St. Louis with comparable cargoes fo buffalo skins. Long and difficult transportation routes had always restricted the Canadian fur trade to small, high-quality furs; it did not take long for the Indians to realize that Americans offered a more generous source of desirable imports in exchange for buffalo skins.

During the 1820s, in order to combat the new rivalry from the Americans, the Hudson's Bay Company and the North West Company merged their Canadian trade and drastically cut their labour force. Most of the men released were Métis, halfbreeds who had been born on, and move with, the frontiers of the fur trade. They had inherited Cree, Ojibwa, and other native traditions through their mothers and were exposed to various degrees of European values carried by their English, Scottish, and French fathers. Neither accepting nor accepted by either of the two parental societies, the growing Métis population gradually acquired a distinct ethnic identity of its own. By 1830 the size of the population group allowed – and preferred – Métis marrying Métis. As they developed an identifiable culture there emerged a distinct Métis style in their decorative arts.

The lower Red River region became the cultural centre of these people after their release by the trading companies, though considerable numbers of them could be found near every trading post on the Northern Plains. In long trains of squeaking Red River carts, the Métis set out on their annual expeditions, hunting buffalo and trading with Indians and whites. Among the latter were an increasing number of British and American tourists, artists, and sport hunters, eager to acquire souvenirs of the Wild West.

The Red River Métis specialized in the manufacture of colourfully ornamented horse gear and fancy "western" garments, such as coats, moccasins, and a variety of bags and pouches. These items were purchased by the Indians, as eager white travellers, who preferred to acquire their souvenirs from "real" Indians. As a result, most Métis art preserved in museums is mistakenly identified as originating from various Indian tribes; their Métis origin is rarely recognized.[158]

The study of Métis art is complicated because their art style influenced native artisans all over the Northern Plains. Through the trade of Métis

116.
Wooden board, Plains Ojibwa, mid-19th century. Courtesy of the Trustees of the British Museum, London 2252. L:48; W:13 (approx.)

This board was used in rituals of the Wabano cult. It was acquired near Fort Carlton, Saskatchewan, in the late 1850s.

117.
An Indian Scalp Dance. Watercolour painted by Peter Rindisbacher in the 1820s while in southern Manitoba. Hudson's Bay Company Collection, Lower Fort Garry, Parks Canada.

craft products, the intermarriage of Métis with the Indians, and the migrations of these people into the most remote corners of the greater northwest, the Métis put their stamp on the art of practically every tribal group of the Northern Plains and the Northwest Territories. Indeed, Métis art history can be viewed as a distinct cycle: originating in the dreams and hands of Indian women, and elaborated by their Métis daughters and granddaughters, it again inspired the creativity of Indian artisans.

Geometric patterns in loom-woven quillwork revealed the Cree component in Red River Métis art of the 1820s.[159] In subsequent decades floral patterns in silk and bead embroidery gradually increased. Roman Catholic mission schools were the main source of these French embroidery patterns; the floral murals in the cathedral at St. Boniface were also copied by Métis women. The fine work of these women earned the Métis their Indian name, "Flower Beadwork People." Utilizing the brilliant colour scheme of early quillwork and bilaterally symmetrical floral designs, Red River Métis art conveys a sparkling delicacy. The embroidered skin mittens made for Lord Elgin in the 1840s suggest a bouquet of flowers. They were presented to him by the Métis, who had played a crucial role in the destiny of the Canadian West (Figure 118).

When the export of buffalo hides became economically feasible, the

118.
Mittens, Red River Métis type, c. 1850.
From the collection of the Earl of Elgin and
Kincardine, KT, CD, Scotland. L:24; W:15

Floral patterns quillworked on white
buckskin mittens were popular among the
Métis.

fate of the Plains Indians was sealed; between 1830 and 1870 the buffalo
dwindled from an estimated thirty million to a few thousand. The native
world, grown rich and colourful with the imports of the fur traders, col-
lapsed when the trade pulled out. The Grasslands had changed into empty,
open space, awaiting the creation of a new world.

During the last desperate resistance of the native people, the Northwest Rebellion of 1885, an unknown Indian sketched his memories of
happier days on twelve sheets of paper.[160] Sketches of this type were
produced by many native artists on the Central and Southern Plains,
continuing the highly developed tradition of painted war records; but
on the Northern Plains, this art style had remained comparatively primitive
and sketches on paper were extremely rare. The artist of this series could
have been one of the American Sioux who had taken refuge in Saskatchewan; however, the pictured ceremonial regalia shows many elements
distinctive of the people of the Northern Plains. Most probably the artist
belonged to one of the Assiniboin bands that straddled the international
border.

While museum specialists study these and similar details of an
impressive past, native artists prove they did not vanish with the buffalo
herds. They survived, by the power of their dreams.

Ted J. Brasser

No Little Variety
of Ornament
Northern Athapaskan
Artistic Traditions

One summer's night in 1770, a small band of Northern Athapaskan Dogrib Indians was surprised by enemy Cree. During the fight, all the Athapaskans were killed, except for three young women. They were taken prisoner and travelled the long distance by canoe to the home territory of their captors. A year later, one of the young women resolved to escape. She set off on foot, intending to rejoin her people several hundred kilometres to the northwest. Progress was slow, the terrain difficult, and the route uncertain. The onset of autumn found her far from human habitation, somewhere south and east of Great Slave Lake. She faced the long, dark, bitterly cold northern winter alone, equipped with only a knife, an awl, and a few caribou sinews.

Apparently undaunted by her predicament, she set about making preparations for the winter. She built a small shelter and from the caribou sinews made snares with which she captured hare for food and clothing. She made a pair of snowshoes and, in anticipation of the melting of lake ice in the spring, began work on a fish net of twisted willow bark.

By one of the most amazing coincidences in history, her personal epic of courage and ingenuity became intertwined with one of the great sagas of exploration in the North — Hudson's Bay Company Samuel Hearne's third expedition in search of the Coppermine River. Travelling with a group of Chipewyan, Hearne had left Fort Churchill, on Hudson Bay, on December 7, 1770, and reached the lower Coppermine River eight months later. On February 11, 1772, during the return journey, his party came upon an unfamiliar snowshoe track, which led them to a tiny hut and the solitary but healthy and apparently content woman. Impressed with her courage, skills, and self-reliance, the Indian men spent the night in wrestling matches to determine which could take her as his wife. Hearne recorded his impressions in a vivid account, which later formed part of his published journal. What struck him most forcibly, and still intrigues the reader of his account two centuries later, is the fact that this woman, who had been without human contact for seven months and who could not anticipate seeing another person for several more months, if ever, and for whom mere survival must have been a daily challenge, had gone to considerable effort to decorate her fur clothing. Hearne's wonderment jumps off the page:

> It is scarcely possible to conceive that a person in her forlorn situation could be so composed as to be capable of contriving or executing any thing that was not absolutely necessary to her existence; but there were sufficient proofs that she had extended her care much farther, as all her clothing, besides being calculated for real service, shewed great taste, and exhibited no little variety of ornament. The materials, though rude, were curiously wrought, and so judiciously

119. (opposite)
Interior of a Dogrib lodge, by Emile Petitot, c. 1860 (1891:286).

The woman on the left wears a dress of tanned skin bound at the waist by a belt of woven quillwork with long fringes, and a hood of trade cloth. She carries her infant on her back. A decorated knife sheath and trade knife are suspended from her neck. The men wear skin clothing: fringed shirts with quillwoven epaulettes, and thigh-high fringed leggings worn with moccasins. (Note the similarity to the man's clothing illustrated in Figure 139.) Three wear headbands of woven quillwork with feathers inserted along the top edge. The two figures on the right wear Hudson's Bay Company blankets.

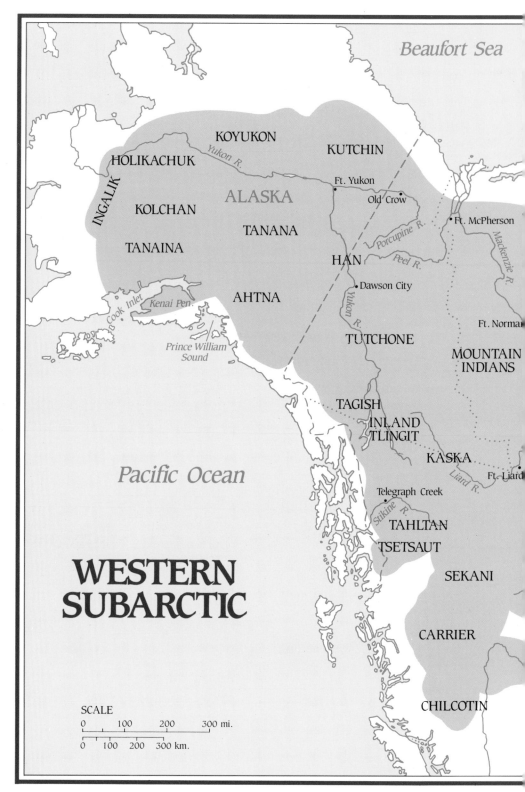

Beaufort Sea

KOYUKON

KUTCHIN

HOLIKACHUK

Yukon R.

Ft. Yukon

ALASKA

Old Crow

Ft. McPherson

INGALIK

KOLCHAN

Porcupine R.

Peel R.

Mackenzie R.

TANANA

TANAINA

HAN

Dawson City

Ft. Norman

AHTNA

Cook Inlet

Kenai Pen.

Yukon R.

TUTCHONE

MOUNTAIN
INDIANS

Prince William
Sound

Pacific Ocean

TAGISH

INLAND
TLINGIT

KASKA

Ft. Liard

Liard R.

Telegraph Creek

Stikine R.

TAHLTAN

TSETSAUT

SEKANI

WESTERN
SUBARCTIC

CARRIER

CHILCOTIN

SCALE

0   100   200   300 mi.

0   100   200   300 km.

120.
upper left: High-ranking Carrier man wearing ceremonial wig of dentalia, human hair and sea-lion whiskers. (Morice, 1895:174)
lower left: Yellowknife leader, Akaitcho, and his son. Coloured lithograph based on a lost 1821 watercolour by Robert Hood. Public Archives of Canada C-5149.
upper right: "Saveeah," a Kutchin leader. Sketch by Alexander Hunter Murray at Fort Yukon, 1847-1848. (Murray 1910:89)
lower right: "Women of the Etcha-Ottine or Slave tribe," by Emile Petitot, c. 1860. (Petitot 1888)

placed, as to make the whole of her garb have a very pleasing, though rather romantic appearance.[1]

This remarkable story is a microcosm of much that is central to Northern Athapaskan culture. For most Athapaskans most of the time, life was hard. A harsh climate, difficult terrain, and the generally seasonal and cyclical availability of animal resources imposed severe restrictions on people's activities. Survival and a harmonious relationship with the land and its other inhabitants were made possible through the delicate inter-meshing of a simple but effective technology, an intimate knowledge of the natural environment, and a system of ritual and taboo for dealing with the spirits that were thought to control the world. Personal traits such as those exhibited by the Dogrib woman — resilience, flexibility, and an ability to handle problems of survival independently — were critically important in this society.

Most groups moved frequently in search of food and the raw materials required for clothing, tools, and weapons. Little could be carried that was not essential for survival, nor was there leisure to produce luxury items. Yet people often went to considerable trouble to decorate them-selves, their clothing, tools, utensils, and containers. Occasionally, the craft worker's skill and aesthetic sense combined in objects of rare beauty. Against the background of Subarctic environment and Northern Athapaskan life-style, such expressions of creative energy stand out in sharp relief.

In decorating utilitarian objects, Athapaskan artisans were satisfy-ing a fundamental human need for aesthetic expression. They were also communicating messages to their fellow men and to the spirits, the non-corporeal inhabitants of their world. Much of the original purpose and meaning of Northern Athapaskan art has been lost through the passage of time and the disruptions to native society that followed contact with whites. The artefact record itself is very incomplete: there are, to cite just a few examples, almost no documented early contact period gar-ments from groups in the interior of British Columbia or east of the Rocky Mountains, no remaining Carrier caribou antler jewellery (although we know it was being produced as late as the 1890s),[2] and no decorated animal-skin medicine bags from the Kutchin. There are several reasons for such gaps. Difficulties of climate and of access to the Northern Athapaskans, combined with their semi-nomadic life-style and relatively simple material culture resulted in these people being largely ignored by early collectors. (For much the same reasons, ethnological work was not begun until well into the twentieth century.) Collectors' indifference is understandable, for Athapaskans never produced a great number of "things." Most of what they made was needed for survival; when it had served its function it was abandoned, destroyed, or reworked into some-thing else. An individual's material wealth was reckoned in beads and clothing, and these were frequently buried or cremated with him.

Decorated objects such as those shown in this exhibition are, there-fore, only fragments of a unique cultural heritage, a heritage that Athapaskans themselves have preserved more in myth, song, and dance than in material possessions. Nevertheless, these fragments can, in con-junction with accounts and illustrations by early fur traders and missionaries and with twentieth-century ethnological studies and native writings, tell us much about traditional culture and its change through time.

"The Land is an Old Friend"

The Physical and Spiritual Environments of Northern Athapaskans

> Being an Indian means being able to understand and live with this world in a very special way. It means living with the land, with the animals, with the birds and fish, as though they were your sisters and brothers. It means saying the land is an old friend and an old friend your father knew, your grandfather knew, indeed your people have always known.[3]

The native inhabitants of the interior of northwestern North America speak variants of a language known as Northern Athapaskan. Their ancestors probably crossed from Siberia into Alaska at least 4,500 hundred years ago;[4] over the centuries, their descendants gradually dispersed east and south from Alaska and the Yukon. By the time of contact with white men and the start of their recorded history, Indians today known as Northern Athapaskan (or, in Canada, Dene) inhabited a large part of northwestern North America, including the Subarctic interiors of Alaska (and a small section of southwestern Alaskan coastline), the Northwest Territories and Yukon Territory, as well as the northern parts of British Columbia, Alberta, Manitoba, and Saskatchewan. These Indians had no formal political tribes, and often referred to themselves as simply "the people." However, twentieth-century scholars have, for practical purposes, distinguished some twenty-six "tribal" groups, generally on the basis of shared territory, similar dialect, and social contact.[5]

The Northern Athapaskan homeland is the *taiga*, a vast northern forest broken by myriad lakes and rivers, rising in the west to a chain of high mountains and plateaux and bordered to the north by Arctic tundra. It is a land of immense variety, encompassing both lowland muskeg and alpine meadow. The climate, too, is one of extremes: long, very cold, dark winters alternate with short, bright, warm summers. Precipitation falls mainly in winter, as dry powdery snow. Animal life includes caribou, moose, musk-ox, mountain sheep and goats, and smaller game such as hare, beaver, muskrat, and porcupine. A marked cyclical fluctuation in numbers characterizes many of these species. The waterways support more than thirty kinds of fish and provide stopping places for a variety of migratory waterfowl. The forests are mainly coniferous — spruce, fir, and pine — but birch and poplar are also present, as are shrubs, such as labrador tea and cranberry.

The native inhabitants of this inland forest evolved a way of life uniquely adapted to its terrain, climate, and resources. Since Athapaskans lived by hunting and fishing, and since much of their food supply was seasonal and migratory, small, family-based groups had to travel frequently. The technology used to exploit the environment was not intricate, but it was highly effective because it was combined with an intimate knowledge of the behaviour and life cycles of the plants and animals needed for survival. Snares, deadfall traps, bows, arrows, and spears were the main devices used in the capture of game and they were equally well-suited for taking large and small animals. Snowshoes permitted travel in winter, and bark canoes, dug-outs, frame boats covered with rawhide, or rafts were used in summer, according to the nature of the waterways and the availability of raw materials. All groups covered great distances on foot, carrying their household goods with them on their backs or, in winter, dragging them behind on wood or skin toboggans.

The land could not support a large human population. Everything depended upon the success of the hunt. Large game animals, particularly caribou and moose, provided not only food, but also skins for clothing and lodges, sinews for thread, snares, and bowstrings, and bone and antler for awls, scrapers, and arrow and spear points. When the caribou did not follow their accustomed migration paths, or when secondary food sources such as hare were at a low point in their cycles, people suffered great privation. Starvation was a constant threat, particularly in the bitter cold of midwinter, when game was difficult to hunt and the fish were deep under the lake ice, and in the early spring, when stored food resources were depleted but migratory birds and animals had not yet returned to the land.

The lives of the people were thus intimately and irrevocably linked with the climate, the seasons, and the land and water and their non-human occupants. During the millennia, the Athapaskans developed beliefs and behaviour patterns that enabled them to live in harmony with their unpredictable physical world, and the beings in it. For, like other native North Americans, Athapaskans perceived the universe to be inhabited by a multitude of spirits. Every animate and inanimate object had its spirit. Among the most powerful spirits were those of the animals, on whom survival depended. When man was successful in the hunt, it was because the spirit of the animal permitted it to be taken. A hunter returning home empty-handed would not say, "I had no luck with bear or beaver," but rather, "Bear or beaver did not *want* me."[6] Good relations with animal spirits were critical to survival, and much time and energy was invested in ritual and taboo designed to please and placate these spirits. Through dreams and vision quests, individuals sought the assistance of the spirit world and a special relationship with the spirit of a particular animal or other natural phenomena who would help them throughout life.

Animals were treated with respect, lest their spirits become offended and withhold themselves from humans. For example, Dogrib and Yellow-knife Indians thought that the caribou would leave the country forever if sticks or stones were thrown at them, and their bones must be treated with care — thrown in the fire or put up in a tree so that dogs could not chew on them.[7] Bears, although economically far less important, were held in awe because of their great spiritual as well as physical powers. To appease its spirit, the Tutchone of the Yukon cleaned the skull of a slain bear, decorated it with feathers, hung it in a tree, and sang special songs to it.[8] Women did not touch fresh bear skins or eat bear flesh.

Conducting one's life so as not to offend the spirit world was the responsibility of every Athapaskan, but the pattern of ritual and taboo was nowhere so striking or elaborate as it was for women of menstruating age. Such women, and particularly girls at puberty, were thought capable of giving the greatest offence to animal spirits, for during their menses women were believed to be imbued with enormous spiritual power. Only through correct observance of a clearly defined set of rituals and taboos could a woman avoid angering the animal spirits and bringing harm to herself and her community. For months following her first menstrual period, a girl lived apart in a specially constructed shelter, attended and instructed by close female relatives. She wore a large skin hood, which hid her face and obstructed her vision, for were she to inadvertently look upon men or game this would have disastrous consequences for the hunt. Only dried foods from which the animal spirits had departed could be eaten, and small amounts of water taken through a bone tube. When her people moved camp, she had to break her own trail; if she walked in a man's track, his success at hunting would suffer. Although the special hood was worn only by girls at puberty, throughout their lives, during menstrual periods and at childbirth, women were expected to observe food and behavioural restrictions.

A sense of group kinship with animals prevailed, as well as one of individual relationships. Athapaskan stories tell of a long-ago time when animals spoke and behaved like humans and when it was difficult to differentiate animals from men. Origin myths frequently revolve around the marriage or encounter of an ancestral human, male or female, with an animal who could assume human form. For example, a Chipewyan myth recounts the story of Ttathe Dene, the first man, who was assisted in making snowshoes by a ptarmigan. He captures her, she turns into a beautiful woman, and from their union the first Chipewyan are born.[9] Another widespread story describes the marriage of a woman with a dog who appears to her in the guise of a handsome young man. The Dogrib Indians believed themselves to be the descendants of this couple.

"Images of Imaginary Beings"
Northern Athapaskan Engraving and Painting in Prehistoric and Early Contact Times

a

b

c

121.
Incised decoration:
top: Mountain-sheep horn ladle, with incised and red-ochred designs. University Museum of Archaeology and Anthropology, Cambridge 22.951.B. L:22.5
bottom: Caribou horn armband. Peabody Museum, Harvard University 31-63-10/K96. Photograph by Hillel Burger. D:10
left: Bird bone drinking tube. Peabody Museum, Harvard University 05-7-10/64525. Photograph by Hillel Burger. L:24.2

Decorated objects often seem to record a dialogue between man and the spirit world. The precise nature of the messages communicated is buried in the past, but historical accounts, ethnographic studies, and the artefacts themselves provide hints as to their original purpose and content. Incising patterns in horn or bone and accentuating the designs by rubbing red ochre or charcoal into them was a widespread and apparently ancient Northern Athapaskan artistic tradition. Archaeological and early ethnographic collections contain the most carefully executed and technically sophisticated examples of this technique, although it survives into modern times in some areas in the decoration of horn spoons and scrapers, and in the designs scraped on birchbark containers. In most cases, decorative motifs are geometric and appear to be non-representational, but at least some of them may be highly stylized representations of animal or plant forms, and symbolic of associated spirit powers. There are a few instances of realistic motifs; for example, crudely drawn animal representations on a few skin scrapers from southern Yukon Territory,[10] and an intriguing, bi-facially decorated "snowshoe needle" from a late-prehistoric Kutchin site near the Mackenzie Delta, which is incised with figures possibly representing two muskrat, a beaver, and caribou beside a lodge or hill.[11]

A variety of artefacts — arm bands, tump-line spreaders, clubs, bowls, spoons, necklace pendants, scrapers, and drinking tubes — display incised decoration (Figure 121). Bone scrapers and reamers from prehistoric sites in the Yukon Territory, for example, are decorated with fine lengthwise grooves, which have small, regularly spaced notches cut along their edges.[12] A nineteenth-century skin scraper is incised with a precise pattern of paired transverse lines alternated with paired diagonal lines, the lower diagonal line being regularly notched along the underside.[13] The intent of such decoration has not been recorded, but similar incised designs on bone skinning tools from the Eastern Subarctic have been explained:

> A stimulus comes to the hunter in one of his dreams to try his luck for beaver. Should he succeed in his excursion, he then "pays for" the admonition by decorating one of the tools used in preparing the flesh or hide of the animals so obtained.[14]

122.
Pendants, probably for shaman's neck-ring, Tutchone, mid-19th century. Canadian Museum of Civilization, National Museums of Canada, Ottawa JaVg 2:93-101. L:10 (longest)

The decoration of ritual equipment with incised motifs strongly suggests that at least some of this ornament was more than merely decorative. Some Kutchin groups wore "special carved wood arm bands . . . in connection with death rites."[15] Koyukon mourners wore "hoops of birch wood around the neck and wrists, with various patterns and figures cut on them."[16] The hollow-bone drinking tubes that girls used during puberty seclusion were frequently decorated with parallel incised lines and cross-hatching.

Perhaps the clearest indication of a spiritual symbolism inherent in some forms of incised decoration is its presence on shamans' necklace pendants from the northern interior of British Columbia (Figure 122). On the northern Northwest Coast, elaborate and complex pendants in various animal forms embodied "the spirit power of the shaman's zoomorphic assistants."[17] Presumably, neighbouring Athapaskan examples served a similar function. The Athapaskan pendants, while relatively simple in both form and decoration, show considerable diversity in shape and incised motif. The most common shape is lanceolate, although other forms occur, including stylized human figures. The shape of some pendants seems to echo in miniature Nootka whalebone clubs from the south coast of British Columbia. Incised decoration is usually done on both sides.

There are spurred and waved lines that are also found on other artefacts from the same region; other design elements suggest Northwest Coast art. These may simply reflect cultural diffusion from the coast: Athapaskan groups with Northwest Coast contacts were strongly influenced in many facets of their culture by their dominant neighbours. At the same time, the presence of some remarkably similar bone pendants in Beothuk collections from Newfoundland suggests that this is, rather, a regional expression of a very old northern artistic tradition.

Some of the finest Athapaskan incised work appears on a series of clubs collected in early contact times from the Tanaina and Ahtena of Alaska (Figure 123).[18] Used mainly for hand-to-hand combat, these clubs are made of the main stem and first tine of a caribou antler.[19] The hand grip is sheathed in tanned skin, which, in at least some cases, was originally decorated with porcupine quillwork and fringes. Some examples have iron and copper inserts along the spine, and glass bead inlays. The incised work consists of fine, precisely delineated, symmetrically arranged patterns, which have been enhanced by rubbing with ochre. Motifs are geometric, "zigzags and triangles, crosshatching, spurs and related forms, parallel and oblique broken lines, and meanders."[20] Some designs resemble those of the Bering Sea Eskimo: a raised waved line worked down the length of the club or along the middle of the tine appears on their tools as a tooth motif.[21] Similar precise data for the designs of the Pacific Eskimo neighbours of the Tanaina are unfortunately lacking. One can only speculate on the meaning of the Athapaskan incised patterns. Repeated lines could represent a war record or tally of animal kills; other motifs could be stylized representations of spirit assistants. There is no evidence to prove or disprove such theories.

Painting was evidently another old and important form of Subarctic Athapaskan artistic expression. Roots, fungi, flowers, berries, and minerals provided the artisan with a variety of colours. Red, usually obtained from ochre (hematite), and black from charcoal, were preferred. These were undoubtedly appreciated for their decorative qualities, since they produced strong, highly constrasting colours. Equally important, however, were the spiritual associations of these colours. Red ochre, highly valued and treated with respect, was imbued with particular spiritual power. The Kutchin, for example, left sinew, beads, or something else of value when they took ochre from the ground.[22] Ochre was applied to both wood and skin in ways that strongly suggest an appeal to the spirit world. The skin lodges of the Slavey were commonly painted with an encircling band of red, which formed a protective ring around the habitation and its occupants.[23] A Slavey man "would paint the manifestation of his 'medicine' on the outside of the bow of his canoe so that the canoe might see where to go and not upset, on the point, or crest of his snowshoes, under the head of his toboggan, and on his drum."[24]

Almost a century and a half before Mason made these observations, Samuel Hearne noted that Chipewyan men painted wooden shields in black and red, in preparation for an attack on Inuit:

> . . . some with the figure of the sun, others with that of the moon, several with different kinds of birds and beasts of prey and many with the images of imaginary beings. . . . On enquiring the reason for their doing so, I learned that each man painted his shield with the image of that being on which he relied most for success in the intended engagement. Some were contented with a single representation; while others . . . had their shields covered to the very margin with a group of hieroglyphics, quite unintelligible to every one except the painter.[25]

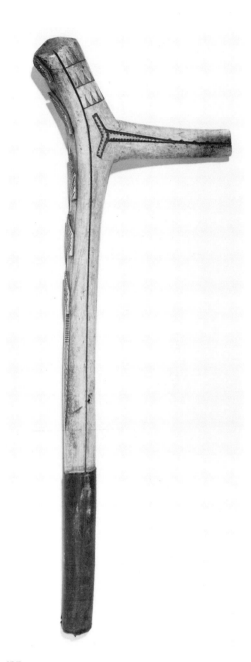

123.
Tanaina type, mid-19th century Club, made from the stem and first tine of a caribou antler, decorated with incised geometric patterns. Staatliche Museen Preußischer Kulturbesitz, Museum für Völkerkunde, Berlin, FRG IV-A-9475. L:56; W:18

124.

Charlie Yahey, Beaver Indian, with drum depicting the cosmos, painted by Kayan, about 1915. Photograph courtesy of Mr. Robin Ridington, Vancouver.

The painting on the drum represents the dreamer's magic flight to the world beyond the sky. "Creation began at the centre of the cross; the lines slanting outward from it lead to the hatched patch to heaven, discovered by the culture hero on his vision quest. . . .'' (Ridington 1981-354).

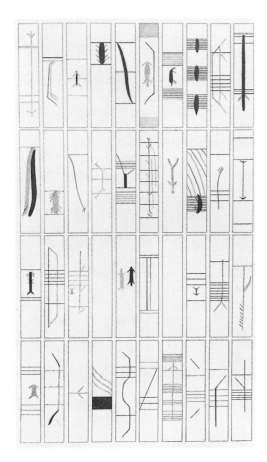

125.

Decorated gambling sticks, Tahltan. The names given to the designs were recorded as follows:

top row (l-r): arrow, canoe in water, man, fresh water crab, fire, bear in water, dog, lakes, leg, musk rat.

second row (l-r): fire, rock, man's eye, caribou horn, mouse, man's trail, man, osprey, ptarmigan, arrow.

third row (l-r): crab, porcupine, hook, mink, ?, beaver, rope, ?, a stick across the trail, fish net, lynx.

fourth row (l-r): fox, canoe, teeth, black bear, sheep, moose, arrow, belly, mooseskin rope, ground hog.

G.T. Emmons *The Tahltan Indians*, 1911, plate xix. University of Pennsylvania Museum publication.

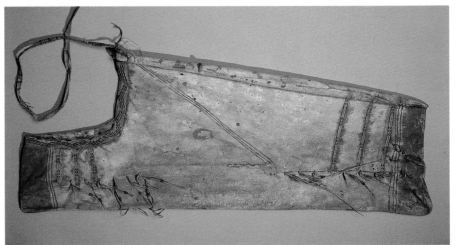

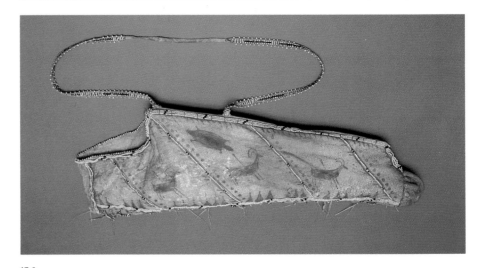

126.

Quivers:

middle: Tanaina type, probably collected from either Prince William Sound or Cook Inlet, Alaska, during Captain Cook's third voyage, 1778. University Museum of Archaeology and Anthropology, Cambridge 22.981. L:84; W:33

bottom: Tanaina type, collected in 1889. Collection du Musée d'ethnographie, Geneva, Switzerland K1564. L:75; W:25

No painted shields exist today, but the painting found on twentieth-century shamans' drums and Tahltan gambling sticks may be similar. Shamans' drums from Southern Yukon Athapaskan groups were painted with "crest animals or representations of shamanistic spirits."[26] A drum from the Beaver of northeastern British Columbia, painted about 1915, depicts the magic flight of a shaman (through dreaming) to the world beyond the sky (Figure 124).[27] The Tahltan gambling sticks are of beautifully finished wood, painted in red and black. Some designs are functional: encircling lines and bands represent the value and name of each stick. Other motifs include simple, highly stylized representations of an "animal form or natural object intimately associated with the life of the people" (Figure 125).[28] These may have represented the spiritual assistants of the sticks' owners, painted in an appeal for success in the game.

As we shall see, red ochre was also extensively used in face painting and skin-costume decoration. In most cases, such painting consisted of simple lines and dots applied in conventional locations, but there are occasional highly stylized motifs. A notable exception is a small group of early quivers, painted with realistic images of animals and humans (Figure 126 bottom). The paintings show profile views of hunters armed with bows and arrows and rifles, and of animals — caribou, mountain sheep, and smaller animals — painted solidly in red. Such quivers are generally poorly documented, but they appear to date from the mid-nineteenth century, and to originate with Alaskan Athapaskan groups; one example has a reliable Tanaina provenance.[29] In 1882, images similar to those on the quivers were observed painted in red and black on Ingalik grave boxes, where they were said to represent "scenes of hunting and fishing in the life of the deceased."[30] It should be noted that both Ingalik and Tanaina Athapaskans are located adjacent to Eskimos who characteristically produced realistic representational art.[31] The Athapaskan quivers may have been painted as a kind of advertisement of hunting prowess. At the same time, picturing a sought-after animal may reflect the desire for success in the hunt.

"Their Best Apparel"
Northern Athapaskan Clothing and Adornment of the early Contact Period

> . . . they all arrived slowly singing harmoniously . . . dressed in their best apparel for the occasion, consisting of white or new dressed skin coverings, Leggings Fringed, painted and garnished with Porcupine quillwork, bunches of Feathers stuck wildly into the Hair of their Heads which hangs in great luxuriance round their Capot.[32]

Northern Athapaskan artistic expression centred on self-adornment and clothing; the body provided a convenient, ever-present, highly visible background. Writing about the Ingalik, a Russian observer in the interior of Alaska in the 1840s noted that "all the natives are passionately fond of finery and bright colours," and this statement could well have applied to all Northern Athapaskans.[33] Across the Western Subarctic, at the time of contact with whites, the native peoples painted and tattooed their bodies, dressed their hair with grease, ochre, beads, and feathers, and derived considerable satisfaction from possessing and wearing beautiful clothing.

Tattooing was accomplished by piercing the skin with a porcupine quill or fine sharp bone, then slowly drawing a sinew coated with charcoal under the surface. The custom appears to have been widespread. Women were tattooed more often than men, sometimes apparently as

127.
Male figurine, Tanaina, collected by Russian scientist Voznesenskiy, Kenai Peninsula, 1841. The Museum of Anthropology and Ethnography named after Peter the Great, Leningrad 2667-15. H:35

young as ten years old.[34] While there may well have been a link with the attainment of womanhood, this has not been clearly documented. Facial tattoos were most common and were considered a mark of beauty. Among the Kaska and Kutchin, men had their upper arms tattooed as a tally of enemies killed. The Kutchin and Carrier also tattooed specific parts of the body as a preventive against or cure for weakness or disease.[35] Tattooing may also have indicated group affiliation: Chipewyan men and women had "blue or black bars, or from one to four straight lines on their cheeks or forehead, to distinguish the tribe to which they belong."[36] Among the Tahltan, and other groups with strong ties to the Northwest Coast, tattooed designs could also pertain to clan affiliation. Carrier facial tattooing had no apparent reference to totem crests, but chest tattooing did, and forearm tattooing generally referred to a "personal totemic animal revealed in a dream, . . . the bearing of whose symbol was supposed to create a reciprocal sympathy and a sort of kinship between the totem and the tattooed individual."[37]

Few details of facial tattooing patterns exist, but they generally consisted of straight single or parallel lines, often applied vertically on the chin, or radiating from the corners of the mouth.

Face painting was a more common, if less permanent, form of body decoration. Very little is known, however, about the precise nature of Athapaskan facial painting. Red and black were the main colours. The raw material (generally ochre or charcoal) was in each case reduced to fine powder, then usually mixed with water and applied with a finger to the face. It seems that people very often painted their faces just to make themselves look attractive or distinguished for important or festive occasions. Men painted their faces more frequently than women:

> Each man has hanging to his neck two small bags containing black lead and red earth for painting themselves (their faces), each one paints according to his own fancy, most commonly the upper parts of the cheeks and around the eyes are black, a black strip along the top of the nose, the forehead is covered with narrow red stripes, and the chin with strips of red and black.[38]

As with tattooing, members of some groups indicated clan affiliation through the use of particular designs.[39] A doll collected in 1841 from the Tanaina, with facial painting of vertical and horizontal bars and small dots in black against an overall red background, provides a rare glimpse of this method of self-adornment (Figure 127).

The inherent symbolic or spiritual power of red and black is clearly evident in some instances of facial painting. In 1771, Hearne recorded how Chipewyan men painted their faces — "some all black, some all red, others with a mixture of the two" — in preparation for an attack on an Inuit camp. The same men, returning to their camp some days later, were in a spiritually vulnerable state, having taken the lives of other humans. They carefully painted the lower half of their faces with red ochre before allowing food or drink to pass their lips.[40] Tahltan shamans who had acquired special knowledge of the birth process from their spirit-helpers would paint red the body of a woman undergoing difficult childbirth.[41] The association of the colour red with blood, fire, warmth — life itself — is probably ancient and world-wide,[42] and it is no surprise to find such colour symbolism apparently prevalent among Northern Athapaskans. The meanings of the colour black in face painting are less evident. Among some groups of Northern Athapaskans, it seems to have been associated with anger, death, and sorrow. Men of several groups used it as war paint, Tanaina mourners and Tutchone widows painted their faces black,[43] and the Ingalik painted a black band across a dead person's eyes in preparation for burial.[44]

Hair dress was another striking and diverse form of self-adornment. Northern Athapaskans generally seem to have considered well-cared-for, carefully arranged, and decorated hair to denote distinction and status and to be an important aspect of overall appearance.[45]

Probably the most elaborate hair-dos were those found among western groups. Some Tanaina, Kutchin, and Han men, for example, wore their hair long, bound at the nape of the neck with a band of dentalium shells. The hair was greased, the parting marked with red ochre, and fine bird down sprinkled liberally overall. Feathers stuck in the back were said to indicate clan affiliation.[46] Hair was generally worn long. Cut or singed hair was a sign of grief, and cutting off a man's long hair was a mortal insult.[47]

In general, men seem to have paid greater attention to hair dress than women, although the hair of Carrier women impressed Alexander Mackenzie:

> . . . the hair of the women was tied in large loose knots over the ears, and plaited with great neatness from the division of the head, so as to be included in the knots. Some of them had adorned their tresses with beads, with a very pretty effect.[48]

Fewer details on hair dress are available for Athapaskan groups farther to the east. Slavey men and women tied their hair and decorated it with feathers.[49] Some early illustrations show Hare and Dogrib men with their hair cut very short in a circle around the crown, sometimes decorated with white down (Figure 128).

Nose ornaments, earrings, necklaces, hair ties, and pendants were also worn by men and women. These were often made of imported, and therefore precious, materials such as dentalium and abalone shells, glass beads, and copper. Hair dress, facial painting, tattooing and ornaments must have combined in a musical and colourful display that artefacts can only hint at. Fortunately, some early descriptions are wonderfully evocative. In 1807, a fur trader, Willard-Ferdinand Wentzel, described young Slavey men dressed to impress:

> [They] tie their hair, wear ornaments, such as feathers, beads in their ears, and paint or tattoo their faces. . . . Around their head, they wear a piece of beaver, otter, or marten skin decorated with a bunch of feathers before and behind. . . . Their robes and capots are ornamented with several bunches of leather strings garnished with porcupine quills of different colours, the ends of which are hung with beaver claws. About their neck they have a well-polished piece of caribou horn, which is white and bent around the neck; on their arms and wrists they tie bracelets and armbands made also of porcupine quills; around their waist they have also a porcupine quill belt curiously wrought and variegated with quills of different colours.[50]

The most important element of personal adornment was clothing. For Northern Athapaskans, clothing was far more than an efficient body covering that provided effective protection from cold in winter and insects in summer. Most people appear to have derived considerable aesthetic enjoyment from well-made, beautifully decorated clothing, and such garments were a source of pride for both maker and wearer. It was in the construction and decoration of clothing that the technical skills and artistic talents of Northern Athapaskan women were given fullest expression.

Clothing made from choice skins, richly embellished with quillwork and rare and costly beads and shells, reflected a man's wealth, his hunting and trading abilities, and his wife's skills as skin dresser and seamstress. Clothing was also an indicator of social standing, as hunting success brought prestige in Athapaskan society. Those who could afford

128.
Kurratah, a Hare Indian, winter 1825-1826. Watercolour over pencil by George Back. Public Archives of Canada C93034.

them travelled with a set of "dress" clothes, which they put on in camp or in anticipation of a meeting with other natives or fur traders.[51]

Underlying the aesthetic appreciation of clothing and the use of clothing to proclaim wealth and social standing were some very interesting attitudes concerning the relationship between an individual and his clothes. Clothing seems to have been a "second skin," closely linked to the soul and personality of its owner.[52] It played an important role at certain life crises, particularly during a girl's puberty observances and at death. The special large skin hood worn by girls in puberty seclusion has already been referred to. A girl wore old clothing while "under the hood": at the termination of puberty seclusion, she was given a new set of clothes, symbolizing the end of childhood and the beginning of a new life as an adult. Tahltan and Tutchone girls, and possibly those of other groups in aboriginal times, wore an elaborately decorated neck ring to mark the attainment of womanhood and readiness for marriage (Figure 129). To leave this life dressed in one's best apparel appears to have been a universal Athapaskan desire: "Their one concern is that they may go to their grave in their best clothes, and a doomed Indian bends every effort to gather together some finery in which to be buried."[53]

129.
Girl's neck ring, Tahltan, c. 1900. National Museum of Natural History, Smithsonian Institution, Washington, D.C. 248388.
W:30; D. 26

"This ring, which is the most highly prized of the ornaments of the woman, is worn as a sign of maturity after the period of confinement following puberty, for about a year, but never after marriage." (Emmons 1911:105)

The concept that a person's clothing could be manipulated to do him either good or harm also appears to be widespread. Among the Carrier, for example, one treatment for curing involved stuffing the moccasins of a sick person with feather down and hanging them up for the night. If the down was warm in the morning, this meant the "wandering soul" had returned, and the moccasins would be quickly placed back on the feet of the sick person.[54] To the north, a Tutchone, Tagish, or Tanaina shaman would predict the condition of a sick person by taking a piece of the individual's clothing and sleeping on it.[55] Personal clothing could also be manipulated if it fell into the hands of an enemy. By being "hidden in certain unlucky places, by the side of dreaded reptiles or their skins, amidst the mutterings of imprecatory words," the clothing could bring its owner harm.[56]

Clothing could become imbued with the abilities of the owner and these abilities could be transferred to a new owner. Thus, among the Koyukon, "the old trousers of good runners are much sought by young men, who expect to acquire by using them, the running qualities. Mothers also beg for these, and out of them make pants for their boys, which will give to these the *K'ot* or running ability."[57] A similar attitude towards clothing prevails among the modern Koyukon. The ethnologist Richard Nelson, who spent the winter of 1976 in Koyukon territory, noted that:

> Putting on another person's mittens can either take away his luck or give him yours. Once I was travelling with a man whose hands became painfully cold, so I offered him my extra mittens. He finally took them, explaining that since I was leaving Huslia I could get along without luck in things like trapping. But a short while later he decided to take them off and endure the cold instead.[58]

Clothing belonging to another could even confer on the new wearer the protection accorded its owner. Early in the nineteenth century, the trader Daniel Harmon recorded that among the Carrier a criminal could seek sanctuary in the house of a chief and, if permitted to stay, could not be molested. Protection would end, however, as soon as the wrongdoer left the house, unless the chief permitted him to wear one of his garments:

> This garment of the Chief, will protect a malefactor from harm, while he wears it; for no person would attack him, while clothed with this safe guard, sooner than he would attack the chief himself; and if he should, the chief would revenge the insult, in the same manner as if it were offered directly to himself.[59]

Not surprisingly, given this close connection between an individual and his clothing, garments were treated with care and respect. Male and female clothing was stored and washed separately, lest a man's garments become tainted with menstrual blood, which would have dire consequences for his hunting.[60] Clothing left lying around was susceptible to the machinations of one's human enemies and to the influence of evil spirits. Exchanging or giving away personal garments was a matter of some import. Among the Han and Kutchin, an exchange of garments symbolized close friendship between individuals, or, in a formal situation such as the meeting of leaders from different groups, peaceful intent.[61]

Northern Athapaskan clothing generally took the form of a fitted two-piece outfit (Figures 130 and 131). The upper garment, a pullover shirt or tunic, reached to a man's mid-thigh or knee; women wore theirs longer. The lower garment was long leggings or trousers sewn to a moccasin-like foot covering. Hoods, caps, and other head coverings were almost always separate from the upper garment.[62] Mittens, suspended by cords around the neck, were a part of male and female winter and summer costume. (Gloves were not worn by pre-contact Athapaskans, except perhaps by those living in the extreme west, such as the Tanaina and Ingalik). Traditional garments did not have pockets: face paints, fire-making equipment, charms, and other small personal belongings were carried in bags and pouches suspended from the neck or looped under a waist belt.[63] A robe was worn overall.

Caribou and moose were the universally preferred clothing materials. These animals provided large hides, which, when tanned, were flexible, durable, and attractive. Summer clothing was of de-haired skin, winter clothing of furred skin — preferably of caribou hide, which was both warm and light. In winter, two layers of skin would be worn — an inner layer with the fur against the body, and an outer layer with the fur to the outside.

Young babies were diapered with soft moss and wrapped in furs or tanned skin. In the eastern part of the region, they were carried on the mother's back, inside her dress, supported by a broad belt. In many

130.
Kutchin man. Watercolour by Edward Adams, 1850-1854. Courtesy of the Glenbow Museum, Calgary AE58.31.1.

131.
Shirt and moccasined pants, Tanaina type, c. 1830. Völkerkundlishe Sammlungen im Städt Reiss-Museum, Mannheim, FRG V-AM-3219 a, b. Shirt: L:123; Pants: L:98

western groups, mothers also carried their infants in a chair-like birch-bark backpack or other forms of stiffened carriers. Once able to walk, children were clothed in miniature versions of adult garments, with hoods and mittens often sewn to the shirts to ensure maximum protection from the environment.

There were, of course, regional variations on this general clothing pattern, as people responded to local climate and resource differences and to contact with neighbouring non-Athapaskan natives. In central British Columbia, for example, Carrier had limited access to caribou and moose. Traditionally, they wore garments pieced from the skins of smaller fur-bearing animals, or from salmon. Further to the northeast, the Beaver and the Hare Indians derived their names from dressing almost exclusively in the furs of those animals. Inland Tlingit, Tutchone, Ahtena, and Sekani as well as other groups wore skirts and robes of groundhog and ground-squirrel skins. In Alaska, Athapaskan groups such as the Ingalik and Koyukon adopted many clothing styles from their Eskimo neighbours.

Early ethnographic collections contain some intriguing garments, which reflect regional clothing developments. For example, an early nineteenth-century shirt type that appears to have originated with the Tanaina differs in several respects from "classic" Athapaskan garments. It is of rectangular cut, has coarse stitching and quillwork, and parallel, horizontal front decorative panels (Figures 132 and 134). Such shirts, and other garments (particularly the combination lower garment), were traded by the Tanaina and interior Athapaskan groups to Tlingit, and sometimes appear in early illustrations of Northwest Coast natives (Figure 135).

In the early contact period, garments were decorated with ochre, moosehair, porcupine and bird quillwork, skin fringes, dentalium shells, and natural seed beads. Everyday clothing was far less decorated than was dress clothing, and winter garments were less elaborately decorated than summer garments. De-haired skin obviously lent itself to the application of ornament, and summer was the time for large gatherings at

132.
Shirt, Tanaina type, c. 1800. Courtesy of the Trustees of the British Museum, London, 1982 Am 28.16.

Three examples of this early type have been located: two in Leningrad and this one. All are constructed of heavy skin in a basically rectangular cut, decorated with five to seven panels of quillwork across the front, the backs undecorated. The quillwork is rather coarse in technique, consisting of relatively wide lanes, wrapping around a foundation of bird and/or rawhide. On this example, the heavy ochring inside and out suggests waterproofing for a wet coastal climate.

133.
Woman's summer dress clothing, Kutchin type, late 19th century. Manitoba Museum of Man and Nature, Winnipeg H4-38.30. Dress: L:140; W:120

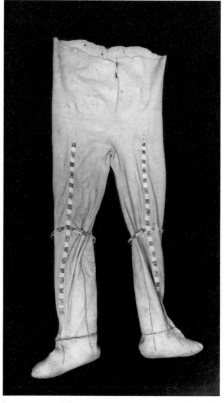

134.
Shirt, Tanaina. The Museum of Anthropology and Ethnography named after Peter the Great, Leningrad 633-31. L:127

This shirt was collected by Yuri Lisianskiy, who spent the winter of 1804-1805 on Kodiac Island. In Lisianskiy's published journal, an entry for May 1805 records the collection of clothing: "We had hardly finished the stowage of our cargo, when furs were brought to us from the Bay of Kenay, or Cook's River. There were also some curious dresses of the natives, several of which I purchased from curiosity." (Lisianskiy 1814:187). This is probably the earliest documented example of Northern Athapaskan clothing.

135.
Tzachey, a Tlingit chief in Norfolk Sound (wearing the same type of garment as in Figures 132 and 134). Watercolour by Sigismund Bacstrom, 1793. From the collection of Mr. and Mrs. Paul Mellon, Oak Spring, Uppersville, Virginia.

fish camps and trade rendezvous — occasions for which elaborately decorated dress clothing would be much in demand.

A discussion of Athapaskan clothing decoration leads inevitably to the question of whether such ornamentation was purely decorative or had greater meaning for the people who made and wore the garments. One would certainly expect the latter to be the case, given the close personal links between an individual and his clothing, and the importance attached to achieving spiritual harmony with animals. The propitiation and honouring of animal spirits through the decoration of animal-skin clothing is well known from other native North American societies,[64] but is difficult to document for Subarctic Athapaskans. The fear of offending animal spirits is implicit in the conscientious care given personal clothing, but there is very little explicit evidence that the quillwork, ochre, beads, and fringes applied to clothing were intended specifically to communicate with animal spirits.

There is, however, some support for the view that, in a general sense, costume decoration was intended to please spirits as well as humans. Much early clothing from Athapaskan groups west of the Rocky Mountains has at least a small amount of red ochre decoration. This may also have been true of pre-contact Eastern Athapaskan clothing, although fur-trade-era examples do not have this form of decoration. Ochre was appreciated for the physical protection it provided: mixed with grease, it was an effective waterproofing agent and preservative for skin and wood. Thus, snare and pack lines and snowshoe frames were stained red; and ochre was sometimes smeared on skin clothing to keep it from becoming hard and stiff when wet. Red ochre was, however, valued more for its decorative abilities and spiritual power. On garments, it outlines vulnerable points, shirt and dress neck and wrist openings, hemlines, and seams. Such markings sometimes appear on the inside of the garment, and they may simply represent pattern markings drawn on the skin before it was cut.[65] However, their function was probably spiritual as well as practical. It is interesting to compare this feature of Athapaskan clothing with similar painting on garments from an interior Salish group in southern British Columbia. Among the Thompson River Indians, such painting was said to be "for ornament . . . to hide the seams, also because it is customary to paint for protective or good luck purposes, where there is a joining or parting. These lines are sometimes called 'earth lines.' "[66] Some Athapaskan mittens and gloves have red ochre covering the tips of the fingers and delineating the bone structure of the hand (Figure 136).

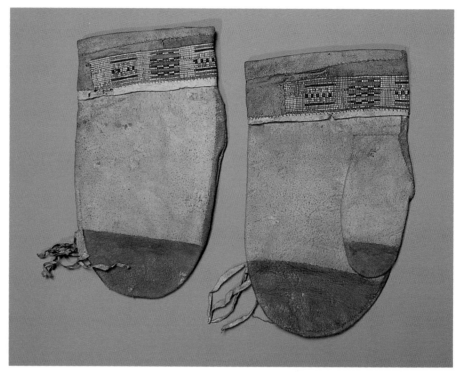

136.
Mittens, Tanaina, probably collected by the Russian scientist, T.G. Voznesenskiy, on the Kenai Peninsula in 1841. The Museum of Anthropology and Ethnology named after Peter the Great, Leningrad. 2667.13. L:23; W:13

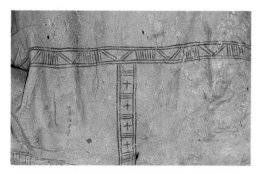

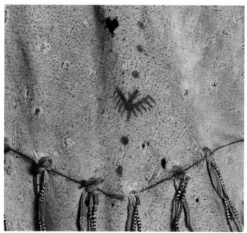

137.
Painting on clothing:
top: Shirt (detail, upper back), Tanaina type, c. 1800. Canadian Museum of Civilization. National Museums of Canada, Ottawa VI-Y-5.
bottom: Shirt (detail, upper back), Tanaina type, c. 1830. The small bird motif painted with red ochre is an unusual feature and probably represents a clan symbol or spirit helper of the garment's wearer.
Völkerkundlische Sammlungen im Städt Reiss-Museum, Mannheim, FRG V-Am-3219.

While the ochre is usually applied either in a solid colour block or in straight or dotted lines, somewhat more specific motifs occasionally appear. An early, possibly Tanaina, shirt has bands of red-ochred geometric patterns across the shoulders and upper back (Figure 137 top). Some shirts and dresses of the Tanaina and Ahtena have a vertical line that flares to a three-pronged fork pattern at its upper end, drawn in ochre down the middle of the lower skirt, front and back. This same mark is found incised on a wide variety of Bering Sea Eskimo artefacts, where, in some contexts, it is thought to represent a raven's foot and to signify membership in the raven "clan."[67] Tanaina and Ahtena also had clans associated with raven, and a similar meaning for this motif on their garments is entirely possible. Another Alaskan Athapaskan garment, a man's shirt that may be Tanaina, has a small bird motif drawn in ochre on the back (Figure 137 bottom). Perhaps it represents a spirit-helper or clan symbol of the garment's owner. Hints in the literature affirm that other groups, for which there are no extant examples, also painted their clothing. In 1793, Alexander Mackenzie noted a Carrier guide wearing a painted beaver robe.[68] Early-twentieth-century Tahltan recalled that designs in red and black were sometimes drawn on clothing, but asserted that such designs were not the result of dreams. Shamans, however, "occasionally painted marks or designs on clothing which had connections with dreams or manitou."[69]

Porcupine quillwork was another major form of Athapaskan costume decoration. The quills were sorted according to size and dyed by boiling with various plants and berries, then flattened by being held between the teeth and pressed between a finger and a thumb-nail drawn down their length. A variety of techniques was used to apply the prepared quills to garments, and regional preferences are apparent. Some early Tanaina garments have parallel, horizontal lanes of rather coarse quillwork in which quills are wrapped around a rawhide or bird-quill filler.[70] Checkerboard and stepped-triangle motifs are common. The small bird motifs worked into two of the quilled bands on an early-nineteenth-century, probably Tanaina, garment are an extremely rare example of a realistic, identifiable image executed in quillwork (Figure 138 top).[71]

Later garments collected from Alaskan Athapaskan groups and those living in contiguous parts of the Yukon Territory and northern British Columbia are decorated with a form of woven quillwork in which the warp strands of sinew are anchored at either end to the tanned skin forming the base for the work. The flattened quills are woven in and out of these warp strands. An additional sinew weft follows each row of quills, passing over and under the warp in an opposite pattern, so as to hold the weave together.[72] Collections of Tanaina, Ingalik, and Ahtena clothing from the 1840s show very fine quillwork of this type as front and back yoke decoration, at the sleeve ends of shirts and dresses, and at the wrists of mittens and gloves, as well as on hoods, knife sheaths, and quivers (Figure 138 bottom).[73] Motifs consist of one or two geometric design units repeated in a symmetrical arrangement, usually in dark-brown and ochre-red dyed quills against a natural white background. This technique appears to have extended east as far as the Kutchin, where it appears but rarely. Much more common among the Kutchin appears to have been appliqué quillwork; flattened and folded quills were stitched directly to the garment, using sinew thread, in parallel rows.[74] Kutchin designs tend to be simple, with crosses and triangles as popular motifs (Figure 138 left).

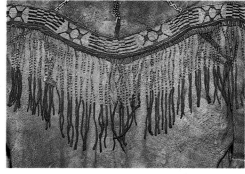

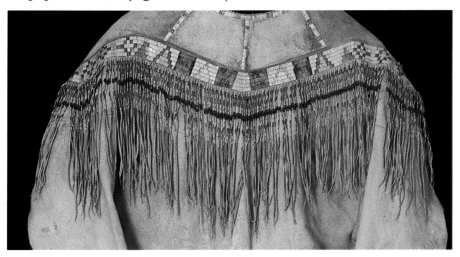

138.
Quillwork on clothing:
top: Shirt (detail, front panel), Tanaina, 1804-1805. The Museum for Anthropology and Ethnography named after Peter the Great, Leningrad 561.3.
bottom: Shirt (detail, quillworked breast-band), Ingalik, 1843-1844. The Museum of Anthropology and Ethnography named after Peter the Great, Leningrad 537.22.
left: Shirt (detail, quillworked breastband), Kutchin, 1860. The Trustees, National Museums of Scotland, Edinburgh 564.

Attempts to reconstruct the details of pre-contact Eastern Athapaskan costume decoration are difficult because so little well-documented material remains. Women were apparently adept at loom-woven quillwork: ". . . the Cinchures of garters are of Porcupine Quills wove with Sinews & are the neatest thing of the Kind that ever I saw."[75] A bow loom, formed from a bent stick and strung with a warp of sinew threats, was used for this work, and the completed weaving was sewn to a backing of tanned skin. Belts, headbands, baby-carrying straps, and wristlets were produced in this manner, and very probably similar woven bands were sewn to pouches and garments.[76] A man's costume with quill-woven bands sewn to the shoulders may represent an early clothing style from the Great Slave Lake area (Figure 139). Appliqué quillwork appears on some early pouches and on babiche bags, and very probably was used on clothing as well.[77] A few early specimens suggest that early designs may have been very simple: for example, a horizontal, zigzag line or repeated diamonds in coloured quills against a natural white quill background occurs on early belts and pouches. The intricate patterns of small, repeated geometric figures, which appear in fur-trade-period loom-woven quillwork from the Eastern Athapaskan area may be a later development reflecting increased exposure to Cree and Métis work.

Obviously, the techniques of woven and appliquéd quillwork lead to a geometricization of motifs; perhaps such designs developed from stylized representations of animals or other animate or inanimate beings whose protection or assistance was sought by the wearer of the garment. Undoubtedly, specific patterns were referred to by particular names by Athapaskan craftswomen just as, for example, Tlingit basket makers had names for particular motifs. Whether the application of a particular pattern to a particular garment was a statement of affiliation or a communication with the spirit world, however, is something we will probably never be able to prove. Most early clothing artefacts, although beautifully constructed and decorated, seem curiously impersonal: quillwork designs are repeated, albeit in different combinations, from one costume to the next; like other decoration, such as ochre painting and fringes, quillwork is applied in conventional locations. The fact that during the early-fur-trade period quillwork was frequently replaced by glass beads in greatly simplified patterns suggests that any symbolic significance that had been attached to particular motifs was lost by the time of contact.

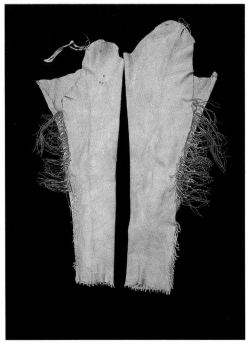

139.
Man's shirt and leggings, probably from the Lake Athabasca/Great Slave Lake Region, mid-19th century type. McCord Museum, McGill University, Montreal M7066, M7067. Shirt: L:81; Leggings: L:90

In 1807, fur trader George Keith described Slavey men's clothing: "Their summer dress consists of a leather shirt with long fringes before and behind, neatly garnished with coloured moosehair and porcupine quills . . ." (1889-1890 (2) 92) Note the similarity with the men's garments depicted in Figure 147.

It is possible that many examples now preserved in museums, although Athapaskan in origin, may never have been intended to be worn by a particular individual. In several areas, clothing was an important element in long-established native trade networks[78] and garments were undoubtedly made up expressly for trade. Furthermore, early descriptions indicate that it was largely through hair dress, facial painting, jewellery, and a variety of attached plant and animal talismans that an individual added his own personal touches to a basic costume. The Koyukon wore "Necklaces of bear's claws and teeth, sable tails, wolf ears, bands of beads and dentalia, embroidery of dyed porcupine quills, small ermine skins, hawk and eagle feathers, beaver's teeth . . . and the bright green scalps of the mallard."[79] Much of such added ornament must have served as a form of identification with the individual's sources of power. A description of a Tanaina shaman's costume states this explicitly:

> The shaman's costume is ornamented sometimes by the addition of painted designs, feather armbands, and necklaces of teeth, claws or feathers of the animal with which the medicine man stands in special relation through his dreams.[80]

Again, it may have been in a general rather than specific sense that quillwork addressed the spirit world. Rare, direct evidence is found in Samuel Hearne's account of Chipewyan men returning to camp in a state of ritual impurity, having killed a group of Inuit. The women immediately set to work to make "a suit of ornaments for their husbands, which consisted of bracelets for their wrists and a band for their forehead, composed of porcupine quills and moosehair, curiously wrought on leather."[81] These quillwork ornaments were but one element in a pattern of ritual and taboo designed to pacify the spirits of the dead. The ornaments were ultimately burned, presumably as an offering to placate the spirits, along with pipe stems and dishes used during the taboo period.[82]

"From the Land of the Ghosts"
Decorative Art in the Fur-Trade Era

> On landing, Fraser's men, to impress the natives with a proper idea of their wonderful resources, fixed a volley with their guns, whereupon the whole crowd of Carrier fell prostrate to the ground. To allay their fears and make friends, tobacco was offered them, which, on being tasted, was found too bitter, and thrown away. Then, to show its use, the crew lighted their pipes and, at the sight of the smoke issuing from their mouths, the people began to whisper that they must have come from the land of ghosts, since they were full of the fire wherewith they had been cremated.[83]

During the late-eighteenth and early-nineteenth centuries, white explorer-traders extended their quest for furs into the most remote and inaccessible regions of northern North America. Most of the Subarctic Athapaskans they encountered had never before seen white men, although word of these strangers and their marvellous technology had often preceded them to the interior. The first meetings of white man and Indian were generally marked by mutual respect, curiosity, and caution, as well as by a spirit of reciprocity. Each had something the other wanted. The native people were quick to recognize the potential of the white man's technology: guns, iron tools, cloth, and beads would make day-to-day life easier and materially richer. The white traders knew that without the Indians' assistance and knowledge, they had little hope of making their way through difficult, unknown territory or of reaping the rich fur harvest of the north country.

Direct contact with Europeans came first to those Dene closest to Hudson's Bay Company posts in the east. Some Chipewyan had had occasional contacts with traders on Hudson Bay by the end of the seventeenth century, and in 1717 Prince of Wales Fort (later Churchill) was established expressly to encourage Chipewyan to trade. On the West Coast, Tanaina, the only Athapaskans living on salt water, approached Captain Cook's ship in 1778, anxious to exchange furs for iron. By the late eighteenth century, traders from the east were penetrating deep into

Athapaskan territory, along the Mackenzie River and in the Peace River country and northern interior British Columbia, making contact with eastern Kutchin, Mountain, Hare, Slavey, Beaver, Sekani, and Carrier groups. During the same period, Russians were establishing trading posts that brought them into contact with some interior Alaskan groups. American and British trading vessels were plying west-coast waters in a highly lucrative and competitive trade, initially for sea-otter skins and, as the sea otter became scarce, for mainland furs. These were obtained indirectly from interior Athapaskans: coastal Eskimo, Eyak, Tlingit and Tsimshian acted as middlemen.

Most of the early contacts were brief and sporadic: trading ships came and went, as did overland expeditions. Interior groups were discouraged from coming to posts on the periphery by distance and by intermediary native groups who jealously guarded their lucrative positions as middlemen in the trade. Hoping to overcome these barriers and to more efficiently tap the rich fur potential of the northern forest, competing fur traders established a series of permanent trading forts in the heart of Athapaskan territory during the late eighteenth and early nineteenth centuries.

Involvement in the fur trade and regular exposure to fur-trade "society" resulted in a number of important modifications to traditional Athapaskan culture. Goods that had reached Athapaskan hands in small quantities were now available in greater variety and number. In exchange for beaver, fox, marten, and other furs and by supplying forts with meat and fish, native hunters could obtain guns, knives, axes, files, chisels, copper kettles, steel needles, awls and scissors, beads, woven cloth, ready-made garments, embroidery silks, and ribbons. Yet, although European technology in some instances made it easier to procure food, shelter, and clothing, contact with whites threatened the very existence of the native people: foreign diseases such as smallpox, influenza, and measles destroyed large segments of the population within a few decades of initial contact.

Participation in the fur trade brought Athapaskans into contact with new cultures, life-styles, and belief systems. At the trading post they might encounter the white trader (often of Scottish heritage) and his assistant, company engagés (packers, canoeists, and boatmen) from a variety of cultural backgrounds – Indians from eastern Canada (mainly Cree and Iroquois), French-Canadian voyageurs, and Red River Métis – and representatives of diverse Athapaskan groups. Missionaries – mainly Roman Catholic and Anglican in Canada, and Russian Orthodox and Anglican in Alaska – soon followed the fur traders into most areas, and by the late 1880s most Athapaskans were at least nominally Christian.

The consequences of contact with whites and participation in the

140.
Container, Slavey type, c. 1860. McCord Museum, McGill University, Montreal. ACC 1514. D:17

fur trade were obviously important and far-reaching. Nevertheless, until well into the twentieth century, many groups continued to live in a manner not radically different from that of old. Most people spent much of the time "in the bush," coming in to the trading post two or three times a year to exchange furs and provisions for supplies and luxury goods, and to socialize. Survival and success in life still depended on bush skills, on hunting and trapping abilities. Traditional animistic beliefs coexisted with Christianity.

The fur trade had its most obvious impact on the aboriginal material culture. As early as 1859, fur trader Robert Campbell was writing from Fort Chipewyan that, "You will be perhaps surprised to learn, that even in this Northern District the 'Indians' appreciate the convenience of the articles of sivilized (sic) usage so much, that hardly a trace now remains of their former dress, domestic utensils, or weapons of war, or the chase."[84] A few traditional crafts disappeared rather rapidly as non-indigenous substitutes became available. Spruce-root basketry, for example, was a dying art by 1860 in the Mackenzie River and Great Slave Lake area (Figure 140).[85] Copper kettles required no effort to produce, and were more durable and more efficient for boiling water and cooking food. Usually, however, trade goods augmented, rather than replaced items of native manufacture. Iron was preferred for arrowheads, knives, and awls, but stone, bone, and antler continued to be used for these items. Guns supplemented the native bow and arrow, spear, and club, but within some groups at least were more a prestige item than an efficient hunting and fighting weapon.[86] European technology could not better some indigenous products: snowshoes (Figure 141), netted babiche game bags (Figure 142), and flexible, tanned skin footwear were perfectly adapted to the northern climate and life-style.

Some traditional skills in working stone, bone, and skin had to be adapted to accommodate newly acquired habits and economic activities. The use of tobacco was first introduced to Athapaskans by the Eskimo, who obtained it through trade networks from Asia.[87] Supplies were greatly increased with the expansion of the fur trade, and smoking became, for both men and women, a popular pastime and a symbol of friendship and well-being. The limited supply of foreign-made pipes was soon augmented by locally made versions (Figures 119 and 120). Those from the Great Slave Lake and Mackenzie River area, for example, sometimes

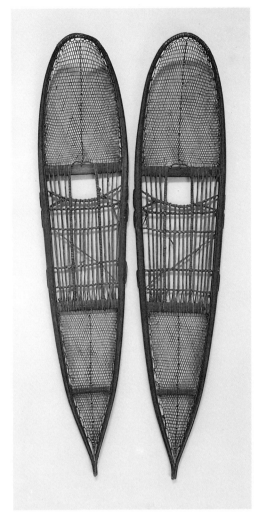

141.
Snowshoes, Kutchin, collected by Richard G. McConnell at Lapierre House, Yukon Territory. Canadian Museum of Civilization, National Museums of Canada, Ottawa VI-I-10. L:15

Staining of snowshoe frames with ochre was common, as was the application of ochre in a line of dots down the centre of the mesh.

142.
Netted babiche game bag, Great Slave Lake-Mackenzie River type, mid-19th century type. Canadian Museum of Civilization, National Museums of Canada, Ottawa VI-Z-62. W:59.5

Made of babiche and smoked skin, such bags are usually decorated through appliqué or woven porcupine quillwork across the top and through alternation of netted patterns, colouring of babiche in horizontal lines, and the attachment of hair or (later) wool tassels.

143.
Man's summer dress clothing, Kutchin, collected in Eastern Alaska by Bernard R. Ross, 1862. The Trustees, National Museums of Scotland, Edinburgh 848.12. Shirt: L:135; Knife: L:37

imitated in stone the form of clay pipe traded by the Hudson's Bay Company. The use of dog teams to service long trap lines was also introduced to Athapaskans via the fur trade, along with an equipment of carioles, harnesses, whips, and blankets, all of which were soon being produced locally.

Adornment styles and the shape, materials, and decoration of clothing and related accoutrements reflect most clearly the impact of the fur trade on Northern Athapaskan culture. Facial painting, tattooing, and elaborate hair dress were discouraged by traders and missionaries, and often were given up soon after contact. Clothing changed radically and rapidly, particularly among those groups most closely associated with the trading posts, although for a time old and new fashions coexisted, and new materials were simply added to traditional items. The Kutchin, for example, were slower than many other Athapaskan groups to give up their traditional dress, but placed a high value on glass beads and dentalium shells, available from Russian traders in Alaska as well as being imported by the Hudson's Bay Company. These glass and shell beads replaced porcupine quills on shirts, trousers, and knife sheaths and formed a highly visible, concentrated form of wealth (Figure 143).

Within a few decades, however, white (unsmoked) skin clothing decorated with geometric patterns of porcupine quills, red ochre, and fringes strung with natural seed beads gave way to Euro-Canadian-influenced garments of heavily smoked skin or cloth decorated with elaborate, multicoloured floral beadwork or silk embroidery, and silk-ribbon appliqués. New materials, patterns, and techniques were applied to such traditional items as mittens, garters, baby-carrying straps, and bags, but just as often they were used in the construction of apparel without antecedent in the aboriginal culture: for example, short cloth leggings, dog blankets, tabbed pouches, and European-styled jackets. In many cases, the contrast between traditional and fur-trade-era decorated material is so striking that, at least on the surface, there seems to be no thread of continuity between the two. Clearly, an intriguing story of cultural exchange and adaptation lies behind these dramatic post-contact developments in Northern Athapaskan decorative art.

The establishment of permanent trading posts in Athapaskan territory made it relatively easy for native craftswomen to obtain Euro-Canadian fabrics, decorative materials, and clothing. Clothing and its decoration would obviously be influenced by what the trading store had in stock. But the ways in which these new materials were incorporated into the native wardrobe reflect influences beyond the shelves of the trading post.

Fur-trade personnel and the coming and going of the fur brigades exposed Athapaskans to apparel and adornment that were a composite of native, Métis, and Euro-Canadian tastes. Ever fashion-conscious, Athapaskans liked much of what they saw. The origins of many elements of post-contact Northern Athapaskan costume are to be found among other groups involved in the fur trade. This can be seen most clearly in clothing developments at the centre of the northern fur-trade industry; that is, in the Great Slave Lake and Mackenzie River area. Knowledge of pre-contact native clothing from this area is incomplete, but an assemblage of distinctively decorated garments, bags, and pouches from the mid-nineteenth century appears to combine traditional and fur-trade-era elements (Figure 144). The earliest documented specimen is a Slavey "ornamented leather gown" collected at Fort Simpson in 1860 (Figure 145). A similar garment appears in a drawing of Slavey women done by the Catholic missionary Emile Petitot in the early 1860s (Figure 120). Petitot was obviously very taken by the clothing of Slavey women. He

144.
top: Baby bag, Slavey type, collected
c. 1870. Canadian Museum of Civilization.
National Museums of Canada, Ottawa
VI-N-112. L:57
left: Pipe bag Slavey type, mid-19th century
type. The Trustees, National Museums of
Scotland, Edinburgh 1928.269. L:41
bottom: Bag, Slavey type, mid-19th century
type. W:35. McCord Museum, McGill
University, Montreal. ME 938.1.20. W:35

describes a dress made of smoked moosehide of a beautiful saffron-yellow colour, hanging below the knee and tightly belted around the middle. This dress was bordered with black and red cloth; white, blue, and red glass beads; fringes hung with copper buttons; swan's leg bones, deer hooves, and porcupine quills — all of which, according to Petitot, gave the young women a "lively and elegant" appearance.[88]

Several examples of this type of dress have been preserved. They exhibit certain structural features, such as shoulder seaming, collars, cuffs, and front-opening edges, that are clearly the result of European influence. Other elements, such as the use of tanned moose or caribou skin, the cut and decoration of the lower skirt, and the presence of decorated yokes, front and back, are reminiscent of traditional clothing of the Kutchin and some Athapaskan groups farther to the west. Access to non-traditional sewing materials is clearly evident in the decoration of the Slavey garments. The yoke is enlarged and elaborated to form a detachable or semi-detachable cape extending over the upper back and shoulders. It is heavily decorated, particularly on the back, with cloth appliqués, glass beads, yarn tassels, triangular pieces of tin, and skin fringing. Bead-decorated cloth epaulettes extend over the shoulders, and printed cotton fabric is commonly used as an edge-binding. There is a preference for juxtaposed red and dark-blue wool cloth, and the border

145.
Woman's dress (back view), Slavey, collected by Bernard R. Ross at Fort Simpson, NWT, 1860. The Trustees National Museums of Scotland, Edinburgh, 55837. L:124.5

between these two colours is frequently delineated by white beads in distinctive patterns.

This type of dress was bound at the waist by a belt of loom-woven quillwork with a long skin fringe, some strands of which were threaded with large glass beads and hollow bones (Figure 146). Such belts (obviously without the glass beads) are probably a very old costume element.

The Slavey appear to have had a penchant for fringes: early in the nineteenth century, a trader described Slavey women as being ''sometimes covered with fringes . . . almost from head to foot.''[89]

With these dresses, women and girls wore rectangular hoods of black, navy, or red stroud with ribbon appliqués in contrasting colours.[90] These show little relation in form or materials to traditional head coverings. However, cloth hoods decorated in distinctive regional styles were popular among the Indians of central and eastern Canada during most of the nineteenth century. The Athapaskan woman's hood probably derives from a more elaborately decorated Cree version, introduced to the far Northwest by James Bay Cree employed as boatmen and packers in the fur trade.

In Petitot's illustration, the woman's dress is knee-length, belted at the waist, and worn with a close-fitting lower garment (probably a slightly modified version of the traditional combination legging-moccasin), with fringed garters below the knee, decoration around the ankle, and a cloth overlay on the moccasin vamp. Petitot's sketch brings to mind Samuel Hearne's eighteenth-century account of a Chipewyan woman who, in the middle of winter, belted her dress "so high" that she froze her thighs

146.
Loom-woven quillwork belt, Athapaskan type, mid-19th century type. By courtesy of the Trustees of the British Museum, London 1921.11-4.1. L:85.5

and buttocks: "she took too much pains to shew a clean heel and good leg; her garters being always in sight . . ."[91] This early type of garment seems to have been replaced during the third quarter of the nineteenth century by short cloth leggings bordered with overlay-stitch beadwork and ankle-wrap moccasins decorated with floral bead or silk motifs.

Changes in men's clothing during this period tend to parallel those of the women. A Chipewyan-Métis man painted by Emile Petitot in 1862 is wearing a smoked skin shirt decorated with fringes and cloth epaulettes, cuffs, and a front placket (Figure 147). As with women's dress of the same period, two contrasting colours of cloth are juxtaposed and white beads are used as an outlining. Leggings are also of smoked skin, fringed up the outer leg.

Jackets of a European cut made of heavily smoked skin decorated with fringes and porcupine quillwork, bead appliqué, or silk embroidery (Figure 148), and dark-wool cloth leggings with floral beaded, knee-high side panels and ribbon rosettes (Figure 149) became increasingly popular among fur-trade personnel including whites, Métis, and Athapaskan men, in the Great Slave Lake and Mackenzie River area during the second half of the nineteenth century. Blanket "capotes" were an even more common Athapaskan man's garment during this period. As with women's dress, the common foot covering was the ankle-wrap moccasin, frequently decorated with floral silk embroidery or, somewhat later, beadwork (Figure 150).

These and later nineteenth-century eastern Athapaskan clothing examples reflect an increasing divergence from traditional styles and, most particularly, a growing preference for multicoloured floral patterns, worked in glass and faceted metallic beads on dark cloth (often wool cloth or velvet) backgrounds (Figures 152, 153, and 155). These developments can be traced to two important, interconnected influences: the mission school and the Métis.

Mission schools were established at several points in the Northwest Territories during the late nineteenth and early twentieth centuries. The Grey Nuns arrived in Fort Providence in 1867, at Lake Athabasca in 1874, and at Fort Resolution in 1903.[92] They established schools where native women and girls were taught Euro-Canadian domestic skills such as embroidery, sewing, and knitting in addition to catechism, reading, and mathematics.

The Métis population of the Northwest Territories was composed of the local descendants of white men (usually Scottish fur traders) who had taken native women as wives, and another group who traced their origins to the Red River area of Manitoba.[93] Métis families had emigrated west and north from the Red River throughout the nineteenth century. What was a gradual movement towards new and unsettled frontiers became a virtual exodus after the rebellions of 1870 and 1885. These people brought with them a love of gay, colourful clothing, and a decorative art heritage that reflected both their mixed Indian-white background and the needlework instruction provided by nuns in mission schools.[94] Sioux and other Plains Indians knew them as the "flower beadwork people." They produced a vast quantity of beautifully decorated equipment and apparel for their own use and for sale, and they continued these traditions in the north.

As they had done farther south, Subarctic Métis became cultural and linguistic intermediaries between the world of the white man and that of the Indian. The men were commonly employed in freighting and boating during the summer and with trapping during the winter; they also found jobs as interpreters and as hunters and guides for expeditions into the

147.
Chipewyan-Metis man, St. Joseph Mission, Great Slave Lake. Watercolour by Emile Petitot, 1862. Courtesy of Mme. Fanny Olivier, Marseilles.

148.
Jacket, collected in the Fort Nelson-Fort Liard-Fort Resolution area, 1906-1925. Courtesy of the Royal Ontario Museum, Toronto 955.177.23. H:66

Men's jackets that combined European and native materials, styling, and decorative techniques were the height of fur-trade fashion during the late 19th century. The style may have originated with a cloth military-style coat presented to Indian leaders in the mid-19th century by the Hudson's Bay Company, and soon copied in locally available materials by Athapaskan seamstresses.

149.
Leggings, man's, probably Slavey or Slavey-Métis, collected at Hay River, NWT, 1896-1908. Courtesy of the Glenbow Museum, Calgary AC 351 a, b. L:66

country. Métis families tended to settle in or near the forts; and Métis women and girls, more so than their native counterparts, could avail themselves of the needlework instruction offered by the nuns and of the sewing and decorative materials in the trading store.[95]

Métis women created a great amount of beautifully decorated material during the last half of the nineteenth century and the beginning of the twentieth century.[96] Much of their work is characterized by elaborate, carefully planned and executed floral silk-and-bead embroidery patterns; by an aesthetically pleasing combination of colours and materials on a single item; and by an overall high standard of craftsmanship.

In the North, many Métis intermarried with Athapaskans; this, as well as their life-style, brought them into contact with a great range of native groups. Athapaskan women were quick to admire, emulate, and absorb into their handwork new techniques, materials, and fashions. A broad regional style developed, "an amalgam of Indian, Canadian voyageur and Métis styles, tempered by what the trading post had in stock."[97]

Just how closely these decorative-art developments were associated with the centre of fur-trade, Métis, and mission-school activity can be seen by comparing turn-of-the-century Subarctic Métis and Athapaskan material from the Great Slave Lake and Mackenzie River area with that of the Tahltan, an Athapaskan group from the northern interior of British Columbia. The Tahltan were relatively isolated from many of the influences

150.
Decorated moccasins:
left: Slavey c. 1913. Canadian Museum of Civilization, National Museums of Canada, Ottawa VI-N-70. L:25.5
centre: Yellowknife, 1900-1911. Canadian Museums of Civilization, National Museums of Canada, Ottawa VI-S-7 a, b. L:25
right: group unknown, Mackenzie River-Great Slave Lake region, collected c. 1870. Canadian Museums of Civilization, National Museums of Canada, Ottawa VI-Z-80. L:24.5

151.
Tahltan ceremonial gear, collected by G.T. Emmons, 1903:
left: Bag. American Museums of Natural History, New York 16/9518. Bag: L:20.5; Strap: L:57
right: Knife sheath. National Museum of Natural History, Smithsonian Institution, Washington, D.C. 248442. Sheath: L:33; Strap: L:36

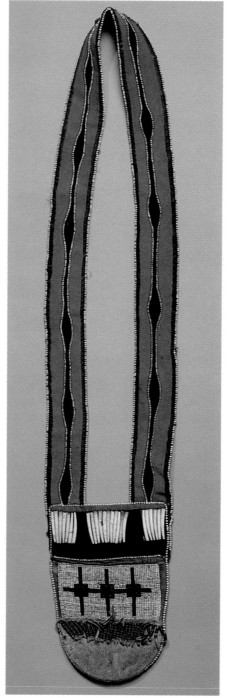
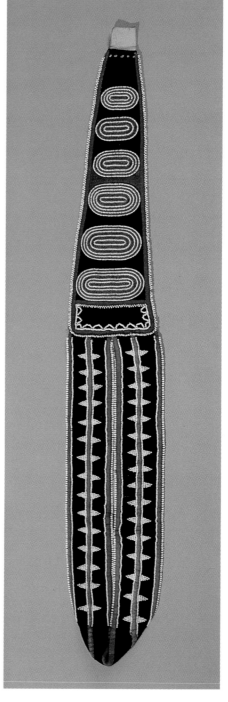

152. (opposite)
Woman's dress with detachable cape and belt, Great Slave Lake-Mackenzie River type (possibly Slavey), collected c. 1900 from the Fort Chipewyan area. Provincial Museum of Alberta, Edmonton H73.55.1 Dress: L:119; Belt: L:80

This magnificent outfit is a late development of a clothing style that first appears in the Great Slave Lake-Mackenzie River area about 1850 (see Figure 144). In its general features the style has remained remarkably consistent over half a century but the decorative shoulder cape is now fully detachable, and it and the cuffs made of black velvet are profusely decorated with floral beadwork.

153.
Baby bag, Kutchin, 1900-1911. Canadian Museum of Civilization, National Museums of Canada, Ottawa VI-I-5. H:55

of the fur trade. For most of the nineteenth century, coastal Tlingit aggressively resisted any attempt to undermine their favourable situation as middlemen in the trade between the interior Athapaskan groups and white traders on the Pacific coast. This, together with the difficulty of maintaining trading posts so far removed from eastern supply depots, effectively limited permanent fur-trading posts in Tahltan territory. The gold rush in the Cassiar district in 1873 and the much larger Klondike gold rush in 1898 finally broke the Tlingit monopoly, and foreigners — miners, other natives, fur traders, and missionaries — flooded into Tahltan territory.[98] By the early twentieth century, traditional everyday clothing had virtually vanished, replaced with ready-made Euro-Canadian garments. Ceremonial gear often consisted of Chilkat blankets, headdresses, and knives (all traded from coastal Tlingit). However, the Tahltan made very distinctive pouches, knife sheaths, and cartridge belts (Figure 151).[99] Although executed mainly in woven cloth and glass beads, these artefacts are worked in designs that probably echo very old decorative traditions. Certain motifs seem to be stylized plant and animal forms; others have counterparts in incised decoration of antler, horn, and bone; yet others suggest coastal Tlingit influences. The designs bear little or no resemblance to the floral designs influenced by the fur trade, Métis, and mission school that Athapaskan groups to the north and east were producing at this time.

Why did most Northern Athapaskans so readily and rapidly abandon artistic traditions that had been an integral part of their culture for centuries? Disruptions to native society as a result of disease and missionization paved the way for a relinquishing of old ideas and activities. Equally important was practicality. Native manufactures — coiled and bark basketry, woven quillwork, skin clothing — required tremendous time and energy from the craft worker. European technology, metals, fabrics, decorative materials, and ready-made garments significantly eased the lives of Indian women, who were the principal artisans and artists of Northern Athapaskan society. The new products in the trader's store must have appeared as irresistible time- and labour-saving innovations to these women. Moreover, the bright colours and new textures of the imported goods would have had great visual and tactile appeal, and the usefulness of wool as a light, warm, and washable covering was quickly recognized.

Beyond these practical and aesthetic considerations, the possession of Euro-Canadian products, and particularly the wearing of the latest fur-trade fashions, signified social status and prestige. As in pre-contact times, clothing reflected hunting and trapping abilities, trading skills, and personal wealth: "To become Fort hunter is the ambition of a northern Indian, for the situation is at once an acknowledgement of his skill, and places the finest and gayest clothing at his command."[100] Looking one's best, "appearing to advantage," particularly when in contact with people outside one's immediate circle, continued to be very important. Before arriving at the trading post, dog teams would be halted, people would change into their best clothing, which had been brought along for that purpose, hair and faces would be tidied, and the dogs would be adorned with brightly decorated "tuppies" and "standing irons" replete with ribbons, feather plumes, and fox tails (Figure 155). The team would make the final run with an impressive flourish, "dashing up to the big house, with cracking whips and jingling bells."[101]

White traders, who stood to gain if the natives pursued beaver and muskrat for furs rather than moose or caribou for garments, encouraged Athapaskans to adopt clothing acquired wholly or in part at the post. They capitalized on traditional attitudes towards clothing by presenting native leaders with special garments such as a red cloth military-style coat,[102] and by rewarding good hunters with blankets, shirts, cloth dresses, and "capotes."[103] As well, the fur trade generated a market for certain native manufactures, which became a source of income for some Athapaskan women. The manufacture of some products – moccasins, mittens, and snowshoes – was stimulated by the fur trade, while other items, such as spruce-root basketry and incised antler jewellery, for which there was limited demand or appreciation, were produced increasingly rarely.

The fur traders were dealing with a people long accustomed to trading in commodities. Native trade networks had existed in North America long before the arrival of white men, and many raw materials and finished

154.
The Fur Trader. Oil on canvas, by an anonymous artist, c. 1855. Courtesy of the Glenbow Museum, Calgary AN.55.31.3.

This painting bears a striking similarity to an oil painting depicting the soldier-surveyor, John Henry Lefroy in the Fort Chippewyan area in 1843 (Private Collection, England). The Glenbow Museum's painting depicts a different individual but in all other respects appears to be a copy of the Lefroy painting. The identity of the man in this painting is not known, but he resembles George Back, the explorer-artist who, as a member of the first and second Franklin overland expeditions, was in Fort Chipewyan in 1820, and again in 1825.

155.
above: Standing iron, for dog harness, Athapaskan-Metis type, late 19th century. McCord Museum, McGill University, Montreal ME966X.111.5 and 6. L:24; W:6
left: Dog blanket, or *tuppie,* collected by A.J. Stone in the Mackenzie River area, 1902. American Museum of Natural History, New York 50-3921. L:45; W:37

The practice of decorating sled dogs with gaily embroidered blankets or *tapis* (which became known as "tuppies") originated with the Red River Métis during the first half of the 19th century. The fashion diffused to the north with the fur trade. Sled dogs decked out with tuppies, standing irons of ribbons, pompoms and feathers, and large jingle bells were said to like their gay, musical adornments, and to be inspired by them "much as a Highland regiment is by its pipes" (Archer 1929:35).

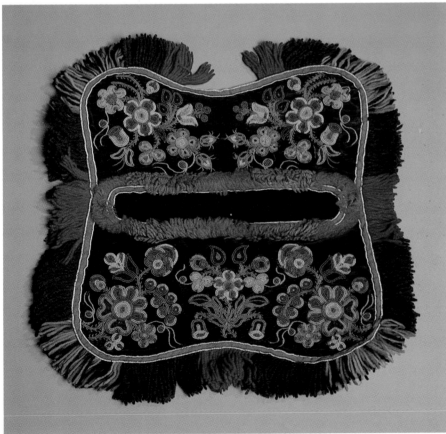

products ended up far from their point of origin. Athapaskans were astute bargainers who knew what they wanted, and white traders tried to have popular items in stock.

In the fur-trade era, as in prehistoric times, when people of differing cultures met, there was always potential for intercultural exchange. Northern Athapaskans were traditionally predisposed to "borrowing" from other cultures that which was practical or attractive, and to modify or adjust foreign technologies, social structures, and artistic traditions to suit their own needs.[104] In fact, cultural flexibility and adaptibility may well have been the keys to successful survival in a harsh, demanding, and unpredictable natural environment. Seen in this light, it is perhaps not surprising that Northern Athapaskan artisans responded with such resilience and creativity to the impact of the fur trade — not surprising, but nevertheless remarkable and somehow poignant. The bright and lively beaded and embroidered garments, dog blankets, and baby bags of the fur-trade era came from a people in the midst of social and cultural upheaval, a people suffering from drastic population losses. Yet they express the same love of beauty, the same delight in colour, texture, and symmetry, and the same striving for technical excellence that is apparent in earlier collections. The material evokes in the viewer feelings of awe and admiration similar to those Samuel Hearne must have felt when he met, locked in a lonely struggle for survival in the Subarctic wilderness, the Dogrib woman, who had decorated her fur garments with "great taste" and "no little variety of ornament."

Judy Thompson

Pretending to be Caribou

The Inuit Parka
as an Artistic Tradition

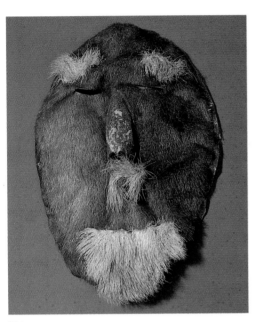

156.
Sealskin mask, male, Iglulik Inuit, collected
1921-1924. National Museum of Denmark,
Department of Ethnography, Copenhagen
P27.740. L:25.5; W:16.5

Although long known as "Eskimos," the native population of the Canadian Arctic refer to themselves as "Inuit," which means "the human ones." The forefathers of contemporary Inuit migrated into the Canadian Arctic from Northern Alaska about 1000 A.D. in pursuit of the bowhead whale. Spreading quickly across the continent to Greenland, they settled coastal areas of the Canadian Arctic, eventually displacing or, perhaps, absorbing an earlier Arctic population known as the Dorset culture.

Survival was the primary and overriding concern of the Inuit: survival through the propitiation of the spirit forces controlling the environment; survival through their dependence on the animals for food, shelter, and clothing; and, on an elemental level, survival through the union of male and female and the regeneration of human life. This fundamental concern permeated the traditional culture of Inuit and was made manifest in the design of Inuit art and material culture.

As European explorers discovered, the Inuit of the Canadian Arctic occupied the most severe environment of the North American continent. The Arctic winters were long and marked by frigid temperatures, high winds, and unexpected storms. From late fall through to spring, the sea was covered by several feet of ice and the land, buried under a thick cover of snow, seemed devoid of life. Above the Arctic Circle, the sun disappeared entirely from late November until early January. This was a period of great apprehension.

But the winter environment was not as barren as it seemed. Small animals burrowed beneath the snow; pregnant polar bears carved out their birthing dens; and Inuit families gathered in snow houses heated and lit by the oil lamp. As the caribou and other animal species upon which the Inuit relied for food migrated south, the hunter's attention turned to the ringed seal. One of the few species to remain in the Arctic throughout the year, the seal was the primary food source for Inuit during the winter. With the help of his dogs, who sniffed out the breathing holes of the seal, the hunter, clothed in thick caribou furs, waited at the breathing hole for the seal to reappear. The difficulty of winter hunting and the scarcity of animal resources ensured that hunting taboos were rigidly observed during the dark winter months.

In contrast, spring and summer were marked by an influx of bird and animal species, who returned to give birth to their offspring. Flocks of geese, as well as ducks, loons, and other birds sought out the solitude of northern lakes, ponds, and marshy areas, or the crevices of cliffs to lay their eggs and nurse their young. Herds of caribou were led by the pregnant females seeking the refuge of the tundra to drop their calves. During the summer, when land and sea abounded with new life, the sun never set below the horizon.

This dichotomy between the hardship of winter and the regenerative spirit of summer – and its parallel in the disappearance and reappearance of the sun – was marked by a pair of rituals celebrated annually in the Eastern and Central Canadian Arctic. The first ritual, held before the onset of darkness, was dedicated to Nuliajuk or Sedna, the spirit who monitored the release of sea animals to the Inuit. The celebration sought to ensure Nuliajuk's good will during the difficult winter ahead.

The key figures in this ritual were two men who dressed in women's parkas and wore sealskin masks marked with female facial tattoos.[1] These men, known in southern Baffin Island as *qailertetang*, carried a man's sealing harpoon in the right hand and a woman's skin scraper in the left. The ethnographer Franz Boas described the ritual on Baffin Island:

> Silently, with long strides the *qailertetang* approach the assembly, who, screaming, press back from them. . . . They match the men and women in pairs and these pairs run, pursued by the *qailertetang*, to the hut of the woman where they are for the following day and night man and wife (*nulianititijung*).[2]

This ritual release of conjugal bonds suggests a celebration of fecundity and the regeneration of life. Nuliajuk, progenitrix of sea life (and, in some regions, the mother of all peoples other than Inuit), looked with favour upon this practice. In a time of fear, the ritual served as a symbol of hope, a foreshadowing of the life that would again replenish the earth.

The return of the sun, a harbinger of winter's end, was also celebrated in villages across the Canadian Arctic. When the sun finally rose above the horizon, the fire in the lamp of each igloo was extinguished and later rekindled. As the American explorer Charles Hall reported: " 'New sun – new light,' implying a belief that the sun was at that time renewed for the year."[3] Among the Copper people, it was an old woman of the village who extinguished the light;[4] while among the Iglulik Inuit:

> . . . children must run into the snow huts and put out the lamps, so that they can be lighted anew; this is called *suvſɔraiſut*: those who blow out. The new sun must be attended everywhere by new light in the lamps.[5]

The selection of elderly women and young children is significant: the former represented the passing of life and the latter its regeneration. In the southern area of Baffin Island, however, ". . . two men start out, one of them dresses to represent a woman and go to every house in the village, blowing out the light in each."[6] This combination of two men, one dressed as a woman, recalls the *qailertetang*, the central figures of the Nuliajuk festival. In both celebrations, the appearance of a costumed figure, simultaneously male and female, revived the primeval time preserved in Inuit oral history:

> There was once a world before this, and in it lived people who were not of our tribe. But the pillars of the earth collapsed, and all was destroyed. And the world was emptiness. Then two men grew up from a hummock of earth. . . . A magic song changed one of them into a woman, and they had children. These were our earliest forefathers, and from them all the lands were peopled.[7]

Thus, the participation of a male and transformed male-female in the annual relighting of the lamp recalled the primordial ancestry of Inuit. The presence of these ancestral figures at the Nuliajuk ritual, the pairing of men and women, and the release of conjugal bonds renewed the event of creation.

The dichotomy between male and female and the ritual efforts to unify the two for procreation was a basic tenet of the traditional world-view,

157.
Sealskin mask, female, Iglulik Inuit, collected 1921-1924. National Museum of Denmark, Department of Ethnography, Copenhagen. P27.741. L:26; W:16.5

These skin masks replicate those worn in the autumn festival dedicated to Nuliajuk (also known as Taleelayo or Sedna), the spirit guardian of sea animals. The festival, traditionally celebrated in the Eastern and Central Canadian Arctic, was led by a pair of masked figures, usually two men, one (or both) of whom was dressed as a woman. The celebration sought to win the good will of Nuliajuk, ensuring an abundant supply of sea animals during the dark months of winter hunting.

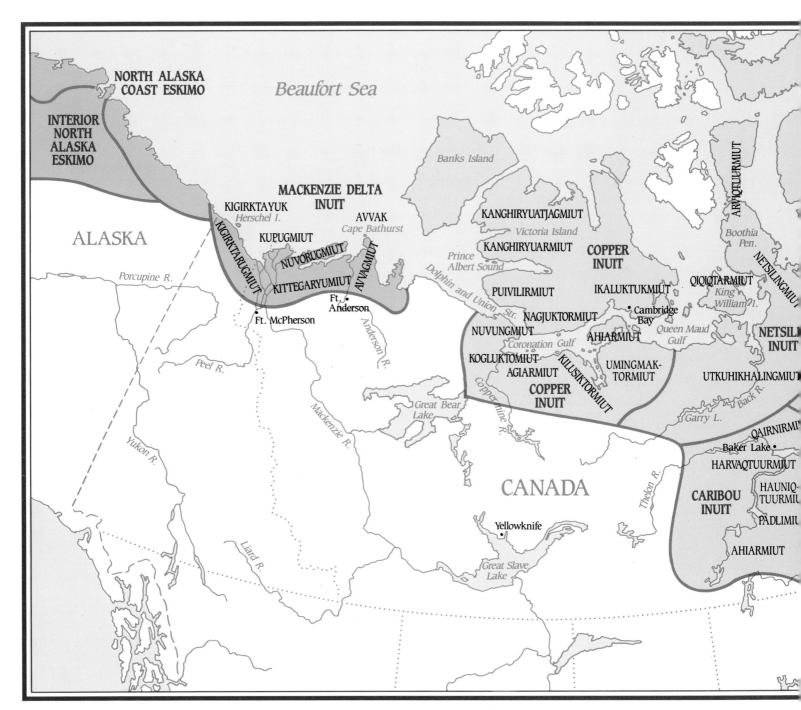

expressed not only in Inuit mythology but also in the material culture.[8]
This profound concern with the regeneration of human and animal life
reveals the strength of the survival ethic in the traditional culture.

Man and Animal

The Inuit world-view was strongly influenced by the relationship between
man and animal. With few vegetal resources, Inuit depended on the
animal for survival. So intimate was this relationship between man and
animal that Inuit mythology told of a time when "man could become
an animal and an animal could become a human being."[9]

In the Canadian Arctic, Inuit relied primarily upon the caribou and
seal for food and material for clothing, for summer tents, and for coverings for kayaks and umiaks. Caribou fur was made into sleeping blankets;
its antlers were used to make hunting equipment; its sinews were used

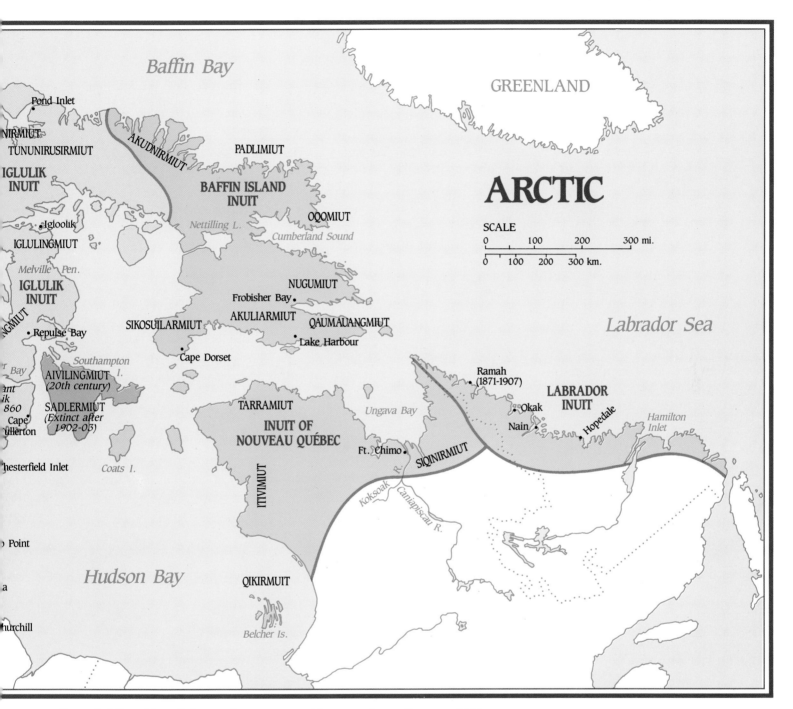

as thread. The skin of the seal was treated in a variety of ways. With the fur left on, the sealskin was water-resistant and could be made into clothing and boots, especially for the wet spring months. Shaved, air-dried, and softened by scraping, the skin of the bearded seal was impermeable; it provided waterproof material for boots. Seal intestine was also used as waterproof clothing for kayakers; gut-skin jackets were made in the Iglulik area and, until the late nineteenth century, in Ungava.[10] The bladder of the seal was inflated and used as a float attached to the harpoon. In earlier times, inflated sealskins were also used as a means of transportation.[11]

Walrus, whale, polar bear, musk-ox, fox, wolf, and other smaller species, especially landfowl and waterfowl, provided a variety of food and raw material in areas of the Canadian Arctic. Of particular importance to both the economy and Inuit cosmology was the dichotomy between land and sea hunting, which dominated the annual cycle.

Two spirit forces oversaw the division between land and sea. Nuliajuk was the guardian of marine animals. Although her name and details of her origin differed from region to region, her existence was known eastward to Greenland and westward to Alaska and Siberia. Species of sea mammals were formed from the severed joints of her fingers; thus she controlled the release of these animals to the Inuit. Hunters and their families took every opportunity to ensure her good will, for she was easily offended when a hunter failed to show respect for the soul (*inua*) of the animal he killed. Her punishment was merciless: she withheld all sea animals from the hunters' harpoons.

The caribou fell under the care of another spirit, and an intense jealousy was said to exist between Nuliajuk and the guardian of the caribou.

> . . . there were no caribou at the time when [Nuliajuk] lived on earth; and therefore she hates the caribou and they have another mother, "*atianak ikveqArput*" : "they have another with whom they are."[12]

Therefore, a strict regimen of rules and regulations was observed to keep separate land and sea products. Certain practices were followed and taboos observed to ensure the beneficence of Nuliajuk and her terrestrial counterpart. For example, equipment used in marine hunting could not be used on land. Clothing used to hunt sea mammals had to be buried near the coast; hunters could not take it inland when hunting caribou.[13] Caribou-skin clothing could not be sewn after the first walrus or seal had been killed in the fall. If the sewing had not been completed by the time the family moved on to the sea ice, a special sewing hut had to be built on shore.[14] And the flesh of walrus, whale, and seal could not be eaten on the same day as caribou meat.[15]

Traditionally, Inuit believed that the animal surrendered itself to the hunter who showed respect for its soul. Only the flesh of the animal

158.

Drag handle, Mackenzie region. Musée d'ethnographie, Neuchâtel, Switzerland VI-152. L:11.5

This drag handle, collected c. 1867 by the Oblate missionary, Emile Petitot, is carved as two opposing bear heads. The bear was the most respected predator in the Inuit world; its likeness on an object suggested that the bear's predatory skills were transferred to the hunter.

was taken; its soul was reclothed in the flesh of another animal to return again to the weapon of the hunter.[16]

The hunter's wife and family also played an important role in maintaining the relationship between hunter and animal. When the hunter returned with his prey, work ceased and all attention was turned to the animal. The hunter's wife welcomed the seal with a drink of fresh water, for it was believed that it was the animal's thirst for unsalted water that allowed it to be captured. The animal was butchered and a prescribed distribution of food to family, friends, and those in need was followed.

The close relationship between hunter and animal was an important design source in the manufacture of Inuit hunting equipment. Extraordinary care was taken in the construction of this equipment as a sign of respect towards the animal. In addition, animal imagery was often used in the design of hunting equipment, for it was believed that the attributes of the animal were symbolically embraced within an object designed in its image.[17] A bone drag handle (Figure 158) is carved in the form of two opposing bear heads; the bear was the most respected predator in the Arctic. Toggles, carved in a naturalistic manner, represent swimming bears (predators) and caribou (prey). Perhaps the most conventional example of animal imagery appears in the finely modelled ivory fish hooks collected from the Mackenzie area in the Western Canadian Arctic.[18] These hooks were carved in the image of a fish with two blue beads for eyes. (The beads were traded through Alaska from Russia.) A third bead or a lead figure of a fish or whale was often implanted in the underbelly, suggesting a symbolic scoring of the prey.

159.
Kayak on Windy Lake, Hudson Bay, Caribou Inuit region, c. 1908-14. Courtesy of the Glenbow Museum, Calgary NA1338-124.

This style of kayak was used to pursue caribou as they crossed the lakes and rivers of the interior of the Central Canadian Arctic. The wooden frame, covered with scraped caribou skin, was designed with upraised horns at the prow and stern. Long, narrow, and extremely lightweight, this style of kayak demanded exceptional skill and balance on the part of the kayaker.

A compelling example of the influence of animal imagery is the design of the Central Arctic kayak. Used exclusively on inland lakes, it has been suggested that this kayak derived its form from the figure of the loon. In the Canadian Arctic, as well as in Greenland and Alaska, the loon was a powerful spiritual image for the kayaker. Its keen eyesight, sharp beak, and tenacious spirit made it a formidable predator.

> When the loon settled in the water, there was no faster water bird. . . . What was more obvious than using the loon as a model for a rapid craft! . . . The kayak bow was shaped like the loon's head with its spearhead-like beak. At the stern, the vessel ended with a little upright tail.[19]

In contrast, the kayak used by the Caribou Inuit, while retaining the beak-like prow, had an upturned stern resembling the tail of a long-tailed duck (Figure 159).[20] Kayak attachments of the Central Arctic used to hold in place the hunter's weapons were carved from bone in the shape of water birds. Iglulik tradition dictated that the prow of the kayak be no wider than the space between the tusks of a walrus: a hunter attacked by an aggressive walrus could direct the prow between its tusks.[21] A Greenland legend records the use of the prow as a weapon to ram a seal or whale.[22] This ingenious technique mimics the loon's use of its beak as a spear-like weapon. Traditionally, the kayak was an essential part of the hunter's tool kit. As such, it has been perceived as an extension of the hunter's body, and its design has been described in parallel terms.[23]

The rich oral history of the Inuit and their traditional belief system provided evidence of a cosmology composed of paired opposites: light and dark, male and female, man and animal, land and sea—simultaneously separate and joined entities expressed in the spiritual and intellectual culture and made manifest in daily life. These dualities and the tension between them infused the material culture, giving shape and form to artefacts, which in turn projected a sense of Inuit cultural identity.

An essential element of Inuit material culture was the parka. Made from the fur of the caribou or seal, the parka marked the wearer as a member of a hunting culture. It identified the gender of the individual and the community from which he or she came. The conventional style of the parka within a community and the design elements incorporated in the parkas of men and women across the Canadian Arctic reveal the parka to be a statement not only of the individual but, more emphatically, of Inuit survival and cultural identity.

The Inuit Parka: Function and Metaphor

Across the Canadian Arctic, the furs of caribou or seal were preferred as clothing material. The long hairs of the caribou fur were hollow and trapped the air, thus providing exceptional insulation for the wearer. For this reason, caribou fur was worn especially during the fall and winter months. In the eastern coastal regions, however, sealskin was preferred during spring and summer, as it was more water-repellent.

Traditionally, the parka was worn in two layers. The inner layer, known as the *atigi*, was made so that the fur faced the wearer's body; the outer layer, the *qulittaq*, had the fur facing out. The *atigi* was usually of a simpler pattern than the *qulittaq*. Often it was made from the furs of young caribou or seal, soft material to have next to the body. The more complex pattern of the outer parka included inserts of contrasting fur that enhanced specific design elements.

These design elements distinguished the form of men's parkas from that of women's: the man's parka served as a metaphoric reference to the animal and to the man's role as hunter; the woman's parka, with its characteristic pouch (*amaut*), in which the wearer carried her infant, symbolized the maternal role of the woman.

Although the distinction between men's and women's parkas was universal across the Canadian Arctic, the form and appearance of the parka differed in the three main geographical areas of the Canadian Arctic: the Mackenzie in the west; the Copper, Netsilik, Iglulik, and Caribou regions in the Central Canadian Arctic; and southern Baffin Island, Labrador, and northern Quebec in the east. Moreover, stylistic differences in parka design within these three geographical areas allowed one to tell the region, and even the community, from which a person came.

The Man's Parka: Camouflage of the Hunter

The function of the man's parka was twofold: it offered protection from the physical forces of nature and symbolically and metaphysically assisted him as a hunter. In the Eastern Canadian Arctic, the hunter's parka

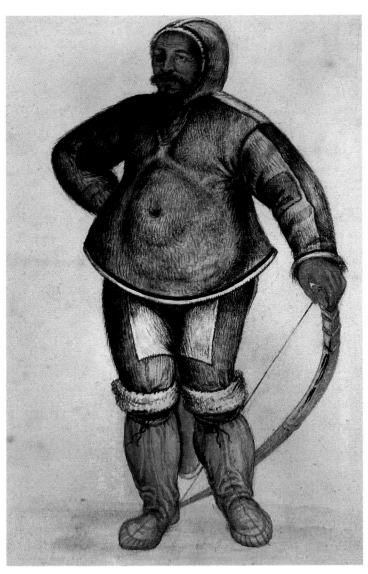

respected the fundamental division between land and sea. Ideally, the hunter dressed in caribou furs to pursue the caribou and in sealskin when he hunted seals on the spring ice or from the kayak. Clothing made from the skin of the animal being hunted not only camouflaged the hunter but assisted him in identifying with the animal. George Best, an officer on the Frobisher expeditions in the late sixteenth century, noted:

> They are good fishermen, and in their small boats, and disguised with their sealskin coats, they deceive the fish [seals? whales?], who take them for fellow seals rather than deceiving men.[24]

The two watercolour drawings that survive from the Frobisher expedition of 1577 show the style of clothing worn by men and women in the Eastern Canadian Arctic at the time of European contact (Figure 160). The man's and the woman's parkas were made from sealskin; each featured a long back tail, a metaphoric reference to the animal and to the Inuit as a hunting culture. This tail disappeared from men's parkas in the Eastern Canadian Arctic, probably due to the influence of the jacket styles of explorers, traders, and whalers. It remained on the woman's sealskin parka, however, and may be seen on contemporary parkas worn in southern Baffin Island, Southampton Island, Labrador, and Nouveau Québec.

160.
Drawings of Inuit man and woman with child, captured by Frobisher Expedition, 1577. Watercolour, attributed to John White. Courtesy of the Trustees of the British Museum, Department of Prints and Drawings.

These two drawings, the earliest illustrations of clothing styles from Baffin Island, reveal that both men's and women's parkas in the early contact period featured a long back tail. This design element later disappeared from men's parkas in the Eastern Canadian Arctic; however, it has been retained on women's parkas throughout the region to the present day.

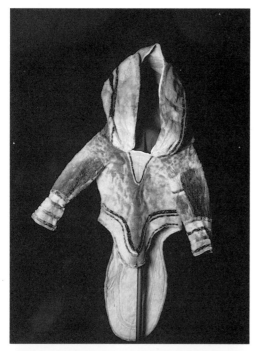

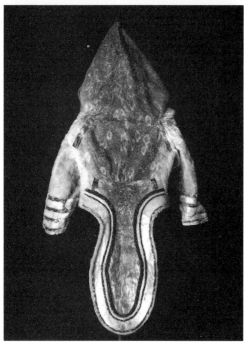

161.
Sealskin woman's parka, Eastern Canadian Arctic, front and back views, collected in 1902. American Museum of Natural History, New York 60/4661. L:136; W:90

Lightweight and water-resistant, sealskin (rather than caribou) parkas were preferred in the coastal areas of Baffin Island, Labrador, and Nouveau Québec during the spring and summer months. The curvilinear tail creates a metaphoric reference to the seal, stressing the importance of maritime hunting in the Eastern Canadian Arctic.

This style of tail is apparent on the woman's sealskin parka collected in the early twentieth century by Captain George Comer (Figure 161). The curvilinear shape of the tail, reiterated by a double line of dark sealskin, magnifies the form of a seal's tail. This metaphoric reference — and stylistic similarity — is also seen in the small tails found on men's and women's parkas in Greenland. It alludes to the importance of maritime hunting for Inuit throughout the Eastern Canadian Arctic and Greenland.[25]

The form and style of the caribou parkas of the Central Canadian Arctic were markedly different from those to the east and west. Within the regions occupied by the Iglulik, Netsilik, Caribou, and Copper Inuit, the parkas worn by men and women formed a stylistic pair. Although specific design elements differentiated the parka of a man from that of a woman, the parkas of both sexes projected metaphoric references to the caribou and to the importance of inland hunting.

The parka style worn in the Copper area seems to have served as the prototype for the Central Arctic parka. The man's parka exhibited the most explicit zoomorphic references in the region (Figure 163). Caribou ears were typically found on the peaked hood, and a long back tail, inset with white fur strips outlining an animal's tail, was a common design element on parkas in the Copper region. The features of the hunting parka "gave a stooping Eskimo so close a likeness to a caribou that it sometimes deceived his dogs hauling on the sled behind him and spurred them on to greater effort."[26]

The parkas in the Copper region were exceptionally well-tailored; narrow strips of white caribou fur were used to articulate important design features. Typically, parkas were made from the light, short-haired summer fur of the caribou. Many of those in museum collections are decorated with broad panels of white caribou fur inset over the chest. These insets, which contrast sharply with the rich dark fur of the caribou, are often edged with narrow strips of ochre-stained caribou hide and dark sealskin. The shape of these panels differentiated between a man's parka (rounded) and a woman's parka (sharply angular).

Implicit references to the caribou were incorporated in the design of the Copper man's parka. The white spot of fur found on the back of most men's parkas was a symbolic reference to the caribou tail;[27] the lengths of dehaired caribou hide, hung in pairs along the tail panel of the parka, were replaced each spring in anticipation of the return of the caribou.[28]

The hunting parka of the Copper area also carried explicit references to the hunter's role as predator. The long back panel was often marked with an inset tail design that created a metaphoric reference to a long-tailed land predator, such as the wolf.[29] Moreover, the back of the hunter's parka was often marked with the winter pelts of three ermines, a carnivore which, despite its small size, is one of the most successful and cunning predators in the Arctic. The pelts were arranged in a uniform manner, "one attached to the back of each shoulder and the third spaced halfway between them at a somewhat lower level."[30] The ermine, considered an exceptionally potent amulet, protected an individual from his enemies.

In the Netsilik, Iglulik, and Caribou regions of the Central Canadian Arctic, the parka resembled that of the Copper Inuit, but it was made from a thicker fur of caribou captured later in the season, which provided greater warmth. In addition, the front of the parka was lengthened, and the back tail broadened, with wide bands of white caribou fur (*pukiq*). This offered greater protection to the wearer's body than did the parka of the Copper area. Although contact with European and American explorers, whalers, and traders seems to have brought about a shorten-

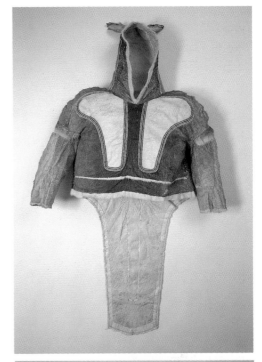

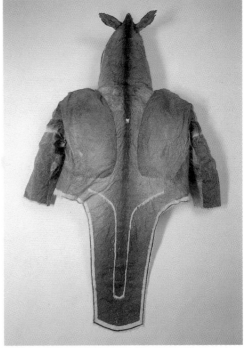

162.
Man's parka, Netsilik Inuit, back view.
Ethnographic Museum, University of Oslo
15.769. L:130; W:60

This Netsilik Inuit parka, collected by the
Norwegian explorer, Roald Amundsen,
1903-1905, is exceptionally well-tailored
with an elaborate design of light and dark
caribou fur inset in the back. It is made
from a thicker fur than the Copper Inuit
parka (Figure 163); broad bands of white
fur added along the edges have lengthened
the front and broadened the back tail, thus
increasing the parka's heat-retaining
qualities. Such alterations, however, begin
to obscure the explicit zoomorphic
references apparent in the parka design of
the Copper Inuit.

163.
Sealskin man's parka, Copper Inuit
(Kilusiktomiut), front and back views, col-
lected 1913-1916. Canadian Museum of
Civilization, National Museums of Canada,
Ottawa. IV-D-960. L:140; W:71

The rounded shape of the chest panels,
edged in ochre-stained hide and sealskin,
identify the wearer as male. The caribou
ears on the hood and stylized predator tail
on the back panel create zoomorphic
references that aid the hunter on a
functional and symbolic level in the pursuit
of his prey.

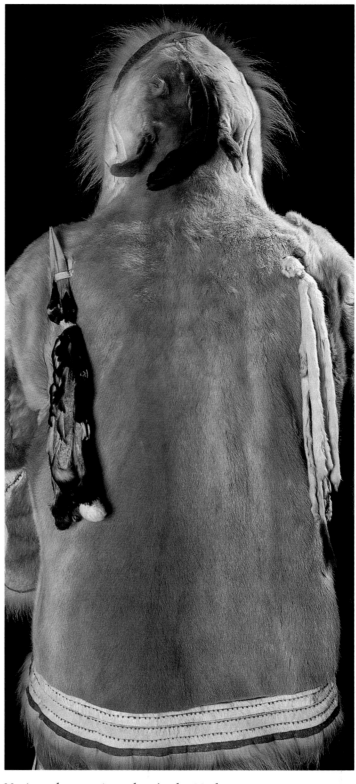

164.
Man's parka with trousers and boots, Northern Alaska/Mackenzie region type, front and back views, collected 1902. Art Gallery and Museum, Glasgow 02.8bk. L:170.5; W:76.0

Men's and women's parkas in the Mackenzie region followed the parka style of Northern Alaska. This outfit, noted as a "Chief's" costume, includes a hooded caribou fur parka, matching fur trousers, and boots with fur uppers and sealskin soles. Attached to the parka back are various references to spiritual power: the skin of a loon, an eagle feather, an ermine pelt, and a pair of caribou ears.

ing of the back tail, especially in the coastal areas of the Central Canadian Arctic, nineteenth-century drawings by John Ross and George Lyon in the Netsilik and Iglulik areas attest to its historical presence.[31]

The Netsilik parka, collected by the Norwegian explorer Roald Amundsen, illustrates the design modifications noted above (Figure 162). Wide bands of white caribou fur and long fringes of caribou hide have been used to lengthen the front and back of the parka. An elaborate design created by alternating strips of light and dark fur marks the back of the parka. The rectangular insert in the centre back corresponds to the spot of white fur representing the caribou tail on the Copper parka.

Parkas from the Caribou region also showed an elaboration of the Copper parka design. Among the Qairnirmiut, three panels of contrasting white and dark fur were often inserted in the back of the parka. The number and location of these panels recalled the Copper attachment of three ermine pelts, perhaps signalling a transformation from naturalistic to abstract references of spiritual protection.

The form of parka worn in the Mackenzie area is distinct from that of the Eastern and Central regions of the Canadian Arctic. Following the parka style of Northern Alaska, the man's parka was made from caribou fur or from the fur of smaller mammals such as ground squirrel or muskrat (Figure 164). The parka was hooded, evenly hemmed, and trimmed with tiers of the white fur of the Siberian reindeer, a valued commodity in the Western Arctic. A pair of trousers of the same fur as the parka and a pair of boots with fur uppers and soles made from scraped sealskin completed the hunter's outfit.

Although the Mackenzie parka did not incorporate the traditional back tail panel of the Central and Eastern Canadian Arctic, it did include a parallel metaphoric reference: Mackenzie area hunters commonly attached the tail of a predatory animal to the back of their parkas. "Many a warrior

165.
Kanneyuk and Kila, two Dolphin and Union Strait girls in full dress, 1916. Canadian Museum of Civilization, National Museums of Canada, Ottawa 51250, 51251.

Women's parkas in the Copper Inuit area followed a highly conventional style. Made from the thin summer fur of the caribou, the parka was designed with broad shoulders; a roomy back in which to carry a child; and a long, narrow (or short, V-shaped) front flap, or *kiniq*. These design features alluded to the woman's maternal role; they were characteristic design elements of women's parkas throughout the Central Canadian Arctic.

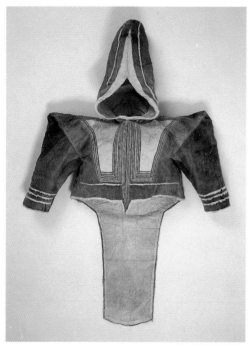

166.
Woman's parka, Copper Inuit, collected 1916. Canadian Museum of Civilization, National Museums of Canada, Ottawa. IV-D-748. L:136; W:75

Within the Copper area, men's and women's parkas were stylistically similar. Both were short-waisted with a long rectangular back panel marked with the outline of a predator's tail. Certain features distinguished women's parkas from those of men: the long hood, accentuated shoulders, angular chest panels, and, most notably, the *kiniq*. In the Copper area, the *kiniq* was either a small, triangular vulvic reference (as in this example) or a long, narrow appendage suggesting an archetypal reference to the phallus. In either case, the *kiniq* served as a symbol of procreation and maternity.

will be seen wearing below his back the tail of a white wolf, of a black fox or of a wolverine."[32]

The parkas of the Mackenzie and northern Alaska were marked by triangular, tusk-like gussets, which originally attached the hood to the body of the parka. This was a reference to the walrus, whose strength and aggressive behaviour when riled made him a formidable opponent. This allusion to the walrus was also carried forth in the labrets worn by men throughout the Western Arctic. The labret was a stone or ivory disc fitted into a hole cut at either end of the lower lip. These cuts were made at puberty; small wooden plugs were inserted until the wounds healed. As a boy matured, he adopted larger and more elaborate labrets, as a sign of his prestige in the society. Together with the tusk-like gussets on the front of the parka, the labrets reinforced the image of the walrus.[33]

These tusk-like gussets are also visible in the drawing of the woman captured by the Frobisher expedition during the sixteenth century (Figure 160). In addition, the single throat gusset apparent in the drawing of the man's parka from the Frobisher expedition (Figure 160) and on the sealskin woman's parka from the Eastern Arctic collected in the early twentieth century (Figure 161) is also found on parkas from the Mackenzie area.[34] Comparable design features in such widely separated geographic regions may indicate a prehistoric link between the parka designs of the Eastern and Western Canadian Arctic. The absence of these design features in the Central Canadian Arctic may provide an important clue regarding the early migration routes of Inuit across the Canadian Arctic.

Despite stylistic differences between the three geographical regions of the Canadian Arctic, the hunting parka everywhere emphasized the relationship between man and animal in a hunting society. By dressing in the furs of the animal he hunted, and by incorporating zoomorphic references in the design of the parka, the Inuit hunter identified himself with the animal world around him. Through the design of his parka, the hunter became both predator and prey.

The Woman's Parka: A Symbol of Maternity

The woman's parka, the *amautik*, also incorporated references to the animal, but these references were subordinate to emphases on the maternal role of the woman in Inuit society. The pouch (amaut), incorporated within the back of the woman's parka, allowed a mother to carry her child. In the woman's parkas of the Central Arctic, the *amaut* could be enlarged with additional pieces of fur; as the infant grew, the *amaut* expanded to accommodate the child. The *amaut*, therefore, was both functionally and symbolically a second womb, enabling the child to benefit from an intimate bonding with the mother.

Women's parkas in the Canadian Arctic were also identified by a short apron flap, called a *kiniq*. In the Central and Eastern regions, the *kiniq* suggested a windbreaker or covering on which a woman could lay her child. The *kiniq* found on women's parkas in the Copper area, however, indicates that its original function was a symbolic one, a reference to procreation and to the regeneration of human life (Figures 165 and 166).

The Copper area *kiniq* appeared in two distinct forms. The first is a narrow appendage approximately twenty or thirty centimetres long with an inset design of two parallel lines extending down the centre (Figure 165). This style suggests an archetypal reference to the phallus, to procreation, and, thus, to the maternal role of the woman.[35]

The second style of the *kiniq* was a short triangular appendage extending just below the waist of the parka. It recalls the pelvic markings inscribed on wooden female figures of the prehistoric period. This pelvic (or vulvic) reference was reiterated by the white gusset in the front of women's trousers and the edges of women's leggings, which created "a series of more or less symmetrical triangles inside one another, all having the bottom edge of the coat for their bases."[36]

167.
Two Young Inuit Women, Labrador. Reproduced in *The Labrador Eskimo*, 1916. by E.W. Hawkes. Canadian Museum of Civilization, National Museums of Canada, Ottawa 42535.

Across the Canadian Arctic, inserts of contrasting fur articulate important design elements in the parka. In this photograph, arched strips of fur on the parka front create a rounded uteral reference over the woman's womb. This design feature is found on women's parkas in the Eastern and Western Canadian Arctic.

168.
Woman's parka, Caribou Inuit (Qairnirmiut), front view, collected 1904. Canadian Museum of Civilization, National Museums of Canada, Ottawa IV-C-628. L:180; W:68; Hood: L:70

The woman's parka (*amautik*) was fitted with a back pouch (*amaut*) in which to carry a child; the broad shoulders allowed an infant to be passed from the *amaut* to the breast without leaving the warmth of the parka. Among the Iglulik, Netsilik, and Caribou Inuit, an edging of broad bands of white fur around the apron flap (*kiniq*) and back tail softened the sharper, more angular lines of the Copper Inuit woman's parka (Figures 165 and 166).

Among the Netsilik, Iglulik, and Caribou Inuit, the women's parkas were designed with a long, full, apron-like *kiniq*, heavily fringed with strips of caribou hide (Figure 167).[37] The strong vertical orientation of the *kiniq*, created by the dark centre line of brown caribou fur, was softened by wide borders of white caribou fur, which gave the *kiniq* a full, rounded appearance. Despite this elaboration, the *kiniq* still maintains a pronounced vertical (phallic) orientation.

In contrast, the *kiniq* on women's parkas in the Eastern Canadian Arctic often showed a female or uterine reference. In the photograph published by E.W. Hawkes in his study, *The Labrador Eskimo* (1916), light-coloured strips of fur inset in the *kiniq* create this uterine reference over the womb of the female (Figure 167). This design is also apparent in a photograph taken in 1876 of a family group at Great Whale River in Nouveau Québec (Figure 169), in other period photographs, and on several women's parkas (including beaded parkas) from Labrador, southern Baffin Island, and Nouveau Québec in museum collections.

Parkas from the Mackenzie region were of Northern Alaskan design; women's parkas had long, scalloped panels forming the front apron and

169.
Eskimo Group, Great Whale River (Poste-de-la-Baleine), Nouveau Québec. Canadian Museum of Civilization, National Museums of Canada, Ottawa.

Taken in 1876, on the east coast of Hudson Bay, this photograph demonstrates the design similarity among women's parkas of the Eastern Canadian Arctic. Two of the women's parkas exhibit the same uteral reference seen in Figure 167.

back tail; strips of light-coloured caribou fur creating a uterine reference are inset on the front apron flap (Figure 170). Women's parkas in the Mackenzie area also exhibited references to the animal and to spiritual protection. For example, a parka from the collection of the Royal Ontario Museum[38] features two elongated triangular gussets, vestigial references to "hood roots."[39] The retention of this design element after it was no longer functional alluded to the symbolic "walrus tusks," discussed earlier. The light-coloured inserts on the back of the Mackenzie-area parkas[40] suggest an abstract figure, perhaps a form of spiritual protection. Other elements of spiritual protection are found in the attached ermine pelts and solitary eagle feather.[41]

These animal references, however, were secondary to the design features that symbolized the woman's maternal role. Despite differences in the form and appearance of women's parkas in the Eastern, Central, and Western Canadian Arctic, the significant features — the *kiniq* (apron) and the *amaut* (baby pouch) — were universal elements, symbolic references to procreation. Thus, while the hunting parka of the man projected references to the animal and the role of the hunter, the woman's parka emphasized the duality of male and female and the union of the two for the regeneration of human life.

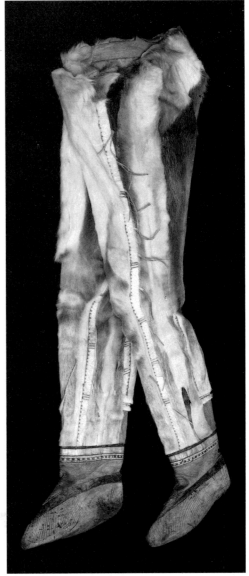

170.
Woman's parka and trousers, Mackenzie region (Inuvialuit), collected in 1895. The Trustees, National Museums of Scotland, Edinburgh 1895,407.

Women's parkas in the Mackenzie area followed the Northern Alaska style with deeply scalloped front and back flaps, edged with strips of cream-coloured fur, russet-stained hide, and snips of coloured cloth. This extraordinary parka was obtained at Fort MacPherson from the wife of To-gwa-tzuk ("Little Ice Chisel"), a prominent Inuit leader in the Mackenzie region. An eagle feather and ermine pelt are attached to the back.

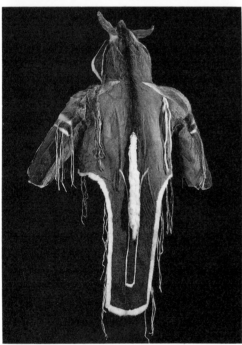

171.
Boy's parka, Copper Inuit, front and back views. Collected 1916-1917. Canadian Museum of Civilization, National Museums of Canada, Ottawa IV-D-1259. L:89; W:37

This young boy's parka follows the style of the adult male Copper Inuit parka with caribou ears attached to the hood and a stylized animal tail inset in the back panel. The outlined chest panels, however, emphasize the boy's novice status; the ermine skin on the back attests to his need for spiritual protection.

The Child's Parka: Symbol of Maturation

In traditional Inuit society, the relationship between man and animal was established at the moment of a child's birth: the skin of a bird or other animal was used to cleanse the birth fluids from the infant's body, thereby transferring the protection and attributes of the animal to the newborn child. For example, the skin of a raven ensured that the child would be the first to arrive at a fresh kill; like the raven, the child would always find food, no matter what the season. The birth skin was a powerful amulet and a piece was often sewn into the child's first article of clothing.[42]

Young children were dressed in a one-piece outfit known as an *atajuq*. Made from the fur of a caribou fawn, it suggested a correlation between the child and the young caribou. The tiny antler buds attached to the hood of the *atajuq* reinforced this relationship and made the child look "just like a little caribou."[43]

As in all societies, play was an important factor in introducing children to their social roles and responsibilities within the culture. Traditionally, an Inuit mother playing with her infant son would pantomime the motion of the kayaker gliding swiftly over the surface of the water. Later, a father would carve model harpoons, bows and arrows, sleds, and other hunting equipment for his son's play. Young girls entertained themselves with miniature stone lamps and cooking pots, carefully tending their play hearths in imitation of their mothers.

Children's clothing followed the parka style of adults of the same sex, emphasizing the role the child would assume. For example, a young girl wore a miniature *amautik*, in which she often carried a doll, a puppy, or even small rocks, so that she could sense the presence of an infant behind her. If the youngster baby-sat for an infant brother or sister, her *amaut* was enlarged to hold the child.

In the Central Canadian Arctic, the style of a young girl's parka changed as she matured. The closely cut hood she had worn as a child, and the short back tail and *kiniq*, gradually grew longer and fuller. When she was an adolescent, her parka did not incorporate an *amaut*: its absence symbolized her unmarried state.[44]

The design and decoration of a boy's parka alluded to his prospective role as a hunter and to the relationship between man and animal. A boy's formal training began at the age of seven or eight, when he first accompanied his father on hunting expeditions. The capture of his first large animal, such as a caribou or seal, was cause for communal celebration. The animal was butchered by the boy's mother and other women in the camp, and shared with as many people as possible.

The boy's parka, collected in the Copper area, contains explicit animal references: a pair of caribou ears are attached to the hood, and the long tail of a predatory animal is inset in the back panel (Figure 171). The simple outline of the chest panels that will mark the boy's adult parka emphasize his novice state. The single ermine-skin amulet on the back acknowledges childhood as an extremely vulnerable state, requiring spiritual protection.

The extraordinary precautions taken to ensure the well-being of an Inuit child were poignantly expressed in the parka of Tertaq, a young Netsilingmio boy, collected in the early 1920s (Figure 172). The parents of young Tertaq attached no less than eighty amulets to the boy's parka, including twelve caribou ears sewn over the back and shoulders to bring the boy luck in hunting; the feet of a red-throated loon to make him a fast kayaker; the snout skin of a caribou to make him as sure a kayaker as the caribou is a swimmer; a tern's head to make him a good salmon fisher; a claw from the fore-flipper of a seal to give him strong arms; two drag lines for seals, belonging to his father and elder brother, to bring him luck while sealing; the hair of an old man sewn to the hood at the temples to bring him strength; and the stump of a flensing knife that had once belonged to a shaman to give him ability as a shaman.[45]

Amulets safeguarded the child during the vulnerable period of childhood. As well, design changes in a boy's parka alluded to his development as a hunter, just as a young girl's parka paralleled her preparation for marriage and child-bearing.

The Role of the Shaman

Traditionally, each individual in Inuit society was responsible for maintaining a personal relationship with the spiritual world. Strict observance of taboos, the knowledge of magic songs and magic words, and the power of one's amulets symbolized an individual's search for balance between the natural and supernatural worlds.

In times of communal crisis, however, the entire community would turn to the *angakkuq*, an individual specially called and trained in shamanism. The *angakkuq* was the intermediary between the natural and supernatural worlds, between the sacred and the profane. The responsibilities of the *angakkuq* were varied:

> They must be physicians, curing the sick. Meteorologists, not only able to forecast the weather, but also able to ensure fine weather. This is effected by travelling up to Sila [the spirit force that controlled the environment]. They must be able to go down to Takanakapsaluk [Nuliajuk] to fetch game. . . . They must be able to visit the Land of the Dead under the sea or up in the sky in order to look for lost or stolen souls. . . . Finally, every great shaman must . . . exercise his art in miraculous fashion in order to astonish the people and convince them of the sacred and inexplicable powers of the shaman.[46]

The Apprenticeship of the Shaman

A prospective *angakkuq* was often called through a personal crisis, such as an illness or a vision. A novice appealed to an established *angakkuq* for instruction in the shamanic tradition and language. The novice would say, "*Takujumagama*" ("I come to you because I desire to see").[47]

The calling of the Iglulik shaman, Aua, was predicted when he lay within his mother's womb. His mother had already suffered several miscarriages; learning of her pregnancy, she announced, "Now I have again that within me which will turn out no real human being." The shaman, Ardjuaq, called upon her helping spirits to assist Aua's mother during her pregnancy; but she did not abstain from work the day after the invocation, and her action brought on premature birth pangs. It was Aua's strong reaction to this and other breaches of taboo while still within his mother's womb that forewarned of his role as an *angakkuq*. Throughout his youth, his life was marked with specially imposed taboos, to be followed by him and his family. Aua recalled:

> Everything was thus made ready for me beforehand, even from the time when I was yet unborn; nevertheless, I endeavored to become a shaman by the help of others; but in this I did not succeed. I visited many famous shamans, and gave them great gifts, which they at once gave away to others; for if they had kept the things for themselves, they or their children would have died. This they believed because my own life had been so threatened from birth. Then I sought solitude, and here I became very melancholy. . . . Then, for no reason . . . I felt a great, inexplicable joy, a joy so powerful that I

172.
Young boy's parka, Netsilik Inuit (Netsilingmiut). National Museum of Denmark, Department of Ethnography, Copenhagen P29.501. L:62

The amulets attached to this parka were designed to protect the child and assist him in developing his prospective skills as a hunter and kayaker. The parka, which was collected by Knud Rasmussen in the early 1920s, belonged to a young Netsilingmio boy named Tertaq. The number of amulets, more than eighty in all, attest to the vulnerable state of childhood and the need for spiritual protection.

173.
Shaman's belt, Caribou Inuit (Padlimiut).
National Museum of Denmark, Department
of Ethnography, Copenhagen P28.254. L:93

This belt, collected from a Padlimiut female
shaman in 1922-1923 is made of short
strips of red stroud, white caribou fur, and
a series of small wooden toggles. These
toggles are miniatures of those attached to
the woman's belt used to hold a child
within the mother's parka. Their appearance on the belt suggest the shaman's
role in assisting women in childbirth.

174.
Shaman's belt, Netsilik Inuit, collected
1903-1905. Ethnographic Museum, University
of Oslo 16.169. L:92; W:2

This amulet belt is made up of a series of
minature knives carved in antler. The knife
symbolized the shaman's ability to combat
evil spirits; its miniature size imitated spirit
implements.

175. (opposite)
Dance costume, Copper Inuit (Ahunga-
hungarmiut), National Museum of Denmark, Department of Ethnography,
Copenhagen. P.30.1. L:120; W:99

The Copper Inuit were the only group in
the Canadian Arctic retaining the vestige of
a specially designed dance costume.
Hoodless, and cut in a dress-like fashion,
this garment was worn with a separate
dance hat (see Figures 176 and 177). The
garment was collected in 1923 on Victoria
Island by the Danish ethnologist, Knud
Rasmussen.

could not restrain it, but had to break into song, a mighty song, with
only room for the one word: joy! joy! And I had to use the full strength
of my voice. And then in the midst of such a fit of mysterious and
overwhelming delight I became a shaman, not knowing myself how
it came about. . . . I had gained my *qaumaneq*, my enlightenment,
the shaman-light of brain and body . . . imperceptible to human
beings, but visible to all the spirits of earth and sky and sea, and
these now came to me and became my helping spirits.[48]

One of Aua's helping spirits was his namesake, a female spirit that lived
by the seashore; the second was a shark that appeared beside him while
he was in his kayak.

. . . it came swimming up to me, lay alongside quite silently and
whispered my name. I was greatly astonished, for I had never seen
a shark before; they are very rare in these waters. Afterwards it helped
me with my hunting, and was always near me when I had need of it.[49]

The Vestments of the Shaman

The typical sign of the shaman in the Canadian Arctic was the shaman's
belt, often made up of short strips of white caribou fur, red stroud, and
other coloured cloth, as well as small gifts. The belt was the creation
of the shaman and an important symbol of his or her power. A belt
of a Padlimiut shaman of the Caribou area features numerous miniature
toggles carved of wood (Figure 173). The toggles imitate those on the
belt of a woman's parka, which secure a child within the *amaut*. The
toggles on this shaman's belt emphasize her critical role in helping women
in childbirth.[50]

A belt collected from the Netsilik area features various styles of model
knives carved in antler, attached to a long piece of hide (Figure 174).
The Inuit knife, the *pana*, was used to build a snow house, to butcher
meat, and to protect oneself against enemies. "The *pana* could also be
used as an amulet. Even the Bible talks of 'double-edged swords' penetrating anything and being more effective than real swords."[51] The shaman's
pana represented his or her ability to combat evil spirits.

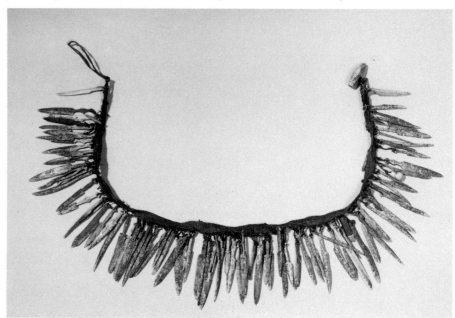

The prevalence of shaman's belts and the widespread acceptance of
the belt as the sole identifying mark of the shaman may have obscured
the traces of shamanistic costume in the Canadian Arctic. Although evidence of this tradition appeared across the Arctic, it seemed particularly
strong in the Copper region.

176.
Dance hat, Copper Inuit, collected c. 1915. University Museum, University of Pennsylvania, Philadelphia NA 4233. L:33; W:17

Drum dances were major social events, held especially to welcome the arrival of visitors. Among the Copper Inuit, a specially designed dance hat, made of alternating strips of white fur and ochre-stained hide, was worn by the dancers. This hat is unusual in that it shows a pair of loon beaks, rather than a single one; a white ermine pelt is attached to the crown. While performing, the dancer rotated the ermine pelt in a swirling motion above the head.

177.
Woman's dance hat, Copper Inuit, collected 1901-1902. Courtesy of the Trustees of the British Museum, London 1903.6-15.1. L:30

The Copper dance hat appeared in two styles: a circular skull-cap design and the more typical bonnet-shaped hat (Figure 176). Both were crowned with an upright loon's beak from which hung an ermine pelt. The skull-cap style, reported to have been worn by women, is extremely rare.

This was the only region in the Canadian Arctic that retained a dance costume of a pattern different from that of men's and women's parkas. The dance costume was hoodless and cut in a dress-like pattern. The ritual function of one such costume is emphasized by the eight ermine skins attached to the shoulders and across the back of the garment (Figure 175).

The Copper area also retained the tradition of a special dance hat (Figures 176 and 177), which presumably accompanied the hoodless dance costume. During the historical period a small number of these hats existed within a community, and various dancers would borrow them during the drum dance. The style of the hat was similar throughout the Copper region. It was bonnet-shaped and made of an alternating pattern of narrow strips of white caribou fur, dark sealskin, and ochre-stained caribou hide. The crown was fitted with the upright beak of a yellow-billed loon, from which hung the white winter pelt of an ermine; the hat was tied beneath the chin.

A rare style of dance hat was a circular skull cap apparently worn by women (Figure 177).[52] One example is made with a crown of concentric circles of alternating white caribou fur and ochre-stained leather. The sides of the hat are formed by vertical bands that repeat the alternating pattern. A loon's beak adorns the crown of the hat, and a fragment of ermine skin is still attached.

The loon's beak and the ermine skin were universal features of the Copper dance hat. The loon was admired for its song and for the beauty of its dance in the courtship ritual.[53] Its breeding plumage was also the subject of an Inuit fable, in which the loon was decorated by the hand of raven. The loon seems to symbolize the artistic element of human nature — a love of dance, music, and personal adornment. The loon also had mystical attributes: its skill as a diving bird may suggest an association between the loon and Nuliajuk at the bottom of the sea.[54] This

association may also explain why the loon's beak adorned the dance hat.

The ermine was a powerful amulet that guarded an individual against his enemies. It was universally regarded as a potent helping spirit of the shaman, as it was both "smart and sneaky."[55] The attachment of the ermine skin to the Copper dance hat, to the dance costume, and to men's hunting parkas may have been to protect the individual against unexpected attack by human or spiritual forces. This protection was especially necessary during the drum dances held to welcome visitors — often strangers — or when several neighbouring groups gathered to socialize or trade. In the Copper area, a drum dance was often the moment to settle a long-standing grudge.[56] A myth recorded in Northern Alaska, however, also claims that Ermine was responsible for introducing the drum dance to his fellow Inuit at a time when men knew no joy. "They toiled, they slept, they awoke again to toil. Monotony rusted their minds."[57] Captured by a young eagle, who was also human, the boy was taught to drum and dance by Mother Eagle. When he returned home, he built a feast hall like the eagles' and filled the larder with meat. He invited all the people he could find and they danced until the light of morning. But as the guests left, ". . . they all fell forward on their hands and sprang away on all fours. They were no longer men but had changed into wolves, wolverines, lynxes, silver foxes, red foxes — in fact, into all the beasts of the forest."[58] Could the ermine pelt on the Copper dance

178.
Dance Costume, Copper Inuit, front view, possibly collected 1931
National Museum of Natural History, Smithsonian Institution, Washington, D.C.
418,613. L:120; W:55.5

Although similar in design to the previous Copper dance costume (Figure 175), certain features of this garment also suggest a shamanic function. The naturalistic outline of a predator's tail alludes to the integration of human and animal worlds, and the ability to pass from one to the other. In addition, the rounded (male) chest panels are coupled with a linear design of white caribou fur on the front, found exclusively on the woman's *kiniq* (see Figure 165). This coexistence of human/animal and male/female design features emphasizes the transforming powers of the shaman.

179.

Attuock. Pastel drawing by Nathaniel Dance, 1773. The Knatchbull Portrait Collection, England.

This pastel drawing portrays Attuock, one of five Inuit from the southern coast of Labrador who were brought to England in 1773 by Captain George Cartwright. Identified as a "priest" (or shaman), Attuock appears to be dressed in a cloth parka with a panel of beadwork encircling each arm and a series of hide strips attached to the parka. These strips apparently symbolize his shamanic profession.

hat be a reference to this mythic origin of dance — and a reminder of the transformative powers of man and animal?

A particularly unusual garment from the Copper area has been described as a "dancing costume" (Figure 178). Like the costume described earlier (see Figure 175), it is hoodless and cut in a dress-like pattern. However, two important design elements seem to indicate that it was made for a shaman. The first is an inset of white caribou fur on the back outlining a long animal tail. This outline is more naturalistically shaped than that on conventional parkas of the Copper area. It may allude to the duality of man and animal and to the mythic time recorded in Inuit oral tradition when "a person could become an animal and an animal could become a human being. . . . Now, only the greatest shamans can do that."[59]

As well, there are both male and female design elements on the parka. The white chest panels are shaped like those on a man's parka, yet the inset design of white caribou fur on the front of the parka corresponds to that found exclusively on the *kiniq* of the woman's parka (see Figure 165). This combination suggests the androgynous state of the shaman. Indeed, it reflects the moment of Inuit creation when a magic song changed one of two men into a woman in order to people the earth.

The only fully documented shaman's garment (Figure 180) was collected from Qingailisaq, an Iglulik shaman, and father of the shaman Aua. The parka follows the hoodless, dress-like design of the Copper dance costumes. The hem, however, is cut into deep scallops and heavily fringed. White caribou fur (*pukiq*) is inset into the dark-brown fur body of the garment in many patterns: there are two helping spirits over the shoulder blades; a pair of human hands on the front chest; chevron patterns over each shoulder and in two vertical columns on the back; three circular motifs across the front and back; and an alternating pattern of light and dark around the collar and along the hem. A small human figure cut in dark caribou fur is set in a white rectangle. Long fringes of white caribou fur hang from the back of the garment; short tassels of the same fur, their ends wrapped in red cloth, hang from the centres of the circular motifs.

A specially designed hat and a pair of mitts accompany Qingailisaq's costume. Covering the head and hands was a traditional means of safeguarding the body from contact with spirit forces. The protection of head and hands figured prominently in burial customs. For example, those mourning the death of a relative kept their heads and hands covered;[60] and, for a full year following the death of an infant, the mother was required to cover her head when outdoors.[61] Finally, when Qingailisaq told of how he came to create his costume, "the women who were near covered their heads with their hoods, for fear of [his] protecting spirit."[62]

Qingailisaq's costume had a supernatural source. One account of the costume's origin was recorded in the 1920s by Aua.[63] As his father was butchering the meat of a caribou he had killed, he was approached by four men. "All were big men, and they looked just like ordinary human beings, save that they had nostrils like those of the caribou." Qingailisaq recognized them as mountain spirits, *iŁeraq* or *ijiqqat*.[64] One of the spirits was searching for his son, whom the group feared had been killed by humans. The oldest fell upon Qingailisaq, suspecting him of the murder, but the *angakkuq* resisted the assault; finally, persuaded of his innocence, the strangers departed "in friendship and mutual understanding."[65]

> My father, who was a great shaman, went home and had a dress made like that of the *iŁeraq*, but with a picture of the hands in front, on the chest, to show how the *iŁeraq* had attacked him. . . . [It] is the only *iŁeraq* tunic ever made by human hands.[66]

The second version of the story, recorded by the collector of the garment, George Comer, is quite different.

> One day when [the shaman] was caribou-hunting near the peninsula Amitoq, he killed three caribou. On the following day he saw four large bucks, one of which was very fat. He struck it with an arrow and . . . [its] antlers and skin dropped off, its head became smaller and soon it assumed the form of a woman with finely made clothes. Soon she fell down, giving birth to a boy, and then she died. The other caribou had turned into men, who told him to cover the woman and child with moss so that nobody should find them. . . . The men told him to return to his people and to tell them what had happened, and to have his clothing made in the same way as that of the woman.[67]

The parka created by Qingailisaq was identical to that worn by the caribou woman, "with the exception of the representation of her child, which he added to it. The hands, represented in white skin, are intended to ward off evil spirits. The animal figures represented on the shoulders were explained to represent 'children of the earth.'"[68]

Certain details on this outfit are similar to details on Siberian shamans' costumes. For example, the shamans' heads and hands are covered by ritual garb. Images of helping spirits are attached to the costume; valuable ritual fabric — white caribou fur and red cloth — are used; elaborate fringes, tassels, and chevron patterns (references to braiding) are found in the costumes. The outfit of the Iglulik shaman, like those of his Siberian colleagues, derived from a vision or supernatural experience. Further examination of museum collections will undoubtedly uncover additional examples of Inuit shamanistic clothing and shed more light on this important feature of traditional Inuit cosmology and material culture.[69]

European Contact and its Influence on Parka Decoration

Inuit usually depended on the resources in their own region for constructing objects required for survival. Trading among Inuit groups, however, ensured the distribution of valuable raw materials across the Canadian Arctic. Wood, for example, was a rare and precious commodity, required for kayak frames, sleds, hunting equipment, and domestic utensils. Valuable copper for arrowheads, soapstone for lamps and cooking pots, and various furs and skins were also traded from region to region. The acquisition of objects through trade also conferred prestige upon the owner; perhaps for this reason trade items for personal adornment were especially prized.

The Mackenzie-area Inuit drew upon the extensive trade network of Alaskan Inuit to obtain blue beads from Siberia. These were used in labrets, earrings, and hairdressing, as well as in the decoration of needle cases and other objects (such as men's pipes) of particular importance to the owner. Pacific dentalium shells, obtained through the trade routes of neighbouring Athapaskan groups, were also used in earrings and hairdressing (Figure 181).

In the Eastern and Central Canadian Arctic, contact with Europeans provided an array of objects for personal adornment and parka decoration. Coloured cloth, metal coins, and tiny beads of coloured glass were especially valued. Seamstresses used the new objects in the conventional forms of decoration inherited from past generations.

Such a development can be seen in hair design. Styles of hairdress-

180. (over)
Shaman's vestments, Iglulik Inuit (Iglulingmiut), front and back views, collected c. 1902. American Museum of Natural History, New York 60/4440. L:96.5; W:52

Traditionally, the shaman (*angakkuq*) served as the intermediary between the natural and supernatural worlds. This hoodless garment, accompanied by a separate hat and mitts, is the only fully documented shaman's costume from the Canadian Arctic. Collected from Qingailisaq, an Iglulik shaman, its design derives from the shaman's encounter with mountain spirits: the hands show how he was accosted by these spirits; the two polar bears (or giant caribou) over the shoulder blades allude to his helping spirits. The existence of this costume suggests a prehistoric tradition of shamanic costume in the Canadian Arctic, probably with roots in Siberia.

ing and customs related to the treatment of the hair revealed a spiritual significance. In the Iglulik area, for example, the hair was associated with the soul. Therefore, anyone who cut his hair cut away a part of his soul.[70] Hair trimmings were never discarded but were burned or saved and often incorporated into women's hair-styles.[71] This latter practice also existed in the Mackenzie area.[72]

Hair-styling in the Central Canadian Arctic and the Mackenzie area was similar: women usually parted their hair in the middle to form a long plait or tail on each side of the head. In the Mackenzie area, the plaits were wrapped with strings of white and blue seed beads;[73] in the

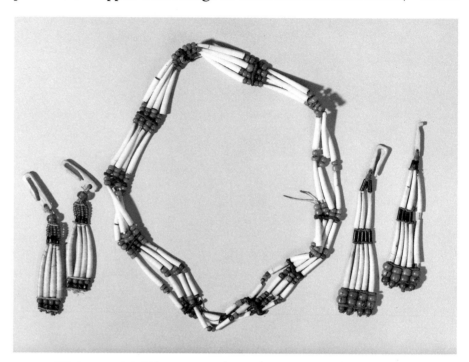

181.
Earrings (two pairs) and headdress, Mackenzie region (Inuvialuit). Courtesy of the Royal Ontario Museum, Toronto HC 1400, HC 1402, HC 1403.

These earrings and headdress reveal the Alaskan and Athapaskan influence in the personal adornment of the Mackenzie region. The earrings are made of dentalium shells from the Pacific and imported glass beads. The circular headdress follows the style worn by Kutchin men in the Athapaskan area.

182.
Atgaratuq, Igjugarjuk's wife. National Museum of Denmark, Department of Ethnography, Copenhagen.

The flow of European trade items into the Canadian Arctic during the late 19th and early 20th centuries strongly influenced the clothing style and personal adornment of the Inuit. This photograph, taken in the 1920s, shows a Padlimiut woman from the Caribou region, her hair wrapped in hairsticks covered with beaded cloth. She also wears a brass browband with long tassels of beads attached to either side. The cloth shawl draped over her caribou fur parka reveals the influence of European trade in the dress styles of the Central Canadian Arctic.

Central Canadian Arctic, the hair was wrapped around a length of wood, antler, or bone, then covered with alternating strips of light and dark caribou fur. The introduction of stroud cloth and beads during the nineteenth century changed the materials but not the form of hair-style. Coloured stroud, usually decorated with beads in triangle motifs, replaced the traditional caribou-fur hair-stick coverings (Figure 182).

The availability of beads during the eighteenth and nineteenth centuries encouraged the production of elaborately beaded ear ornaments worn by Inuit women in Labrador. Long lengths of beads arranged in horizontal colour bars were attached to a cap of depilated sealskin. A thin loop of sinew sewn to the cap apparently fitted over the woman's ear. Caubvic, a Labrador woman brought to England in 1773, wears a pair of these ornaments in a drawing by Nathaniel Dance (Figure 4).[74]

The oldest and most pervasive form of personal decoration among Inuit women, however, was tattooing. In the Mackenzie area, women's tattoos were apparently confined to the chin and forehead;[75] in the Central and Eastern Canadian Arctic, women were more extensively tattooed on the face and body. Two drawings collected from the Netsilik area illustrates the tattoo patterns applied to a woman's face, arms, hands, and thighs (Figure 183). Women in the Ungava region of Nouveau Quebec were once elaborately tattooed "with curved lines and rows of dots on the face, neck, and arms, and on the legs up to mid-thigh. . . . [until] some shaman declared that a prevailing misfortune was the result of tattooing."[76]

183.
Drawing of female tattooing by Arnarulunguaq, Netsilik region. National Museum of Denmark, Department of Ethnography, Copenhagen.

In the Central Canadian Arctic, women were extensively tattooed on the face, arms, hands, and thighs. The lines and geometric patterns were made by drawing a needle, followed by a sinew thread coated with a mixture of soot and blubber, under the skin's surface. Among the Netsilik Inuit, a tattooed woman earned the rewards of the afterlife, for she had endured pain for the sake of beauty.

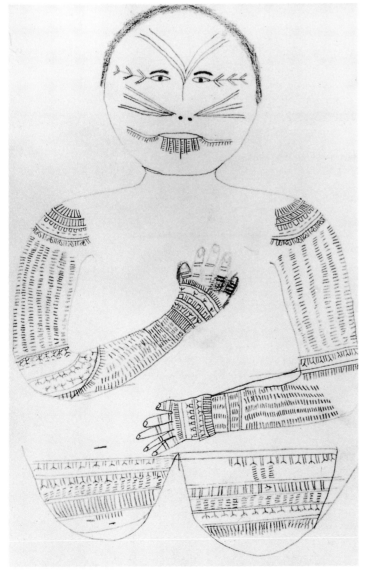
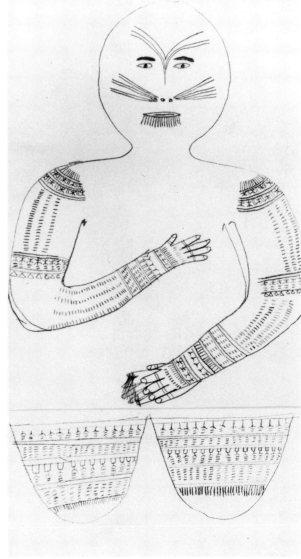

184.
Woman's beaded inner parka, Iglulik Inuit (Aivilingmiut), collected 1911. University Museum, University of Pennsylvania NA 2844.

In the Central Canadian Arctic, elaborate beaded designs were worked out on coloured stroud panels and attached to the chest, shoulders, hood, and wrists of the woman's parka. Beadwork designs were highly individual, the unique invention of the seamstress. This Aivilingmiut parka shows the work of a talented graphic artist. The emblem on the hood depicts a topsail whaling schooner, perhaps the *Era*, mastered by Captain George Comer, the whaling captain who collected this garment (F. Calabretta, in Driscoll 1984).

Women were tattooed during adolescence. In the Ungava region, the candidate was secluded for four days, during which she was tattooed on the face and body by an old woman versed in the art. "When the girl returns to the tent it is known that she has begun to menstruate."[77] In the Copper area, "the process was commenced a year or so before marriage and completed a year or two afterwards."[78]

Tattooing was extremely painful. An older woman, often a relative, made the patterns by drawing a needle and a length of sinew coated with the soot of the oil lamp under the surface of the skin. When the wound healed it left a permanent bluish-grey mark. Dot patterns, which were particularly prevalent in the Eastern Canadian Arctic, were made by pricking the skin with a sharply pointed instrument, then rubbing in a bit of lamp soot.

The Netsilik Inuit believed that tattooing had a deep spiritual significance. Only beautifully tattooed women could join the most able hunters in the rewards of the afterlife, for tattooing proved that a woman was willing to suffer pain for the sake of beauty.[79] In Iglulik, tattooing was also related to childbirth, for the tattooing on a woman's thighs ensured that the first thing a newborn infant would see would be something of beauty.[80] This association of tattooing with menstruation, marriage, and childbirth emphasized the "life-giving" significance of this ancient tradition.[81]

Tattooing and the Inuit Parka

In the Central Canadian Arctic, tattooing marked the joints of the shoulder, elbow, and wrist. The joints were marked with a series of simple geometric shapes inscribed within a multi-tiered cluster of horizontal lines. Similarly, in the decoration of the woman's outer fur parka the seamstress inserted horizontal bands of contrasting fur into the shoulder and wrist of the parka sleeve as a symbolic reference to the joints.[82]

This correspondence between tattooing and parka decoration was made clear in the beaded parkas of the Central Canadian Arctic. The beaded panels on the Aivilingmiut parka mark the major design elements of the parka (Figures 184 and 185). They outline the front chest panels, the *kiniq* or apron flap, the back tail, the upper shoulder, and the wrist, as well as the centre panel and outer edge of the hood. The placement of beaded panels at the shoulders and wrists, and the simple geometric motifs set between pairs of horizontal lines, recall traditional tattooing styles. As beads became more readily available throughout the nineteenth and twentieth centuries, Inuit seamstresses in the Central Canadian Arctic imitated tattooing in devising a style of beadwork decoration that would preserve the symbolic significance of tattooing. Through beadwork — and, on the outer parka, the use of white caribou fur — the seamstress drew attention to those design elements of the women's parka that alluded to life: the *kiniq* as a symbolic reference to procreation; the tail as a reference to the animal, the source of life; the chest or breast panels as a reference to nurturing; the joint-markings as a reference to the skeleton, the final source of life.[83]

The Parka as an Artistic Tradition

The origin of the form and design of the Inuit parka lies hidden in the shadows of Inuit prehistory. The conventional nature of Inuit culture, however, has preserved the form of the parka from generation to generation. Even today, although the Inuit parka is most often made of imported duffel and covered with an outer shell of cotton drill or nylon, the traditional form of the parka remains. The persistence of this form, as well as its function, craftsmanship, and symbolic imagery establish the parka as an artistic tradition.

In terms of function, the construction of Inuit clothing was determined by two basic factors: the demands of the environment and the resources available. Despite limited resources, the Inuit devised ways of treating available material to satisfy various needs.

The treatment and multiple uses of sealskin illustrate this point. As we have seen, water-resistant sealskin with the hair left on was often used in clothing and boots for spring and summer. Water-resistant boots with a sealskin upper and scraped skin sole were worn during the early spring, while the snow was still dry. Waterproof boots, needed during

185.
Woman's beaded, caribou amautik, Aivilingmiut. Collected at Cape Fullerton in 1906. American Museum of Natural History, New York 60/5758. L:136; W:68

This elaborately beaded parka, collected by Captain Comer, is the creation of Niviatsianaq, nicknamed "Shoofly" by American whalers. Although the placement of beadwork on the parka follows a conventional pattern, the depiction of the crouched hunter with his rifle aimed at a caribou is the unique design of Niviatsianaq. This pictorial scene, coupled with that in Figure 184, reveals the increasing influence of outside contact and trade in the Canadian Arctic during the early 20th century.

warm weather, were made from the scraped skin of the bearded seal (*ugjuk*) and skilfully sewn with watertight seams, in which the needle did not puncture the outer surface of the skin. "Men commonly tested a new pair of waterboots by standing in water, and unmercifully scolded their wives if the result proved unsatisfactory."[84]

Sealskin was also used for tents, kayak covers, storage bags, water buckets, and harpoon lashings. The thin parchment-like intestine, lightweight and waterproof, provided windows for snow houses, sails for *umiaks*, and clothing for kayakers. Thus, by recognizing the inherent attributes of materials at hand, and by devising methods of treatment to alter or enhance these attributes, Inuit designed specific objects that responded to the demands of the environment. This functional response, however, only partially explains the form and significance of the Inuit parka.

As an artisan, the Inuit seamstress ranked among the most innovative and skilful craftspeople in the world. Within the community, "an outstanding seamstress enjoys genuine esteem."[85]

The skill of a seamstress was judged by her treatment of skins; her ability to match furs for colour, tone, and texture; her mastery of various stitches; and the rhythmic pattern of her stitches. Frequently, sewing ability passed from generation to generation within families, for it was only under the guidance of an experienced seamstress that a young girl learned the fundamentals and mastered the finer techniques of the art.

In the Netsilik area, when a young girl began to sew she was given a ring made from the skin of the salmon: her stitches were to be as rhythmic as the pattern of scales on the salmon.[86] This parallel between a seamstress's stitches and the patterns of nature suggest her responsibility to reshape and reconstruct the resources available so that Inuit were able to exist in a more favourable relationship with nature.

In sewing a kayak cover, the seamstress transformed man into a new species of waterfowl, allowing him direct access to the sea animals created by Nuliajuk. By sewing the seams of scraped seal or caribou skins with a watertight stitch, she made the kayak cover as impermeable as the skin of the eider ducks, geese, and loons that were the hunter's companions on the inland lakes and open sea. Similarly, by tailoring the parka from the furs of the animal being hunted, the seamstress created the hunter's physical and metaphysical identification with the animal.

In her construction of the parka, the Inuit seamstress continued an inherited tradition of form and style. She was not only a gifted artisan but also a guardian of Inuit cultural identity, expressed in real and symbolic terms, consciously and unconsciously, in the design of the parka.

As an artistic tradition, the parka reflects essential cultural ideas regarding the relationship of Inuit to the world around them, between man and animal, male and female. The parka exists as a formal, multivalent statement of survival: survival of the individual, protected from the elements; and survival of Inuit culture, basically, through dependence on the animal, the source of life, and ultimately, through the union of male and female, and the regeneration of human life.

Bernadette Driscoll

Silent Speakers
Arts of the
Northwest Coast

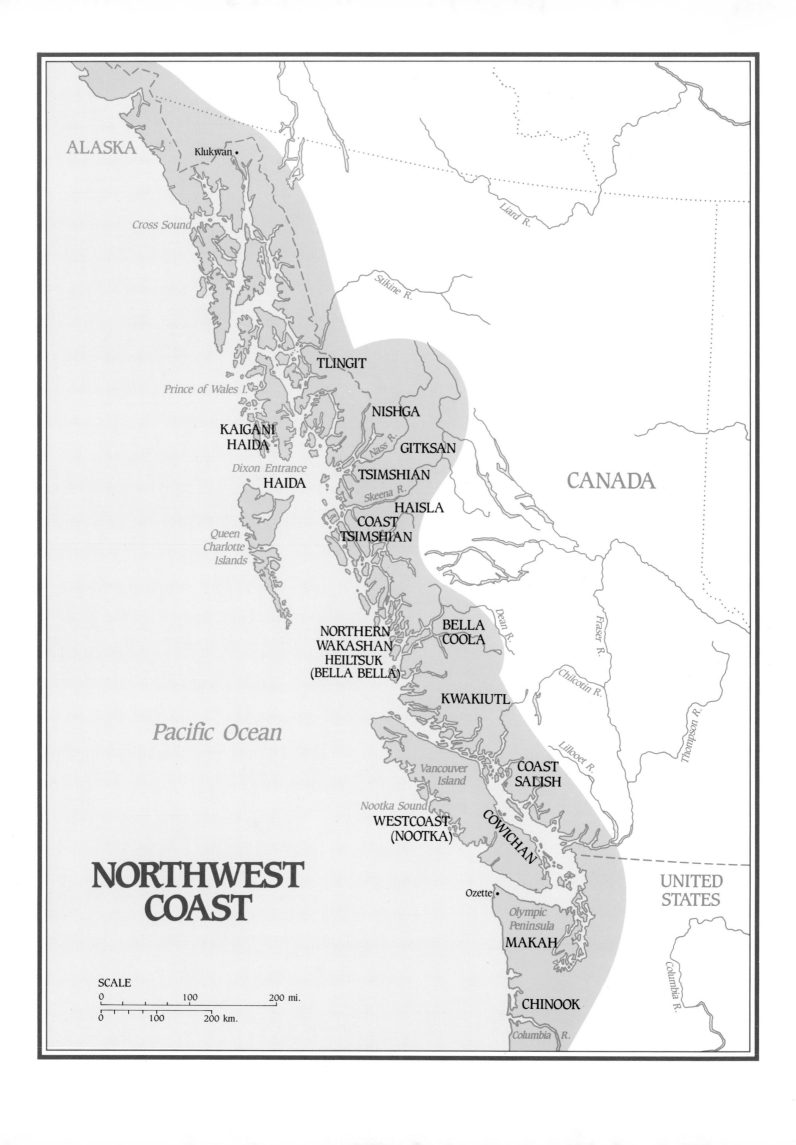

ALASKA

Klukwan •

Cross Sound

Stikine R.

Liard R.

TLINGIT

Prince of Wales I.

NISHGA

KAIGANI
HAIDA

Nass R.

GITKSAN

Dixon Entrance

TSIMSHIAN

HAIDA

Skeena R.

CANADA

HAISLA
COAST
TSIMSHIAN

*Queen
Charlotte
Islands*

Dean R.

Fraser R.

NORTHERN
WAKASHAN
HEILTSUK
(BELLA BELLA)

BELLA
COOLA

Chilcotin R.

Pacific Ocean

KWAKIUTL

Lillooet R.

Thompson R.

*Vancouver
Island*

COAST
SALISH

Nootka Sound

WESTCOAST
(NOOTKA)

COWICHAN

UNITED
STATES

Ozette •

*Olympic
Peninsula*

NORTHWEST
COAST

MAKAH

CHINOOK

Columbia R.

SCALE

| 0 | 100 | 200 mi. |

| 0 | 100 | 200 km. |

Columbia R.

Overture

Art can never be understood, but can only be seen as a kind of magic, the most profound and mysterious of all human activities. Within that magic, one of the deepest mysteries is the art of the Northwest Coast — a unique expression of an illiterate people, resembling no other art form except perhaps the most sophisticated calligraphy. If it were the product of some great urban civilization, it would have still been an amazing creation, the result of a constant dialogue between a rigidly structured convention and the questing genius of the artists, controlled and amended by a cool, sometimes ironic, intellect.

Being what it really was, the work of a handful of sea hunters living in tiny communities, it exists as one of the most inexplicably dazzling facets of human creativity. It was made to serve the compulsive need to proclaim the power and prestige of the old aristocrats, a power which might extend in some instances over as many as a hundred individuals; and yet so strong was their conviction of that power that even today it radiates undiminished from the great works of the past, whether they be as exquisitely small as a goat-horn spoon handle or as monumentally huge as a totem pole, or if you like, monumentally small or exquisitely huge.

It is buried now, that old powerful magic, under the wrinkled grey curtain of age, beneath the sterile canopy of the museum, the meaningless pile of words of the experts. But it is still there, as strong as ever, a renewing force for all of us if we can learn to use it. It can never give us what it gave those for whom it was created, the sure conviction of their own worth, but it can assure us through its residual magic, of possibilities still attainable for us and our kind. With a little effort, this much we can understand.[1]

Haida artist Bill Reid's hitherto unpublished but eloquent writing helps to place the arts of the Northwest Coast in a deservedly unique historical and cultural context. Claude Lévi-Strauss, pre-eminent among twentieth-century anthropologists, has compared the arts of the Northwest Coast with the classic arts of Greece and Egypt.[2] Indeed, the art of the Northwest Coast rivals that produced anywhere in the world, both in quantity, which was prodigious,[3] and in aesthetic quality, which still delights us today.

Several factors permitted and encouraged these artistic outpourings, among them the natures of the peoples who first arrived on the Pacific Coast and the skills they brought with them, skills that grew and diversified in their rich new surroundings.

The earliest Northwest Coast peoples settled some ten to twelve thousand years ago along a twisting coastline studded with islands and inlets extending from Yakutat Bay, in Alaska, to the valley of the Columbia River. They arrived by various routes from what was probably an Asiatic homeland, bringing with them several cultural traditions. Recent archaeological evidence suggests that some were maritime people who worked with wood and subsisted on marine resources, and who navigated the rugged, often stormy, coast. Others undoubtedly followed the river valleys from the interior to the coast.[4]

The creative skills and traditions they brought with them were modified and adapted to the new environment of the Northwest Coast, and eventually, elaborate societies developed that were encountered by eighteenth-century European explorers. An indication of how rich and varied the cultures of the Coast had become by that time is the wide linguistic diversity: six separate linguistic groups, several dozen languages,[5] and innumerable dialects, many understandable only to residents of the immediate area.

The main linguistic divisions by which the various groups are identified are, from north to south, the Tlingit; the Haida; the Tsimshian (whose speakers are the Coast Tsimshian, the Nishga, and the Gitksan); the Wakashan-speaking people – the Haisla, the Xaihais, the Heiltsuk or Bella Bella, the Kwakiutl (or Kwakwa ka' wakw, meaning Kwakwalla speakers), the West Coast (Nootka or Nuu-Chah-Nulth), and the Makah; the Salishan speakers – the Bella Coola and the Coast Salish; and finally the Penutian speakers, the Chinook.

As they differed in language and other cultural characteristics, so they each had several versions of an origin myth to account for their own existence as well as that of the world in which its members lived. Within the single ethnic group of the Kwakiutl, for example, which comprised twenty-eight tribal subgroups, each had its own origin myth. These tales tell of supernatural ancestors who came down from the sky, or up from the sea or the underworld, in the form of a thunderbird or another fabulous being, and assumed human form by removing their masks or costumes. Their descendants became the human members of the tribes. A Nimpkish (Kwakiutl) tale says that, after the flood, the former people were transformed into animals and stones. When the waters had receded, the giant halibut Nemyya'likyo (Only One) rose from the depths of the ocean carrying on his back the first man, whom he put ashore at Qulkh before returning to the depths. The man looked around on earth and saw no one. Therefore he called himself Nemokyustalis, Being-the-only-one-to-emerge-on-shore-from-the-Ocean-Depths.[6]

First Encounters

From the European perspective, history on the Northwest Coast begins with the first dated and recorded meetings with the natives in the mid-eighteenth century. There may have been earlier native contacts made with non-literate maritime people, such as the inhabitants of the Aleutian Islands and those of northeastern Asia. But as far as the "civilized" world was concerned, until more than a couple of hundred years ago, the Northwest Coast of America was completely unknown. The first European visitors to the Northwest Coast were seafarers and explorers sent to map this unknown region. Their tales of enormous wealth to be found in the newly discovered lands encouraged fur hunters and traders to follow.

In the north, Russian explorers and traders moved farther east along the Aleutian Islands year after year; they reached Tlingit territory, in what is now mainland Alaska, in 1741.

The Spanish had established settlements in Mexico and California, and feared that the Russians' momentum might carry them right down the coast. Spain therefore dispatched a series of expeditions northward to counteract Russian penetration and to secure its own territorial rights.[7]

In the summer of 1774, off what is now called Langara Island, in the northwest corner of the Queen Charlotte archipelago, the Juan Perez expedition was welcomed by a flotilla of large Haida canoes, many as long as Perez's frigate, *Santiago*. The paddlers sang and scattered eagle down on the water, a traditional Northwest Coast sign of peace. The natives exchanged dried fish for trival, but to them exotic, items with the ship's crew. Trade between the Northwest Coast natives and the Europeans had begun.[8]

Later in exchange for knives and almost anything made of iron, the natives offered sea-otter pelts, fur clothing, woven and ornamented blankets, cedar-bark mats, basketry hats, and a variety of carved dishes, boxes, rattles, and spoons (Figure 186).

For a few years after this friendly exchange, the main trade was in sea-otter pelts, which commanded very high prices in China. Other commodities and numerous "artificial curiosities,"[9] the now-famous "art objects" of the Coast, found their way into the holds of the 450 or so trading vessels. Explorers such as Perez and Cook — the first serious collector on the Northwest Coast, in 1778 — and later Malaspina (1792), Vancouver (1792 to 1794), and Lisiansky (1804), were on "government-sponsored expeditions, prompted by exploratory, scientific, and diplomatic purposes."[10] Not only did they gather samples of Northwest Coast artistic

186.
Double-headed bird rattle. West Coast, collected in 1778. University Museum of Archaeology and Anthropology, Cambridge 22.948. L:35; W:20; H.12

The elegant simplicity of this rattle is characteristic of many 18th-century Wakashan sculptures.

187. (opposite)
Trophy-head effigy, Wakashan, collected in 1778. South African Museum, Cape Town 2361. W:22; H:27

A ritual gift from the natives to the newcomers.

188.
Slat armour, collected in 1778. University Museum of Archaeology and Anthropology, Cambridge 22.950 b. L:28; W:42; H.52

The warrior's equipment consisted of body armour made from wooden slats laced together with sinew, and worn over an elk-hide tunic, a heavy wooden helmet, a curved and bent wooden collar, and slat armour greaves.

expression, some of which are pictured here; they also described the characteristics of Northwest Coast native life in their diaries and logbooks: the extraordinary plank houses handsomely decorated "with a kind of frieze work,"[11] the large, seaworthy dug-out canoes, the abundance of preserved food, the class stratification, the dress and demeanour of people, the varied attitudes towards trading their "gods,"[12] and their sophisticated dealings with strangers and traders.[13]

Although trade brought with it new diseases and firearms that made native intertribal warfare increasingly deadly, the early maritime fur trade has been perceived as having a positive impact on Northwest Coast culture, particularly its art, for trade added riches to a society already organized around wealth.[14] New tools and guns increased the natives' productive efficiency. The new wealth strengthened existing social and economic systems as the chiefs became richer. More wealth led to more and bigger potlatches; the more active ceremonial life, in turn, increased the need for artistic products. The character of ceremonial life was altered after contact as well. The new diseases may have caused a rapid turnover in leadership. Frequent potlatches and feasts were needed to initiate new leaders.[15] Moreover, some decorated artefacts were no longer made. The *atlatl* (or spear thrower) and warrior gear such as slat armour, visors, bows, and so on had become obsolete after contact (Figures 188 and 208).

We do not know exactly the role of pre-contact iron tools in the distinc-

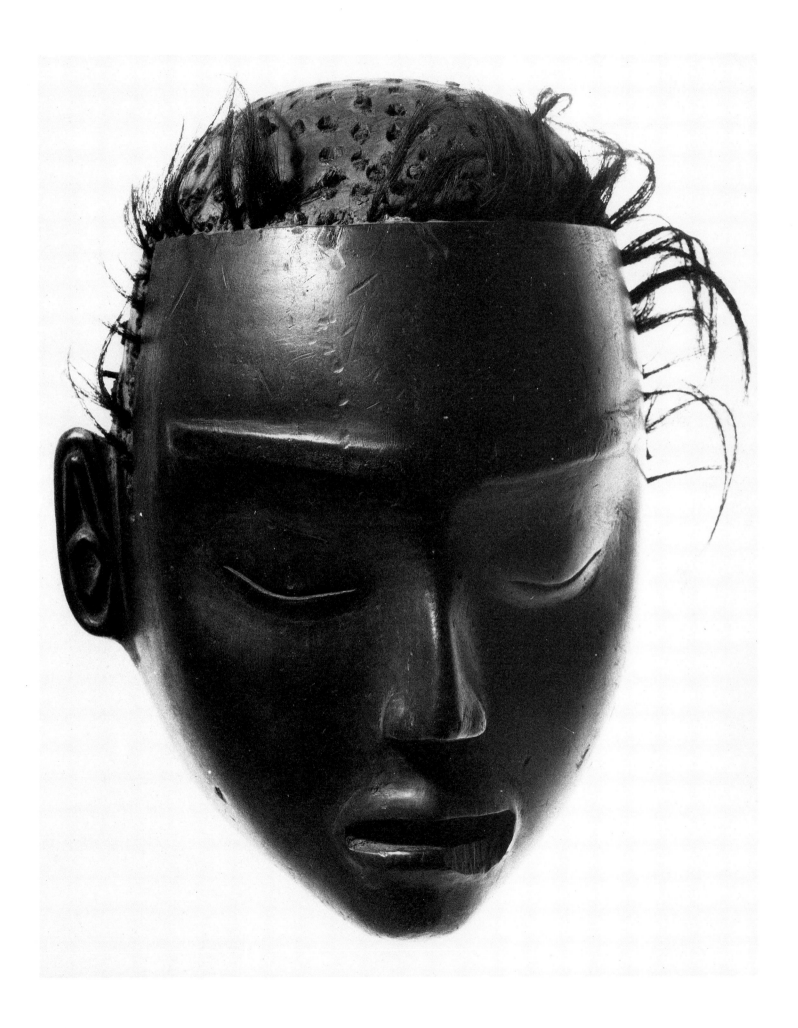

tive styles in existence at the time of contact, or in prehistoric times,[16] but new iron tools obviously allowed artisans to work faster while maintaining or refining the quality of their products (Figure 189). Totem-pole carving, for example, could be more complex, and artisans enjoyed a period of great creativity.

The production of artefacts for the European market had begun before the end of the eighteenth century,[17] and continued through the nineteenth century, "the golden age"[18] of Northwest Coast art. During this period, some types of Haida argillite carvings originated and thrived, while traditional artistic production, diversity, and styles continued.

189.
Heraldic sculptures characteristic of northern groups. Haida village of Ninstints (Anthony Island), British Columbia, declared a "World Heritage Site, of importance to the history of mankind," by UNESCO in 1980. Photograph by C.F. Newcombe, 1901. Courtesy of the British Columbia Provincial Museum, Victoria.

In their eagerness for European metal, the Northwest Coast natives seemed willing to part with many things, from vital war implements (Figure 206) to secret-society items.[19] One of Cook's officers describes how the natives at Nootka Sound would bring "strange carv'd heads, & place them in a conspicuous part of the Ship, & desire us to let them remain there, & for these they would receive no return."[20] One such powerful carving, a very sensitively executed trophy head, is now in the South Africa Museum; it was left in Cape Town by Cook on his return to Europe (Figure 187).

This odd gift, like all Northwest Coast art forms, is rooted in two complementary elements of Northwest Coast culture: it fulfills a social function and reveals a meaning. To understanding it and, by extension, eighteenth- and early-nineteenth-century Northwest Coast artistic expression, it is necessary to consider three intimately related components: context, form, and content. These are the essentials of all art forms, if we consider art, like other natural and human activities, to be based on a system. The aesthetic standard of any artwork depends on its context, form, and content combining to form an ordered, consistent whole. The context of Northwest Coast art production includes life-style, social structure, wealth, and world-view. An understanding of the iconography and iconology of the Northwest Coast embedded in this belief system and world-view will give us a deeper appreciation of this distinctive art style, its local variations, and that hidden dimension, meaning.

Context, Form, and Content

The coastal peoples enjoyed environmental conditions that provided a wide range of workable raw materials. The most important was the wood of the western red cedar (*Thuja Plicata*), which grew abundantly along the coast except in the far north. Yellow cedar (*Chamaecypary Noot-kaensis*), alder (*Alnus*), yew (*Taxus Brevifolia*), and several other coniferous and deciduous trees yielded workable wood, bark, and roots. Abundant animal life provided hides, sinews, wool, bones, antlers, horns, and shells. Some were gathered locally; others were traded.[21] Peoples on the Coast also shared the ingenious technology of steaming wood, used in the manufacture of dug-out canoes and bent-corner boxes; an economy based on fishing resources; and a set of beliefs related to supernatural beings and guardian spirits. Yet the area was not homogeneous in its cultural development. Distinctive northern and southern social contexts, meeting roughly at Bella Bella, produced unique artistic styles. Among the northern groups are the Tlingit, Haida, Coast Tsimshian, Nishga, Gitksan, and Bella Bella. The southern groups may be represented by the Kwakiutl, West Coast, and Coast Salish, and their northern linguistic relatives, the Bella Coola.

190.
Interior of a Westcoast House at Friendly Cove. Watercolour by John Webber, 1778. Peabody Museum, Harvard University 41-72-10/499. Photograph by Hillel Burger.

The house posts are reminiscent of a carved miniature post collected on Cook's third voyage and now located in Berlin (IV.B.265).

Context

Why have some Northwest Coast societies produced more or better-designed artistic expressions than others? It is often suggested that sufficient leisure time to play with techniques and forms is a prerequisite for high art, and that only when the economic base is productive is leisure time afforded. Hence art has been held to depend upon the production of foods in excess of subsistence needs.[22] Yet the Coast Salish culture, for example, produced neither the range nor the complexity of objects made farther to the north or west — only one mask type, the Swaixwe, was produced during historic times — despite the fact that their technology, skills, and economy were similar to those of the northern groups. Thus, although increased leisure time may foster the development of the arts, it does not cause it; other factors play a part.[23] For art develops in the cultural complexity usually associated with sedentary societies that have a relatively reliable subsistence base and an extensive division and specialization of labour.[24] Here again, Northwest Coast society is a remarkable phenomenon.

191.
Hat, West Coast, collected in 1778.
Courtesy of the Trustees of the British
Museum, London NWC 6. D:27; H:28.5

192.
Effigy of a whale fin, Wakashan (Makah),
c. 1600. Makah Cultural and Research
Center, Neah Bay, Washington.

Made from several pieces of red cedar sewn
together and inlaid with some 700 sea-otter
molar teeth arranged to depict the thunderbird in the centre.

The Rise of Northwest Coast Culture

Northwest Coast people were fishermen, hunters, gatherers, and pre-
servers; but their societies little resembled the other hunting and gathering cultures represented in this book. The other cultures were made of
nomadic and egalitarian people, who shared food and other products,
who sharply divided labour according to gender, who had a rather limited
material culture, and who had no specialized artisans. By comparison,
Northwest Coast settlements tended to be permanent; the people left their
winter villages only for such seasonal activities as salmon fishing and
shellfish gathering. This permitted the development of complex societies,
hierarchically structured from slaves to the proud and wealthy aristocrats
who commissioned talented specialists to produce original works of art,
mainly for important ceremonial events.

To maintain a settled existence based on marine-fauna resources,
it was necessary to develop sophisticated technologies both to harvest
great quantities of seasonally available foods and to preserve the harvest
for later use. The staple of all coastal peoples, the Pacific salmon, was
supplemented by other fish and shellfish, wild fruits, and sea and land
game. Highly sophisticated methods of capturing fish — a male activity —
and preserving them — a female activity — were developed. Preserving
was the key factor, for it reduced the need to leave the community for
fresh supplies; stable groupings of people could form permanent or semi-
permanent communities. Large durable wooden dwellings, both utilitarian and prestigious, were decorated with permanent monumental sculptures. Luxury goods of all kinds could be accumulated, from food supplies
to manufactured objects, such as carved storage chests, mountain-goat
and fur-seal robes, and woven capes. Finally, the refinement of existing
skills, such as wood carving and bark and wool weaving, was
encouraged.

The watercolour of the Nootka Sound house interior by John Webber
(Figure 190), the official artist for Cook's expedition, clearly illustrates
the life-style of these people. The floor space of their huge dwelling is
organized into separate areas for sleeping, food preparation, storage, and
so on. Some of the occupants wear cloaks and wrapped-around skirts
of shredded cedar bark. Like most coastal peoples, they are barefoot.
Dried and smoked fish hang on racks from the roof. Some people are
boiling food in a wooden box; the water is heated with hot rocks. Two
carved house posts display the owner's crest.

In this everyday domestic scene, most of the ritual objects are out
of view in their storage chests along the walls of the house; but there
is one important symbolic item visible, to the right of the figures on the
platform. It is in the shape of the dorsal fin of a whale. The parallel lines
of white dots probably represent a decoration of shell or tooth inlay. A
similar effigy made from several pieces of red cedar sewn together was
discovered in the rich Ozette archaeological site on the Olympic Peninsula
in Washington State.

We do not know whether they were the only native group to hunt
whales, but it is certain that only the people of the West Coast of
Vancouver Island attached such ceremonial significance to the killing of
these great animals. The right to hunt was reserved for the noble chiefs,
who gained considerable acclaim for each successful hunt. Long ritual
purification rites prepared the hunter for his dramatic encounter with "this
high born lady," as the whale was addressed. With a harpooner in the
bow, several canoes participated in the hunt. Many harpoons, each
attached to an inflated sealskin float, were planted in the body of the
prey. When the animal became exhausted, the chief dispatched it at close
range with a long lance. Such a whaling scene is a decorative element

193.
Helmet, Tlingit. Collected at Yakutat in
1791. Museo de Americas, Madrid 1290.
L:37; W:12.5; H:25

This helmet, painted black, red, white, and
green, possibly represents a seal.

of high status on the eighteenth-century West-Coast-style chief's hat,
woven of cedar bark and decorated with an overlay of surf grass
(*Phyllospadix Torreyi*) (Figure 191).

With great effort, the dead whale was towed to shore, where it was
greeted ceremonially. The whale was then butchered in a prescribed ritual
manner. The chief would receive first the most important part, the saddle:

> First to be cut off was the whaler's special and large piece, the saddle
> of skin and blubber of the dorsal fin back of the head. . . . Eagle
> feathers were stuck in a row on top and white down was sprinkled
> on in honour of the whale. The whale was appeased, for being taken,
> by ceremonies performed around its saddle.[25]

The saddle was later cut into thin strips and boiled. The oil was stored
in sea-lion bladders, which were decorated with eagle feathers for winter
feasts.

The massive house visited and recorded by Webber was the home
of a wealthy whale-hunter chief; the saddle was a symbol of his hunting
activities, and, by extension, of his wealth, power, and rank.

One determining factor of egalitarian and non-egalitarian societies
is the existence or absence of storage foods. Preservation — that is, transforming food into a more durable product — allows food to be monopolized
or exchanged through inter-group relationships. Social inequalities become
possible when the old rule of sharing no longer exists.[26]

In the non-egalitarian Northwest Coast societies, the old obligation
to share was transformed through the "potlatch," a complex ceremony
during which different types of preserved foods and manufactured objects
were given as gifts. The need and desire to share surplus food grew into
a striving for social position through the control and display of wealth.
(The actual sharing was less important than the ostentatious way of
asserting or raising the donor's prestige.) Chiefs spent years accumulat-
ing enough wealth to give a potlatch.

Wealth thus redistributed emphasizes differences in rank, and
ultimately leads to the possibility of control of labour and production by
certain individuals. Such control by leaders, combined with a sense of
ownership or territoriality, may lead to hostilities between groups. Head-
hunting and warfare are evidenced by trophy-head collection and weapons
such as stone, antler, and whale-bone clubs, daggers, and warrior outfits

consisting of a war helmet, visor, and slat armor worn over a leather tunic (Figures 188 and 193).

Although all the societies were hierarchical and based on wealth, it was not necessarily the groups with the greatest amount of natural resources that produced the greatest art.

> . . . the most spectacular art production occurred in the least hospitable region and the bountiful Salish area nurtured the least imposing arts. It has been suggested that the more locally concentrated resources in the north influenced the development of the concept of rank and privilege, which in the last analysis is the direct motivation for much northern heraldic art.[27]

A greater abundance of totem poles existed in the north than in the south, for example; but another equally important factor must also be taken into consideration: social structure.

194.
Ceremonial interior screen from Kitwankul village (Skeena River). Canadian Museum of Civilization, National Museums of Canada, Ottawa 62244.

The dragonfly is a decorative motif, not a crest, while the two men are crests of the clan *Wudaxhayetes*. Under the beak (which was added the last time it was used, c. 1850), swansdown with red cedar bark was suspended.

Northwest Coast Social Structure

Social factors determined the production of art works in the north, where art was created to express social position. In the south, the motivation was more religious and spiritual. We do have comprehensive descriptions and interpretations of the shamanic and religious aspects of Northwest Coast arts as displayed during the Winter Ceremonial and in other contexts;[28] yet no systematic correlation of art styles with social and economic structures has been done. Nevertheless, stylistic differences can be explained in terms of the social structures that inform much of Northwest Coast art.

The northern groups shared, with minor differences, many structural features — division into several social units, called phratries; descent traced through females only, and children assigned membership in their mother's kin group; residence after marriage with the husband's maternal uncle; potlatch; and ranking systems. Men and women had to marry outside their own social unit. A social unit comprised clans made up of lineages of close kin. Each status group had its own origin myths and legends, and symbols or crests, which its members would wear on suitable occasions.

The crests are made up of named, totemic representations, depicted as natural and supernatural animals, humanoid creatures, natural

195.
Interior of Chilkat (Tlingit) chief's house at Klukwan. Winter and Pond photographers, 1900. Courtesy of the British Columbia Provincial Museum, Victoria.

It is as if the Tlingit universe is encompassed in this extraordinary display of wealth.

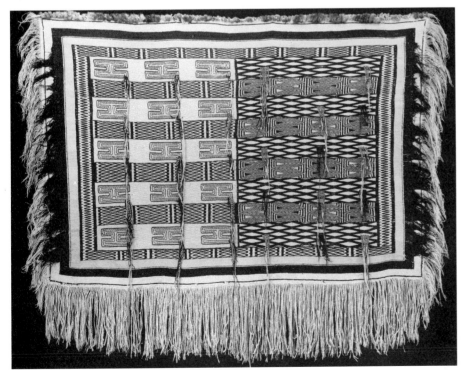

196.
Blanket, Tlingit, c. 1800. Peabody Museum, Harvard University 09-08-10/76401. Photograph by Hillel Burger.

The "Swift" blanket, named after its collector, Captain Benjamin Swift of Charlestown, Massachusetts, displays elaborate geometric patterns.

phenomena such as clouds and rainbows, plants (fireweed, for example), and celestial bodies, such as the moon, the sun, and the stars. They appeared on totem poles, house fronts, interior house screens, ceremonial headdresses, frontlets, and robes, and were tattooed on faces and bodies (Figure 194). Sixty-two Haida crests[29] and ninety-nine Tsimshian crests have been identified.[30]

Much heraldic art in the north was displayed at mortuary potlatches held to commemorate the death of a chief and recognize his successor. Building a new house and raising the house frontal pole was another important occasion on which crest art was displayed.

Chiefs and nobles, like the nobility of mediaeval Europe, commissioned art works for important social display. "It is as though the heraldic idea had taken hold of the whole life and had permeated it with a feeling that social standing must be expressed at every step by heraldry."[31]

A late-nineteenth-century photograph taken in the Tlingit village of Klukwan shows a Chilkat chief surrounded by his material possessions (Figure 195). In the background a monumental carved and painted screen represents the "rain wall," whose symbolism remains obscure;[32] it is flanked by two elaborately carved house posts representing mythical creatures and their exploits. At the foot of the screen lies the fourteen-foot long "wood worm" ceremonial dish, a prominent crest among the Tlingit. On a platform below, many crest symbols can be seen on helmets, clan hats, painted leather tunics, a Chilkat woven apron displaying a beaver crest, an ermine cape, animal and humanoid masks, hats, and chests containing sacred paraphernalia. It is as if the Tlingit universe is encompassed in this extraordinary display of wealth.

The southern groups had a different social structure. Ranked lineages or houses were the principal social units; descent was through both parents, as in European societies; and after marriage the new couple would generally reside in the neighbourhood of the husband's father. Southern groups did share their northern neighbours' concepts of rank, wealth, and the display of wealth.

Among the created objects of greatest value were the blankets referred to in the north as "Chilkat blankets" and in the south as "chief's blankets." They could be worn only by those entitled to them by rank; they were a type of currency (Figure 196).

Because the blankets could be cut up or unravelled and rewoven, they could be divided and recombined. Occasionally, a Chilkat blanket would be transformed into several new garments, such as aprons and leggings. The finely woven blankets, called objects of "bright pride," were also coveted because they were rare.

The blankets were not made after the introduction of Hudson's Bay blankets, but a new wealth item, copper plates, became a valuable item of exchange. Like Chilkat blankets, they could be cut and pieced back together. Moreover, both share a three-part design abstractly based on the human body.[33]

There were more potlatch occasions in the south than in the north. As in the north, potlatches marked death, succession, *rites de passage*, house building, and pole raising; but they were also associated with marriage.[34]

Initiation into dancing societies was always associated with potlatching. Dancing societies, apparently centred among the Bella Bella, diffused north (with least impact among the Tlingit)[35] and south (with least impact among the West Coast and the Salish)[36] during the mid-nineteenth century. Among the theatrical Kwakiutl, elaborate dramas were performed representing the abduction by supernatural beings of individuals who had inherited the rights to perform and, subsequently, their return, freshly endowed with spectacular ceremonial privileges.

197.
Noohlmahl (Fool) mask, Kwakiutl, 19th century. Courtesy of the Trustees of the British Museum, London 1944. Am. 2.145. H:33; W:25

The fool dancer is a member of the *Hamatsa* (Man Eater) secret society. His face is encircled by a mane of curvilinear ribs.

The numerous Kwakiutl secret-society masks, worn only by men,[37] take the form of human, animal, and mythical characters, and include transformation masks and puppets (Figure 200). One of these characters is the Fool, *Noohlmahl*. Everywhere, fools have played a prominent and indispensable role; they deride the self-important and deflate the pompous. They make the overwhelming comic, and thus manageable. This concept was highly developed within the theatrical rituals of the Kwakiutl.

This mask represents *Noohlmahl*, the fool dancer, a member of the Hamatsa (Cannibal) secret society, who had specific powers and functions (Figure 197). Membership in the *Noohlmahl* fraternity derives from visions or dreams of unearthly spirits who hate order. As a result, the *Noohlmahl* conduct is violent, unpredictable, and "contrary." Filthy and rude buffoons with grotesque, comedic masks, distorted by huge noses from which mucous constantly runs, strike out with their clubs, endangering life and property. (In their contemporary manifestations, the *Noohlmahl* have lost their violence; they retain their relevance only as figures of fun and eccentricity in the dignified Winter Ritual).

198.
Pair of painted screens depicting four episodes of the Raven Cycle, Tlingit, mid-19th century. Denver Art Museum, Colorado 1939. 140. PT1-3 a, b. L:410; H:165.

Coast Salish societies seem to have possessed far less wealth in the form of titles, ceremonial privileges, and crest uses than their northern and western counterparts. Consequently, they had fewer formal indications of social position. There seems also to have been a narrower range from high to low.[38] Nonetheless, the chief's prestige stemmed from his possession of group properties.

All Coast societies included chiefs, nobles, commoners, and slaves. The slaves formed a uniform subgroup, but it seems that the members of other groups "occupied a series of social positions that were graded in minute steps from high to low. . . . It is impossible to mark off a fixed point separating noble from commoner."[39] Despite the apparent rigidity of the system, persons could alter their status slightly, and improve that of their children and other dependent relatives.

Northwest Coast societies differed in their degree of stratification and flexibility, although the northern societies were generally more rigid than those in the south.

> . . . if there is any tendency of societies to cluster it is near the center. . . . Even in this central group, however, any two societies can be compared as to their relative nearness to the two poles, and their art styles can then be investigated to see whether they differ in the predicted direction.[40]

One theory holds that a relationship exists between matrilineal kin groups and achievements in plastic arts. Societies that trace descent through the mother rather than the father may "generate an emotional climate predisposing the men to aesthetic expression."[41] In such cases, art can be seen as a mechanism by which inner societal tensions are relieved. Another study relates art styles to three aspects of social relations: social hierarchy, the relative prestige of the sexes, and the form of marriage.[42]

While the choice of variables and criteria in these studies can be criticized, their findings are stimulating. For example, significant association exists between stratified social systems and asymmetry in art.[43] In this context, Northwest Coast art poses an interesting paradox. Almost every Northwest Coast two- or three-dimensional creation shows perfect bilateral symmetry, yet much of the decoration of these items is asymmetrical. The Northwest Coast artist often made the decorations on opposite sides of a three-dimensional object (which cannot be seen at the same time and, logically, should be symmetrical) different in many details, while keeping the general structure of the designs enough alike

that they would appear to be fully symmetrical to the casual viewer. The result is a paradox, an asymmetrical symmetry. For example, the end paintings on all-purpose storage chests were hardly ever mirror images, often differing radically in their orientation and treatment. But they appear symmetrical until examined carefully.

The Tlingit raven screens of Sitka are also fine examples of this illusion, as all design elements are visible at once (Figure 198). The screens depict four episodes in the raven legend. At first glance, all four ravens appear to be identical except that two face one way and two the other. Upon closer observation, however, one can see that the raven images are far from identical.

If social stratification does lead to asymmetry in art, and if the absence of such stratification gives rise to the use of symmetry, how can Northwest Coast designs be simultaneously symmetrical and asymmetrical? The answer may be that such designs occur when "the existence of a class of persons which are associated with more than one ranked group serves to blur the distinctions between the various groups in the stratification system."[44]

Among the Kwakiutl, for example, a noble person can belong simultaneously to several ranked *numayms* (descent groups) in order to increase his or her potlatch positions. Moreover, the first four children born to a Kwakiutl noble family are noble; the other siblings are of lower rank.

Although all Northwest Coast societies were stratified and showed the use of asymmetry in their art works, the greater the number of cross-affiliations, society memberships, or other situations in which social stratification becomes blurred, the more likely symmetry and asymmetry will be found simultaneously in art.

However, heraldic art forms were not merely passive reflections of the social order; they were also agents of ideology and affected social interaction. These objects could be manipulated by their owners to create not only esteem and power, but also confusion and disorder. As an evocation of social values, they could express challenge; and they could, if only for a moment, threaten the existing social order.

> . . . if any chief learned that one of his crests had been adopted by a chief of a family that was considered of lower rank, he would put the latter to shame, and by giving away or destroying more property than the other chief could muster, force him to abandon it.[45]

Thus Northwest Coast aesthetic phenomena are far from purely aesthetic. Not only were they indispensable in promoting economic exchanges; they were also instruments of power, as they reflected the structures of the society.

World-View

> Their world view is their picture of the way things in sheer actuality are, their concept of nature, of self, of society. It contains their most comprehensive ideas of order.[46]

People from all over the world have attempted to explain the unknowable by constructing a supernatural world. And they talk about this world in their myths and legends. These stories, which tell the adventures of supernatural beings that have magical powers, deal mostly with marriage alliances and access to wealth. But journeys into the underworld or into the celestial realm inform us also of the cosmological world of the Northwest Coast natives.

A general overview of Northwest Coast cosmology as revealed in mythology will help unravel at least one mystery: the meaning of the gift left by the natives on Cook's ship (see p. 208).

At the heart of traditional Northwest Coast beliefs lies the general conception of a universe divided into several cosmic realms — Sky (Above), Land (Nearby), Ocean (Below), Underworld (Underneath) — each inhabited by a pantheon of supernatural beings endowed with specific supernatural powers. All species of animals and plants are regarded as supernatural beings; nature is supernatural by definition. Its animals and plants offer their life and flesh in sacrifice to humans. Therefore, animals must be treated with ritualized respect to ensure that they return and allow themselves to be killed for the sake of future humankind. Ceremony surrounded the whale and bear hunts, salmon and halibut fishing, and other forms of finding provisions.

The World Above, or Upper World, is a realm inhabited by birds, such as ravens, eagles, and cranes, and by celestial bodies, such as the moon, sun, stars, winds, and clouds. Great mythic creatures — the thunderbird and its relatives — also live in this part of the cosmos. West Coast people portray the thunderbird as a huge man living on a far-off mountain who puts on an eagle-like costume to hunt whales. "His belt is the lightning snake, which when dropped flashed down to earth."[47] Thunder is created by the flapping of the thunderbird's wings.

Among the northern groups, raven held a prominent role in Northwest Coast mythology. Myths can be classified into several categories, the most important of which is the raven cycle. The raven's primary role as a cultural hero is not so much to create things as to change them, or to make them happen. He is more a transformer, a trickster, than a creator. He carries with him all the cleverness, curiosity, wit, humour, dignity, and despair of all humankind. He makes people laugh at themselves and cry at the same time, showing how their greatness is overlaid by vanity. He is energy unfolding as he flies or transforms himself at will to better suit his plot, playing tricks on the unknown ruler of the universe, who may be himself. Being caught at his own game sometimes makes him look pathetic and miserable. How can bad things happen to demi-gods?

As a transformer, he is responsible for the present order of the universe. He discovers mankind, acquires and controls food, and brings the light into the world. Episodes from the raven myths were and still are represented on carved totem poles throughout the Coast and on some other two- and three-dimensional works of art (Figure 198).

The World Nearby is the familiar land, the sea shores and beaches where people lived. The forest is less familiar and associated with darkness. It is inhabited by all the land-animal species we know — mink, bears, wolves, mountain goats, and others — as well as by powerful antisocial spirits such as the Kwakiutl female ogre, *Dzonokwa*, and the Haida, Kwakiutl, and West Coast Wild Man of the Woods. This is also the realm of the Kwakiutl *Baxbakwalanuxsiwae*, Man-Eating Spirit, a central character in the Winter Ritual.

The ocean is the World Below, populated by salmon, sculpins, red snapper, octopus, halibut, and sea mammals. Several gigantic aquatic monsters or spirits also live there, in houses similar to those of the human realm: the five-finned killer whale and sea wolf of the Haida, the Kwakiutl *Sisiutl* (or Double-headed Serpent), and giant octopus and sharks, which are capable of swallowing dug-out canoes.

The World Below is governed by a mighty demi-god, a sea monster, master of the wealth of the ocean. To the Tlingit, he is *Qonagedet*, to the Haida *Qonagada*, and to the Kwakiutl *Gomogwa*.

Finally, the World Underneath, situated at the bottom of the ocean, is the realm of ghosts and of the dead.

In myth time, humans and animals shared the same faculties and could communicate with each other. Moreover, they could exchange physical forms. Killer whales (which are sea-mammal hunters reincarnated) remove their killer-whale apparel to put on their human outer trappings, for example.

The power of these creatures of aboriginal myth lies in their ability to cross the otherwise unbridgeable boundary between the supernatural and human worlds. Consequently, the amphibian creatures, like frogs and sea snakes, and other creatures that inhabit several cosmic realms, such as land otters, octopuses, and birds, played a special role in facilitating communication between the several layers of the cosmos. Invested with their own specific powers from more than one realm, they become privileged spirit-helpers, particularly of the shaman (Figure 199).

Of all the artistic traditions in the world, those of the Northwest Coast have been the most successful in giving convincing representations of that supernatural universe in which the human kingdoms and the species were still merged.

The master of the undersea world, *Qonagedet, Qonagada*, or *Gomogwa*, brings power and wealth, most often in the form of copper plates and abalone shells, to those lucky enough to see him. Sometimes he emerges from the water in the shape of a big house painted and decorated with abalone shells, sometimes as an enormous self-paddling

199.
Shaman's grave guardian, Tlingit, late 19th century. American Museum of Natural History, New York E2208.

This figure has been carved to represent a spirit in the form of a man: over the head is a frog spirit; over each shoulder and around the hips are river-otter spirits; "yakes," or spirits, form the knee-caps.

war canoe, also elaborately decorated and painted.

The first European ships must have been an incredible sight to the natives. Not only were the ships visually awesome, but they also brought riches: all the wealth of *Qonagadet*. People thought the strangers were supernatural creatures coming back from the country of the dead, as the myths recounted, and they incorporated the event into native oral traditions. In 1874, when Father Brabant established a mission at Hesquiat, he was told that the ancestors of the West Coast people first believed that the *Santiago* was a canoe that had "come back from the land of the dead with their bygone chiefs."[48] Knowing this, it is easier to interpret the meaning of the gift of a trophy head to Cook's ship. The head, the image of death, was to be returned to the land of the ghosts. (All the coastal nations had cults of the dead to whom they made offerings and sacrifices.)

Some aspects of southern world-view were expressed through metaphors. Among the Kwakiutl, for example, death, represented by *Baxbakwalanuxsiwae* (Man-Eating Spirit), is expressed in terms of devouring; life — creation and order — is expressed in terms of vomiting. The two metaphors become one, a metaphor of passage: transformation — from death to life or reincarnation, from rich to poor, from giver to receiver, from non-initiate to initiate.[49] Transformation underlies every cultural aspect of Kwakiutl society, and appears to some extent in all the societies of the Coast.

Nowhere else in the world has the concept of transformation been epitomized as on the Northwest Coast in the so-called "Transformation Masks," where two creatures, sometimes more, occupy the same space at the same time. The Kwakiutl excelled in these masks. One mask, when closed, represents an eagle; open, it reveals a human face in the centre, possibly *Gomogwa*, the undersea mythic monster, master of all aquatic wealth (Figure 200). The inner profiles of the eagle mask are painted to represent *Sisiutl*, the double-headed serpent. The top and lower parts attached to the mask are painted with aquatic anatomical features belonging to *Gomogwa*.

Another fundamental metaphor related to the concept of transformation is that of the container, for transformations occur in containers, whether they are mouths, stomachs, bowls, dishes and chests, houses, coffins, canoes, or capes. Containers are the vehicles of transformation. Elaborately decorated or plain, boxes and bowls, seal dishes, chests, and other containers were practical receptacles; they also encapsulated Northwest Coast philosophy (Figures 201 and 202).

Form

Northwest Coast artisans were designers as well as artists. House builders, canoe makers, totem-pole carvers, bark and wool weavers, box makers, and chest painters all understood the relations of space and form, the two principles of design.

> Every design problem begins with an effort to achieve fitness between two entities: the form in question and its context. The form is the solution to the problem; the context defines the problem.[50]

Design does not refer to form alone, but to the achieving of harmony or perfect balance of form and its context. For example, a mask is part of the greater whole, the ritual for which it was created. In a dance performance, the form of the mask may be related to the movements or gestures of the dancer, the rhythm of the accompanying music, or the words of the song. Moreover, the mask is only part of a whole costume.

Alone, a mask is without context, divorced from its artistic premise.

The fusion of form and context appears in a single object, as well. For example, a Haida wooden bowl collected by Dixon in 1787 is carved in the shape of a human or animal-like creature lying on its stomach (Figure 201). It is formed of a set of organized elements, shallowly engraved, which convey the intended shape. The "rightness" of the form depends, as it did in the case of the mask, on the degree to which it fuses form with context, without effort or friction. This presupposes a perfect understanding by the artist of the form-to-be and its context.

Another example of such harmonious design is the northern dugout canoe. Critical to the rich way of life enjoyed by the Northwest Coast people, these very elegant craft were the key that unlocked the treasure chest of the North Pacific. It is as though perfect function created perfect beauty. The final and vital shape of this eighteen-foot boat (Figure 203) is achieved by shaping and steam-spreading a hollowed-out log.[51] It is a dynamic line, expressive of contained energy and tension. This particular example is finished by exquisite hand-adzing, which creates a texture like that of finely woven fabric.

200.
Transformation mask, Kwakiutl, late -19th century. Denver Art Museum, Colorado 1951.228.

Closed, the mask represents the Eagle; when open it reveals a human face in the centre, possibly *gomogwa*. The inner profiles of the eagle mask are painted to represent *Sisiutl*.

201.
Bowl, Haida, collected in 1787, displaying northern two-dimensional surface decoration. Courtesy of the Trustees of the British Museum. London NWC 25.

Canoe makers were also great carvers of other objects, and the sensibility they developed while creating their graceful craft was carried over to their other works, bringing with it a tension and an expressiveness engendered by the dialogue between the material and the makers.

Was the primal image of the canoe printed or embedded in the consciousness of the earliest artisans? Did this lead to the many canoe-shaped dishes or bowls we find in the world museums (Figures 204 and 205)? Or did the canoe-dish concept have symbolic significance of its own, possibly related to that of plenty?[52] How can we explain the significant number of eighteenth- and early-nineteenth-century canoe miniatures, wrongly identified as canoe "models" in art catalogues? Were they toys, as they seem to have been classified at times? Were they early tourist items?

202.
Bowl, late-18th century, carved in wood in the shape of a humanoid figure lying on its stomach. Underneath each palm is a frog. Courtesy Field Museum of Natural History, Chicago 18359. L:29.5; W:18; H:14.7

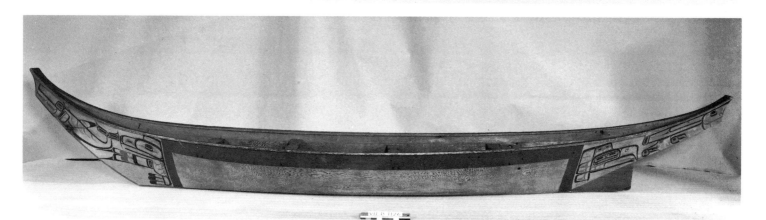

203.
Canoe, Haida, collected in 1878. Canadian Museum of Civilization, National Museums of Canada, Ottawa VII-B-1126. L:571.5

The exterior is painted with raven and whale designs on the stern and a crouching animal and bird on the bow.

Many of them are exquisitely executed and painted, fully equipped with realistically carved paddlers, dressed and with human hair; some are shown holding shaman rattles. Could they have been used by shamans during their visionary journeys to ensure successful fishing or sea-mammal hunting? The peoples of the Northwest Coast knew that whales and other sea mammals have the power to transform their bodies into canoes.[53] Perhaps the canoe miniatures represent the outer forms of these powerful sea creatures. If so, they may be yet another symbol of transformation and another means of acquiring wealth, in this case, the wealth from the sea.

The Origins of Form

The origins of Northwest Coast art are still largely unknown, and the factor that permitted it to flourish is also responsible for there being scanty evidence of its early stages. The warm, moist climate of the Coast encouraged the lush rain forest that provided most of the materials from

204.
Canoe-shaped bowl, Tlingit, 19th century. National Museum of Natural History, Smithsonian Institution, Washington, D.C. 9244. L:47; W:15; H:14.5

which this art was made; it also assured the rapid decay and disappearance of all but the most recent examples. Obviously, however, this sophisticated and refined mode of expression is the culmination of a long evolutionary process, during which profound conceptual and stylistic changes occurred.

A few precious specimens have survived: those made from stone and a few that have been preserved by becoming buried in mud and silt beneath fresh water. Although this is a very scanty record, it contains sufficient evidence to show that this refined art extends back at least 4,500 years.[54]

Powerful sculpture has a long tradition in both northern and southern areas of the Coast. Stone bowls (Figure 205), plain or decorated, some carved in animal forms, were used by both groups, as were the stone war clubs sometimes called "slave killers." The club collected at Nootka Sound by Cook is an excellent example of West Coast stone art[56]. It is made of a single piece of hard stone: "both the wolf's head at the striking end and the bird at the pommel end are in traditional West Coast style."[55] A considerable amount of human hair seems to have been glued to the top of the wolf's head; traces remain of both an adhesive substance and hair. Similarly shaped weapons made of yew wood with striking blades of stone were also found at Nootka Sound. Another weapon, a Tlingit club of yew wood, was collected by Malaspina at Yakutat (Figure 206). It represents an animal's head decorated with human hair and opercula-shell teeth; it is executed in the northern form-line style. The blade is made of dark-green stone, or nephrite, and the handle is wrapped with black and white bird quills.

Two of the most refined and exquisite stone sculptures of the Northwest Coast were produced in late prehistoric or early historic times by the Tsimshian living near the mouth of the Skeena River (Figure 207). They are both sensitively carved human-face masks. Although collected by different people in two locations, they obviously are intended to function as a pair — one fits perfectly inside the other. In spite of their great weight, they were meant to be worn in a ritual performance. The eyes of one mask are open, those of the other closed, indicating a kind of transformation.

The oldest surviving wooden object is probably this proto-Salish *atlatl*

205.
Stone bowl, Haida, prehistoric. McCord Museum, McGill University, Montreal 1205 a. L:43; W:23; H:15 (approx.)

Executed in characteristic northern form-line style, this bowl attests to the maturity and full development of this style in prehistoric times.

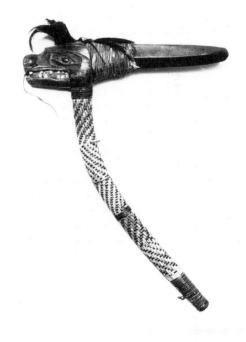

206.
Warrior club, Tlingit, 18th century. Collected by Malaspina. Museo de Americas, Madrid 1219 L:56; W:35

Carved of yew wood, with a blade of dark green nephrite and a handle wrapped with black and white bird quills.

or spear thrower (Figure 208). Radio-carbon dating indicates that it is approximately 1,700 years old.[57] Its powerful composition and finely detailed execution seems to depict a "feathered or plumed sea-monster rearing over a human head, the eyes of both inlaid with white shell or stone."[58] If this is representative of the works of the past era, it must have been an extremely rich one, indeed. The most ancient sculptures and engravings in bone, antler, and stone show that there are strong general similarities in style along the entire coast, "all showing hints of a developing 'form line' structure, a characteristic convention of historical Northwest Coast art."[59]

Form: a Synthesis of Form

Particularly striking in Northwest Coast art are the form and variation, within a common tradition, that exhibit "basic conceptual features, such

207.
Stone mask, Coast Tsimshian. Collected by I.W. Powell in 1879. Canadian Museum of Civilization, National Museums of Canada, Ottawa VII-C-329. D:23

as the raised positive-recessed negative concepts, and some formal features such as crescent and T-shaped reliefs, the so-called Northwest Coast eye of varying forms, and the skeletal representations, especially ribs and joint marks."[60] Northwest Coast art can be seen as variations upon the single essential underlying principle of form-line art.

The most dominant element of two-dimensional northern Northwest Coast art is the network of curvilinear connected tapered lines, usually painted black, that form the basic structure of the work, named by Bill Holm "primary formline": "The characteristic swelling and diminishing linelike figure delineating design units."[61]

Primary form-line not only delineates the form, but *is* the form itself. The other elements — secondary form-lines and tertiary elements — provide highlights and detail, but remain subservient to the dominant form-line. The form-line is rather like calligraphy — both delineate the subject while *creating* it: they are both the subject and its representation.

Characteristic northern form-line provides a positive structure of a basic form, which is then relieved by secondary and tertiary elements. These are, like "the holes in doughnuts, negative spaces." The unpractised eye often sees the negative space and motifs rather than the basic form. This eighteenth-century Spanish watercolour of a Tlingit clan hat (Figure 209) shows, in its oversimplification of the design elements, how much the European was unfamiliar with this art form. Form-line is equally influential, if somewhat less apparent, in three-dimensional works.

208.
Atlatl or spear-thrower, proto-Salish, 1700 B.P. Museum of Anthropology, University of British Columbia, Vancouver A7021.
Photograph by W. McLennan. L:39.3

This atlatl depicts a feathered or plumed sea monster rearing over a human head.

209.
Sombrero tejido y pintado del gefe de Mulgrave. Watercolour by Spanish artist José Cardero. Museo de Americas, Madrid 2.256.

This painting of a Tlingit wooden clan hat shows oversimplified three- and two-dimensional decorations.

210.
Bent-corner box, 19th century. American Museum of Natural History, New York 19/1233.

This box is painted with two-dimensional northern style designs displaying great virtuosity in terms of conception, execution, and composition.

The Logic of Form

Form-line is governed by "rules" or conventions, which allow sufficient variation in treatment to express individualism; without this freedom within the rules, Northwest Coast art would have been merely a static system of icons.

Although the rules as we perceive them — such as the use of form-lines, colour arrangements, and the space to be treated, and their relation one to the other — were probably not codified, they were so deep in the consciousness of people that it would be unthinkable, especially for artists, not to incorporate them into their work.

The rules of Northwest Coast artistic expression, like the syntax of a language, were applied often with great virtuosity. As Bill Reid and Bill Holm have pointed out, virtuosity calls for "the courage to take it beyond the point your mind tells you is logical."[62] Within the range — wide but not infinite — of the possibilities within rules and their implicit logic, could the artist create "out of tune" works? The aesthetic is not only a matter of logic. Rules can always be defied; but when it is done by a true artist, rules and logic are transcended and the result is a masterpiece.

Such virtuosity can be seen in a painted wooden bent-corner box (Figure 210). The lower-right quadrant of each side of the box is a black background over-painted with red primary form-lines. Sides one and three and sides two and four share orientation and composition but differ in many details. The rules have been played with to achieve an incredible *tour de force* in which all elements fit perfectly together to create superb visual harmony.

Although we may never be able precisely to delineate or to comprehend the limits of the artist's iconographic freedom of expression, this box clearly shows that artistic beauty relates to "the balance between courage to go beyond logic, and at the same time, to hang in there with tradition."[63] The complex, intellectual, and unspoken rules were rigidly applied and maintained, yet innovation — not radical, but within the tradition — was the artist's challenge to the rules.

Among the few objects produced by Northwest Coast artists in which rules have been abandoned completely are unsmokeable pipes with no function or meaning except as art objects for the tourist market, and the prestigious copper plates used in the context of potlatches. Both types of objects date from the nineteenth century.

Principle of Design and Representation

On the Northwest Coast, sculpture and two-dimensional art provide the fundamental means of artistic expression. Sculpture tended to be realistic, while two-dimensional art forms are more symbolic and "decorative." Art created by males — sculpture and two-dimensional art — has a representational intention; art created by females — weaving and plaiting — is non-representational.

Northwest Coast two-dimensional art displays the following characteristics: abstraction rather than realistic representation; exaggeration or miniaturization of certain anatomical features; bilateral and "asymmetrical symmetry"; and splitting. (In addition to being split, the subject is sometimes dislocated into elements that are recombined according to the rules of convention rather than of nature.)

Another common characteristic of Northwest Coast art is the visual pun, the "illogical" transformation of design details into new representations. On one sixty-foot Haida canoe, the painting on the bow represents a wolf and its cub; the stern is decorated with the wolf's hind legs and its tail, which seems to turn into a mosquito (Figure 211).

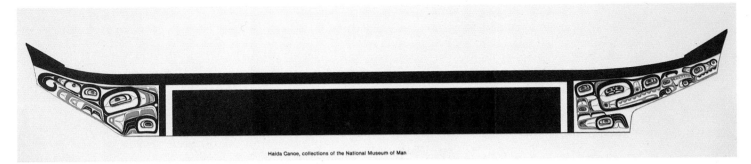

Haida Canoe, collections of the National Museum of Man

211.
Canoe, Haida. Canadian Museum of Civilization, National Museums of Canada, Ottawa. Colour rendering by W. McLennan.

The painted design of the stern of this sixty-foot canoe is an example of visual punning: the wolf's tail turns into a mosquito.

212.
Frontlet, Tlingit, collected in 1791. Museo de Americas, Madrid 1310. H:16; W:17

Carved in the shape of a humanoid face, the frontlet has an eagle nose-beak and a wide open mouth (perhaps of a shark) inlaid with opercula.

A final characteristic is the suppression of all non-essential elements, anatomical parts, and details. It culminates, in three-dimensional works, in a synthesis so complete that a specific part becomes the whole, a kind of visual synecdoche. For example, the addition of a killer-whale fin to any creature, human or animal, suggests that the work represents the aquatic mammal itself. The Tlingit frontlet collected by Malaspina shows an extremely expressive human face, carved and painted, with sheet-iron inlay in the eye's pupils, dotted with an eagle-beak nose; the lower part of the headdress shows a wide mouth inlaid with opercula (Figure 212). This mouth belongs, certainly, to a mythic being unknown to us; yet this single feature is sufficient to represent the entire creature.

213.
Mountain-sheep horn rattle. Cowichan (Coast Salish), 18th century. Museum for Ethnology. Rotterdam, the Netherlands 34818. L:32 (approx.)

The rattle is elaborately carved on both sides with thunderbird and fish representations.

214. (opposite)
Spindle whorl, Coast Salish, late 18th century (?). Private collection, New York. D:21.9

The whorl is elaborately carved in Coast Salish two-dimensional style with its characteristic use of "form surface" (as opposed to northern "form-line"), crescents, and parallel lines for feathers and wings.

Two-dimensional designs and paintings were not used only on flat surfaces; they were also used on curvilinear, three-dimensional creations — totem poles, bowls, masks, combs, rattles, and shaman charms (Figures 215).

For the purist, classic northern form-line art style, in all its intellectual complexity, vanishes south of the Heiltsuk. What then is taking place among the Coast Salish and the Wakashan-speaking people? The stylistic expressions of the south — those of the Kwakiutl, the West Coast, and the Coast Salish — are indeed different, and worthy of consideration in their own right.

The paintings on Salish spirit-canoe figures and boards exhibit frequent use of parallel lines and rows of dots, which do not appear in northern painting.[64] Some engravings on spindle whorls, horn bracelets, rattles, and combs, such as T-shapes and crescents, show concepts and designs characteristic of northern art, although they do not conform to the form-line art style we have discussed. Not only are the form-lines themselves different; so is the treatment of decorated surface, which often shows a larger amount of empty space than do northern pieces. "What these Salish pieces seem to have is a *form surface*, that is, a connected uniform surface whose perimeter is marked by an incised line or by a cut and conjunction with another, lower surface."[65]

One of the greatest known spindle whorls (Figure 214) illustrates the difference between Salish and northern art forms:

Round faces like this and bodies in unlikely places are typical of the Salish. . . . Another thing . . . not found in the North, is the repetition of both a series of little reliefs and a series of parallel lines. So we end up with a more geometric handling of the whole space. . . . A higher percentage of Salish figures have naturalistic proportions — straightforward representation, rather than the stylization more noticeable in the North.[66]

Another remarkable Coast Salish specimen dating from the eighteenth century is a horn rattle carved on both sides with thunderbird representations, now in Rotterdam (Figure 213). One side of the rattle shows the bird's head in profile, its wings, and other small creatures, perhaps fish. The whole surface is an asymmetrical composition. The other side shows bilateral symmetry, and is amazing complex. Two full-length profiles of birds in flight meet in the centre of the rattle, creating a face; the birds are the eyes. Above each bird profile is a powerful thunderbird head, also in profile, which forms the eyebrows.

This masterpiece of Coast Salish art displays curvilinear form surfaces as well as more geometric elements, such as parallel lines depicting feathers, and repetitive decorative elements, such as circles and crescents.

The principles of southern form-surface art also apply to pre-contact Wakashan West Coast and Kwakiutl art, although northern influences can clearly be seen, especially in nineteenth-century pieces. (Some Kwakiutl artists "incorporated the superficial trappings of the sophisticated northern system, but without ever completely bowing to its exacting rule."[67] Although this style appears to conform to the northern rules governing the use and arrangement of form-lines, eye-shapes, and U-forms, it differs quite markedly from its model (Figure 200).

Tribal Variations: the Music Metaphor

Northwest Coast art, like all art forms, has often been compared to language; both art and language are systems of communication. Northwest Coast art functions as a visual language on at least two levels — semantic and formal. From a semantic point of view, this heraldic art

215.
Bear rattle, Haida, 19th century. Courtesy of the Trustees of the British Museum, London 5930 H:17; D:13

This wooden sculpture is a good example of Haida style, showing great concern with composition.

216.
Pipe, Haida, 19th century, carved of yew wood. Berne Historical Museum, Berne de W.74.403.1. L:38.5; W:2.6; H:7

217. (opposite)
Headdress, Tlingit, early 19th century. The Museum of Anthropology and Ethnography named after Peter the Great, Leningrad 2448-20. W:15; H:21

This sitting-beaver headdress is complete with eagle down, flicker feathers, a crown of sea-lion whiskers, and mummified red-shafted flickers.

form reveals highly symbolic content, translating social values and "thought into matter." From an iconographic point of view, because Northwest Coast artistic composition results in the organization of structural elements according to rules and conventions, it is a kind of visual grammar.

It occurred to me that perhaps we could compare Northwest Coast art style and another non-verbal mode of expression to create a rough model, to illuminate the secrets and complexities of most Northwest Coast art works. Music seems most likely to provide analogies, for several reasons. Music is highly articulated, and is at least as complex as Northwest Coast art. It follows rules of composition, and repeated motifs can convey rhythm and movement. Finally, music is a "sensuous object, which by virtue of its dynamic structure can express the forms of vital experience which language is particularly unfit to convey."[68]

To recognize that a certain object has been made by Tlingit rather than, say, Salish artists is intuitively to assimilate the rules governing the work from its most common characteristics. On the other hand, "a good metaphor implies an intuitive perception of the similarity in dissimilars."[69]

We have said that northern Northwest Coast art can be best described as variations on a single theme, and that it is rigorously structured. The form-line art can be seen as a variation on a single note — the form-line. The primary form-line is the main theme or *cantus firmus*, the melodic line. The secondary form-line and tertiary elements would be the counterpoint.[70] From the simple elements at his disposal, the composer creates complex combinations and contrasts between counterpointed variations and the basic theme. So it is for the Northwest Coast artist.

The northern form-line style can be said to be analogous to baroque music. Both are ordered by well-defined rules governing complicated composition, and both are built on a limited range of possibilities. The emphasis is not on innovation but on the creative use of established forms. The main themes, embellished and commented on by additional elements, give substance and completeness to the entire composition (Figure 215). This carved wooden pipe shows reiterated motifs, each a variation of the others, which together produce rich, tightly knit harmonious textures, which we associate with the baroque period.

As the music of the baroque era differs from region to region in Europe, while sharing essential basic similarities, so the different northern regions where form-line art is found demonstrate stylistic variations consistent with slight but obvious distinctive cultural characteristics.

Haida style is very conservative and shows great concern with composition. The wooden pipe and horn spoon handles shown here clearly illustrate this principle (Figure 216).

Typical of Tlingit style are the rounded contours and continuous lip bands, often with the addition of copper inlay for lips, nostrils, and eyebrows, and hair inset on the upper part of the face. This perhaps results in a more lyrical and flamboyant style (Figure 217).

Tsimshian face style shows a bony structure with pyramidal cheeks. The "expression of fleshy forms and tightly drawn surface skin over these bony structures"[71] are typical of Tsimshian features (Figure 207).

Of all the Northwest Coast groups, the Bella Bella are perhaps the least known to anthropologists and other students of the culture. And yet it seems they occupied a pivotal position not only geographically but also artistically, as innovators and major producers of artistic creations. Bella Bella style and its superb handling of the classic form-line conforms to the northern form-line conventions. This masterly handling of form-line as a basis for creation, as displayed in this nineteenth-century seat (Figure 218), is in other cases almost obscured by the untrammelled use of the decorative and colourful embellishments.

It is tempting to compare nineteenth-century Wakashan style with the music of the Romantics, for Kwakiutl artists (and, to a lesser degree, artists on the West Coast) took established forms and splashed them around with great abandon and exuberance (Figure 200). The more direct and naturalistic and less sophisticated art style of the Salish would be reflected best in early European music (Figures 213 and 214).

The other distinctive Northwest Coast style is that of the Bella Coola. It is the result of a number of influences, for example Kwakiutl and Salish, and incorporates the northern rules in a very distinctive and bold way that defies an analogy with music (Figure 219).

218.
Chief's seat, Bella Bella, commissioned and collected by Jacobsen in the 1880s.
Staatliche Museen Preußischer Kulturbesitz, Museum für Völkerkunde, Berlin, FRG IV-A-2475/76/77. L:137; W:87

The undoubted Bella Bella provenance has proved valuable in the attributions of Bella Bella artworks.

Content

Attempting to explain cultural products whose meaning derives from a way of thinking different from our own is always dangerous. In preliterate societies, art forms are highly symbolic: they simultaneously represent, define, and manifest their subject. In recent years, however, interest has grown among symbolic anthropologists to interpret the forms and meanings of Northwest Coast traditional artistic productions.[72] Analysis of these creations reveals them to be the result of several components: form

219.
Sun mask, Bella Coola. Etnografiska
Museet, Stockholm 04-19. D:52 (approx.)

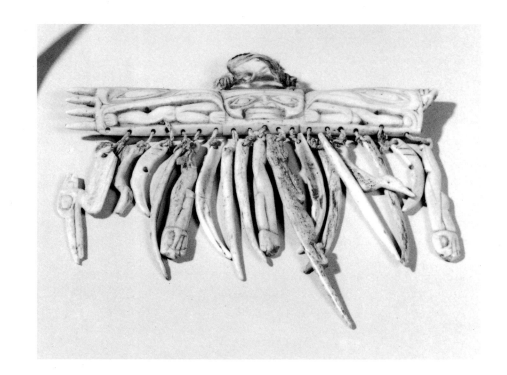

220.
Shaman's charm, 19th century. National Museum of Natural History, Smithsonian Institution, Washington, D.C. 89021. L:14; W:17.8

The top section of this charm is carved with bird figures, and many of the seventeen suspended ivory figures represent shore birds, water birds, and other amphibious creatures, all considered important spiritual beings because they apparently crossed the barriers between different cosmic realms.

221.
Spruce root hat, Tlingit, collected c. 1800-1820. The Peabody Museum of Salem, Massachusetts E3647. W:58.8; H:40

The elaborate painting represents a bird crest. It is crowned with six basketry cylinders, usually referred to as "potlatch rings."

(the way of expressing meaning), context, and content (the meaning itself).

Early Northwest Coast artefacts convey or communicate information to us through some formal, tangible, perceptible qualities. In order to read this information, we must consider several related layers: the nature of the material and how it was handled by the maker; its relationship to space, time, and language; and the metaphysical element of substance and causality.

Traditionally, the natural materials selected for specific purposes were never chosen accidentally. Materials possessed quasi-magical powers and virtues that generated a work of art. The created object was an emanation of the chosen material. A dug-out canoe or a bent-corner box derived much of its shape from the nature of the raw material from which it was made. Most Tlingit shaman charms used in healing ceremonies were carved out of ivory or bone because bones have numerous shamanic connotations (Figure 220).[73] Other associations governed the use of red cedar bark, copper, or mountain-goat wool.[74] The material or colour chosen depended on the culture's system of classification. Among the Kwakiutl, black, red, and white were used during the red cedar-bark ceremony, and objects or things connoting these colours were worn during phases of some rites of passage because of their symbolic associations.

However, the artisan's creative gesture was not reduced to mere execution. Born of the chosen material, gesture and material belonged to the same creative moment. An artisan would carve away enough of a red cedar log to let the inner content he had foreseen reveal itself.

Finale:
Form, Context, and Content Reunited

The raison d'être of an object is to communicate messages aesthetically and semantically. Form and content, signifier and signified, are one.

> To attempt to determine whether a bowl was made to look like an animal or the animal was distorted to become a bowl is a fruitless task. They grew together: the bowl became animate and its animation gave reason for its being a bird as well as a bowl.[75]

The character of an object is also a part of the language that evoked it. In Kwakiutl, for example, the word *tlakwa* means copper, a plate made of copper, and the colour red. The naming of an object connected it to the surrounding symbolic and physical world, and to the speaker.

Finally, these artefacts were not "objects" in the strict etymological sense of "things thrown before or against the mind." Rather, they were things that shared the space and time with their makers and consumers. Ceremonial crafted objects were considered powerful, symbolically efficient, and permanent creations through which human beings gave their actions spatial and temporal dimensions beyond their own limits.

To reveal their social identity, Northwest Coast people were associated with specific uniquely styled ornaments or insignia, labrets (lip plugs), nose rings and earrings, headdresses or frontlets, helmets, belts, adorned capes and hats, speaker staffs, clubs, and rattles (Figures 191 and 221). The result was a very rich and beautiful whole made of individual creations. These ornaments and accessories constituted the wealth of the clan or the group, its sacred property, and the rights to these belongings were, and still are, jealously guarded.

In Northwest Coast costumes there is a very close association between apparel — dress, ornaments, and decorations — and social category.

Apparel is an important indication of social classification, differentiating, classifying, and ordering in the same way that titles do. Hence, it forms a "second skin" through which the individual manifests his or her primary identity.[76]

Ornaments and dress create a para-linguistic means for each individual to exhibit his or her participation as part of a social unit, a phratry, a clan, or a group of names. But they also go beyond words or names: they are icons through which the identity can be physically explained, changed, and transformed during social transactions.[77] A Haida individual, for example, who might say, "I am a five-finned killer whale from the eagle phratry," would be entitled to wear some ornaments or to decorate his belongings with five-finned killer whale and eagle representations. Not only do these attributes offer visual proof of who their owners are by affirming and confirming their identities; they also reinforce their owners' ideas of who they *think* they are. The attributes translate their owners' dreams into matter and mediate between supernatural and human worlds.

Northwest Coast art was a fluent visual and symbolic language, whose variation and subtlety were shared by those who made the art and those who cherished it. Art forms were meaningful to everyone and imbued with social, cosmic, and mythic resonances. Any ceremonial crafted object was a "total phenomenon," a visible container of myth, an aesthetic concentrate of latent meaning and energy; it made tangible the invisible. A dish carved with a crest image was a vessel, a heraldic symbol, and a mediator "between the natural, biological act of eating and the human cultural act of feasting."[78] Such objects ". . . become a kind of shining language in which a society formulates its conception of the universe and its cultural philosophy."[79] It was art such as this that the first travellers to the Northwest Coast were privileged to witness.

Martine J. Reid

Notes

All references to the catalogue of the exhibition entitled *The Spirit Sings* are indicated by "Catalogue" followed by the region and number designations of the object.

Introduction

1. Several of the objects discussed in the text and in the exhibition come from areas outside the political boundaries of Canada. These objects come, however, from groups with cultural traditions contiguous with those historically found within Canada.

2. *The Canadian Encyclopedia,* p. 212. 1981 census figures record 491,000 peoples of Native descent in Canada. Other Canadian government and academic surveys estimate the Métis and Non-Status Indian population to be between 700,000 and 1,000,000 thus raising the native population to about five per cent of the total Canadian population.

3. MacGregor 1985: 217.

4. MacGregor 1985: 217. Italics original.

5. Leacock: 10.

6. See page 148.

7. See page 191.

8. See page 42.

9. Levine: 57. Italics added.

10. Leacock: 5.

11. Leacock: 4.

12. Cole 1985: 58.

13. Cole 1985: 66ff.

14. Halpin 1965.

15. As quoted in Sotheby's October 23, 1982 catalogue.

Atlantic Coast

All subheads in this essay are taken from *Poems of Rita Joe*. Halifax: Abenaki Press, 1978.

1. Story from Mary Doucet Newall (Doucette Noel, born *ca.* 1800 in Newfoundland. Told by her daughter and granddaughter to Elsie Clews Parsons 1925, 38: 73.

2. The late Wisconsinan glaciation.

3. MacDonald 1968.

4. Tuck 1984: 27.

5. Tuck 1976.

6. Hewson 1978; Howley 1915: 256.

7. Bernard Francis, Micmac Language Institute, has provided correct spellings and translations for Micmac words used herein, using the Francis-Smith Orthography.

8. Lescarbot 1907, I: 79

9. Possibly the Scadouc River; the name *Souricoua* appears only once in the historical record (Champlain 1922, I: 169), and may derive from Basque *zurikoa*: "of the white men" (Bakker n.d.), as the river was a sixteenth-century trading rendezvous and route from the Northumberland Strait into the Bay of Fundy.

10. *Mi'kmaq*, the unpossessed core form of *nikmaq*, was not used in speech (Bernard Francis, personal communication 1986).

11. Dr. Peter L. Paul, Andrea Bear Nicholas, personal communication 1986.

12. Howley 1915: 174.

13. Micmac name *Lkimu*: "He Sends."

14. Maillard 1863: 209-309.

15. Maillard 1863: 300.

16. Maillard 1863: 304.

17. LeClercq 1910: 84.

18. Howley 1915: 252.

19. Champlain 1922, I: 101.

20. Maillard 1863: 301-304.

21. Lopez 1986: 8.

22. Swinton, in Taylor, Swinton 1967: 37.

23. Howley 1915: 125.

24. Tanner 1979: 92.

25. Vastokas 977: 95.

26. LeClercq 1910: 95.

27. Pulling 1792: 6.

28. Whitehead 1982.

29. LeClercq 1910: 146-149,152.

30. Whitehead 1982.

31. Catalogue E 20; British Museum 2583.

32. Catalogue E 12; Newfoundland Museum VIII-A-392a,b.

33. Whitehead 1985: NFLDMUS VIII-A-413. Gender identification is speculation on the part of the author. Catalogue E 10; Newfoundland Museum VIII-A-413.

34. Remaining claw is Black Guillemot (*Cepphus grylle*), originally red.

35. Champlain 1925, II: 14-15.

36. Adney, Chapelle 1964: 70.

37. Burrage 1906: 348-349.

38. Adney, Chapelle 1964: 70,101.

39. Marshall n.d.: unpaginated.

40. Marshall n.d.: unpaginated.

41. Marshall n.d.: unpaginated.

42. Marshall n.d.: unpaginated.

43. LeClercq 1910: 100.

44. Alika Webber, personal communication 1986.

45. Lescarbot 1914, III: 99.

46. Turnbull 1976,4: 50-62.

47. Rand 1894: 225.

48. Magnusson, Pálsson 1965: 65-67.

49. Dr. Birgitta Linderoth Wallace, personal communication 1986.

50. Sauer 1968: 50.

51. Prins, Whitehead n.d.; the Cartier transcription (Lescarbot 1911,II: 45) reads "*Napeu* (Micmac for male, male bird, cock), *ton* (*tou* with the u reversed) *damen* (*dameu* with the u reversed) *assur tah* (thought to be Portuguese pidgin).

52. Quinn 1962: 339-340.

53. Lescarbot 1911, II: 28.

54. Howley 1915: 10.

55. Quinn 1962: 339.

56. Cell 1982: 117.

57. Howley 1915: 12-13.

58. Pastore n.d.

59. Cell 1982: 193-194.

60. Cell 1982: 74.

61. Cell 1982: 76.

62. Pastore n.d.: 1.

63. Harper 1956,1957.

64. Gyles 1869: 45.

65. Lescarbot 1914, III: 32.

66. Lescarbot 1914, III: 32.

67. Bourque, Whitehead 1986.

68. Bailey 1969.

69. Maillard 1863: 278-279.

70. Howley 1915: 29.

71. Pastore 1984.

72. Pastore n.d.: 20.

73. Pulling 1792: 3-6.

74. Howley 1915: 20.

75. Howley 1915: 72-90.

76. Howley 1915: 92.

77. Howley 1915: 93.

78. Howley 1915: 91-103.

79. Howley 1915: 129.

80. Howley 1915: 225.

81. Howley 1915: 229.

82. Howley 1915: 191-192.

83. Howley 1915: 195.

84. Howley 1915: 222.

85. Howley 1915: 193-194.

86. Ingeborg Marshall, personal communication 1986.

87. British Museum 2583.

88. Catalogue E 23; British Museum LL3.

89. Catalogue E 9; National Maritime Museum NMM AOA330.

90. Ingeborg Marshall, personal communication 1986.

91. Catalogue E 24; McCord Museum ACC 1141 a-c.

92. Dr. David Keenlyside, personal communication 1986.

93. Marshall 1974: 147.

94. Marshall 1974: 144; Marshall 1978: 139-254.

95. Child's age established by Dr. Sonja Jerkic, Memorial University of Newfoundland, personal communication via Dr. Ralph Pastore 1986.

96. Catalogue E 13; Newfoundland Museum VIII-A-387.

97. Catalogue E 11; Newfoundland Museum VIII-A-412.

98. Hubbard 1983: 160.

99. Perley 1843: 127.

100. Denys 1908: 448.

101. Catalogue E 109; Ashmolean Museum n.n.

102. Whitehead 1982: 133.

103. LeClercq 1910: 96.

104. Denys 1908: 412-413.

105. Dièreville 1934: 167.

106. Gyles 1869: 22.

107. Whitehead 1982.

108. Catalogue E 94; National Maritime Museum CK-Vi-X-55 M63/61.

109. Catalogue E 48; Naprstkovo Museum 22273.

110. Museum of Victoria X8938.

111. Whitehead 1982.

112. Catalogue E 29-E 34; New Brunswick Museum 983.47.2. 1-6.

113. Whitehead 1982.

114. Catalogue E 68; British Museum 76/772.

115. Catalogue E 4; Pitt Rivers Museum 1886.1.869.

116. MacGregor 1983.

117. Blom, Blom 1983: 174.

118. Blom, Blom 1983: 61,163,46,296,336,341.

119. Blom, Blom 1983: 47.

120. Blom, Blom 1983: 142.

121. Gesner 1848: 119.

122. Mary Doucet Newall (Parsons 1925,38: 73)

123. Wallis, Wallis 1955: 424.

124. Maillard 1758: 64.

Woodlands

1. Densmore 1910: 86.

2. The metaphorical quality of Indian oratory was admired by many observers, from Charlevoix, who commented on the ''variety of turns and phrases'' (1761: 300), to Carver, who wrote that ''their style is adorned with images, comparisons and strong metaphors'' (1778: 261).

3. For further background information about the historical development, and social and economic systems of the Woodlands peoples, the reader is referred to the detailed discussions of each group in Volumes 15 and 6 of the *Handbook of the North American Indian* (Trigger 1976 and Helm 1981). The vast Woodlands region, which as an ecological and cultural zone encompasses eastern North America from the Atlantic coast to the Mississippi, can be subdivided in a number of ways. This essay will focus on the northern portion of the Woodlands, roughly corresponding to the modern national boundaries of Canada. The Iroquois of New York State and the Ottawa, Ojibwa, and Potawatomi of northern Michigan, Wisconsin, and Minnesota will be included in the discussion because of their close historical ties to and intermittent occupation of lands now within Canada. The exclusion of other art traditions from consideration, such as those of the Delaware and New England Indians, the Sac and Fox, Menomini, Winnebago, Miami, and Shawnee results from the practical need to limit the discussion. The artistic expressions of these groups are closely related to those of the more northerly peoples and could well be included in a similar study of broader scope. The Maritime region is also technically a subdivision of the Woodlands, although its distinctive artistic developments have been dealt with separately here.

4. Beltrami 1828: II, 225. The accuracy of the model is further borne out by the match between its contents and Schoolcraft's listing of canoe contents as also including ''blankets, guns, fishing apparatus, and dogs,'' together with a rolled-up sail (1820: 69, 80).

5. Speck 1914.

6. Graham 1969: 190.

7. Museum für Völkerkunde, Frankfurt-am-Main, FGR. NS 35032. Permission to illustrate this object was refused by the Museum.

8. Sagard 1939: 66. On Ottawa tapestry-woven mats, see also Feest 1984: 15-16.

9. Thwaites 23: 211.

10. From the late seventeenth century through the early nineteenth, Iroquois towns in central New York State were the major area of refuge for groups of New England, Delaware, Ohio Valley, and southern Great Lakes Indians. Some of these refugee peoples later moved to Ontario with the Six Nations (Hauptman 1980).

11. The Nipissing were using ''collars and scarfs'' of wampum in 1642-43 (Thwaites: 23, 217), and Charlevoix found

them in use among the Mississauga in 1720 (1761: 369), as did La Vérendrye among the Swampy Cree in 1734 (1927: 173). Carver and Long report wampum in general use among the Ojibwa at the end of the eighteenth century (Long 1791: 47; Carver 1778: 242).

12. Trigger 1976: 76.

13. Tanner 1984; Webber 1983. Catalogue W 85.

14. The use of concentric circles to represent the sun among the Iroquois has recently been discussed by Oberholzer 1986, Chap. 4.

15. Brasser 1976: 23.

16. Catalogue W 61.

17. Thwaites 6: 163.

18. See, for example, "Canot à loutaouase," f. 23, p. 18 in "Les Raretés des Indes" (*Codex Canadensis*), Thomas Gilcrease Institute of American History and Art, Tulsa, Oklahoma.

19. Kohl 1860: 150-151.

20. Johnston in Masson 1889-90: II, 153.

21. Thwaites: 6, 175-177; Cameron in Masson 1889-90: II, 259.

22. Sagard 1939: 186.

23. A cult associating eagle-like predatory birds with the rain-bringing Thunderers and with warfare appears to have its roots in the prehistoric Mississippian cultures of the Southern Woodlands. Such beliefs probably spread to the Iroquois from the central Great Lakes at the very beginning of the early historic period through the calumet dance, but remained most explicitly expressed among the Central Great Lakes peoples (Fenton 1953).

24. This scene is depicted on a pouch in the United States National Museum, No. 154,012.

25. Charlevoix 1761: I, 356.

26. Catalogue W 38 and W 98.

27. Thwaites: 7, 23.

28. Catalogue W 6 and W 65.

29. Thwaites 5: 161. See also Wallace 1958.

30. See Speck 1977: 197 and Densmore 1929: 78-86.

31. Thwaites: 23, 155.

32. Cameron, in Masson 1889-1890: II, 261.

33. Graham 1969: 164.

34. Jones 1861: 72.

35. Charlevoix 1761: I, 338.

36. Graham 1969: 164.

37. Speck 1977: 193.

38. Thwaites: 12, 17.

39. Catalogue W 80, W 81 and W 101.

40. See Maurer 1986.

41. Brasser 1980.

42. Thwaites 24: 135.

43. Thwaites: 11, 263.

44. Hickerson 1963.

45. The Midewiwin is known among the West Main Cree but did not extend into the eastern Cree region or to the Iroquois.

46. The artistry that could inform totemic marks was noted by Isaac Weld: "their signatures consist of the outline . . . of the different animals whose names they bear. Some of the signatures at the bottom of these deeds were really well executed, and were lively representations of the animals they were intended for." 1799: 395.

47. Fenton 1940; Catalogue W 42.

48. Thwaites: 13, 263.

49. Thwaites: 13, 231.

50. Beltrami 1828: II, 251; Turner 1894: 299.

51. Thwaites: 17, 209.

52. Turner 1982: 16.

53. Graham 1969: 164-165.

54. Biggar 1924: 268.

55. Le Beau 1738: II, 55-60.

56. Sagard 1939: 102.

57. Sagard 1939: 257.

58. Catalogue W 65

59. Catalogue W 72.

60. Long 1791: 6-7.

61. A deerskin shirt collected by Jasper Grant about 1806 in the region of Detroit shows no European influence in construction or materials and is probably a rare example of the pre-contact shirt type. (Phillips 1984: cat. 1,2).

62. Perrot in Blair 1911: I, 77.

63. Late-eighteenth-century writers report that by that period Indians around the Great Lakes wore cloth garments except for leggings and moccasins (Weld 1799: 379). Alexander Henry described reaching a band of Minnesota Ojibwa in 1764 that had been cut off from trade goods for some time and were wearing deerskin garments. "It was not long, after my goods were dispersed among them, before they were scarcely to be known for the same people," he wrote (1901: 190).

64. Weld 1799: 380-381. Catalogue W 133.

65. Weld 1799: 379.

66. Hind 1863: II, 99.

67. McKenzie in Masson 1889-90: II, 412. Although there are no documented hide garments in museum collections that can be firmly attributed to the Montagnais or East Main Cree, it is probable that some painted clothing identified as Naskapi may have been made by these peoples. A coat in the Museum of Mankind, London (no. 2613, ill. King 1982: 41) and a shirt collected by George Catlin in the United States National Museum (386,521) display the painted striped patterns described by early visitors to the Montagnais.

68. It was earlier thought that the full-skirted Naskapi coat was adapted from European frock coats. As this style is later than the earliest example of Naskapi fitted coats, however, the latter now appear to be an aboriginal clothing type. (Dorothy Burnham, personal communication.)

69. Thwaites: 7, 15.

70. Turner 1894: 292.

71. Isham 1949: 110. Graham describes the outer coat as sleeveless (1969: 145).

72. Skinner 1912: 53-56.

73. Isham 1949: 110; McKenzie in Masson 1889-90, II: 413; Grant in Masson 1889-90: II 318-319.

74. Graham 1969: 149.

75. Catalogue W 13, W 14 and W 15.

76. Graham 1969: 149.

77. Thwaites: 7, 15.

78. Graham 1969: 146. Catalogue W 24 and W 25.

79. Catalogue W 30.

80. In the early seventeenth century, Le Jeune considered

the question of the origin of these hoods and concluded, with Jesuit logic, that they were post-contact because Native people did not seem to know how to make them and bought them ready-made, although they did make their own leggings and sleeves from uncut trade cloth (Thwaites: 7,11).

81. Catalogue W 26 and W 27.
82. Catalogue W 7 and W 8.
83. Tanner 1979: 141.
84. Speck 1977: 28. For associations between beads and berries in the Northeast, see Hammel 1983.
85. Weld 1799: 395-396.
86. Champlain 1922-1936: I, 108.
87. Grant in Masson 1889-90: II, 317.
88. Charlevoix 1761: II, 40.
89. Thwaites: 5.
90. Sagard 1939: 64.
91. Quaife 1958: 237.
92. Anna Jameson, visiting Henry Schoolcraft and his wife at Mackinaw in the 1830s, found the dress of the men to be ''very various'' in contrast to that of the women, which was ''more uniform'' (1838: III, 29).
93. Quaife 1958: 227.
94. Speck 1977: 197; Tanner 1979: 102-103; Brasser 1982. Catalogue W 33.
95. In the Eastern Subarctic, symbolic ornamentation was applied to the straps used to carry home game. Carver also refers to the *metump* used to draw the toboggan in central and eastern Canada as ''made of leather and very curiously wrought'' (1778: 331).
96. Perrot in Blair 1911: I, 78.
97. Perrot in Blair 1911: I, 76.
98. Hamell 1982.
99. Oberholzer 1986, Chap. 7.
100. Hamell 1983.
101. Sagard 1939: 191-92.
102. Thwaites: 42, 39.
103. Thwaites: 5, 243.
104. Sagard 1939: 66.
105. Quaife 1958: 233.
106. Graham 1969: 149; Le Beau 1738: II, 53.
107. Thwaites: 5, 230.
108. Sagard 1939: 65.
109. Carver 1778: 227.
110. Graham 1969: 165.
111. Le Beau 1738: II, 62.
112. Graham 1969: 150.
113. Thwaites: 54. 139-143.
114. Thwaites: 21, 197.
115. Graham 1969: 144.
116. Phillips 1984.
117. Thwaites: 44, 295.
118. Feest 1987 forthcoming: 285-290.
119. Catalogue W 16 and W 17.
120. Whiteford 1986.
121. Catalogue W 56.
122. Tanner 1984.
123. Sagard 1939: 162.
124. Maurer 1986a.

125. The phrase ''figure-ground reversal'' has been used by Hammel in his discussion of the Iroquois antler combs (1979).
126. Mathews 1978: 188.
127. Vescey 1983: 109-110.
128. Thwaites: 55, 237.
129. Thwaites: 15, 17.
130. Champlain 1922-1936: 3, 133-35.
131. Graham 1969: 151.
132. Hamell 1983: 12.
133. Johnson in Masson 1889-90: II, 169.
134. Thwaites: 50, 265-267.
135. Vescey 1983: 131; Thwaites: 5, 177; Thwaites: 6, 163.
136. Catalogue W 138.
137. Jameson 1838: III, 146.
138. Phillips 1986.
139. Hamell 1979.

Plains

1. The following interpretation of the creation is based upon myths shared by the Blackfoot, Sarsi, Plains Cree, Ojibwa, and to some extent, by the Atsina. Referred to as Old Man (Napi) by the Blackfoot, the cultural hero's name in Cree myths is Wisakedjak, identical with Nanabozho in Ojibwa traditions. Primary sources for these myths are Wissler and Duvall, 1908; Simms, 1904; Bloomfield, 1930; Kroeber, 1907; Vecsey, 1983; Curtis, 1911, 1928.
2. Grinnell 1962: 141.
3. Brasser 1982: 317.
4. McLuhan 1971: 136.
5. Wissler and Duvall 1908: 126.
6. Grinnell 1896: 286.
7. Catlin 1973, II: 134.
8. Catalogue P 36 and P 37.
9. Catalogue P 39.
10. Brasser 1982: 309.
11. Paulson 1952: 64.
12. Coues 1897 II: 513,527.
13. Schuster 1952: 45.
14. Snow 1976: 86; Syms 1979: 63.
15. Reeves 1970: 159; Kehoe 1979: 23.
16. Snow 1976: 86; Gordon 1979: 63.
17. The excellent essays on Mississippian culture consulted were in Brose, Brown, and Penney, 1985.
18. Bruner 1961:201; Burpee 1927: 314.
19. Snow 1976: 89.
20. Ewers 1954: 431-433.
21. Ibid., 433.
22. Ibid., 435.
23. Lessard 1984.
24. Ewers 1958:202; Lowie 1916: 911,940,952.
25. Burpee 1927:312; Ewers 1954: 433.
26. Bain 1901:309; Syms 1979: 294.
27. Syms 1979.
28. Isinger 1971.
29. Mulloy and Lewis 1944.
30. Pohorecky 1970: 28.
31. Godsell n.d.: 335.

32. Swanton 1952: 281. Dusenberry 1960: 48.

33. Bruner 1961: 201.

34. Forbis 1977.

35. Curtis 1911: 69; Cooper 1956: 166.

36. Forbis 1970: 27; Kehoe 1979; Brumley, 1987.

37. Kehoe 1979.

38. Forbis 1970: 32; Kehoe 1959; Dempsey 1956.

39. Steinbring 1970: 247.

40. Forbis 1970: 36.

41. Richard Forbis (1970: 37) suggested a relationship with the medicine rocks used in Mandan and Hidatsa rituals. See also Maximilian 1906, 23: 33.

42. Brasser 1976: 22.

43. Keyzer 1977.

44. Leechman, Hess, and Fowler 1955.

45. Ibid., 39; Keyzer 1977: 51.

46. Keyzer 1977: 55.

47. Ibid., 35.

48. Wintemberg 1939:177. The outlining by dots of the Roche Percée petroglyphs is also unusual.

49. Morton 1929: 47.

50. Descriptions of Plains Indian history until recently repeated the early assumption that the western expansion of Cree Indians from their James Bay homeland started only after and due to the fur trade. In view of increasing archaeological evidence to the contrary this viewpoint is no longer tenable. Cree Indians infiltrated Manitoba by 900 A.D., and had reached the lower Saskatchewan River by 1600 A.D., if not already a century earlier. See Wright 1971; Meyer 1981; Brasser 1982. Similar corrections are required with regard to the original location of the Assiniboin Indians, assumed to be east of Lake Winnipeg. Several studies have associated these Indians with southwestern Manitoba since 900-1000 A.D. See Andersen, 1970; Syms, 1979; Brasser, 1982.

51. Ewers 1955:13

52. Ibid., 14.

53. Glover 1962: 241.

54. Ewers 1955: 18.

55. Burpee 1927: 25.

56. Isinger 1971.

57. Capes 1963: 116; Habgood 1967: 22; Syms 1979: 304. Gordon 1979: 80.

58. Andersen 1970.

59. Ewers 1955: 16; Curtis 1928: 177; Godsell n.d. II: 99.

60. Tefft 1965: 168.

61. Glover 1962: 241.

62. Burpee 1908: 111.

63. Coues 1897,II: 724.

64. Feder 1964: 16.

65. Glover 1962: 238. Italics added.

66. Bain 1901:312. Ewers 1955: 310.

67. Ewers 1955: 300.

68. Lessard 1984: 63.

69. Catlin 1973, I: 100.

70. Ibid., 100.

71. Bain 1901: 305, 312. The resemblance of western Cree and Assiniboin in dress and other apparel was noticed by most later observers as well.

72. Feder 164.

73. Feder 1984.

74. Wissler 1915: 71.

75. Catalogue P 68.

76. Catalogue P 50.

77. Krickeberg 1954: 177.

78. Catalogue P 53.

79. Burpee 1927: 332.

80. Lehmer 1971: 158,170.

81. Lessard 1984.

82. Wissler 1915.

83. Wissler 1915.

84. Ewers 1945: 39.

85. Catlin 1973, I: 46. Ewers 1945: 14.

86. Ewers 1939: 14.

87. Morrow 1975.

88. Catalogue P 67.

89. Ewers 1939: 34.

90. Catalogue P 27.

91. Maximilian 1906,23: 101.

92. Catalogue P 6.

93. Lessard 1984: 65.

94. Glover 1962: 51.

95. Ewers 1945: 44.

96. Lessard 1984: 63.

97. Glover 1962: 257.

98. Ewers 1945: 54.

99. Krickeberg 1954: 78.

100. Catalogue P 8.

101. Maximilian 1906,23: 114,197. Krickeberg 1954: 80.

102. Wilson 1887: 191.

103. Wissler and Duvall 1908: 131.

104. Wissler 1912: 111.

105. Wissler and Duvall 1908: 65.

106. Coues 1897, II: 514.

107. Brasser 1976: 22.

108. Bloomfield 1930: 137.

109. Maximilian 1906,23: 75,101.

110. Kroeber 1908: 196.

111. Wissler 1912: 122.

112. Brasser 1984.

113. Glover 1962: 244.

114. Hector and Vaux 1860: 257.

115. Ewers 1958: 203. Glover 1962: 266. Shimkin 1953: 407.

116. Curtis 1911: 76.

117. Cooper 1956: 166.

118. Wissler 1912: 147.

119. Harper 1971: 144.

120. Harper 1971: fig. 68.

121. Snow 1976: 68.

122. Catalogue P 60.

123. Harper 1971: 150.

124. Wissler 1912: 141.

125. Ibid., 1912: 150.

126. Ibid., 1912: 136.

127. Ibid., 1912: 194.

128. Doughty and Martin 1929: 19.

129. Fenton 1953: 161.
130. Ibid., 1953: 186-89.
131. Brasser 1980.
132. Annual Archaelogic Report, Toronto 1914: 74.
133. Brasser 1976: 39.
134. Ewers 1958: 167.
135. Krickeberg 1954: 131, pl. 43.
136. Shimkin 1953: 408.
137. Ewers 1958: 174.
138. Ibid., 1958: 175.
139. Wissler 1918: 241.
140. Ewers 1945: 20.
141. Wissler and Duvall 1908: 131.
142. Ibid., 1908: 83. Wissler 1912: 214.
143. Grinnell 1962: 259.
144. Wissler 1905.
145. Ibid., 1905.
146. Harper 1971: 139.
147. Vecsey 1983: 178.
148. Carver 1778: 270-78,286.
149. Phillips 1984: 26.
150. Ritzenthaler 1953: 228.
151. Ibid., 1953: 243. Vecsey 1983: 145.
152. Catalogue P 47.
153. Ewers 1986: 128.
154. Catalogue P 76.
155. Ewers 1986: 170. Lamb 1970: 138.
156. Vecsey 1983: 192.
157. Brasser 1985: 221.
158. Ibid., 1985: 225.
159. Ibid., 1985: 225.
160. Catalogue P 48.

Subarctic

1. Hearne 1958: 169.
2. Morice 1895: 170.
3. Richard Nerysoo of Fort McPherson, quoted in Berger, Thomas R. *Northern Frontier Northern Homeland: The Report of the Mackenzie Valley Pipeline Inquiry.* Vol. 1 Minister of Supply and Services, Canada. 1977 p. 94.
4. Krauss and Golla 1981: 67.
5. Helm 1981: 1-4.
6. Morice 1905: 204.
7. Pike 1892: 56.
8. McClellan 1970: 37.
9. Petitot 1970: 123.
10. For example, Royal Ontario Museum Catalogue Numbers HK2328, and HK2330, collected by G.T. Emmons.
11. Gordon and Savage 1974: 181.
12. Leblanc 1984: 322; Morlan 1973: 301.
13. Catalogue S 19 (ROM HK2392). A similar pattern appears on a drinking tube (Figure 121), and on Carrier birchbark basketry; for example, MM Am13A(9).
14. Speck 1935: 217.
15. Osgood 1936: 99.
16. Dall 1898: 94.
17. Jonaitis 1978: 62.
18. These clubs are described and illustrated in Siebert 1980; also in Troufanoff 1970.
19. Troufanoff 1970: 155.
20. Troufanoff 1970: 159.
21. Fitzhugh and Kaplan 1982: 68.
22. Osgood 1936: 93.
23. Mason 1946: 26.
24. Mason 1946: 26.
25. Hearne 1958: 96-97.
26. McClellan 1975: 295.
27. Ridington 1978: 50.
28. Emmons 1911: 90.
29. Siebert 1980.
30. Jacobsen 1977: 104.
31. Dr. Catharine McClellan, personal communication, 1986.
32. Samuel Black's account of meeting, in July 1824, a group of Tahltan who had never seen white men (Black 1955: 108).
33. Zagoskin 1967: 246.
34. Osgood 1936: 162; Honigmann 1954: 66.
35. Osgood 1936: 46; Morice 1895: 181.
36. Mackenzie 1970: 151.
37. Morice 1895: 181.
38. Murray 1910: 86.
39. Osgood 1936: 141.
40. Hearne 1958: 99.
41. Teit 1956: 100.
42. Cordwell 1979: 49.
43. Lisianskiy 1968: 189; Dr. Catharine McClellan, personal communication 1986.
44. Nelson 1978: 28.
45. See, for example, Slobodin 1981, on the Kutchin.
46. Osgood 1936: 53; Dall 1898: 108.
47. McKennan 1959: 84; 1965: 46.
48. Mackenzie 1970: 338.
49. Wentzel 1889-90: 1: 86.
50. Wentzel 1889-90: 1: 86.
51. Murray 1910: 85; Richardson 1851: 382.
52. McClellan has been the first anthropologist to state this explicitly: in her monograph on the Tagish, Tutchone, and Inland Tlingit, she describes a ''pervasive notion of the intimate connection between the individual and his clothing'' (1975: 300). While no other anthropologist has pursued this concept in any depth, information gleaned from a variety of historical and ethnographic sources suggests that McClellan's findings regarding clothing attitudes and Athapaskans of southern Yukon Territory could well apply to many, if not all, Athapaskan groups.
53. McKennan 1959: 144.
54. Morice 1890: 158.
55. Osgood 1936: 179; Dr. Catharine McClellan, personal communication 1986.
56. Morice 1905: 208, in reference to the Carrier.
57. Jetté 1911: 259.
58. Nelson 1983: 27.
59. Harmon 1957: 249-51.
60. McClellan 1975: 301.
61. Osgood 1936: 166; Schmitter 1910: 17.
62. Only one example of an adult shirt with attached hood

was located: Museum of the American Indian 20/9087, a "Kutchin" man's shirt.

63. See, for example, Catalogue S 25 and S 26 (CMC VI-D-163; SWM482).

64. Brasser 1982: 18; Speck 1935.

65. McClellan 1975: 302.

66. Teit, collection notes, Canadian Ethnology Service.

67. Fitzhugh and Kaplan 1982: 84.

68. Mackenzie 1970: 338.

69. Teit 1956: 74.

70. See also Catalogue S 1 and S 2 (IE 561.3; CMC VI-Y-5).

71. See Catalogue S 1 (IE 561.3).

72. Orchard 1984: 38.

73. See, for example, Catalogue S 3, S 4 and S 10 (NMF VK172, VK 180, and VK 188).

74. Orchard 1984: 35.

75. Mackenzie 1970.

76. For examples of loom-woven quillwork, see Catalogue S 29 and S 37.

77. See Catalogue S 25 and S 36 (CMC VI-D-163, VI-Z-62).

78. See, for example, Vanstone 1982; Whymper 1869: 162-163.

79. Dall 1898: 94.

80. Osgood 1937: 77.

81. Hearne 1958: 133.

82. Such sacrifice of personal property may also have been a means of thanking a spirit assistant for success in war or hunting. Morice describes a similar custom among western Athapaskan groups: ". . . if success attended his efforts he would sometimes thank it (the spirit-helper) by destroying in its honour any piece of property on hand, food or clothing, or in later times tobacco, which he would throw into the water or cast into the fire as a sacrifice." (Morice 1905: 205).

83. Carrier account of first meeting with Simon Fraser, July 26, 1806, as told to Father A.G. Morice, probably during the late 1880s (Morice 1905: 62).

84. Correspondence, Robert Campbell to George Wilson, 5 May 1859, NMS.

85. "Remarks on a collection of specimens of aboriginal art from the Mackenzie River District." Forwarded to the Industrial Museum of Scotland 1862 by Bernard R. Ross.

86. Krech 1981: 79.

87. Dr. Catharine McClellan, personal communication, 1986.

88. Petitot 1888: 374.

89. Keith 1889-90: 2-292.

90. See Catalogue S 4 (NMS 558.42).

91. Hearne 1958: 48.

92. Duchaussois 1919.

93. Slobodin 1966.

94. Brasser 1985.

95. Thompson 1983: 43; Duncan 1982: 124,125.

96. See Osgood 1932: 65; Cameron 1910: 321; Russell 1898: 169-80; Whitney 1896: 60.

97. Helm et al. 1981: 154.

98. McClellan 1981: 394.

99. Emmons 1911.

100. Simpson 1843: 77.

101. Russell 1898: 98.

102. Murray 1910: 90; Simeone 1983.

103. Krech 1984: 110-113.

104. This can be seen most clearly on the perimeters of Athapaskan territory. Alaskan Athapaskans, for example, adopted housing, clothing, shamanistic practices, and elaborate ceremonies involving masks from their Eskimo neighbours. In the northern interior of British Columbia and in southern Yukon, ceremonial clothing, potlatching, and mythology were among several features of Athapaskan life influenced by Northwest Coast culture. In Alberta, in historic times, Athapaskan-speaking Sarcee moved out of the boreal forest into a Plains environment and adopted a wholly Plains culture. These are extreme examples, but a general receptiveness to outside influences prevailed throughout the Athapaskan culture area.

Arctic

1. See also Royal Ontario Museum HC 2311, HC 2283 and HC 2284; Catalogue A 21, A 22 and A 23.

2. Boas 1964: 197; See also Hutchison (1977) for a structural analysis of the Sedna (Nuliajuk) festival recorded by Boas.

3. Quoted in Boas 1964: 199.

4. Harry Egotak, personal communication, Holman, 1986.

5. Rasmussen 1929: 183.

6. Boas 1964: 199.

7. Rasmussen 1929: 252-253.

8. See, especially, Saladin d'Anglure 1975; 1977a; 1977b; 1978a; 1978b; 1980 for an insightful consideration of male/female imagery in Inuit intellectual and spiritual culture.

9. Rasmussen 1931: 208.

10. Gut-skin jackets from the Iglulik area were collected by William Parry and George Lyon, 1821-23. These are in the collection of the Royal Scottish Museum but were too fragile to consider for this exhibition. A gut-skin jacket from Ungava, collected by Lucien Turner in 1882-84, is in the Smithsonian Institution. For a detailed description, see Turner 1979: 56-58.

11. In 1824 George Lyon published an engraving of a young man from the Sadlermiut on Southampton Island astride a float of inflated sealskins which he used to reach Lyon's ship. See Lyon 1824. In addition, Inuit in southern Baffin Island provided an inflated seal bladder to their colleague captured by the Frobisher Expedition in 1577 (Figure 160). "We suspected, however, that it was sent to him so that he could escape by swimming." (Quoted in Kenyon 1975: 67).

12. Rasmussen 1929: 67.

13. Boas 1907: 122.

14. Boas 1907: 148; Rasmussen 1931: 180.

15. Rasmussen 1929: 193.

16. Rasmussen 1931: 165-166.

17. See, especially, Fitzhugh and Kaplan, 1982 for a discussion of spiritual aspects of hunting technology in 19th-century Bering Sea Eskimo culture.

18. Royal Scottish Museum 559.9; 1142.29; 1142.32; Catalogue A 78, A 74, A 77.

19. Rosing, 1981.

20. Rosing 1981: 151.

21. George Qulaut, personal communication, 1987.

22. Rosing 1981: 152.

23. In Nouveau Québec the bow of the kayak was called *usuujaq*, ''that which resembles a penis'' (Saladin d'Anglure 1975: 63).

24. Quoted in Kenyon 1975: 115.

25. Women in Labrador were prohibited from moving about too much while their husbands were whale hunting, for the movement of their parka tails was believed to influence that of the whales, making the whales difficult to capture (Taylor 1986: 126).

26. Jenness 1946: 12.

27. Ibid., 1946: 12.

28. Mark Emerak, personal communication, Holman, October 1982.

29. George Swinton, personal communication, 1986.

30. Jenness 1946: 46. Jenness describes these as ''lemming'' skins, but a thorough examination of Copper clothing collections has revealed these attachments to be exclusively ermine skins.

31. Lyon 1824; Ross 1835.

32. Savoie 1971: 204.

33. Fitzhugh and Kaplan, 1982.

34. See, for example, the women's parka from the Royal Scottish Museum 1895.407; Catalogue A 2. In contrast, the Mackenzie woman's parka from the Royal Ontario Museum (HC 2345) shows two triangular gussets.

35. The term *kiniq* is related to other linguistic terms associated with procreation: *kinerservik*: the snow hut or tent in which a woman gives birth; *kinersertuq*: a woman occupying the birth house. See Rasmussen 1931: 258; also Driscoll 1980: 14-15; Driscoll 1983: 100-105.

36. Jenness 1946: 35.

37. Canadian Museum of Civilization IV-C-628; Catalogue A9.

38. Royal Ontario Museum HC 2267.

39. Hatt 1969: 38.

40. Royal Scottish Museum 1895: 407; Catalogue A 2 and Royal Ontario Museum HC 2267. This is a common feature of women's parkas in the Mackenzie area.

41. Royal Scottish Museum 1895: 407; Catalogue A 2. A single eagle's feather is also attached to the man's parka (Figure 164) from the Western Arctic, in the collection of the Glasgow Museum 02.8bk; Catalogue A 1. The head of a loon and the winter pelt of an ermine are also attached to this parka.

42. Rosie Igaliyuk, personal communication, Igloolik, 1978.

43. Melanie Tabvatah, personal communication, Eskimo Point, 1978.

44. Annie Napayok, personal communication, Eskimo Point, 1978.

45. Rasmussen 1931: 271-272.

46. Rasmussen 1929: 109.

47. Rasmussen 1929: 111.

48. Rasmussen 1929: 118-119.

49. Rasmussen 1929: 119.

50. A similar belt belonging to a Padlimiut female shaman is in the collection of the Manitoba Museum of Man and Nature (H5.21.40). In addition to strips of red and white stroud, the belt contains numerous attachments of minature hats and mitts. These are said to be gifts given to the shaman by women wishing to bear children.

51. Myra Kukiiyaut, quoted in Driscoll 1982: 46.

52. Birket-Smith 1945: 150 and 157.

53. Helen Kalvak, personal communication, Holman, 1982.

54. Sproull-Thomson 1979: 487; Maxwell 1985: 292.

55. Helen Kalvak, personal communication, Holman, 1982.

56. Harry Egotak, personal communication, Holman, 1986.

57. Rasmussen 1932b: 9.

58. Rasmussen 1932b: 15.

59. Rasmussen 1931.

60. Boas 1964: 206.

61. Boas 1964: 203; see also Rasmussen 1929: 198.

62. Boas 1907: 509.

63. Rasmussen 1929: 205-206.

64. Saladin d'Anglure 1983.

65. Rasmussen 1929: 206.

66. Rasmussen 1929: 206.

67. Boas 1907: 509.

68. Boas 1907: 509.

69. Driscoll 1983: 192-217.

70. Rasmussen 1929: 182.

71. Rasmussen 1929: 182.

72. Whittaker 1937: 143.

73. Whittaker 1937: 143.

74. A pair of beaded hair ornaments from Labrador are preserved in the Völkerkundemuseum Herrnhut, Staatliches Museum für Völkerkunde Dresden 67793; catalogue no. A 61.

75. Whittaker 1937: 143.

76. Turner 1979: 43-44.

77. Turner 1979: 44.

78. Jenness 1946: 52.

79. Rasmussen 1931: opp. 312.

80. Saladin d'Anglure, film, *Igloolik*.

81. Rothschild 1985.

82. These inserts of contrasting fur do not appear at the site of the joint; they are ''displaced'' joint marks, as described by Schuster 1951. In fact, in the Copper woman's parka, the three narrow stripes of white caribou fur are clustered at the wrist—in number, if not in location, they correspond to the three joints of the arm: shoulder, elbow, and wrist. George Swinton, especially, has discussed the bands of the parka sleeve as joint references.

83. Driscoll 1984a.

84. Jenness 1946: 25.

85. Rasmussen 1931: 193.

86. Rasmussen 1931.

Northwest Coast

1. Bill Reid 1981. Unpublished Ms.

2. Claude Lévi-Strauss. 1943: 175-183.

3. According to George MacDonald, 1986, there are some 500,000 Northwest Coast objects in world museums (personal communication).

4. Carlson 1983: 13-32; Fladmark 1982: 95-156, 1986.

5. Fladmark 1986: 6

6. Boas 1975: 218.

7. Gormly 1977: 8.

8. E. Gunther 1972: 6-7.

9. As called by eighteenth-century explorers.

10. Douglas Cole 1985: 1.

11. Cook, in E. Gunther 1966: 15.

12. Cole 1985: 3.

13. Cole 1985: 3-4; Fisher 1977.

14. Duff 1964: 57; Wike 1951.

15. As suggested by Wyatt (personal communication).

16. Early explorers noticed that Northwest Coast natives had already some iron tools. The iron was most likely obtained by way of Native trade routes from Asia or from shipwrecks stranded on the beach.

17. Cole 1985: 5.

18. Duff 1964: 59.

19. Cole 1985: 3-5.

20. Cole 1985: 5.

21. Sea-mammal ivory, whalebone, goat horn, and dentalia shells were available only locally and had to be traded.

22. W. Wolfe 1969: 4.

23. Suttles 1983: 86-87.

24. A.W. Wolfe, op.cit. p. 39.

25. Arima 1983: 44.

26. A. Testart 1979: 99-108.

27. Holm 1972: 78.

28. E. Gunther 1966; Boas 1895; Drucker 1940.

29. Swanton 1909: 114-115.

30. Boas 1916: 503-6.

31. Boas 1955: 280.

32. For an interpretation of it see G. MacDonald 1984: 126-27.

33. Martine de Widerspach-Thor (Reid) 1981: 157-174.

34. Rosman and Rubel 1971: 175-207.

35. M.F. Guedon 1984: 36.

36. M.F. Guedon, op.cit.

37. For a reappraisal of the relationships between masks and women on the Northwest Coast, see M. Reid 1986.

38. Drucker 1955: 127.

39. Drucker 1955: 124.

40. J. Fisher 1971: 143-44

41. Wolfe, op.cit, 29-44.

42. Fisher, op.cit.

43. This finding supports a previous seminal study by Lévi-Strauss (1967) who, while considering Caduveo facial paintings in relation to Caduveo social structure, found that social hierarchy (the Caduveo being the remnants of a culture called Mbaya, divided into heriditary castes) tends to increase the use of asymmetry in art. This could be read as follows:

symmetry	=	egalitarian societies (or less stratified societies)
asymmetry	=	stratified societies (or more stratified societies)

44. M.P. Caroll 1981: 208.

45. Swanton 1909: 108.

46. C. Geertz 1973: 126-27.

47. Arima 1983: 8.

48. Kendrick 1986: 36.

49. This particularity of swallowing enabled us to explain why Hamatsa masks are birds in an environment that does not lack for carnivorous and ferocious animals. Also carnivorous but toothless (that is, incapable of chewing) birds express, in their nature, the very image of swallowing and regurgitation (Dzonakwa, the child-eating female ogre, is also toothless.) M. Reid 1981.

50. C. Alexander 1979: 18-19.

51. From Bill Holm and Bill Reid (personal communication). Also from my own observation during the manufacture of a fifty-foot Haida canoe.

52. Boas 1895.

53. Sapir 1910-1912: VI, 8.

54. Fladmark 1986.

55. Holm 1983b: 97.

56. Catalogue No. 33.

57. Fladmark 1986: 88.

58. Fladmark, op.cit.

59. Fladmark, op.cit.

60. Hom 1983: 33.

61. Holm 1965: 29.

62. B. Holm and W. Reid 1975: 36.

63. B. Holm and W. Reid, op.cit. p.37.

64. Suttles 1983: 71.

65. Kew 1980: 4.

66. Holm 1975: 60.

67. Holm 1972: 82.

68. Langes 1953: 32.

69. Aristotle 1956.

70. Definition of Counterpoint: the art of writing music in several distinct parts or themes proceeding simultaneously, as distinguished from harmony, which depends more for its effects on the composition and progression of whole chords than on the melody of each separate part (so called because the points which formerly represented musical notes were written under or against each other on the lines). Webster 1952: 196.

71. Wingert 1951, in Holm 1983b: 42.

72. Lévi-Strauss 1975; Reid 1981.

73. Jonaitis

74. Reid, M. 1981; 1986.

75. Taylor 1973: 8.

76. Reid, M. op.cit. 1981.

77. Christopher Crocker 1977: 157-179.

78. Jacknis 1973.

79. Turner 1982: 16.

Bibliography

Adam, L.
1936 North-West American Indian Art and its Early Chinese Parallels. Man 36(3).

Adney, T. and Chapelle, H.
1964 The Bark Canoes and Skin Boats of North America. Washington: The Smithsonian Institution.

Alexander, C.
1979 Notes on the Synthesis of Form. Cambridge: Harvard University Press.

Amundsen,R.
1908 The Northwest Passage. Being the Record of a Voyage of Exploration of the Ship ''Gjoa,'' 1903-1907. 2 vols. New York: E.P. Dutton.

Andersen, R.R.
1970 Alberta Stoney (Assiniboin) Origins and Adaptations: a Case for Reappraisal. Ethnohistory, Vol. 17, Nos. 1-2.

Arima, E.Y.
1975 A Contextual Study of the Caribou Eskimo Kayak. Ottawa: National Museum of Man. Mercury Series.

_____.
1983 The West Coast (Nootka) People. British Columbia Provincial Museum. Special Publication 6.

_____.
1984 Caribou Eskimo. In Handbook of North American Indians 5 (Arctic): 447-462. Washington, D.C.: Smithsonian Institution Press.

Aristotle
1956 Poetics. trans. House. Westport: Greenwood.

Armstrong, A.
1857 A Personal Narrative of the Discovery of the Northwest Passage. London: Hurst and Blackett.

Back, G.
1836 Narrative of the Arctic Land Expedition to the Mouth of the Great Fish River, and Along the Shores of the Arctic Ocean in the Years 1833, 1834, and 1835. London: J. Murray.

Bailey, A.G.
1969 A Conflict of European and Eastern Algonkian Cultures, 1504-1700. Toronto: University of Toronto Press.

Bain, J., ed.
1901 Alexander Henry's Travels and Adventures in Canada and the Indian Territories. Boston: Little, Brown. (Reprinted, Edmonton: Hurtig, 1969.)

Bakker, Peter
Early Basque-Amerindian Language Contact in East Canada. In preparation.

Balikci, A.
1964 The Eskimos of the Québec-Labrador Peninsula: Ethnographic Contributions. In Le Nouveau-Québec: Contribution à l'étude de l'occupation humaine. J. Malaurie and J. Rousseau (eds.) Paris: Mouton.

_____.
1970 The Netsilik Eskimo. Garden City, N.Y.: Natural History Press.

_____.
1984 Netsilik. In Handbook of North American Indians 5 (Arctic): 415-430.

Bebbington, J.M.
1982 Quillwork of the Plains. Glenbow Museum, Calgary, Alberta.

Beltrami, J.C.
1828 A Pilgrimage in Europe and America, leading to The Discovery of The Sources of the Mississippi and Bloody River, 2 vols. London: Hunt and Clarke.

Berger, Thomas
1977 Northern Frontier Northern Homeland: The Report of the Mackenzie Valley Pipeline Inquiry, Vol. 1. Minister of Supply and Services, Canada.

Biggar, Henry J., ed.
1924 The Voyages of Jacques Cartier: Published from the Originals with Translations, Notes and Appendices. Publications of the Public Archives of Canada 5. Ottawa.

Bilby, J.
1923 Among Unknown Eskimo. London: Seeley Service.

Birket-Smith, K.
1929 The Caribou Eskimos: Material and Social Life and their Cultural Position. Report of the Fifth Thule Expedition, 1921-24 5(1-2). Copenhagen.

_____.
1945 Ethnographical Collections from the Northwest Passage. Report of the Fifth Thule Expedition, 1921-24 6(2). Copenhagen.

_____.
1959 The Earliest Eskimo Portraits. Folk 1: 5-14. Copenhagen.

Black, Samuel
1955 A Journal of a Voyage from Rocky Mountain Portage in Peace River to the Sources of Finlays Branch and North West Ward in Summer 1824. E.E. Rich, ed. (Publications of the Hudson's Bay Record Society 1B) London: The Hudson's Bay Record Society.

Blair, Emma H., ed.
1911 The Indian Tribes of the Upper Mississippi Valley and Region of the Great Lakes, as Described by Nicolas Perrot, French Royal Commissioner to Canada; Morrell Marston, American Army Officer; and Thomas Forsyth, United States Agent at Fort Armstrong. 2 vols. Cleveland: Arthur H. Clark.

Blodgett, J.
1979 The Coming and Going of the Shaman: Eskimo Shamanism and Art. Winnipeg: The Winnipeg Art Gallery.

Blom, M.H. and T.E. Blom, eds.
1983 Canada Home: Juliana Horatia Ewing's Fredericton Letters. Vancouver: University of British Columbia Press.

Bloomfield, L.
1930 Sacred Stories of the Sweet Grass Cree. National Museum of Canada, Bulletin 60. Ottawa.

Boas, F.
1897 The Social Organization and the Secret Societies of the Kwakiutl Indians. U.S. National Museum Report for 1895. Washington.

_____.
1901-1907 The Eskimo of Baffin Island and Hudson Bay. Bulletin of the American Museum of Natural History 15. New York.

_____.
1916 Tsimshian Mythology. Bureau of American Ethnology Annual Report No. 31. Washington, D.C.

_____.
1955 Primitive Art. New York: Dover.

_____.
1964 The Central Eskimo. Lincoln: University of Nebraska Press. (Originally published in 1888.)

Bockstoce, J.R.
1977 Eskimos of Northwest Alaska in the Early Nineteenth Century. University of Oxford: Pitt Rivers Museum.

Borden, C.
1969 The Skagit River Atlatl: A Reappraisal. Winter 1968-69. B.C. Studies 1.

Bourque, Bruce J. and Ruth Holmes Whitehead
1986 Tarrentines and the Introduction of European Trade Goods in the Gulf of Maine. Ethnohistory 32(4): 327-341.

Brasser, Ted J.
1976 "Bo' Jou Neejee!": Profiles of Canadian Indian Art. Ottawa: National Museum of Man.

_____.
1980 Self-Directed Pipe Effigies. Man in the Northeast. 19: 95-104.

_____.
1982a Pleasing the Spirits: Indian Art around the Great Lakes. Pp. 17-31 in Pleasing the Spirits: A Catalogue of a Collection of American Indian Art. New York: Ghylen Press.

_____.
1982b The Tipi as an Element in the Emergence of Historic Plains Indian Nomadism. Plains Anthropologist, Vol. 27-98, pt. 1.

_____.
1984 Backrest Banners among the Plains Cree and Plains Ojibwa. American Indian Art Magazine, Vol. 10 (1): 56-63.

_____.
1985 In search of Métis art. In The New Peoples. J. Peterson and J.S.H. Brown (eds.), Winnipeg: University of Manitoba Press.

Brose, D.S., J.A. Brown, and D.W. Penney
1985 Ancient Art of the American Woodland Indians. Detroit: Detroit Institute of Art.

Brumley, J.H.
1987 Medicine Wheels on the Northern Plains; a Summary and Appraisal. Edmonton: The Archaeological Survey of Alberta.

Bruner, E.M.
1961 Mandan. In E.H. Spicer, ed., Perspectives in American Indian Culture Change. Chicago: University of Chicago Press.

Burch, E.S., Jr.
1978 Caribou Eskimo Origins: An Old Problem Reconsidered. Arctic Anthropology 15(1): 1-35.

_____.
1979 Ethnography of Northern North America: A Guide to Recent Research. Arctic Anthropology 16(1): 62-146.

_____.
1984 Kotzebue Sound Eskimo. In Handbook of North American Indians 5 (Arctic): 303-319. Washington, D.C.: Smithsonian Institution Press.

Burpee, L.J., ed.
1908 Journal of Mathew Cocking, from York Factory to the Blackfeet Country, 1772-73. Proceedings & Transactions of the Royal Society of Canada, 3rd Series, Vol. 2.

_____.
1927 Journals and Letters of Pierre Gaultier de Varennes De La Vérendrye and his Sons. Toronto: The Champlain Society.

Burrage, H.S., ed.
1906 Early English and French Voyages. New York: Charles Scribner's Sons.

Cameron, Agnes Deans
1910 The New North: Being Some Account of a Woman's Journey Through Canada to the Arctic. New York and London: D. Appleton.

Capes, K.H.
1963 The W.B. Nickerson Survey and Excavations, 1912-15, of the Southern Manitoba Mounds region. National Museum of Canada, Anthrop. Paper No. 4. Ottawa

Carlson, R.L., ed.
1983 Indian Art Traditions of the Northwest Coast. Burnaby: Simon Fraser University Archaeology Press.

Carlson, R.L.
1983a Prehistory of the Northwest Coast. Burnaby: Simon Fraser University Archaeology Press.

_____.
1983b Change and Continuity in Northwest Coast Art. Burnaby: Simon Fraser University Archaeology Press.

Carroll, M.P.
1980 Lévi-Strauss on Art: A Reconsideration. Anthropologica. Vol. XXII, No. 2.

Carver, Jonathan
1778 Travels Through the Interior Parts of North America in the Years 1766, 1767 and 1768. London: Printed for the Author. (Reprinted: Ross and Haines, Minneapolis, 1956)

Catlin, G.
1973 Letters and Notes on the Manners, Customs and Conditions of the North American Indians. 2 Vols. New York: Dover Publications.

Cell, Gillian, ed.
1982 Newfoundland Discovered. London: Hakluyt Society.

Champlain, Samuel de
1922-1936 The Works of Samuel de Champlain. Vols I-VI. H.P. Biggar, ed. Toronto: The Champlain Society.

Charlevoix, Pierre F.X. de
1761 Journal of a Voyage to North America. 2 vols. London: Printed for R. and J. Dodsley.

Clermont, N.
1980 Les Inuit du Labrador méridional avant Cartwright. Études/Inuit/Studies 4(1-2): 147-166.

Cole, D.
1985 Captured Heritage: The Scramble for Northwest Coast Artifacts. Vancouver: Douglas and McIntyre.

Collins, H.B., Jr. et al.
1973 The Far North: 2000 Years of American Eskimo and Indian Art. Washington, D.C.: National Gallery of Art.

———.
1984 History of Research before 1945. In Handbook of the North American Indian 5 (Arctic): 8-16. Washintgon, D.C.: Smithsonian Insitution Press.

Collinson, R.
1889 Journal of H.M.S. Enterprise, on the Expedition in Search of Sir John Franklin's Ships by Behring Strait, 1850-1855. T.B. Collinson (ed.). London: Sampson, Low, Marston, and Rivington.

Cordwell, Justine M.
1979 The Very Human Arts of Transformation. In The Fabrics of Culture: The Anthropology of Clothing and Adornment. New York: Mouton Publishers.

Comer, G.
1910 A Geographical Description of Southampton Island and Notes Upon the Eskimo. Bulletin of the American Geographical Society 42: 84-90.

———.
1921 Notes on the Natives of the Northwestern Shores of Hudson Bay. American Anthropologist 23(2): 243-244.

Cooke, A. and C. Holland
1978 The Exploration of Northern Canada, 500 to 1920: A Chronology. Toronto: Arctic History Press.

Cooper, J.M.
1956 The Gros Ventres of Montana: Part II, Religion and Ritual. Edited by R. Flannery. The Catholic University of America, Anthrop. Series No. 16. Washington, D.C.

Cordwell, Justine M.
1979 The Very Human Arts of Transformation, Pp. 47-75 in The Fabrics of Culture: The Anthropology of Clothing and Adornment. Paris: Mouton.

Coues, E., ed.
1897 New Light on the Early History of the Greater Northwest; Manuscript Journals of Alexander Henry and of David Thompson. 3 Vols. New York:

Crocker, C.
1977 Les réflexions du soi (The Mirrored Self). In L'Identité. Séminaire dirigé par Claude Lévi-Strauss. Figures. Paris: Grasset.

Curtis, E.S.
1911, 1928 The North American Indian. Vols. 6, 18, Norwood.

Dall, William H.
1898 Travels on the Yukon and in the Yukon Territory in 1866-1868. Pp. 1-242 in The Yukon Territory, by William H. Dall et al. London: Downey.

Damas, D.
1972 Central Eskimo Systems of Food Sharing. Ethnology 11(3): 220-240.

———.
1975 Three Kinship Systems from the Central Arctic. Arctic Anthropology 12(1): 10-30.

———.
1984 Central Eskimo: Introduction. In Handbook of North American Indians 5 (Arctic): 391-396. Washington, D.C.: Smithsonian Institution Press.

———.
1984 Copper, Eskimo. In Handbook of North American Indians 5 (Arctic): 397-414. Washington, D.C.: Smithsonian Institution Press.

Damas, D., ed.
1984 Handbook of North American Indians 5 (Arctic). Washington, D.C.: Smithsonian Institution Press.

Danzker, Jo-anne Birnie, ed.
1979 Robert Flaherty, Photographer and Film-maker: The Inuit 1910-1922. Vancouver: The Vancouver Art Gallery.

Deignan, G.
1947 HBC and the Smithsonian. The Beaver (June): 3-7.

Dempsey, H.A.
1956 Stone Medicine Wheels — Memorials to Blackfoot War Chiefs. Journal of the Washington Academy of Sciences, Vol. 46, No. 6.

Densmore, Frances
1910 Chippewa Music, I. Bureau of American Ethnology Bulletin 45. Washington, D.C.

———.
1929 Chippewa Customs. Bureau of American Ethnology Bulletin 86. Washington, D.C. (Reprinted: Johnson Reprint Corporation, New York, 1970).

Denys, Nicolas
1908 The Description and Natural History of the Coasts of North America (Acadia). W.F. Ganong, tr. and ed. Toronto: The Champlain Society.

Dièreville, Sieur de
1934 Relation of the Voyage to Port Royal in Acadia, 1699. J.S. Webster, ed. Toronto: The Champlain Society.

Diószegi, V.
1968 Tracing Shamans in Siberia: The Story of an Ethnographical Research Expedition. Oosterhout, The Netherlands: Anthropological Publications.

Diószegi, V., ed.
1968 Popular Beliefs and Folklore Tradition in Siberia. Bloomington: Indiana University.

Diószegi, V. and M. Hoppál, eds.
1978 Shamanism in Siberia. Budapest: Académiai Kiadó.

Doughty, A.G. and C. Martin
1929 The Kelsey Papers. Public Archives of Canada, Ottawa.

Driscoll, B.
1980 The Inuit Amautik: I Like My Hood to be Full. Winnipeg: The Winnipeg Art Gallery.

———.
1982 Inuit Myths, Legends and Songs. Winnipeg: The Winnipeg Art Gallery.

———.
1983 The Inuit Parka: A Preliminary Study. Unpublished M.A. thesis. Ottawa: Carleton University.

———————.
1984a Sapangat: Inuit Beadwork in the Canadian Arctic. Expedition 26(2): 40-47. University Museum, University of Pennsylvania.

———————.
1984b Tattoos, Hairsticks and Ulus: The Graphic Art of Jessie Oonark. Arts Manitoba 3(4): 13-19

Driscoll, B., ed.
1985 Uumajut: Animal Imagery in Inuit Art. Winnipeg: The Winnipeg Art Gallery.

Drucker, P.
1940 Kwakiutl Dancing Societies. Anthropological Records 2(6). Berkeley: University of California Press.

———————.
1963 Indians of the Northwest Coast. Garden City, New Jersey: The Natural History Press.

Duchaussois, Pierre
1919 The Grey Nuns in the Far North, 1867-1917. Toronto: McClelland and Stewart.

Duff, W.
1964 The Indian History of British Columbia. Volume 1: The Impact of the White Man. Anthropology in British Columbia. Memoir 5. Victoria.

———————.
1983 The World is as Sharp as a Knife: Meaning in Northern Northwest Coast Art. In Indian Art Traditions of the Northwest Coast. R.L. Carlson (ed.) Archaeology Press. Burnaby: Simon Fraser University. 47-66.

Dufour, R.
1975 Le phénomène du sipiniq chez les Inuit d'Iglulik. Recherches Amérindiennes au Québec 5(3): 65-69.

Duncan, Kate
1982 Bead Embroidery of the Northern Athapaskans: Style Design Evolution and Transfer. Unpublished Ph.D. thesis. University of Washington.

———————.
1987 Bead Embroidery, the Art of the Northern Athapaskans. Seattle: University of Washington Press.

Dusenberry, V.
1960 Notes on the Material Culture of the Assiniboin Indians. Ethnos, Vol. 2.

Eber, D.
1973 Eskimo Penny Fashions. North/nord 20(1): 37-39.

Eliade, M.
1964 Shamanism: Archaic Techniques of Ecstacy. Princeton: Princeton University Press. Bollingen Series.

Ellis, H.
1748 A Voyage to Hudson's Bay by the Dobbs and California in the Years 1746 and 1747 for Discovering a Northwest Passage. London: H. Whitridge.

Emmons, George T.
1911 The Tahltan Indians. Philadelpia: University of Pennsylvania Museum, Anthropological Publication 4(1).

Ewers, J.C.
1939 Plains Indian Painting. Palo Alto, California: Standford University Press.

———————.
1945 Blackfeet Crafts. U.S. Indian Service, Indian Handicrafts No. 9.

———————.
1954 The Indian Trade of the Upper Missouri before Lewis and Clark: an Interpretation. Bulletin of the Missouri Historical Society, Vol 10, No. 4.

———————.
1955 The Horse in Blackfoot Culture. Bureau of American Ethnology, Bulletin 159.

———————.
1958 The Blackfeet: Raiders on the Northwestern Plains. Norman: University of Oklahoma Press.

———————.
1986 Plains Indian Sculpture. Washington, D.C.: Smithsonian Institution Press.

Fairbanks, Jonathan and Robert Trent
1982 New England Begins. Boston: Museum of Fine Arts.

Feder, N.
1964 Art of the Eastern Plains Indians. Brooklyn, N.Y.: The Brooklyn Museum.

———————.
1984 The Sidefold Dress. American Indian Art Magazine, Vol. 10 (1): 48-55.

Feest, Christian F.
1984 Ottawa Bags, Baskets and Beadwork. Pp. 12-28 in Beadwork and Textiles of the Ottawa. Harbor Springs, Michigan: Harbor Springs Historical Commission.

———————.
1984 Some 18th Century Specimens from Eastern North America in Collections in the German Democratic Republic. Jahrbuch des Museums für Völkerkunde Leipzig. 37: 281-301. Forthcoming.

Fenton, William
1940 Masked Medicine Societies of the Iroquois. Pp. 397-430 in Annual Report of the Smithsonian Institution for 1940. Washington.

———————.
1953 The Iroquois Eagle Dance: An Offshoot of the Calumet Dance; with An Analysis of the Iroquois Eagle Dance and Songs by Gertrude P. Kurath. Bureau of American Ethnology Bulletin 156. Washington.

Fisher, J.L.
1971 Art Styles as Cultural Cognitive Maps. In Anthropology and Art: Readings in Cross Cultural Aesthetics. C.M. Otten (ed.) Garden City, New Jersey: Natural History Press.

Fitzhugh, William W.
1980 A Review of Paleo-Eskimo culture history in southern Québec-Labrador and Newfoundland. Études/Inuit/Studies 4(1-2): 21-31.

———————.
1984 Images from the Past: Thoughts on Bering Sea Eskimo Art and Culture. Expedition 26(2): 24-39. University Museum, University of Pennsylvania.

————.
1985 The Nulliak Pendants and Their Relation to Spiritual Traditions in Northeast Prehistory. Arctic Anthropology 22(2): 87-109.

Fitzhugh, William W. and Susan A. Kaplan
1982 Inua: Spirit World of the Bering Sea Eskimo. Washington, D.C.: Smithsonian Institution Press.

Fladmark, K.R.
1982 An Introduction to the Prehistory of British Columbia. Canadian Journal of Archaeology. No. 6.

————.
1986 British Columbia Prehistory. National Museums of Canada. Ottawa.

Flaherty, R.
1924 My Eskimo Friends: Nanook of the North. New York: Doubleday, Page.

————.
1979 Robert Flaherty, Photographer and Film-maker: The Inuit 1910-1922. Vancouver: The Vancouver Art Gallery.

Fleming, A.L.
1932 Perils of the Polar Pack: The Adventures of the Reverend E.W.T. Greenshield of Blacklead Island, Baffin Land. Toronto: Missionary Society of the Church of England in Canada.

————.
1957 Archibald the Arctic. London: Hodder and Stoughton.

Forbis, R.G.
1970 A Review of Alberta Archaeology to 1964. Publications in Archaeology No. 1. Ottawa: National Museums of Canada.

————.
1977 Cluny, an Ancient Fortified Village in Alberta. Department of Archaeology, University of Calgary.

Franklin, J.
1823 Narrative of a Journey to the Shores of the Polar Sea, in the Years 1819, 1820, 1821, and 1822. London: J. Murray.

————.
1971 Narrative of a Second Expedition to the Shores of the Polar Sea, in the Years 1825, 1826, 1827. Edmonton: Hurtig. (Originally published in 1828).

Freeman, M.M.R.
1976 Report: Inuit Land Use and Occupancy Project. 3 vols. Ottawa: Department of Indian and Northern Affairs.

————.
1984 Arctic Ecosystems. In Handbook of North American Indians 5 (Arctic): 36-48. Washington, D.C.: Smithsonian Institution Press.

Gabus, J.
1943 Touctou; chez les hommes qui-vivent-loin-du-sel. Neuchâtel, Switzerland: Editions Victor Attinger.

Garfield, V.E. and P.S. Wingert
The Tsimshian Indians and Their Arts. Seattle and London: University of Washington Press.

Gaudet, J.L.
1935 Chief Trader Charles Philip Gaudet. The Beaver (September): 45.

Geertz, C.
1973 The Interpretation of Cultures. New York: Basic Books.

Gesner, Abraham
1848 Legislative Assembly of Nova Scotia Journals. Appendix 24:119. Halifax: Nova Scotia Legislature.

Gilberg, R.
1981 How to recognize a shaman among other religious specialists. Paper presented at Symposium on Shamanism in Eurasia. Budapest.

————.
1984 Polar Eskimo. In Handbook of North American Indians 5 (Arctic): 577-594. Washington, D.C.: Smithsonian Institution Press.

Gilberg, R., ed.
1978 Ander og mennesker. Copenhagen: Nationalmuseet.

Glover, R.
1962 David Thompson's Narrative 1784-1812. Toronto: The Champlain Society.

Godsell, P.H., ed.
n.d. The R.N. Wilson Papers. 2 Vols. Manuscript in the Glenbow Museum Archives, Calgary.

Gordon, Bryan C. and Howard Savage
1974 Whirl Lake: A Stratified Indian Site near the Mackenzie Delta. Arctic 27(3). Pp. 175-188.

Gordon, B.H.C.
1979 Of Men and Herds in Canadian Plains Prehistory. Ottawa: Mercury Series, National Museum of Man.

Gormly, Mary
1977 Early Culture Contact on the Northwest Coast, 1774-1795: Analysis of Spanish Source Material. Northwest Coast Anthropological Research Notes. Vol. 11, No. 7.

Graham, Andrew
1969 Andrew Graham's ''Observations on Hudson's Bay.'' 1767-1791. Glyndwr Williams, ed. Publications of the Hudson's Bay Record Society 27. London: The Hudson's Bay Record Society.

Grinnell, G.B.
1896 Childbirth among the Blackfeet. American Anthropologist, Vol. 9.

————.
1962 Blackfoot Lodge Tales. Lincoln: University of Nebraska Press.

Guédon, Marie-Françoise
1984 La Formation des sociétés secrètes Amérindiennes de la Côte nord-ouest. Recherches Amérindiennes au Québec. Vol. XIV, No. 2.

Gunther, E.
1966 Art in the Life of the Northwest Coast Indian. Portland, Oregon: The Portland Art Museum.

————.
1972 Indian Life on the Northwest Coast of North America As Seen by the Early Explorers and Fur Traders during the Last Decades of the Eighteenth Century. Chicago and London: The University of Chicago Press.

Gyles, John
1869 Memoirs of Odd Adventures, Strange Deliverances, etc. Cincinnati, n.p.

Habgood, Th.
1967 Petroglyphs and Pictographs in Alberta. Archaeological Society of Alberta, Newsletters 13, 14.

Hall, C.F.
1970 Life with the Esquimaux: a narrative of Arctic experience in search of survivors of Sir John Franklin's Expedition. Edmonton: Hurtig. (Originally published in 1864.)

Halpin, Marjorie M.
1965 Catlin's Indian Gallery: The George Catlin Paintings in the United States National Museum, Washington, D.C.: Smithsonian Institution.

Hamell, George R.
1979 Of Hockers, Diamonds and Hourglasses: Some Interpretations of Seneca Archaeological Art. Ms. Paper presented at the Iroquois conference at Albany, New York. October 13-15, 1979.

————.
1982 Part Two: Metaphors They Live By: Light is Life, Mind, Knowledge, and Greatest Being. MSS.

————.
1983 Trading in Metaphors: The Magic of Beads. Proceedings of the 1982 Glass Trade Bead Conference, Charles F. Hayes III, ed. (Research Records No. 16) Rochester, New York: Rochester Museum and Science Center.

Hanbury, D.T.
1904 Sport and Travel in the Northland of Canada. New York: Macmillan.

Hantzsch, B.A.
1977 My Life Among the Eskimos: Baffinland Journeys in the Years 1909 to 1911. L.H. Neatby (ed./translator). Saskatoon: University of Saskatchewan.

Harmon, Daniel W.
1957 Sixteen Years in the Indian Country: The Journal of Daniel Williams Harmon, 1800-1816. W. Kaye Lamb, ed. Toronto: Macmillan of Canada.

Harp, E.
1984 History of Archaeology after 1945. In Handbook of North American Indians 5 (Arctic): 17-22. Washington, D.C.: Smithsonian Institution Press.

Harper, F.
1964 Caribou Eskimos of the Upper Kazan River, Keewatin. Lawrence: University of Kansas.

Harper, J. Russell
1956 Portland Point: Preliminary Report of the 1955 Excavation. Appendix One. Historical Studies No. 9. St. John: The New Brunswick Museum.

————.
1957 Two Seventeenth-Century Copper-Kettle Burials. Anthropologica 4: 11-36.

————.
1971 Paul Kane's Frontier. Toronto: University of Toronto Press.

Harrison, J.D.
1985 Métis, People between Two Worlds. Calgary: The Glenbow-Alberta Institute.

Hatt, G.
1969 Arctic Skin Clothing in Eurasia and America: An Ethnographic Study. K. Taylor (trans.). Arctic Anthropology 5(2): 3-132. (Originally published in 1914.)

Hauptman, Lawrence M.
1980 Refugee Havens: The Iroquois Villages of the Eighteenth Century. Pp. 128-139 in American Indian Environments: Ecological Issues in Native American History. Christopher Vecsey and Robert W. Venables, eds. Syracuse, New York: Syracuse University Press.

Hawkes, E.W.
1916 The Labrador Eskimo. Canadian Geological Survey, Memoir 91, Anthropological Series 14. Ottawa.

Hearne, Samuel
1958 A Journey from Prince of Wales's Fort in Hudson's Bay to the Northern Ocean in the Years 1769, 1770, 1771, and 1772 R. Glover, ed. Toronto: Macmillan. (Originally published in 1795.)

Hector, J. & W.S.W. Vaux
1860 Notice of the Indians seen by the Exploring Expedition under the Command of Captain Palliser. Ethnological Society of London. Transactions, Vol. 1.

Helm, June, ed.
1981 Handbook of North American Indians. 6. Washington, D.C.: Smithsonian Institution.

Helm, June, Edward S. Rogers, and James G.E. Smith
1981 Intercultural Relations and Cultural Change in the Shield and Mackenzie Borderlands. Pp. 146-157 in Subarctic. Volume 6, Handbook of North American Indians. Washington, D.C.: Smithsonian Institution.

Henry, Alexander
1901 Travels and Adventures in Canada and the Indian Territories Between the Years 1760 and 1776. James Bain, ed. Boston: Little, Brown.

Hewson, John
1978 Beothuk Vocabularies. Technical Papers of the Newfoundland Museum 2. St. John's: The Newfoundland Museum.

Hickerson, Harold
1963 The Sociohistorical Significance of Two Chippewa Ceremonials. American Anthropologist 65(1): 1-26.

Hind, Henry Y.
1863 Explorations in the Interior of the Labrador Peninsula, the Country of the Montagnais and Nasquapee Indians. 2 Vols. London: Longman, Green, Historical Index for the Museum of Deerfield Academy. Ms, Pocumtuck Valley; Longman, Roberts and Green.

Höhn, E.O.
1963 Roderick MacFarlane of Anderson River and Fort. The Beaver (Winter): 22-29.

Holm, Bill
1965 Northwest Coast Indian Art: An Analysis of Form. Seattle and London: University of Washington Press.

————.
1972 Heraldic Carving Styles of the Northwest Coast. In American Indian Art: Form and Tradition: Walker Art Center Indians Art Association. The Minneapolis Institute of Arts.

————.
1983 Form in Northwest Coast Art. In Indian Art Traditions of the Northwest Coast. Burnaby: Simon Fraser University Archaeology Press.

Holm, Bill and William Reid
    1975 Form and Freedom: A Dialogue on Northwest Coast
         Indian Art. Houston: Institute for the Arts. Rice
         University Publishers.

Holtved, E.
    1966-67 The Eskimo Myth about the Sea-Woman: A
         folkloristic sketch. Folk 8-9: 145-153.

————.
    1967 Contributions to Polar Eskimo Ethnography.
         Meddelelser om Gronland 182(2). Copenhagen.

Honigmann, John J.
    1954 The Kaska Indians: An Ethnographic Reconstruc-
         tion. Yale University Publications in Anthropology
         51. New Haven, Connecticut.

Hooper, W.H.
    1853 Ten Months Among the Tents of the Tuski with
         Incidents of an Arctic Boat Expedition in Search of
         Sir John Franklin as Far as the Mackenzie River,
         and Cape Bathurst. London: J. Murray.

Howley, James P.
    1915 The Beothucks or Red Indians. Cambridge: Cam-
         bridge University Press.

Hubbard, Mina
    1983 A Woman's Way Through Unknown Labrador. St.
         John's: Breakwater Press.

Hughes, C.C.
    1984 History of Ethnology after 1945. In Handbook of
         the North American Indians 5 (Arctic): 23-26.
         Washington, D.C.: Smithsonian Institution Press.

————.
    1984 Siberian Eskimo. In Handbook of the North
         American Indians 5 (Arctic): 247-261. Washington,
         D.C.: Smithsonian Institution Press.

Hulton, P.H.
    1961 John White's Drawings of the Eskimo. The Beaver
         (Summer): 16-20.

Hulton, P.H. and D.B. Quinn
    1964 The American Drawings of John White, 1577-1590,
         with drawings of European and Oriental Subjects.
         Chapel Hill: University of North Carolina Press.

Hutchinson, E.
    1977 Order and Chaos in the Cosmology of the Baffin
         Island Eskimo. Anthropology 1(2): 120-138.

Isham, James
    1949 Observations on Hudson's Bay, 1743 and Notes and
         Observations on a Book Entitled A Voyage to Hud-
         son's Bay in the Dobbs Gallery, 1749. E.E. Rich,
         ed. Toronto: Published by the Champlain Society for
         The Hudson's Bay Record Society.

Isinger, B.J.
    1971 Saskatchewan Catlinite Tablets. Napao, Vol. 3, No. 1.

Issenman, B.
    1982 Sources for the Study of Inuit Clothing. Unpublished
         monograph in author's possession.

Jacknis, I.S.
    1974 Functions of the Containers. In Boxes and Bowls:
         Decorated Containers by 19th Century Haida,
         Tlingit, Bella Bella and Tsimshian Indian Artists.
         Renwick Gallery of the National Collection of Fine
         Arts. Washington: The Smithsonian Institution
         Press. 16-19.

Jacobsen, Johan A.
    1977 Alaskan Voyage, 1881-1883: An Expedition to the
         Northwest Coast of America (1884). Erna Gunther,
         trans. Chicago: University of Chicago Press.

James, W.C.
    1985 A Fur Trader's Photographs: A.A. Chesterfield in
         the District of Ungava, 1901-1904. Kingston and
         Montreal: McGill-Queen's University Press.

Jameson, Mrs. Anna
    1838 Winter Studies and Summer Rambles in Canada.
         3 Vols. London: Saunders and Otley, Conduit Street.
         (Facsimile ed. Coles Canadiana Collection. Toronto:
         Coles Publishing Co., 1970, 1972.)

Jenness, D.
    1922 The Life of the Copper Eskimos. Report of the
         Canadian Arctic Expedition. 1913-1918. 12(A).
         Ottawa.

————.
    1923 Origin of the Copper Eskimos and Their Copper
         Culture. Geographical Review 13(4): 540-551.

————.
    1925 A New Eskimo Culture in Hudson Bay. Geographical
         Review 15(3): 428-437.

————.
    1928 People of the Twilight. New York: Macmillan.

————.
    1946 Material Culture of the Copper Eskimos. Report of
         the Canadian Arctic Expedition, 1913-1918. 16.
         Ottawa.

Jetté, Jules
    1911 On the Superstitions of the Ten'a Indíans (Middle
         Part of the Yukon Valley, Alaska). Anthropos
         6:95-108. 241-259, 602-615, 699-723.

Joe, Rita
    1978 Poems of Rita Joe. Halifax: Abenaki Press.

Jonaitis, Aldona
    1978 Land Otters and Shamans: Some Interpretations of
         Tlingit Charms. American Indian Art Magazine
         4(1):62-66.

Jones, Peter
    1861 History of the Ojibway Indians; with Especial
         Reference to their Conversion to Christianity. Lon-
         don: A.W. Bennett. (Reprinted Canadiana House,
         Toronto, 1973).

Jordan, R.H. and Susan A. Kaplan
    1980 An archaeological view of the Inuit/European con-
         tact period in Central Labrador. Études/Inuit/Studies
         4(1-2): 35-45.

Kaplan, Susan A.
    1980 Neo-Eskimo Occupations of the North Labrador
         Coast. Arctic 33(3): 646-658.

Kaplan, Susan A. and Kirsten J. Barsness, eds.
    1986 Raven's Journey: The World of Alaska's Native
         People. Philadelphia: The University Museum, The
         University of Pennsylvania.

Kehoe, T.F., and A.B. Kehoe
    1959 Boulder Effigy Monuments in the Northern Plains.
         Journal of American Folklore. Vol. 72.

————————.
1979   Solstice-Aligned Boulder Configurations in Saskat-
        chewan. Mercury Series. Ottawa: National Museum
        of Man.

Keith, George
1889-1890   Letters to Mr. Roderic McKenzie, 1807-1817.
             Pp. 61-132 in Vol. 2 of Les Bourgeois de la Com-
             pagnie du Nord-Ouest: Récits de voyages, lettres et
             rapports in édits relatifs au Nord-Ouest Canadien.
             L.R. Masson, ed. 2 vols. Quebec: A. Coté.

Kemp, W.
1984   Baffinland Eskimo. In Handbook of North American
        Indians 5 (Arctic): 463-475. Washington, D.C.:
        Smithsonian Institution Press.

Kendrick, John
1986   The Men with Wooden Feet: The Spanish Exploration
        of the Pacific Northwest. Toronto: NC Press Limited.

Kenyon, W.
1975   Tokens of Possession: The Northern Voyages of
        Martin Frobisher. Toronto: Royal Ontario Museum.

Kew, J.E.M.
1980   Towards a Formal Analysis of Salish Engraving: A
        Preliminary Examination of Twenty Spindle Whorls.
        Unpublished Paper.

Keyzer, J.D.
1977   Writing-On-Stone: Rock Art on the Northwestern
        Plains. Canadian Journal of Archaeology, No. 1.

King, J.C.H.
1982   Thunderbird and Lightning: Indian Life in North-
        eastern North America 1600-1900. London: British
        Museum Publications Ltd.

————————.
1984   Inuit/Eskimo: People of the North American Arctic.
        Exhibition handlist. London: Trustees of the British
        Museum.

Kohl, Johann G.
1860   Kitchi-Gami: Wanderings Round Lake Superior. Lon-
        don: Chapman and Hall. (Reprinted: Ross and
        Haines, Minneapolis, 1956).

Krauss, Michael E. and Victor K. Golla
1981   Northern Athapaskan Languages. In Subarctic 6
        (67-85), Handbook of the North American Indians.
        Washington D.C.: Smithsonian Institution Press.

Krech, Shepard, III
1974   The Eastern Kutchin and the Fur Trade. 1800-1860.
        Ethnohistory 23(3): 213-235.

————————.
1981   "Throwing Bad Medicine": Sorcery, Disease and
        the Fur trade among the Kutchin and Other
        Northern Athapaskans. Pp. 73-108 in Indians,
        Animals, and the Fur Trade: A Critique of the
        Keepers of the Game. Athens: University of Georgia
        Press.

————————.
1984   The Trade of the Slavey and Dogrib at Fort Simpson
        in the Early Nineteenth Century. In The Subarctic
        Fur Trade: Native Social and Economic Adaptations.
        99-146. Vancouver: University of British Columbia
        Press.

Krickeberg, W.
1954   Altere Ethnographica aus Nordamerika im Berliner
        Museum fur Völkerkunde. Baessler Archiv, Beitrage
        zur Völkerkunde. Berlin.

Kroeber, A.L.
1907   Gros Ventre Myths and Tales. Anthropological
        Papers, American Museum of Natural History,
        Vol. 1. New York.

————————.
1908   Ethnology of the Gros Ventre. Anthropological
        Papers, American Museum of Natural History,
        Vol. 1, part 4. New York.

Lamb, W.K.
1970   The Journals and Letters of Sir Alexander
        Mackenzie. Toronto: Macmillan.

Langer, S.K.
1953   Feeling and Form. New York: Charles Schribner's
        Sons.

Larsen H.
1969/70   Some Examples of Bear Cult among the Eskimo
           and Other Northern Peoples. Folk 11-12: 27-42.

La Vérendrye, Pierre Gaultier de Varrennes de
1927   Journals and Letters of Pierre Gaultier de Varennes
        de la Vérendrye and His Sons . . . Lawrence J.
        Burpee, ed. (Publications of the Champlain Society
        16.) Toronto: The Champlain Society.

Leacock, E.B. and N.O. Lurie, eds.
1971   North American Indians in Historical Perspective.
        New York: Random House.

Le Beau, Claude
1738   Aventures du Sr. C. Le Beau, avocat en parlement,
        ou Voyage curieux et Nouveau parmi les Sauvages
        de l'Amérique Septentrionale. 2 Vols. Amsterdam:
        Herman Uytwerf.

Leblanc, Raymond
1984   The Rat Indian Creek Site and the Late Prehistoric
        Period in the Interior Northern Yukon. Ottawa: Mer-
        cury Series Archaeological Survey Paper 120.
        National Museum of Man.

LeClercq, Chrestien
1910   New Relation of Gaspesia, 1691. W.F. Ganong, tr.
        and ed. Toronto: The Champlain Society.

Leechman, D., M. Hess, R.L. Fowler
1955   Pictographs in Southwestern Alberta. National
        Museum of Canada, Bulletin 136. Ottawa.

Lehmer, D.J.
1971   Introduction to Middle Missouri Archaeology.
        Washington, D.C.: National Park Service, U.S.
        Department of the Interior.

Lescarbot, Marc
1907-14   History of New France. Vols. I-III. Toronto: The
           Champlain Society.

Lessard, F.D.
1984   Classic Crow Beadwork: Upper Missouri River Roots.
        In F.D. Lessard, ed., Crow Indian Art. Mission,
        S.D.: Chandler Institute.

Levine, Stuart and Nancy O. Lurie (eds.)
1968   The American Indian Today. Baltimore: Penguin
        Books.

Lévi-Strauss, Claude
1943   The Art of the Northwest Coast at the American
        Museum of Natural History. Paris: Gazette des
        Beaux-Arts.

_____.
1967 Structural Anthropology. Anchor Books. Garden City, New York: Doubleday.

_____.
1979 The Way of the Masks. Translated from the French by Sylvia Modelski. Seattle: University of Washington Press.

Lisiansky, Urey
1968 Voyage Round the World in the Years 1803, 1804, 1805 and 1806. New York: Da Capo Press.

Long, John
1791 Voyages and Travels of an Indian Interpreter and Trader Describing the Manners and Customs of the North American Indians. London: Printed for the Author.

Lopez, Barry
1986 Arctic Dreams. New York: Charles Scribner's Sons.

Low, A.P.
1906 The Cruise of the Neptune, 1903-04. Report on the Dominion Government Expedition to Hudson Bay and the arctic islands on board the D.G.S. Neptune 1903-04. Ottawa: Government Printing Bureau.

Lowie, R.H.
1916 Plains Indian Age Societies: Historical and Comparative Summary. Anthropology Papers, Vol. 11. American Museum of Natural History.

Lyon, G.F.
1824 The Private Journal of Captain G.F. Lyon of H.M.S. Hecla, During the Recent Voyage of Discovery under Captain Parry. London: John Murray.

MacDonald, George
1968 Debert: A Paleo-Indian Site in Central Nova Scotia. Anthropology Papers No. 16. Ottawa: National Museum of Man.

_____.
1984 Painted Houses and Woven Blankets: Symbols of Wealth in Tsimshian Art and Myth. In The Tsimshian and their Neighbors of the North Pacific Coast. J. Miller and Carol M. Eastman (eds.) Seattle: University of Washington Press.

_____.
1986 Material Culture as Text. Unpublished Paper.

MacGregor, Arthur, ed.
1983 Tradescant's Rarities. Oxford: Clarendon Press.

MacGregor, Gaile
1985 The Wacousta Syndrome: Explorations in the Canadian Langscape. Toronto: University of Toronto Press.

Mackenzie, Sir Alexander
1970 The Journals and Letters of Sir Alexander Mackenzie (1789-1819). W. Kaye Lamb, ed. Cambridge, England: Published for the Hakluyt Society at the University Press.

Magnusson, Magnus and Pálsson, Hermann, trs. and eds.
1965 The Vinland Sagas. Baltimore: Penguin Books Ltd.

Maillard, Abbé Antoine Simon-Pierre
1758 An Account of the Customs and Manners of the Mikmakis and Maricheets, Savage Nations, Now Dependant on the Government at Cape Breton. London: S. Hooper and A. Marely.

_____.
1863 Lettre à Madame de Drucourt. In Les Soirées Canadiennes. Québec: Brousseau Frères. Translated for this publication by M.A. Hamelin, Nova Scotia Museum.

Manning, T. and E. Manning
1944 The Preparation of Skins and Clothing in the Eastern Canadian Arctic. The Polar Record 4(28): 156-169.

Marsh, W.P.
1976 People of the Willow. Toronto: Oxford University Press.

Marshall, Ingeborg C.L.
n.d. Beothuk Ethnography and History. In preparation.

_____.
1974 "A New Collection of Beothuk Bone Pieces." Man in the Northeast 8: 31-56.

_____.
1978 "The Significance of Beothuck Carved Bone Pendants." Canadian Journal of Archaeology 2: 139-254.

_____.
1985 Beothuk Bark Canoes: An Analysis and Study. Mercury Series Paper 102. Ottawa: National Museum of Man.

Martijn, C. and N. Clermont, eds.
1980 Les Inuit du Québec-Labrador méridional/The Inuit of Southern Quebec-Labrador. Études/Inuit/Studies 4(1-2).

Mary-Rousselière, G., o.m.i.
1976 The Paleoeskimo in Northern Baffinland. In Eastern Arctic Prehistory: Paleoeskimo Problems. M. Maxwell, ed. Memoirs of the Society for American Archaeology 31. Salt Lake City.

_____.
1984 Iglulik. In Handbook of North American Indians 5 (Arctic): 431-446. Washington, D.C.: Smithsonian Institution Press.

Mason, J. Alden
1946 Notes on the Indians of the Great Slave Lake Area. Yale University Publications in Anthropology 34. New Haven, Conn.

Masson, Louis F.R.
1889-1890 Les Bourgeois de la compagnie du Nord-Ouest canadien. 2 Vols. Québec: A. Coté et Cie.

Mathews, Zena Pearlstone
1978 The Relation of Seneca False Face Masks to Seneca and Ontario Archaeology. New York: Garland Publishing, Inc.

Mathiassen, T.
1927 Archaeology of the Central Eskimo. 2 vols. Report of the Fifth Thule Expedition 1921-24. 4(1-2). Copenhagen.

_____.
1928 Material Culture of the Iglulik Eskimos. Report of the Fifth Thule Expedition 1921-24. 6(1). Copenhagen.

Maurer, Evan
1986 Representational and Symbolic Forms in Great Lakes-Area Wooden Sculpture. Bulletin of the Detroit Institute of Arts 62, 1: 6-17.

————.

1986 Determining Quality in Native American Art. Pp. 143-156 *in* The Arts of the North American Indian: Native Traditions in Evolution. Edwin L. Wade, ed. New York: Hudson Hills Press.

Maximilian, Prince of Wied
1906 Travels in the Interior of North America. In R.G. Thwaites, ed., Early Western Travels. Vols. 22-24. Cleveland: Arthur H. Clarke.

Maxwell, M.
1984 Pre-Dorset and Dorset Prehistory of Canada. *In* Handbook of North American Indians 5 (Arctic): 359-368. Washington, D.C.: Smithsonian Institution Press.

————.

1985 Prehistory of the Eastern Arctic. Orlando, Fla.: Academic Press, Inc.

McCartney, A.P., ed.
1979 Thule Eskimo Culture: An Anthropological Perspective. Ottawa: Mercury Series, Archaeological Survey Paper 88. National Museum of Man.

McClellan, Catharine
1970 The Girl Who Married the Bear: A Masterpiece of Indian Oral Tradition. Ottawa: National Museum of Man, Publications in Ethnology 2.

————.

1975 My Old People Say: An Ethnograhic Survey of Southern Yukon Territory. 2 pts. Ottawa: National Museum of Man, Publications in Ethnology 6.

————.

1981 Intercultural Relations and Cultural Change in the Cordillera. *In* Subarctic 6 (387-401) Handbook of North American Indians. Washington, D.C.: Smithsonian Institution Press.

McGhee, R.
1972 Copper Eskimo Prehistory. National Museums of Canada. Publications in Archaeology 2. Ottawa.

————.

1974 Beluga Hunters: An Archaeological Reconstruction of the Mackenzie Delta Kittegaryumiut. University of Newfoundland. Institute of Social and Economic Resources. Social and Economics Studies 13. St. John's.

————.

1976 Differential Artistic Productivity in the Eskimo Cultural Tradition. Current Anthropology 17(2): 203-220.

————.

1977 Ivory for the Sea Woman: The Symbolic Attributes of a Prehistoric Technology. Canadian Journal of Archaeology 1: 141-150.

————.

1984 Thule Prehistory of Canada. *In* Handbook of North American Indians 5 (Arctic): 369-376. Washington, D.C.: Smithsonian Institution Press.

————.

1985 Ancient Animals: The Dorset Collection from Brooman Point. *In* Uumajut: Animal Imagery in Inuit Art. B. Driscoll (ed.). Winnipeg: The Winnipeg Art Gallery.

McKennan, Robert K.
1959 The Upper Tanana Indians. New Haven, Connecticut: Yale Publications in Anthropology 55.

————.

1965 The Chandalar Kutchin. Arctic Institute of North America Technical Paper 17. Montreal.

M'Clintock, F.L.
1859 The Voyage of the 'Fox' in the Arctic Seas: A Narrative of the Discovery of the Fate of Sir John Franklin and His Companions. London: John Murray.

McLuhan, T.C.
1971 Touch the Earth: A Self Portrait of Indian Existence. New York: Promontory Press.

Meldgaard, J.
1960 Eskimo Sculpture. London: Methuen.

Meyer, D.
1981 Late Prehistoric Assemblages from Nipawin: the Pehonan Complex. Saskatchewan Archaeology, Vol. 2.

Michael, H.N. (ed.)
1963 Studies in Siberian Shamanism. Toronto: University of Toronto Press.

Miertsching, J.A.
1967 Frozen Ships: The Arctic Diary of Johann Miertsching, 1850-1854. L.H. Neatby (ed. and trans.). Toronto: Macmillan of Canada.

Moore, C.H.
1978 Anguhadluq's Art: Memoirs of the Utkuhikalingmiut. Études/Inuit/Studies 2(2): 3-21.

Morice, Adrien G.
1890 The Western Dénés: Their Manners and Customs. Pp. 109-174 in Proceedings of the Canadian Institute for 1888-1889, ser. 3, 6: 2, 7.

————.

1895 Notes Archaeological, Industrial, and Sociological on the Western Dénés with an Ethnographical Sketch of the Same. Toronto: Transactions of the Canadian Institute 4: 1-222.

————.

1905 The History of the Northern Interior of British Columbia (Formerly New Caledonia). 1660-1880. 3d ed. Toronto: William Briggs.

Morlan, Richard E.
1973 The Later Prehistory of the Middle Porcupine Drainage, Northern Yukon Territory. Ottawa: Mercury Series Archaeological Survey Paper 11. National Museum of Man.

Morrow, M.
1975 Indian Rawhide, an American Folk Art. Norman: University of Oklahoma Press.

Morton, A.S., ed.
1929 The Journal of Duncan McGillivray of the North West Company. Toronto: University of Toronto Press.

Mulloy, W., and O. Lewis
1944 Some Sculptured Artifacts from eastern Montana. American Antiquity, Vol. 9, pp. 334-35.

Murdoch, J.
1892 Ethnological Results of the Point Barrow Expedition. *In* Ninth Annual Report of the Bureau of American Ethnology for the Years 1887-1888. Washington, D.C.

Murray, Alexander H.
1910 Journal of the Yukon, 1847-48. J.J. Burpee, ed. Publications of the Public Archives of Canada 4. Ottawa.

_____.
Open letter from National Congress of American Indians. Washington, D.C.: unpublished. September 26, 1986.

Neatby, L.H.
1984 Exploration and History of the Canadian Arctic. *In* Handbook of North American Indians 5 (Arctic): 377-390. Washington, D.C.: Smithsonian Institution Press.

Nelson, Edward W.
1978 E.W. Nelson's Notes on the Indians of the Yukon and Innoko Rivers, Alaska, James W. VanStone, ed. Fieldiana: Anthropology 70, Chicago.

_____.
1984 The Eskimo about Bering Strait. Washington, D.C.: Smithsonian Institution Press. (Originally published in 1899.)

Nelson, Richard K.
1969 Hunters of the Northern Ice. Chicago: University of Chicago Press.

_____.
1983 Make Prayers to the Raven: A Koyukon View of the Northern Forest. Chicago: University of Chicago Press.

Neumann, E.
1955 The Great Mother: An Analysis of the Archetype. Princeton: Princeton University Press. Bollingen Series.

Nooter, G.W. (ed.)
1984 Life and Survival in the Arctic: Cultural Changes in the Polar Regions. The Hague: Government Publishing Office.

Nungak, Z. and E. Arima
1969 Unikkaatuat sanaugarngnik atyingualiit Puvirngniturngmit: Eskimo Stories from Povungnituk, Québec. Anthropological Series 90, National Museum of Canada Bulletin 236. Ottawa.

Nute, G.L.
1943 Kennicott in the North. The Beaver (September): 28-32.

Oakes, Jill
1987 Inuit Annuraangit/Our Clothes: A Travelling Exhibition of Inuit Clothing. Eskimo Point: Inuit Cultural Institute.

Oberholzer, Catherine
1986 The Iroquois Sun Disc Wand: A Condensed Symbol. Master's Dissertation. Peterborough, Ontario: Trent University.

Orchard, William C.
1975 Beads and Beadwork of the American Indians. New York: Museum of American Indian, Heye Foundation.

_____.
1984 The Technique of Porcupine Quill Decoration Among the North American Indians. Ogden, Utah: Eagle's View Publishing.

Osgood, Cornelius
1932 The Ethnography of the Great Bear Lake Indians.

Pp. 31-97 in Annual Report for 1931, National Museum of Canada Bulletin 70, Ottawa.

_____.
1936 Contributions to the Ethnography of the Kutchin. Yale University Publications in Anthropology 14. New Haven, Conn.

_____.
1937 The Ethnography of the Tanaina. New Haven, Connecticut: Yale University Publications in Anthropology 16.

Oswalt, W.H.
1979 Eskimos and Explorers. San Francisco: Chandler and Sharp.

Parry, W.D.
1821 Journal of a Voyage for the Discovery of a Northwest Passage from the Atlantic to the Pacific: Performed in the Years 1819-1820. London: John Murray.

_____.
1824 Journal of a Second Voyage for the Discovery of a North-west Passage from the Atlantic to the Pacific: Performed in the Years 1821-22-23, in His Majesty's Ships Fury and Hecla. London: John Murray.

Parsons, Elsie Clews
1925 Micmac Folklore. Journal of American Folklore 38, No. 147: 33-55.

Pastore, Ralph
1984 Excavation at Boyd's Cove 1984: The Preliminary Report. Archaeology in Newfoundland and Labrador Annual Report 5: 322-337. St. John's: The Newfoundland Museum.

_____.
n.d. Fishermen, Furriers and Beothuks: The Economy of Extinction. Man in the Northeast. (In Press.)

Paulson, I.
1952 The Seat of Honor in Aboriginal Dwellings of the Circumpolar Zone, with special regard to the Indians of northern North America. In Sol Tax, ed., Indian Tribes of Aboriginal America. 29th Internat. Congress of Americanists. Vol. 3. Chicago.

Perley, Moses
1843 Legislative Assembly of Nova Scotia Journals. Appendix 49: 127. Halifax: Nova Scotia Legislature.

Petersen, R.
1966-67 Burial Forms and Death Cult Among the Eskimos. Folk 8-9: 259-280. Copenhagen.

Petitot, Emile
1888 En route pour la mer glaciale. 2nd ed. Paris Letouzey et Ané.

_____.
1970 Indian Legends of North-Western Canada. Trans. T. Habgood. Western Canadian Journal of Anthropology 2(1): 94-129.

_____.
1981 Among the Chiglit Eskimos. Trans. E.O. Höhn. Boreal Institute for Northern Studies. Occasional Publication No. 10. Edmonton: University of Alberta.

Pharand, S.
1975 Clothing of the Iglulik Inuit. Unpublished manuscript. Ottawa: Canadian Ethnology Service,

National Museum of Man, National Museums of Canada.

Phillips, Ruth B.
1984 Patterns of Power: The Jasper Grant Collection and Great Lakes Indian Art of the Early Nineteenth Century. Kleinburg, Ontario: The McMichael Canadian Collection.

————.
1986 Dreams and Designs: Iconographic Problems in Great Lakes Twined Bags. Bulletin of the Detroit Institute of Arts 62 (1): 27-37.

————.
1986-87 Jasper Grant and Edward Walsh: The Gentleman-Soldier as early Collector of Great Lakes Indian Art. Journal of Canadian Studies 21(4).

Pike Warburton, M.
1892 The Barren Ground of Northern Canada. London and New York: Macmillan.

Pohorecky, Z.
1970 Saskatchewan Indian Heritage; the First Two Hundred Centuries. Saskatoon: University of Saskatchewan.

Prins, Harald and Whitehead, Ruth Holmes
Early Sixteenth-Century Micmac-Portuguese Pidgin in the Gulf of St. Lawrence. In Preparation.

Pulling, G.C.
1792 Some Facts Concerning the Native Indians of Newfoundland. Ms GN1/13/2A. St. John's: Newfoundland Public Archives.

Quaife, Milo Milton, ed.
1958 The Siege of Detroit in 1763: The Journal of Pontiac's Conspiracy and John Rutherfurd's Narrative of a Captivity. The Lakeside Classics. Chicago: R.R. Donnelly and Sons Co.

Quinn, David, ed.
1964 North American Discovery circa 1000-1612. New York: Harper and Row.

Rae, J.
1850 Narrative of an Expedition to the Shores of the Arctic Sea in 1846 and 1847. London: T. and W. Boone.

————.
1866 On the Esquimaux. Transactions of the Ethnological Society of London n.s. 4: 138-153. London.

————.
1963 Correspondence 1844-1855. E.E. Rich (ed.). Toronto: The Hudson's Bay Record Society.

Rand, Silas T.
1894 Legends of the Micmacs. New York: Longmans, Green & Co.

Rasmussen, K.
1929 Intellectual Culture of the Iglulik Eskimos. Report of the Fifth Thule Expedition 1921-24. 7(1). Copenhagen.

————.
1930 Intellectual Culture of the Hudson Bay Eskimos. Report of the Fifth Thule Expedition 1921-24. 7(1-3). Copenhagen.

————.
1931 The Netsilik Eskimos: Social Life and Spiritual Culture. Report of the Fifth Thule Expedition 1921-24. 8(1-2). Copenhagen.

————.
1932 Intellectual Culture of the Copper Eskimos. Report of the Fifth Thule Expedition 1921-24. 9. Copenhagen.

————.
1932b The Eagle's Gift: Alaska Eskimo Tales. I. Hutchinson (trans.). Garden City, N.Y.: Doubleday, Doran.

Ray, D.J.
1975 The Eskimo of Bering Strait, 1650-1898. Seattle: University of Washington Press.

Reeves, B.
1970 Culture Dynamics in the Manitoba Grasslands 1000 BC-A.D. 1700. In W.M. Hlady, ed., Ten Thousand Years of Archaeology in Manitoba. Winnipeg: Manitoba Archaeological Society.

Reid, Bill
1981 Unpublished manuscript.

Reid, Martine J.
1981 La cérémonie hamatsa des Kwagul: Approche structuraliste des rapports mythe-rituals. Ph.D. dissertation. Vancouver: University of British Columbia.

————.
1984 Le mythe de Baxbakwalanuxsiwae: Une affaire de famille. Recherches Amérindiennes au Québec. La Côte Nord-Ouest 14(2): 25-33.

————.
1986 Women and Masks on the Northwest Coast: A reappraisal paper presented at the First Conference of the Native Art Studies Association of Canada, Victoria.

Remie, C.
1984 How Ukpaktoor lost his buttock and what he got in exchange for it: Cultural changes amongst the Arviligdjuarmiut of Pelly Bay, Northwest Territories, Canada. In Life and Survival in the Arctic. G.W. Nooter (ed.). The Hague: Government Publishing Office.

Richardson, Sir John
1851 Arctic Searching Expedition: A Journal of a Boat-voyage Through Rupert's Land and the Arctic Sea, in Search of the Discovery of Ships Under Command of Sir John Franklin with an Appendix on the Physical Geography of North America. 2 vols. London: Longman, Brown, Green, and Longman.

Richling, B.
1980 Images of the "Heathen" in Northern Labrador. Études/Inuit/Studies 4(1-2): 233-242.

Ridington, Robin
1978 Swan People: A Study of the Dunne-za Prophet Dance. Ottawa: National Museum of Man. Mercury Series. Ethnology Service Paper 38.

Ritzenthaler, R.E.
1953 Chippewa Preoccupation with Health. Milwaukee: Milwaukee Public Museum, Bulletin 19, No. 4.

Rosing, J.
1981 The Loon. Folk 23: 151-160. Copenhagen.

Rosman, Abraham and Rubel, Paula
1971 Feasting With Mine Enemy: New York: Columbia University Press.

Ross, J.
1835 Narrative of the Second Voyage in Search of a

North-West Passage, and a Residence in the Arctic Regions During the Years 1829, 1830, 1831, 1832, 1833. Philadelphia: E.L. Corey and H. Hart.

Ross, W.G.
1975 Whaling and Eskimos: Hudson Bay 1860-1915. Canada National Museum of Man. Publications in Ethnology 10. Ottawa.

———.
1984a An Arctic Whaling Diary: The Journal of Captain George Comer in Hudson Bay 1903-05. Toronto: University of Toronto Press.

———.
1984b George Comer, Franz Boas, and the American Museum of Natural History. Études/Inuit/Studies 8(1): 145-164.

Rothschild, K.
1985 Historical Inuit Tattoo Practices: A Preliminary Study. Master's Thesis. Ottawa: Carleton University.

Rowley, S.
1985 The Significance of Migration for the Understanding of Inuit Cultural Development in the Canadian Arctic. Unpublished PhD. dissertation. University of Cambridge.

Russell, Frank
1898 Explorations in the Far North: Being the Report of an Expedition Under the Auspices of the University of Iowa During the Years 1892, '93, and '94. Iowa City: University of Iowa Press.

Sabo, G. and D. Sabo
1985 Belief Systems and Ecology of Sea Mammal Hunting among the Baffinland Eskimo. Arctic Anthropology 22(2): 77-86.

Sagard-Theodat, Gabriel
1939 Father Gabriel Sagard: The Long Journey to the Country of the Hurons [1632]. George M. Wrong, ed. Toronto: The Champlain Society.

Saladin d'Anglure, B.
1975 Recherches sur le symbolisme inuit. Recherches amérindiennes au Québec 5(3): 62-64.

———.
1977a Iqallijuq ou les reminiscences d'une âme-nom inuit. Études/Inuit/Studies 1(1): 33-63.

———.
1977b Mythe de la femme et pouvoir de l'homme chez les Inuit de l'Arctique central canadien. Anthropologie et sociétés 1(3): 79-98. Québec.

———.
1978a L'homme (angut), le fils (irniq) et la lumière (qau); ou le cercle du pouvoir masculin chez les Inuit de l'Arctique central. Anthropologica n.s. 20(1-2): 104-144.

———.
1978b Entre cri et chant: Les Katajjait, un genre musical féminin. Études/Inuit/Studies 2(1): 85-94.

———.
1980a "Petit-Ventre" l'enfant-géant du cosmos inuit: Ethnographie de l'enfant et enfance de l'ethnographie dans l'Arctique central inuit. L'Homme 20(1): 7-46.

———.
1980b Nanuq, super-mâle. L'ours blanc dans l'espace imaginaire et le temps social des inuit de l'Arctique canadiens. Études Mongoles 11: 63-94.

———.
1983 Ijiqqat: voyage au pays de l'invisible inuit. Études/Inuit/Studies 7(1): 67-83.

———.
1984 Inuit of Québec. In Handbook of North American Indians 5 (Arctic): 476-508. Washington, D.C.: Smithsonian Institution Press.

Sapir, Edward
1910-12 Nootka Notes. Unpublished ms. 1237. 526, Canadian Ethnology Service, National Museum of Man, National Museums of Canada, Ottawa.

Sauer, Carl O.
1968 Northern Mists. Berkeley: University of California.

Savoie, D. (ed.)
1970 The Amerindians of the Canadian Northwest in the 19th Century, as seen by Émile Petitot. Vol. 1: The Tchiglit Eskimos. Ottawa: Department of Indian Affairs and Northern Development.

Schlederman, P.
1980 Notes on Norse Finds from the East Coast of Ellesmere Island, N.W.T. Arctic 33(3): 454-463.

———.
1981 Eskimo and Viking Finds in the High Arctic. National Geographic Magazine 159(5): 575-601.

Schmitter, Ferdinand
1910 Upper Yukon Native Customs and Folk-lore. Smithsonian Miscellaneous Collections 56(4). Washington.

Schneider, M.J.
1980 Plains Indian Art. In Anthropology on the Great Plains. W.R. Wood and M. Liberty, eds. Lincoln: University of Nebraska Press.

Schoolcraft, Henry Rowe
1820 Travels through the Northwestern Regions of the United States. (Reprinted, University Microfilms, Inc., Ann Arbor, Michigan, 1966)

Schuster, C.
1951 Joint-Marks: A Possible Index of Cultural Contact between America, Oceania and the Far East. Royal Tropical Institute, Mededeling. 94. Amsterdam.

———.
1952 A Survival of the Eurasiatic Animal Style in Northern Alaskan Eskimo Art. In Sol Tax, ed., Indian Tribes of Aboriginal America. 29th Internat. Congress of Americanists. Vol. 3. Chicago.

Shimkin, D.B.
1953 The Wind River Shoshoni Sun Dance. Bureau of American Ethnology, Bull. 151, Anthrop. Papers No. 41. Washington, D.C.

Siebert, Erna V.
1980 Northern Athapaskan Collections of the First Half of the Nineteenth Century. In Arctic Anthropology 17(1): 49-76.

Simeone, William E., Jr.
1983 The Alaskan Athapaskan Chief's Coat. American Indian Art Magazine, 8(2): 64-69.

Simms, S.C.
1904 Traditions of the Sarcee Indians. Journal of American Folklore, Vol. 17.

Simpson, Thomas
1843 Narrative of the Discoveries on the North Coast of America; Effected by the Officers of the Hudson's Bay Company During the Years 1836-1839. London: Richard Bentley.

Skinner, Alanson B.
1912 Notes of the Eastern Cree and Northern Saulteaux. Papers of the American Museum of Natural History 9(1). New York.

Slobodin, Richard
1966 Métis of the Mackenzie District. Ottawa: Saint Paul University, Canadian Research Centre for Anthropology.

——————— .
1981 Alexander Hunter Murray and Kutchin Hair Style. In Arctic Anthropology 18(2): 29-42.

Smith, David M.
1982 Moose-deer Island House People: A History of the Native People of Fort Resolution. Ottawa: Mercury Series. Canadian Ethnology Service Paper No. 81. National Museum of Man.

——————— .
1984 Mackenzie Delta Eskimo. In Handbook of North American Indians 5 (Arctic): 347-358. Washington, D.C.: Smithsonian Institution Press.

Smith, J.G.E. and E.S. Burch, Jr.
1979 Chipewyan and Inuit in the Central Canadian Subarctic, 1613-1977. Arctic Anthropology 16(2): 76-101.
Sotheby's sale catalogue of Fine American, Indian, African and Duamic Art. New York Galleries. October 23, 1982.

Snow, D.
1976 The Archaeology of North America. New York: The Viking Press.

Soby, R.M.
1969-70 The Eskimo Animal Cult. Folk 11-12: 43-78. Copenhagen.

Speck, Frank G.
1914 The Double-curve Motive in Northeastern Algonkian Art. Anthropological Series 1. Memoirs of the Canadian Geological Survey 42. Ottawa.

——————— .
1931 Montagnais-Naskapi Bands and Early Eskimo Distribution in the Labrador Peninsula. American Anthropologist 33(4): 557-600.

——————— .
1935 Labrador Eskimo Mask and Clown. The General Magazine and Historical Chronicle 37(2): 159-172.

——————— .
1936 Inland Eskimo Bands of Labrador. In Essays in Anthropology in Honor of Alfred Louis Kroeber. Berkeley: University of California Press.

——————— .
1977 Naskapi: The Savage Hunters of the Labrador Peninsula. [1935] Norman: University of Oklahoma Press.

Spencer, R.F.
1984 North Alaska Coast Eskimo. In Handbook of North American Indians 5 (Arctic): 320-337.

Sproull-Thomson, J.
1979a Towards a Definition of Styles and Patterns in Thule Decorative Art. Unpublished M.A. thesis. Ottawa: Carleton University.

——————— .
1979b Recent studies in Thule art: Metaphysical and Practical Aspect. In Thule Eskimo Culture: An Anthropological Perspective. A.P. McCartney, ed. Ottawa: Mercury Series, Archaeological Survey of Canada Paper 88. National Museum of Man.

Stefánsson, V.
1913 My Life with the Eskimo. New York: Macmillan.

——————— .
1914 Prehistoric and Present Commerce Among the Arctic Coast Eskimo. Canada. Geological Survey Museum Bulletin 6. Anthropological Series 3. Ottawa.

——————— .
1919 The Stefánsson-Anderson Arctic Expedition of the American Museum: Preliminary Ethnological Report. Anthropological Papers of the American Museum of Natural History 14(1). New York.

Steinbring, J.
1970 The Tie Creek Boulder Site of Southeastern Manitoba. In W.H. Hlady, ed., Ten Thousand Years Archaeology in Manitoba. Winnipeg: Manitoba Archaeological Society.

Sturtevant, W.C.
1980 The First Inuit Depiction by Europeans. Études/Inuit/Studies 4(1-2): 47-49.

Suttles, Wayne
1983 Productivity and Its Constraints: A Coast Salish Case. In Indian Art Traditions of the Northwest Coast. R.L. Carlson (ed.) Archaeology Press. Burnaby: Simon Fraser University.

Swanton, J.R.
1901 Contributions to the Ethnology of the Haida. Memoirs of the American Museum of Natural History. Vol. 8. New York.

——————— .
1952 The Indian Tribes of North America. Bureau of American Ethnology Bulletin 145. Washington, D.C.

Swinton, G.
1965 Eskimo Sculpture. Toronto: McClelland and Stewart.

——————— .
1972 Sculpture of the Eskimo. Toronto: McClelland and Stewart.

——————— .
1980 The Symbolic Design of the Caribou Amautik. In The Inuit Amautik: I Like My Hood to be Full. Winnipeg: The Winnipeg Art Gallery.

——————— .
1985 Animals: Images, Forms, Ideas. In Uumajut: Animal Imagery in Inuit Art. Driscoll, B. (ed.). Winnipeg: The Winnipeg Art Gallery.

Swinton, N.
1980 La déese inuite de la mer/The Inuit Sea Goddess. Montréal: Musée des beaux arts de Montréal.

Syms, L.
1979 The Devils Lake—Sourisford Burial Complex on the Northeastern Plains. Plains Anthropologist, Vol. 24: 283-308.

Tanner, Adrian
1979 Bringing Home Animals. Social and Economic Studies No. 23. St. John's: Memorial University of Newfoundland.

——————.
1984 Notes on the Ceremonial Hide. Pp. 91-106 in Papers of the Fifteenth Algonquian Conference. William Cowan, ed. Ottawa: Carleton University.

Taylor, J.C.
1974 Foreword: Form and Spirit. *In* Boxes and Bowls: Decorated Containers by 19th Century Haida, Tlingit, Bella Bella and Tsimshian Indian Artists. Renwick Gallery of the National Collection of Fine Arts. Washington: The Smithsonian Institution Press. 7-10.

Taylor, J.G.
1974 Netsilik Eskimo Material Culture: The Roald Amundsen Collection from King William Island. Oslo: Universitetsforlaget.

——————.
1979 Indian-Inuit Relations in Eastern Labrador, 1600-1976. Arctic Anthropology 16(2): 49-58.

——————.
1980 The Inuit of Southern Quebec-Labrador: Reviewing the Evidence. Études/Inuit/Studies 4(1-2): 185-194.

——————.
1984 Historical Ethnography of the Labrador Coast. *In* Handbook of North American Indians 5 (Arctic): 508-521.

——————.
1986 The Arctic Whale Cult in Labrador. Études/Inuit/Studies 9(2): 121-132.

Taylor, William and Swinton, George
1967 Prehistoric Dorset Art. The Beaver. Autumn:32-47.

Tefft, S.K.
1965 From Band to Tribe on the Plains. Plains Anthropologist, Vol. 10, No. 2.

Teit, James
1956 Field Notes on the Tahltan and Kaska Indians: 1912-15. June Helm MacNeish, ed. Anthropologica 3: 40-171. Ottawa.

Testart, Alain
1979 Les Sociétés de chasseurs Cueilleurs. Pour la science. Février 1979, 16. Paris.
The Canadian Encyclopedia. Edmonton: Hurtig.

Thompson, Judy
1983 Turn-of-the-century Métis Decorative Art from the Frederick Bell Collection. American Indian Art Magazine 8(4): 36-45.

Thwaites, Reuben G., ed.
1896-1901 The Jesuit Relations and Allied Documents: Travel and Explorations of the Jesuit Missionaries in New France, 1610-1791; the Original French, Latin, and Italian Texts, with English Translations and Notes. 73 Vols. Cleveland: Burrows Brothers. (Reprinted: Pageant, New York, 1959)

Townsend C., ed.
1911 Captain Cartwright and His Labrador Journal. Boston: Dana Estes and Company.

Trigger, Bruce G.
1976 Children of Aataentsic: A History of the Huron People to 1660. 2 Vols. Montreal: McGill-Queen's University Press.

Trigger, Bruce G., ed.
1978 Handbook of American Indians. Vol. 15: Northeast. Washington, D.C.: Smithsonian Institution.

Troufanoff, I.P.
1970 The Ahtena Tomahawks in the Museum of Anthropology and Ethnography of the Academy of Sciences of the U.S.S.R. Current Anthropology 11(2): 155-159.

Tuck, James
1976 Ancient People of Port-au-Choix. St. John's: Memorial University of Newfoundland.

——————.
1984 Maritime Provinces Prehistory. Ottawa: National Museums of Canada.

Tulurialuk, R.A. and D. Pelly
1986 Qikaaluktut: Images of Inuit Life. Toronto: Oxford University Press.

Turnbull, Christopher
1976 The Augustine Site: A Mound from the Maritimes. Archaeology of Eastern North America 4: 50-62.

Turner, Lucien M.
1894 Ethnology of the Ungava District, Hudson Bay Territory. 11th Annual Report of the Bureau of American Ethnology for the Years 1889-1890: 159-350. Washington.

——————.
1979 Indians and Eskimos in the Québec-Labrador Peninsula: Ethnology of the Ungava District. Québec: Presses Comeditex. (Originally published in 1894.)

Turner, Victor
1982 Introduction. In Celebration: Studies in Festivity and Ritual: 11-30. Victor Turner, ed. Washington: Smithsonian Institution Press.

Ungalaaq, M.A.
1985 Recollections of Martha Angugatiaq Ungalaaq. I.C.I. Autobiography Series 1. Eskimo Point, N.W.T.: Inuit Cultural Institute.

Usher, P.
1971 The Canadian Western Arctic: A Century of Change. Anthropologica n.s. 13(1-2): 169-183. Ottawa.

VanStone, James W.
1974 Athapaskan Adaptations: Hunters and Fishermen of the Subarctic Forests. Chicago: Aldine.

——————.
1984 Exploration and Contact History of Western Alaska. *In* Handbook of North American Indians 5 (Arctic): 149-160. Washington, D.C.: Smithsonian Institution Press.

——————.
1981 Southern Tutchone Clothing and Tlingit Trade. *In* Arctic Anthropology 19(1): 51-61.

Vastokas, Joan
1977 The Shamanic Tree of Life. *In* Stone, Bones and

Skin: 93-117. Toronto: The Society for Art Publications.

Vecsey, Christopher
1983   Traditional Ojibwa Religion and its Historical Changes. Philadelphia: The American Philosophical Society.

Wallace, Anthony F.C.
1958   Dreams and the Wishes of the Soul: A Type of Psychoanalytic Theory Among the Seventeenth Century Iroquois. American Anthropologist 60 (2): 234-248.

————.
1972   The Death and Rebirth of the Seneca. New York: Vintage Books.

Wallis, W.D. and Wallis, R.S.
1955   The Micmac Indians of Eastern Canada. Minneapolis: University of Minnesota.

Webber, Alica Podolinsky
1983   Ceremonial Robes of the Montagnais-Naskapi. American Indian Art Magazine 9, 1: 60-69, 75-77.

Webster, J.H.
1949   Deerskin Clothing. The Beaver (December): 44-47.

Weld, Isaac, Jr.
1799   Travels through the States of North America and the Provinces of Upper and Lower Canada during the years 1795, 1796, and 1797. London: Printed for John Stockdale, Picadilly.

Wentzel, Willard-Ferdinand
1889-90 Letters to the Hon. Roderic McKenzie, 1807-1824. Les Bourgeois de la Compagnie du Nord-Ouest, Vol. 1, 67-153. L.R. Masson, ed. 2 vols. Quebec: A. Coté.

Whiteford, Andrew Hunter
1977   Fiber Bags of the Great Lakes Indians. American Indian Art Magazine 2(3): 52-64, 85.

————.
1986   The Origins of Great Lakes Beaded Bandolier Bags. American Indian Art Magazine 11 (3): 32-43.

Whitehead, Ruth Holmes
1980   Elitekey: Micmac Material Culture from 1600 A.D. to the Present. Halifax: The Nova Scotia Museum.

————.
1982   Micmac Quillwork. Halifax: The Nova Scotia Museum.

————.
1985   Micmac, Maliseet and Beothuk Material Culture in International Collections. Vols. I-IX. MS. Calgary: The Glenbow Museum.

Whitney, Caspar
1896   On Snow-shoes to the Barren Grounds: Twenty-eight Hundred Miles after Musk-oxen and Wood-bison. New York: Harper and Brothers.

Whittaker, C.E.
1937   Arctic Eskimo: A Record of Fifty Years' Experience and Observation among the Eskimo. London: Seeley, Service and Co., Ltd.

Whymper, Frederick
1869   Travel and Adventure in the Territory of Alaska, Formerly Russian America—Now Ceded to the United States—and Various Other Parts of the North Pacific. New York: Harper and Brothers.

de Widerspach-Thor, Martine (Reid)
1981   The Copper Equation. In The World is as Sharp as a Knife. An Anthology in Honour of Wilson Duff. D.N. Abbott (ed.) Victoria: British Columbia Provincial Museum.

Wike, Joyce A.
1951   The Effect of the Maritime Fur Trade on Northwest Coast Indian Society. Unpublished Ph.D. thesis. New York: Columbia University.

Wilson, E.F.
1887   Report on the Blackfoot Tribes. British Association for the Advancement of Science. 57th Annual Report. London.

Wingert, Paul
1951   Tsimshian Sculpture. In The Tsimshian: Their Arts and Music. Publications of the American Ethnological Society. Vol. XVIII.

Wintemberg, W.J.
1939   Petroglyphs of the Roche Percée and Vicinity, Saskatchewan. Transactions of the Royal Society of Canada. Third Series, Section II, Vol. 33.

Wissler, C.
1903   The Whirlwind and the Elk in the Mythology of the Dakota. Journal of American Folklore, Vol. 18: 157-268.

————.
1907   Some Protective Designs of the Dakota. American Museum of Natural History, Anthrop. Papers 11: 21-53.

————.
1912   Ceremonial Bundles of the Blackfoot Indians. American Museum of Natural History, Anthrop. Papers, Vol. 7, part 2.

————.
1915   Costumes of the Plains Indians. Anthrop. Papers of the American Museum of Natural History, Vol. 17, part 2. New York.

Wissler, C., and D.C. Duvall
1908   Mythology of the Blackfoot Indians. American Museum of Natural History, Anthrop. Papers Vol. 2. New York.

Wolfe, A/W.
1969   Social Structural Bases of Art. Current Anthropology 10: 3-44.

Wright, J.V.
1971   Cree Culture History in the Southern Indian Lake Region. In Contributions to Anthropology VII. National Museums of Canada, Bulletin 232. Ottawa.

Zagoskin, Lavrentii Alekseevich
1967   Lieutenant Zagoskin's Travels in Russian America. 1842-1844. Henry N. Michael, ed. (Anthropology of the North: Translations from Russian Sources 7) Toronto: Published for the Arctic Institute of North America by University of Toronto Press.

Acknowledgements

With a project as large and as complex as *The Spirit Sings*, it is difficult to know where to begin to acknowledge those who contributed to it. While we cannot list everyone individually, we do wish to express our sincere appreciation to all those who helped.

To the sponsor of our project, Shell Canada Ltd., we extend our sincere appreciation for their most generous support of *The Spirit Sings*. Their contribution was the largest single donation ever made to any arts project in Canada. The assistance of other supporters – OCO 88 Arts Festival Committee, The National Museums of Canada, The Province of Alberta, the City of Calgary, and the Nova Scotia Museum – is also gratefully acknowledged.

The Board of Governors of the Glenbow-Alberta Institute supported the project at a time when the museum was under severe financial constraints; and *The Spirit Sings* would never have come into being were it not for the unfailing determination of the Glenbow's director. Duncan Cameron enthusiastically embraced the concept and diligently worked to ensure its fulfilment. The Canadian people are indebted to him for his vision of what our museums should be.

We are deeply indebted to the Curatorial Committee who worked on the project and wrote the text of this book. They helped direct its focus and content and laboured long and hard to ensure the high standards that we all envisioned and we were not disappointed. Their unfailing support for the idea and their commitment to make it a very significant event in the Canadian museum, academic, and native community and to ensure its appeal to the Canadian public at large, predetermined the success of the *The Spirit Sings*. The committee included Ruth Whitehead, Judy Thompson, Dr. Ruth Phillips, Ted Brasser, Bernadette Driscoll, and Dr. Martine Reid. A special note of thanks to Bill Reid, who attended some of our meetings and offered seminal insight and wisdom when we were struggling with difficult issues. Dr. Christian Feest of the Museum für Völkerkunde in Vienna, who was a consultant to the project, must be acknowledged for his assistance, particularly during the research stages of the project.

The institutions and individuals that so generously loaned to the exhibition were obviously vital to the success of the project. The institutions that allowed the Curatorial Committee access to their collections during the research stage of the exhibition deserve mention. Everyone involved with *The Spirit Sings* owes a great debt to these people and many others who helped in a variety of ways. Some of these people and institutions include:

CANADA
Robert Janes and Barbara Winter, Prince of Wales Northern Heritage Centre, Department of Culture and Communication, Yellowknife; National Gallery of Canada, Ottawa; Dr. Peter L. Paul, Woodstock Reserve, New Brunswick; Andreas Bear Nicholas, Tobique Reserve, New Brunswick; Bernie Francis, Micmac Language Institute, Sydney, Nova Scotia; Rita Joe, Micmac poet, Nova Scotia; Ingeborg Marshal, Portugals Cove, Newfoundland; Saskatchewan Museum of Natural History, Regina; Ruth McConnell and Eric Waterton, Provincial Museum of Alberta, Edmonton; Alan Hoover, British Columbia Provincial Museum, Victoria; Marilyn Laver, Canadian Conservation Institute, Ottawa; Donat Savoie, Department of Indian and Northern Affairs, Ottawa; Gilbert Gignac, Public Archives of Canada, Ottawa; Dr. David Keenlyside, Dr. J. Garth Taylor, Judy Hall, and Kitty Glover, Canadian Museum of Civilization, Ottawa; Kenneth Lister, Valerie Grant, Trudy Nicks, and Arnie Brownstone, Royal Ontario Museum, Toronto; Conrad Graham, Betty Issenman, Kristen Rothschild, McCord Museum, Montreal; Louise McNamara, Château Ramezay, Montreal; Peter Schledermann, Calgary; Kay Desrochers, Photo Division, National Museums of Canada; Malcolm Wake and Ed McCann, RCMP Museum, Regina; Katherine Pettipas and Doug Leonard, Manitoba Museum of Man and Nature, Winnipeg; Callum Thomson and Jane Sproull Thomson, Newfoundland Museum, St. John's; Dr. Michael Ames, University of British Columbia, Museum of Anthropology, Vancouver; Cheryl Samuels, Victoria; York-Sunbury Historical Society Inc. Museum, Fredericton; Carol Laidlaw and Gary Hughes, The New Brunswick Museum, Saint John; George MacBeath, Fredericton; David Myles, Fredericton; Emelie Seheult, Fredericton; Charles Martijn, Quebec City; Brigitte Petersmann, Halifax; Terrence Heath, former Director, Winnipeg Art Gallery; David Ross, Linda Lazarowich and Edwina Hoogenberg, Lower Fort Garry, Parks Canada; Bruce Ellis and Anna Genereaux, Army Museum, Halifax; Shirlee Anne Smith, Hudson's Bay Company Archives, Winnipeg; Annie Napayok and Charlotte St. John, Eskimo Pt., Northwest Territories; Rhoda Karetak, Inuit Cultural Institute, Eskimo Pt., Northwest Territories; George Qulaut, Igloolik; Agnes Nigiyok, Mabel Nigiyok, Harry Egutak, Elizabeth Banksland and Mary Okheena, Holman, Northwest Territories; Lancy Michel, Saskatchewan; Ernie Hedger, Saskatchewan.

UNITED STATES
Bruce J. Bourque, Maine State Museum; Bruce C. Craig and James Rubinstein, National Museum of Natural History, Smithsonian Institution, Washington, D.C.; Robert Engelstad, Washington, D.C.; Virginia Crawford, The Cleveland Museum of Art; Pamela Hearne, University Museum, University of Pennsylvania, Philadelphia; Suzanne L. Flynt, Memorial Hall Museum, Pocumtuck Valley Memorial Association, Deerfield, Massachusetts; John Grimes, The Peabody Museum of Salem, Massachusetts; Dr. David Penney, The Detroit Institute of Arts, Detroit; Jane Robinson, Florida State Museum, Gainesville, Florida; Dean Zimmerman, The Western Reserve Historical Society, Cleveland; Richard Conn, Denver Art Museum, Colorado; Dr. Stanley Freed and Anibal Rodriquez, American Museum of Natural History, New York; Eulie Wiedsma, Mary Jane Lenz, Lisa Callander, and Natasha Bonilla, Museum of the American Indian, Heye Foundation, New York; Dr. Ian W. Brown, Peabody Museum, Harvard University; Linda Fisk-Jones, San Diego Museum of Man; Dr. James Nason, Thomas Burke Washington State Museum, Seattle; Alabama Department of Archives and History, Montgomery; The Brooklyn Museum; Buffalo Bill Historical Center, Cody, Wyoming; The Paul Dyck

Foundation, Rimrock, Arizona; Dr. Frank A. Norick, Lowie Museum of Anthropology, University of California, Berkeley; Barbara A. Hail, Haffenrefer Museum of Anthropology, Bristol, Rhode Island; Mary Bruton Sandifer, New York; Margaret Stearns, The City of New York; Field Museum of Natural History, Chicago; Florida State Museum, Gainesville; The Kansas City Museum, Missouri; John H. Hauberg, Seattle.

UNITED KINGDOM
Her Majesty, Queen Elizabeth II; Yvonne Schumann and Adrian Jarvis, National Museums and Galleries on Merseyside, Liverpool; Leonard M. Pole, Saffron Walden Museum; Miss Adamson and Mr. Chalmers, Art Gallery and Museum, Glasgow; Lord and Lady Elgin, Dunfermline, Scotland; Alessandro Tana, Brighton Art Gallery and Museum; Dale Idiens and Maureen Barrie, Royal Scottish Museum, Edinburgh; Jonathon King and Trudy Martin, British Museum, London; Anne M. Oakley, Dean and Chapter of Canterbury; Michael Ryan, National Museum of Ireland, Dublin; Mrs. Elizabeth Breckenridge, County Cork, Ireland; Dr. Schuyler Jones and Linda Cheetham, Pitt Rivers Museum, Oxford; Dr. Arthur McGregor, Ashmolean Museum, Oxford; Dr. E.W. McKie, Hunterian Museum, Glasgow; Dr. Paul Sant Cassia, University Museum of Archaeology and Anthropology, Cambridge; Charles Hunt, Marischal College of Aberdeen; Perth Museum and Art Gallery, Perth and Kinross District, Scotland; Robert Headland and Clive Holland, Scott Polar Institute, Cambridge; Dr. George A. Bankes, University of Manchester; Ann Shirley, National Maritime Museum, Greenwich; Michael Hitchcock, Horniman Museum, Glasgow; Sue Giles, Bristol City Museum and Art Gallery; W. Boag, Scottish United Services Museum, Edinburgh; Victoria Gabbitas and June Swann, Northampton Leather Museum; June Bedford, London; Michael Johnson, Walsall; Carol Whitehead, London.

AUSTRALIA
Catherine Thorpe, Museum of Victoria, Melbourne.

NEW ZEALAND
Eileen Brown, House of Memories Museum, Waipu.

EUROPE
Dr Sylvie de la Salle, Musée des Beaux-arts de Chartres; Mme Catherine Lesseur and Mme Viviane Huchard, Musées d'Angers; Dr. H.K. Schmutz, Natural History Collection of the Town of Winterthur; Mme Denise Cornzmusaz, Société du Musée et Vieil Yverdon; Roland Kaehr, Musée d'ethnograhie, Neuchâtel; Daniel Schoepf, Musée d'ethnograhie, Geneva; Dr. Peter Gerber, University Museum, Zurich; Herr und Frau Hans Lang, Indianer Museum der Stadt Zurich; Dr. Ernst Klay, Berne Historical Museum; Dr. J. Kandert, Naprstkovo Museum, Prague; Musées Royaux d'art et d'histoire, Brussels; Father Jozef Penkowski and Father Leonard A. Boyle, Vatican City State; Dr. Helga Rammow, Völkerkunde-Sammlung der Hansestadt Lubeck; Dr. K.O. Meyer, Staatliches Museum für Naturkunde und Vorgenschichte, Damm; Berete Due, Karen Quist, Mr. Ayelson, Rolf Gilberg, Anna Bahnson, Anne Lisbeth Schmidt and Vigdis Vingelsgaard, National Museum of Denmark, Copenhagen; Stephan Augustin and Inge Baldauf, Volkerkundemuseum Herrnhut Pirjo Varjola, The National

Museum of Finland, Helsinki; A.H.G. Rientjes, Amerika-museum, Cuijak, Netherlands; Dr. Gerti Nooter, Rijksmuseum voor Volkerkunde, Leiden; Unni Wikan and Tom Svensson, Ethnograhic Museum, University of Oslo; Dr. H. Israel, Staatliches Museum für Völkerkunde, Dresden; Dr. Ross, Staatliche Schlosser und Garten, Worlitz; Dr. Sara Ciruzzi, Museo Nazionale di Antropologia e Etnologia, Florence, Italy; Dr. Guerra, Museo Civico di Scienze Naturali ''E. Caffi,'' Bergamo, Italy; Dr. Claudio Cavatrunci, Museo Preistorico Etnografico L. Pigorini, Rome; Gudrum Ekstrand, Kungl Livrustkammaren, Stockholm; Dr. Bengt Kylsberg, Skoklosters slott, Balsta, Sweden; Dr. Anna Brita Hellbom, Etnografiska Museet, Stockholm; Irmhild Petersmann, Munich; Dr. Jean-Loup Rousselot, Staatliches Museum für Völkerkunde, Munich; Reiner Beckershaus, Berlin, Federal Republic of Germany; Dr. Corrina Raddatz, Hanover; Dr. Horst Hartmann, Gunther Hartmann, Eva Gerhards, Herr Borbe, and Herr Wedell, Museum für Völkerkunde, Berlin, Federal Republic of Germany; Dr. Karin von Welck, Rautenstrauch-Joest Museum für Völkerkunde, Cologne; Dr. Renate Wente-Lukas, Deutsches Ledermuseum, Offenbach am Main, Federal Republic of Germany; Dr. Christian Feest, Museum für Völkerkunde, Vienna, Austria; Johanna Feest, Vienna; Dr. Henning Bischoff, Voelkerkundliche Sammlungen im Staedt Reiss-Museum, Mannheim, Federal Republic of Germany; M. Jacqueline Linnet, Bibliothèque Sainte-Geneviève, Paris, France; Dr. Christof Romer, Braunschweigisches Landesmuseum, Federal Republic of Germany; Dr. Galena Dzeniskevich, The Museum of Anthropology and Ethnography named after Peter the Great, Leningrad, U.S.S.R.; Dr. Andreas Luderwaldt, Ubersee Museum, Bremen, Federal Republic of Germany.

The outside readers of the essays and the valuable insights that they gave to the authors of the text were most appreciated. These people include: Dr. William N. Fenton; Dr. Michael Ames; Dr. Jack Ewers; Dr. Bea Medicine; Dr. Mark Phillips; Dr. R. Forbis; Dr. Ralph Pastore; Dr. Bruce Bourque; Dr. Kate Duncan; Dr. Bill Holm; Peter Macnair; Dr. Victoria Wyatt; Dr. Leland Donald; Dr. Evan Mauer; Dr. Jim Van Stone; Dr. Katherine MacClelland; Dr. Hugh Dempsey; Mr. George Swinton; Dr. Susan Kaplan; Dr. Bill Fitzhugh; Dr. Parker Duchemin; Dr. James Taylor.

The support and encouragement offered by Charis Wahl, the editor for the book, was most sincerely appreciated by all the authors. She nurtured the essays and their authors to ensure that the text melded to the complete whole that we envisioned. Bob Young integrated text and photographs in a design that sets both off to advantage. Deborah Seed verified the copy.

Many people at Glenbow contributed to the project but two people in particular deserve mention: Anne Williams and Beth Carter. Without their unfailing dedication to the project and cheerful enthusiasm, The Spirit Sings would never have been realized. We owe them a great deal.

This book is dedicated to the native people who created the magnificent objects discussed in this book and those which were included in the exhibition. It is their spirit which continues to sing among the native peoples of Canada today.